Governing California in the Twenty-First Century

FIFTH EDITION

THE POLITICAL DYNAMICS OF THE GOLDEN STATE

J. Theodore Anagnoson
California State University, Los Angeles

Gerald Bonetto
Vice President, Government Affairs, Printing Industries of California

J. Vincent Buck
California State University, Fullerton

Richard E. DeLeon
San Francisco State University

Jolly Emrey
University of Wisconsin–Whitewater

James J. Kelleher
California State University, Dominguez Hills

Nadine Koch
California State University, Los Angeles

W. W. NORTON & COMPANY
INDEPENDENT PUBLISHERS SINCE 1923

W. W. Norton & Company has been independent since its founding in 1923, when William Warder Norton and Mary D. Herter Norton first published lectures delivered at the People's Institute, the adult education division of New York City's Cooper Union. The firm soon expanded its program beyond the Institute, publishing books by celebrated academics from America and abroad. By midcentury, the two major pillars of Norton's publishing program—trade books and college texts—were firmly established. In the 1950s, the Norton family transferred control of the company to its employees, and today—with a staff of four hundred and a comparable number of trade, college, and professional titles published each year—W. W. Norton & Company stands as the largest publishing house owned wholly by its employees.

Printed in Canada.

The text of this book is composed in Berlin with the display set in Interstate.

Book design: Sandra Watanabe

Composition: Achorn International

Manufacturing: Marquis Book Printing

Editor: Lisa Camner McKay

Editorial Assistant: Samantha Held

Project Editor: Caitlin Moran

Senior Production Supervisor, College: Ashley Horna

Marketing Manager, Political Science: Erin Brown

Permissions Manager: Megan Jackson

Photo Editor: Kathryn Bryan

ISBN 978-0-393-93839-5 (pbk.)

W. W. Norton & Company, Inc., 500 Fifth Avenue, New York, N.Y. 10110

www.wwnorton.com

W. W. Norton & Company Ltd., Castle House, 75/76 Wells Street, London W1T 3QT

2 3 4 5 6 7 8 9 0

Contents

Preface

We began this project over a decade ago with a working title asking whether California's political system and its politics were simply "broken." That is, politicians were caught within a system that was so contradictory in its rules, norms, and mores that budgets simply couldn't be passed on time or balanced, programs and departments couldn't be managed under the existing set of rules, and citizen expectations were so out of line with the ability of the political system to satisfy them that the level of negativism and cynicism was about as bad as could be found anywhere in the nation.

We think after a decade of false and halting starts that the picture needs some modification. California has begun to repair its infrastructure. The state has new incentives for politicians to be less ideologically extreme on the right or the left, in particular the "top two" primary system and the commission that is now drawing new districts for the Assembly, the state Senate, and congressional districts every 10 years after the Census. Decision rules in Sacramento still leave much to be desired, but at least a budget can be passed with majority rule instead of having to obtain a two-thirds vote, a rule that necessitated some votes from the minority party and, unfortunately, some pork projects or other incentives to gain those votes. And the nation's strictest term-limit rules have been modified to allow members of the Assembly or state Senate to serve 12 years in a single house before being "termed out" and forced to seek another office outside the state legislature. Hopefully this will increase the level of expertise available among legislators.

At the same time, if the distance to be traveled to reach a political system that would actually "function" and make decisions is one mile, we have gone perhaps 1,000 feet. There still is no way to adjust the tax system without a two-thirds vote, and California's tax system badly needs modernization; its last overhaul was more than 50 years ago. While the economy has moved toward a services base, California's tax system remains based on manufacturing, which was more common a half century ago. The income tax relies much too heavily on the capital gains tax, and that in turn creates revenue peaks and valleys that tempt Sacramento politicians to build the periodic surges of revenue into the base and in turn to run deficits when times are tough.

Proposition 13, passed in 1978, caused a massive centralization of authority in Sacramento over the next decade at the expense of cities, counties, and school districts. As a result, local governments have little authority over their own revenue. State government proved unable to provide local governments with the revenue and authority they needed to deal with the recent recession, financial collapse, and defaulted mortgages that plague certain parts of the state, resulting in a number of local government bankruptcies, and in governments that are not bankrupt, the inability to help people in a genuine time of need. In some dire cases, state government cutbacks combined with the revenue-depleting impacts of home mortgage foreclosures, high unemployment, business failures, and grossly overburdened public sector pension and benefit obligations created local "perfect storms" of economic and political conditions that bankrupted cities like Stockton and still threaten others. The state has been unable to help. The drought of 2013–15 exacerbated existing flaws in California's water policy, and while the state government has proposed several solutions, some controversial, the fact remains that the state's demand for water still drastically exceeds its supply.

In these circumstances, the Fifth Edition of *Governing California in the Twenty-First Century* offers a ray of hope but the reality of a long distance to go. We hope you enjoy our analysis of California's politics, not quite "broken"—but not as yet "fixed" either.

New to this edition, the "Who Are Californians" features present visual snapshots of California's politics and people. These infographics, contributed by Melissa Michelson of Menlo College, shine a light on demographic diversity and political behavior in the state.

We divided the writing of this book as follows:

1. California Government: Promise and Practice—Anagnoson (tanagno@calstatela.edu)
2. The Constitution and the Progressive Legacy—Bonetto (Gerry@piasc.org) and Anagnoson
3. Interest Groups and the Media in California—Bonetto
4. Parties and Elections in California—Koch (nkoch@calstatela.edu)
5. The California Legislature—Buck (vbuck@fullerton.edu)
6. The Governor and the Executive Branch—Buck
7. The California Judiciary—Emrey (emreyj@uww.edu)
8. The State Budget and Budgetary Limitations—Anagnoson
9. Local Government—DeLeon (rdeleon@sfsu.edu)
10. Public Policy in California—Anagnoson

There are websites for the fourth and fifth editions of this book. For the fourth edition, go to http://www.silcom.com/~anag999/g4.html. For the fifth edition site, substitute "g5" (without the quotes) for "g4." The sites contain:

- A link to the publisher's own site for this book.

- A list of *errata*. If you find any error in the book, please email the lead author, J. Theodore Anagnoson, at anag999@silcom.com or tanagno@calstatela.edu.

- The answers to the short answer questions at the end of each chapter.

- PowerPoint slides used by Anagnoson in Spring 2009 to teach an upper division course in California politics. These are up to date only to the end of Spring 2009.

We have constructed, in addition, a test bank for instructors. To gain access to the test bank, visit wwnorton.com/instructors.

We would like to acknowledge the helpful recommendations from professors who have reviewed the book; their comments have assisted us in updating events and materials. For the fifth edition, we thank the following reviewers:

M. Allen Coson, California State Polytechnic University, Pomona
Pearl Galano, California State University, Channel Islands
Kathleen Lee, Humboldt State University
Leonard McNeil, Contra Costa College
Melissa Michelson, Menlo College
Donald R. Ranish, Antelope Valley College
Michelle Rodriguez, San Diego Mesa College
Martin Saiz, California State University, Northridge
Mary Lea Schander, Pasadena City College and Glendale Community College
Wade R. Smith, Sacramento State University
Jamilya Ukudeeva, Cabrillo College
John Vento, Antelope Valley College

We also thank the students who have communicated their comments.

We would be glad to hear from you about the book. Please use the e-mail addresses above to communicate with us.

J. Theodore Anagnoson
Professor of Political Science
California State University, Los Angeles

1

California Government: Promise and Practice

WHAT CALIFORNIA GOVERNMENT DOES AND WHY IT MATTERS

You wake up and drive to work on the freeway, stopping first at the gas station on the corner to fill up and to buy an apple for a morning snack. You then drive across a bridge to get to the university where you attend school, taking general education courses. When you graduate, you consider working for the California Highway Patrol (CHP), a private security guard service, or in the same grocery store where you stopped for your apple. In the evening you go out to a restaurant.

How is the government of California relevant to your day? Your car is built to conform to government safety standards. The freeways are built by the state government to conform to federal and state standards, with a mixture of federal and state money; traffic is monitored by the CHP. The gas station has to meet local safety regulations, and it uses gasoline that conforms to federal standards for automobiles. The grocery store relies on scales that are certified by county government; both imported and domestic fruit must meet U.S. and state Department of Agriculture standards. The bridge is built by government and supposedly maintained by government, although a large proportion of the bridges nationally and in California are behind on their scheduled maintenance. If you attend a K–12 school, the school must comply with state standards for what must be taught at each grade level, as well as tests to determine whether schools are meeting the standards. If you are in higher education, the public university you attend must have a general education program that conforms to state regulations; if you attend a community college, the California State University, or the University of California, the total cost of your education is being subsidized by state funds. If you attend a private college, you might be receiving federal student aid. If you eventually go to work for the CHP, you will work under state laws and regulations. The private security service is regulated by the state as well, and the grocery store must conform to state safety standards. The restaurant is inspected periodically by the local government health department, and in some locations, the department will post the summary score (A, B, C, etc.).

The California Dream?

For almost 200 years, the **California dream** has attracted immigrants from the United States and abroad. Governor Arnold Schwarzenegger, in one of his State of the State speeches (2004), said that California represents "an empire of hope and aspiration," a place where "Californians do great things." To some, the California dream is sun and surf; to others, the warm winter season; to still others, a house on the coast amid redwoods and acres of untrammeled wilderness, or three or four cars per family. Many of these dreams can be summed up in the phrase "freedom from restraints" or "freedom from traditions." These are typical themes in statewide elections and gubernatorial State of the State speeches—evoking the image of an older, less crowded California.

The reality is that some of the dream is attainable for many—California's winter weather is the envy of most of the nation—but much of it is not. One of the themes of this book is the conflict between dreams and reality, between the ideals that we set for ourselves and the reality of our everyday lives. Particularly vivid for politicians is the conflict between our expectations for them and the constraints and incentives with which we saddle them.

Why Study California Politics?

The obvious answer is that you have to: your California history course meets some requirement for graduation or your major, since the State of California decided that every college student should know something about the California Constitution and California government and politics. But more important—why *care* about California politics?

- You are **the residents and voters of the present and future**. The policies and political trends occurring today will impact your lives, affecting everything from university tuition fees to the strength of the job market.

- California politics is plagued by **low levels of participation and turnout**, so much so that the electorate is older, more conservative, wealthier, more educated, and less ethnically diverse than would be the case if every eligible adult voted. So your vote and participation really can make a difference.

- California politics also suffers from **too much interest-group participation and not enough citizen participation**. The general interests of large groups of citizens need to be represented at the table.

That's the narrow answer. A broader answer as to why we study California politics is that California's government and politics are distinctive and worthy of study. How is California different from other states?

- We have much **more cultural diversity** than other states, including a much higher proportion of Latino and Asian residents. By some measures, we are the country's multicultural trendsetter. Our diversity affects our politics, and our solutions to multicultural issues become an example for other states.

- We are **one of the 10 largest economies in the world**. The California economy in 2014, according to the Center for Continuing Study of the California Economy, is the eighth largest in the world, slightly larger than the economies of Russia and Italy and just behind Brazil's. California's large and diverse economy means that we are able, in theory, to weather economic downturns more easily than other states. The fact that economic crises continue to plague California, then, indicates that our tax system is distinctive as well (see below and Chapter 8).

- We are **the most populous state, and we have grown more quickly than other states**. In 1960 New York had 41 members in the U.S. House of Representatives; California had 38. The 2010 census gave California 53 seats, followed by Texas with 36 and Florida and New York with 27 each. California is forced to develop creative solutions to the problems engendered by high growth, such as its varied distribution among the various regions of the state and the need for housing and schools.

- We are **more majoritarian than other states**, meaning that we rely more on the measures for direct democracy—the initiative, the referendum, and the **recall**—that were added to the state constitution by the Progressive movement in 1912. Every state uses majority rule for most decisions, but in a majoritarian state, the public is more likely than elected representatives to make policy decisions.

Consider the following continuum:

majoritarian   republican

A **majoritarian** government is one that is highly influenced by the public at large, through public-opinion polls and measures like the initiative, referendum, and recall that enable the public to decide government policies directly.

A **republican** government is one in which we elect representatives to make our decisions for us, based on the Madisonian model for the federal government.

California government has moved much more toward the majoritarian model than other states. Not only are initiatives to amend the constitution routine but also interest groups often collect signatures for an initiative just to pressure the legislature into voting in their favor. California voters can influence policy in the state more than voters in other states by voting directly on public policies and constitutional amendments that are placed on the ballot.

And Californians like being majoritarian: surveys show that most don't want to restrict use of the initiative in spite of its extensive use and manipulation by

California's extensive use of direct democracy measures, like the referendum, reflects the state's majoritarian character. Here, volunteers from a conservative advocacy group sort through mail containing signatures in support of a referendum to overturn an August 2013 law allowing transgender public school students to use restroom facilities consistent with their gender identities. Opponents of the law failed to collect enough signatures to place the referendum on the November 2014 ballot.

interest groups.[1] A report from the nonpartisan Initiative and Referendum Institute at the University of Southern California lists 352 initiatives in California from 1904 to 2012, placing it second only to Oregon, with 363. Twenty-seven states do not have the initiative at all, and the top five states account for more than half of all initiatives considered from 1904 to 2012.[2]

What Determines the Content and Character of California's Politics?

Three factors shape the content and character of California's politics:

- The underlying demographic and sociopolitical trends that affect California and the other states;

- The rules of the game, as set out in the federal and state constitutions and in state laws; and

- The decisions of voters and politicians.

In Chapters 1 and 2 we will discuss the underlying demographic and sociopolitical trends and the rules of the game. The decisions of voters and politicians, and the way they shape California politics, will be discussed later in the text.

Who Are Californians?

The preamble to the California State Constitution begins, "We, the People of the State of California, . . ." This is fitting for a democratic form of government, which seeks to give voice to the people in the governing of the affairs of their community.

So, who are Californians? Do the demographic characteristics of California differ from those of the United States as a whole? And how have changing demographic and socioeconomic trends contributed to the political challenges that face California voters and politicians? (See the Who Are Californians feature on the next page.)

RACE AND ETHNICITY In many respects, California's population has a notable degree of **racial and ethnic diversity** compared with the U.S. population. **Latino or Hispanic** is not a racial category in the official census, but a separate census question asks about Hispanic or Latino origin. About 17 percent of the United States is Latino, but Latinos make up about 38 percent of California's population. Almost 60 percent of that population is of Mexican heritage.

AGE California's population is relatively young, mostly because of immigration. Immigrants tend to be younger and to have larger families than those who have been residents for longer periods.

EDUCATION Californians are well educated. A greater proportion of Californians have gone to college or completed a bachelor's or higher degree than in the United States in general. Fewer, however, have graduated from high school (81.0 percent versus 85.7 percent for the United States as a whole from 2008 to 2012).

MOBILITY AND FOREIGN-BORN About 60 percent of all Americans live in the state in which they were born, but only 50 percent of all Californians were born in California. In fact, 27.1 percent are **foreign-born**, a much higher percentage than in the United States as a whole (12 percent). Most foreign-born residents are not U.S. citizens; only 46 percent of the foreign-born in both the United States and California are citizens. As one might expect with such a large foreign-born population, only 61 percent of those over age five speak English at home in California, as opposed to 82 percent nationwide. That is a substantial difference by the standards of social science. Many political issues have arisen from this, ranging from debates over whether local store signs should be written in foreign languages to the "English as the official state language" movement.

INCOME The U.S. Census Bureau has estimated California's median household income at $61,400 for 2008–12, about $8,000 higher than the national figure of $53,046. The state poverty rate is almost the same as the national figure: 15.3 percent (California) for 2008–12 compared to 14.9 percent (United States).

GEOGRAPHY Over the last 40 years, the population of California has shifted so that the coastal regions have become significantly more liberal and aligned with the Democratic Party than the inland regions, which in turn have become more conservative and aligned with the Republican Party. These liberal coastal regions include every county on the coast, from Del Norte County near Oregon to Los Angeles County. The Central Valley and Inland Empire (Riverside and San Bernardino counties) are disproportionately Republican. Orange and San Diego counties have been very Republican in the past but less so in recent elections. Local politics, on the other hand, are quite different even among Democratic- or Republican-leaning cities (e.g., San Francisco's local politics are very liberal compared with Los Angeles's more moderate politics).

How Is the California Population Changing?

California's demographics are changing rapidly. The state used to be dominated by non-Latino whites (Anglos), but since 2000 the state has had a majority minority population. Latinos in particular are a fast-growing population, while Anglos and blacks are an increasingly small proportion. The Asian population is also growing in size, albeit more slowly than Latinos. By 2060, less than 30 percent of Californians will be Anglo, while almost half (48%) will be Latino.

At the same time, the total size of the state's population is expected to continue to grow rapidly, from 37.2 million people in 2010 to 52.7 million in 2060. Population density will increase in the state's urban areas as well in inland areas, particularly the San Joaquin and Sacramento Valleys.

Projected Population Growth by Demographic Group

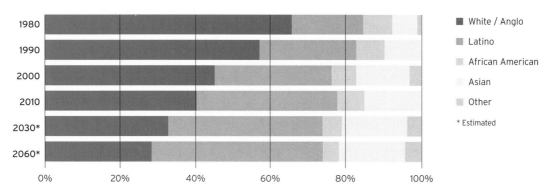

forcriticalanalysis

1. What impact are these shifting demographics likely to have on California politics? Will it change the issues that the state government focuses on? Will it change the issues that are the subject of citizen-driven initiatives?

2. California's coastal regions have traditionally been more densely populated, but rapid population growth and housing costs are increasingly driving populations to settle farther inland. How will this change California politics in the inland counties, particularly in areas traditionally dedicated to agriculture?

Projected Population Growth between 2010 and 2060 by county

SOURCE: U.S. Census Bureau

POPULATION GROWTH Except for the four years from 1993 to 1996, California's population has grown by about 450,000 people per year for more than two decades. The 2010 census listed California's population as 37,691,912; at the end of 2013, the state Department of Finance estimated the population at 38.3 million. California's current rate of growth is approximately 350,000 people per year. This strong and consistent growth means that many of the problems that have plagued the state in the past will continue to do so in the future. Some of these issues include:

- **Housing and Transportation**   Even with the decline brought on by the recession of 2008–09, housing prices in many middle-class areas have skyrocketed since the early 1990s. Many lower- and middle-class people who work in San Francisco's Bay Area must live in the Central Valley, while many of those who work in the Los Angeles area must live in Riverside and San Bernardino counties. In both of these places, commutes of one to two hours each way—if not more—are common. Our transportation systems, built for a much smaller population, have not kept pace with this growth.

- **Schools**   Population growth means more schoolchildren and thus high demand for teachers across the state. Sadly, the state lacks enough fully qualified or credentialed teachers to meet this demand, particularly in many urban areas. Projections of the educational requirements of the future job market indicate that approximately 35 percent of jobs will require a college degree. The University of California, California State University, and community college systems do not produce sufficient numbers of graduates to meet this goal, which means that well-educated migrants from other states will fill these positions. The proportion of students who receive a college degree should be rising to meet future job requirements; instead, it is falling.

- **Immigration**   California has experienced high levels of immigration since the 1950s—so high in some areas that candidates for Mexico's presidency have campaigned here. Between 1970 and 2011 the number of immigrants in the California population increased from 1.8 million to about 10.2 million; 27 percent of the state's current population during that period was foreign-born, a much higher proportion than the 13 percent nationwide. Most immigrants in California are from Latin America or Asia; 4.3 million alone come from Mexico, composing some 43 percent of the total immigrant population in California. Immigrants live in all parts of California, with those from Latin America more likely to live in Southern California and those from Asia in Northern California. Immigrants are younger than nonimmigrant Californians and more likely to be poor, and although some have relatively high levels of education, most are less educated than the native population.[3] Table 1.1 shows the 11 largest countries of origin for immigrants in California in 2006.

As of 2009, there were approximately 2.7 million **undocumented immigrants** in California, according to the Urban Institute, which used the census figures on the foreign-born population and subtracted the numbers of people who are naturalized or here on legal visas and work permits.[4] Undocumented immigrants are a continuing political issue, with politicians arguing over the public services to which

TABLE 1.1 ● Leading Countries of Origin of Immigrants in California, 2009

Country	Number of Immigrants in California	Percentage Naturalized (%)
Mexico	4,308,000	28%
Philippines	783,000	68
China (including Taiwan)	681,000	68
Vietnam	457,000	82
El Salvador	413,000	37
India	319,000	46
Korea	307,000	55
Guatemala	261,000	28
Iran	214,000	76
Canada	132,000	49
United Kingdom	125,000	40

SOURCE: Public Policy Institute of California, "Just the Facts: Immigrants in California" (April 2011), www.ppic.org (accessed 7/17/12).

they should have access: Should they be treated in hospital emergency rooms? Should they be allowed to obtain driver's licenses? Table 1.2 lists the number of undocumented immigrants by state, along with the share they compose of that state's total population. Arizona and California have the highest proportion of undocumented immigrants, at 7.0 percent.

Reflecting the controversies over immigration, both documented and undocumented, in recent years, a number of demonstrations have taken place in California on the immigration issue. These demonstrations have represented different views: against more immigration, in favor of closing the borders, in favor of a "path to citizenship," both for and against the Arizona immigration law of 2010, against housing undocumented children who have been taken into custody before their court hearings, and so forth. At least one of the demonstrations involved over 1 million people, the largest ever seen in Southern California to date. But aside from a 2013 law that allowed undocumented immigrants to obtain driver's permits starting in 2015, little policy action has taken place at the state level.

The Crisis of California Politics

Is California government capable of making the decisions needed for California to thrive and preserve its standard of living through the twenty-first century? The general sentiment among informed observers is that California is hamstrung by voter-approved rules and regulations, some of which are admirable on an individual level but make for a collective nightmare. However, some progress started to

TABLE 1.2 ● Undocumented Immigrants by State, 2009

State	Number of Undocumented Immigrants	Share of State's Total Population (%)
California	2,600,000	7.0%
Texas	1,680,000	6.8
Florida	720,000	3.9
Illinois	554,000	4.3
New York	550,000	2.8
Georgia	480,000	4.9
Arizona	460,000	7.0
New Jersey	360,000	4.1
North Carolina	370,000	3.9
Other states	2,976,000	1.9
All states	10,750,000	3.5

SOURCE: Public Policy Institute of California, "Just the Facts: Illegal Immigrants" (December 2010), www.ppic.org (accessed 7/17/12).

be made during the 2003–2011 Schwarzenegger administration and has continued under present governor Jerry Brown:

- Proposition 11, approved in November 2008, took the power to apportion the districts of the Assembly and state Senate (**redistricting**) away from those bodies and gave it to a citizens' commission. Later, the voters added congressional districts to the duties of the new citizens' commission. In 2012, the first year the new districts were used, they seemed to be fair (that is, not gerrymandered). Future years will establish whether unbiased districts will produce more moderate legislators willing to compromise for the good of the state as a whole, which was the goal of changing the reapportionment method. So far, elections have been more competitive.

- In 2010, the voters opted to change the state's party primary elections to a new **top-two primary** system, used for the first time in June 2012. Under the new system, there is no party primary. Instead the election system is like a swimming or track meet, in which there are preliminary heats and finals. Following the preliminary election, the top two candidates advance to the finals in November, even if they are from the same party or are not in a major party. Third parties such as the Green Party are strongly opposed to the new system, since they rarely finish in the top two candidates in the primary election and thus have no access to the general election ballot during the two months when voter attention is highest.

- In 2010, the voters also approved of a change in the legislative process for approving the state budget: the requirement was once a **two-thirds vote** of the total number of legislators in each chamber, the Assembly and the state Senate, but is now a simple majority (50 percent plus one). The budget approved in June 2011 was the first to use the new system. However, the state constitution still requires a two-thirds majority of both houses of the legislature, plus the governor's signature, to raise or lower taxes.

After the election of Governor Jerry Brown in November 2010, California's frustrating budget stalemate initially continued in spite of the new majority rule, largely because the taxation system has not changed. In June 2012 the budget gap was $16 billion, more than the total revenues received for the general fund in 40 of the 50 states. By mid-2014, however, the budget had a surplus almost as large as the deficit from two years before. The California taxation system is dependent on income taxes paid on **capital gains** (funds received from selling stock); it produced a huge surplus in 2013 and 2014 when the stock market rose, inducing many investors to sell shares. The governor and legislature agreed to use the surplus to build up a "rainy day" fund and to pay off many old bonds issued when the budget was in deficit. In November 2011, the Legislative Analyst's office projected five years of deficits averaging about $8 billion per year, as shown in the left graph of Figure 1.1. A little over two years later, the improvement in the economy produced the projection on the right, showing an average surplus of over $8 billion per year.

The first decade of the 2000s was one long downward trend, the result of difficult and tough decisions. Every college student in California knows some of them, having seen cut after cut to the budgets of the community colleges, the California State University system, and the University of California system. These cuts have been partially replaced by tuition and fee increases. Other reductions have included Medi-Cal (California's medical program for the poor) rate and service reductions, many cost-containment measures in the state programs for the developmentally disabled, and the elimination of the state's local government redevelopment agencies and their state funding (see Chapter 9). Prisoners are being sent from the state prisons to local jails, and many state responsibilities are being passed to the local

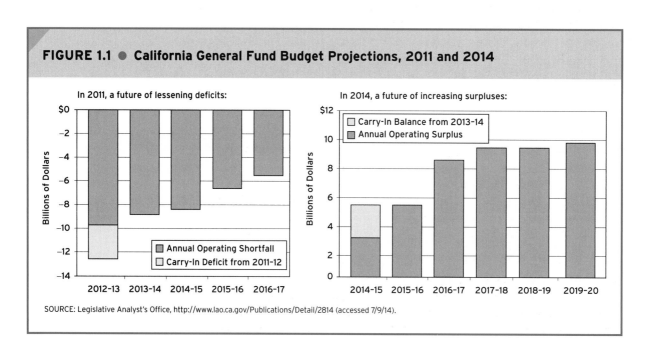

FIGURE 1.1 ● California General Fund Budget Projections, 2011 and 2014

In 2011, a future of lessening deficits:

In 2014, a future of increasing surpluses:

■ Annual Operating Shortfall
□ Carry-In Deficit from 2011-12

□ Carry-In Balance from 2013-14
■ Annual Operating Surplus

SOURCE: Legislative Analyst's Office, http://www.lao.ca.gov/Publications/Detail/2814 (accessed 7/9/14).

level of government. Figure 1.1, on the other hand, shows how drastically California's budget can change when the stock market is high, as it was in 2014. But no one should think that the era of plenty has arrived. California's budget is unduly responsive to the economy and especially to capital gains. When the next recession arrives, and it *will* arrive, revenues will dive again.

California state government thus faces a series of paradoxes. On the one hand, we see progress in cutting the deficit and in making the hard decisions necessary to weather the national economic storm. On the other hand, the difficulty of those decisions and the fact that taxes can be raised only by a two-thirds majority has meant that a budget crisis occurred every year from 2000 to 2012. Every decision in the state government is a budget decision—a decision made solely, or almost solely, on the basis of whether there is enough money and a budget source for the considered activity.

Let us take a closer look at some reasons for the recurring crises despite the promise of California state government.

The Ease of Passing Initiatives

One factor is certainly the ease with which **special interests** collect signatures to propose, campaign for, and sometimes pass initiatives to help their own causes. The initiative was added to the California Constitution by the Progressive movement just after the beginning of the twentieth century as a way to promote the involvement of the public in public policy and affairs. One recent example is Proposition 15 on the June 2010 ballot, which ostensibly allowed taxpayers to have more control over their government but was in fact designed to keep local public utilities from competing with PG&E. Another is Proposition 33 on the November 2012 ballot, which ostensibly allowed insurance companies to give longevity discounts to drivers who had continuous insurance coverage from another insurance company, but was in fact designed to give one insurance company the ability to raise rates on drivers who had lapses in insurance coverage. In general, the initiative has ceased to promote direct democracy for at least the last two decades. It is instead just one more method by which special interests convince voters who are paying little attention to government and politics to enact rules, laws, and constitutional amendments that benefit the particular interest at the expense of the public as a whole.

Term Limits

The **term limit** movement found fertile ground in California in the 1980s and 1990s. Proposition 140 in 1990 imposed what were then the severest term limits in the nation on the legislature and the elected officials of the executive branch, and the voters in many cities in California instituted term limits as well. Part of the statewide anger and consequent push for term limit legislation was directed against Willie Brown, then-Speaker of the California Assembly, whose flamboyant lifestyle and prolific fund-raising raised the ire of voters.

The theory of the term limits movement is that term limits will encourage members of the Assembly and state Senate to pay more attention to their jobs and raise less money for future campaigns, and will make the legislative bodies more welcoming to minority and female candidates. Since term limits have been imposed, the proportion of Latino legislators has indeed risen, but members have much less expertise on the matters they vote on and, by the time they acquire this expertise, they are term-limited out. Additionally, many—perhaps most—members of the legislature spend a good deal of their time in office worrying about their next job and raising funds for those campaigns. Most observers believe that term limits have worsened the legislature, not bettered it.

While voters strongly support term limits, they recently took a step to address some of the institutional problems that have resulted from them. In June 2012, the voters approved Proposition 28, which allows legislators to serve as many as 12 years in the legislature, as long as those 12 years are served in one house. (The previous total service time was actually higher—14 years—but capped at 6 years in the Assembly and 8 in the Senate.) Currently the term limits are 12 years (six terms) for the Assembly, 12 years (three terms) for the state Senate, and 8 years (two terms) for all statewide officials (governor, lieutenant governor, attorney general, controller, secretary of state, treasurer, superintendent of public instruction, insurance commissioner, and the four elected members of the Board of Equalization).

The Two-Thirds Requirement for Raising Taxes

As noted earlier, until the voters passed Proposition 25 in November 2010, California's constitution required a two-thirds vote of the total membership—not just those present and voting—in each house of the legislature to pass the budget. Only three states, Arkansas, California, and Rhode Island, required such a strong supermajority to pass the budget. Proposition 25 lowered the required vote to 50 percent plus one. It will take several years to see if this change makes a substantial difference. So far, the first four budgets passed under the new rules—which financially penalize legislators if the budget is not passed on time—have been passed around June 15, the constitutional deadline. Only the last, however, passed in June 2014, was technically balanced, and only because of the surge in income tax revenues from those who had sold stock in the previous year. A balanced budget clearly requires improvements in the quality of the state's economy and tax system as well as different procedural deadlines.

Herein lies the problem. A two-thirds vote of the absolute number of legislators in both houses of the state legislature is still necessary to raise or lower any tax level. With a Republican Party that refuses to countenance tax increases of any kind (plus the taxpayer groups that promise to sue the instant any tax increase is passed), the burden of balancing the state budget has fallen on low- and moderate-income state residents, who benefit disproportionately from the state programs that have been cut. For higher-income state residents, state services are at least partially irrelevant—their major "service" is a low tax rate, as well as exemptions and deductions that enable some of their income to be taxed at a lower rate.

This may change somewhat in the next few years. The 2012 elections saw the Democrats win a short-lived **supermajority** of seats in the legislature, which meant they had enough votes to raise taxes without any Republican support (see Chapter 5). Raising taxes, however, requires the approval of the governor, and Governor Jerry Brown wanted a balanced budget without additional tax increases beyond those instituted by Proposition 30, approved by voters in November 2012. This proposition enacted a four-year increase in the state sales tax and seven-year increases in the tax rates for citizens making over $250,000 in income (see Chapter 4). The supermajority lasted a little over a year, until early 2014 when three Democrats in the state Senate were suspended over corruption allegations. These developments have had a significant impact, but the two-thirds rule for raising taxes continues to hold sway. The structure of California's tax system has been frozen since the 1960s.

Lack of Consensus on Fundamental Questions

Another reason for California's perpetual state of crisis is the inability of legislators to unify on matters of policy and principle. In order to be effective, a political system must overcome the inertia generated by narrow interests to make decisions that benefit the broader public interest. This is a persistent issue in a large, complex state like California, but in the past, California politicians have been able to overcome the lack of **consensus** to make progress on significant questions. Has California changed? Why do interest groups cause impasse in the 2000s, when their influence was relatively minimal back in the 1970s and 1980s? After all, we have always had interest groups, and we had the two-thirds decision rule for adopting the budget or raising taxes in the legislature from 1935 until 2010. Dan Walters suggests that the blame heaped on the legislature is inappropriate:

> In fact, California's governance maladies stem from the complex, often contradictory nature of the state itself. With its immense geographic, economic, and cultural diversity, California has myriad policy issues, but those same factors also have become an impediment to governance. The state lost its vital consensus on public policy issues, and without that civic compass, its politicians tend to ignore major issues and pursue trivial ones. . . . The real issue is whether the public's anger at Gray Davis will morph into a new sense of civic purpose or whether California is destined to be . . . ungovernable.[5]

So far, the events following the recall of Governor Gray Davis in 2003 have indicated very slow progress, with no "new sense of civic purpose." The same old problems seem to vex California's political class, over and over.

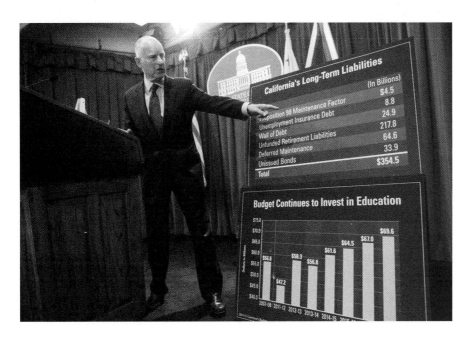

Passing a balanced state budget is a perennially contentious issue in California. However, the budget surplus in early 2014 allowed Governor Jerry Brown to propose a budget for 2014–15 that not only increased state funding for education but also paid off some of the debt that the state had accrued over previous years.

Reform Ideas

In addition to the steps already taken (as discussed earlier), numerous additional reforms have been suggested over the years to address the institutional hindrances to effective California governance. Some of the standard ones are listed here. See how many you agree with as you begin this book.

On the liberal side:

- **Instituting public financing of election campaigns.** This would reduce the impact of money on Assembly, state Senate, and Congressional campaigns, because all or most campaign funding would come from the state, not from interests who want something in return for these donations. It would be difficult to devise a system that would not unduly benefit incumbents, who are typically better known than their challengers. It would also lessen the impact of fund-raising on members of the legislature, some of whom spend up to half their time in Sacramento raising money.

- **Lowering the required supermajority to raise taxes** from two-thirds to some lower, more achievable percentage, such as 55 or 60 percent. This proposal would require an amendment to the state constitution, probably impossible on a tax issue like this unless it is proposed as part of a broad package of tax relief and reform.

- **Restricting the initiative process** to allow more citizen participation and lessening the need to hire professional firms to collect signatures and run initiative campaigns. This would require lengthening the time allowed to collect signatures. Changing an initiative process that California's citizens hold in high regard would be a tough sell, and the industry that sponsors initiatives and makes money from them might oppose it; this would make the campaign expensive.

- **Realigning the tax structure** to match the state's shift from a manufacturing economy to a service-based one (see Chapter 8). The most powerful method for doing this would be to change the sales tax to make it apply to services, like medical and automobile repair bills. In order to pass, this would have to be sold as decreasing the sales tax rate. Several recent commissions have indicated interest, but few politicians want to be associated with the cause.

On the conservative side:

- **Changing the legislature from full time to part time.** This is popular in Tea Party circles. It would severely weaken the legislature's level of expertise on the programs it is expected to enact and oversee.

- **Lowering California's tax rates**, making the system less progressive in the process. This is popular among conservatives, but a tough sell for liberals and Democrats.

- **Improving California's business climate** with lower taxes and fewer regulations. Almost everyone agrees that this goal is laudable, but there is little agreement on what taxes to lower (or how to make up the difference financially) and what regulations to simplify or abolish.

Most of these ideas involve so much controversy that they have little chance of being enacted, at least in the short run. Enacting major reforms such as those just listed is much easier through the ballot box (that is, via an initiative) than it is through the legislature, where constitutional changes require a two-thirds vote of the Assembly and the Senate before being placed on the ballot for ratification.

Conclusion

In this book we are going to consider the real world of California politics and the possibilities, both fascinating and frustrating, of the present, as well as changes that might make the future more positive for both politicians and the public. We will investigate what makes California different from other states and examine its unique political problems, including:

- the inability to balance the budget, year after year.

- the malapportioned districts for the California legislature that, in combination with the primary system, produce legislators who are more liberal than the public on the Democratic side and more conservative than the public on the Republican side. We shall see whether the new top-two primary system and the non-gerrymandered legislative districts make any difference in this area.

- the public's attachment to the strictest term limits in the nation.

- the public's attachment to extreme majoritarianism, which produces the longest ballots in the nation as well as some of the lowest turnout rates.

Our coverage includes subjects that the newspapers and bloggers discuss in great detail as well as some subjects, such as the California tax system and the impact of Proposition 13, that receive little coverage in the media. Welcome to the journey.

A Guide to This Book

Chapter 2, "The Constitution and the Progressive Legacy," deals with California's state constitution and the Progressives, the two crucial factors that defined the shape and direction of today's California government.

Chapters 3 and 4 deal with the bodies outside government that influence what government can accomplish. Chapter 3, "Interest Groups and the Media in California," deals with the groups that are as prevalent and influential in California as they are in our nation's capital. Chapter 4, "Parties and Elections in California," deals with parties and voters, and how both influence government through elections and campaigns.

Chapters 5, 6, and 7 deal with the institutions of government. Chapter 5, "The California Legislature," deals with the legislature, the body we love to hate. We try in this book to understand the legislature and why it functions as it does rather than simply condemn it. Chapter 6, "The Governor and the Executive Branch," asks whether California has become ungovernable. Chapter 7, "The California Judiciary," deals with judges and the criminal justice system.

Chapters 8, 9, and 10 deal with policy problems and governmental structures that are particularly relevant today. Chapter 8, "The State Budget and Budgetary Limitations," addresses taxes, spending, and the California budget, asking whether the budget can be controlled in today's political and policy environment with the tools we have available to us. Chapter 9, "Local Government," deals with local government and its dependency on the state, a dependency that localities are taking action to eliminate in part through the initiative process. Chapter 10, "Public Policy in California," deals with several contemporary public policy problems, illustrating how the institutions and voters have acted in these areas.

Study Guide

FOR FURTHER READING

"California in Crisis." *California Journal* (August 2003): 18–27.

Davis, Mike. *City of Quartz: Excavating the Future in Los Angeles*. New York: Vintage, 1990.

Goldmacher, Shane. "New Rules, New Tactics, in U.S. Races: Lessons Learned in the Free-Spending State Campaigns Now Apply to Candidates Seeking Office at the Federal Level." *Los Angeles Times*, February 24, 2010, p. AA3.

Horwitz, Sasha. *Termed Out: Reforming California's Term Limits*. Los Angeles: Center for Governmental Studies, October 2007. www.cgs.org. Accessed July 17, 2014.

Lewis, Michael. "California *and* Bust." *Vanity Fair*, November 2011.

Mathews, Joe, and Mark Paul. *California Crackup: How Reform Broke the Golden State and How We Can Fix It*. Berkeley: University of California Press, 2010.

McGhee, Eric, and Daniel Krimm. *California's Political Geography*. San Francisco: Public Policy Institute of California, February 2012.

Olin, Spencer C. *California's Prodigal Sons: Hiram Johnson and the Progressives, 1911–1917*. Berkeley: University of California Press, 1968.

Public Policy Institute of California. "Just the Facts: Undocumented Immigrants." San Francisco: Public Policy Institute of California, February 2013. www.ppic.org. Accessed July 17, 2014.

———. "Just the Facts: Immigrants in California." San Francisco: Public Policy Institute of California, May 2013. www.ppic.org. Accessed July 9, 2014.

———. "Research Brief: How Have Term Limits Affected the California Legislature?" No. 94. San Francisco: Public Policy Institute of California, November 2004. www.ppic.org. Accessed July 17, 2014.

Skelton, George. "California's Capitol—The Long View. A Columnist Looks Back on 50 Years Covering the Ups and Downs of Sacramento." *Los Angeles Times*, December 1, 2011.

Slater, Dashka, and Gary Rivlin. "Economy, California on the Brink." *Newsweek*, September 5, 2011, pp. 26–27.

Statewide Ballot Proposition Elections. San Francisco: Field Institute, California Opinion Index, October 2011. www.field.com/fieldpollonline/subscribers. Accessed July 17, 2014.

Walters, Dan. "California Makes It Easier to Cut Taxes Than to Raise Them." *Sacramento Bee*, May 16, 2010.

Wilson, James Q. "A Guide to Schwarzenegger Country." *Commentary* (December 2003): 45–49.

ON THE WEB

California Choices: www.californiachoices.org. Accessed July 17, 2014.

California Forward: "How to Fix California's Government." www.cafwd-action.org/pages/how-to-fix-CA-government. Accessed July 17, 2014.

Center for Governmental Studies: www.cgs.org. Accessed July 17, 2014. A think tank that specifically focuses on promoting citizen participation in government.

The Field (California) Poll: Field Institute. www.field.com/fieldpollonline/subscribers/index.html. Accessed July 17, 2014.

Los Angeles Times: www.latimes.com. Accessed July 17, 2014.

Public Policy Institute of California: www.ppic.org. Accessed July 17, 2014. A think tank devoted to nonpartisan research on how to improve California policy.

Sacramento Bee: www.sacbee.com. Accessed July 17, 2014.

San Francisco Chronicle: www.sfgate.com. Accessed July 17, 2014.

SUMMARY

I. California politics are important for several reasons.
   A. California is the most populous state, has an economy in the top 10 among nations of the world, and has a population more multicultural and diverse than the rest of the nation.
   B. California is strongly majoritarian, and its citizens like it that way.
   C. California is younger than many states, has a greater percentage of college-educated citizens, and is richer than most states.
   D. California has experienced some of the strongest population growth of any state, resulting in a number of political conflicts over the years.
   E. California has more immigrants, and more undocumented immigrants, than any other state, although Arizona has the same proportion of undocumented immigrants.

II. Progress in dealing with California's problems has occurred in the last decade, in spite of the fact that the state is generally considered to be hamstrung by voter-approved rules and regulations.
   A. Redistricting, once the province of the legislature, is now done by a citizens commission. The new districts (used from 2012 forward) seem to have considerably less gerrymandering than the old.
   B. The party primary election system has been changed to the new "top-two" system, in which the two top vote-getters from the primary election, regardless of party, move to the general election for a runoff.
      1. The new system is more like a swim meet or track meet, with a preliminary heat and final, than a party primary.
   C. In 2010 the voters approved a change to the state constitution so that the legislature could approve the state budget by a majority vote, instead of the prior rule of two-thirds of the total membership of each house of the legislature.

   1. The state constitution still requires any tax increase to be approved by a two-thirds vote of each house of the legislature, plus the governor's signature.
   D. These changes have not changed the underlying problems with the state's taxation system, which result in soaring surpluses when the stock market is high and the opposite during recessions.

III. Some reasons for the continual crisis in California state government include:
   A. The ease of passing initiatives. Special interests find the state has a congenial atmosphere in which several million dollars can be spent to collect signatures and fund a campaign to pass a law or change the state constitution in order to benefit the initiative's proposer.
   B. Term limits, in spite of the 2012 change that lengthened the maximum time to 12 years in either the Assembly or the state Senate, still hamper the legislature. By the time legislators learn their jobs, they are often looking for new ones.
   C. The two-thirds vote requirement in the Assembly and state Senate to raise taxes has meant that the only realistic way to balance declining budgets has been to cut services disproportionately used by the lower middle class and the poor.
   D. The lack of consensus on fundamental questions among both politicians and citizens has made it difficult to build the broad consensus that major change requires.

IV. Reform ideas are abundant, but few have the political support necessary for enactment in the short run. Several from both sides of the political spectrum are listed in the text.

PRACTICE QUIZ

1. The budget must be passed by a majority of those present and voting in both chambers of the legislature.
   a) true
   b) false

2. Most states require a two-thirds majority to pass their budgets each year.
   a) true
   b) false

3. According to the text, California's population, the foreign-born population, and the approximate number of undocumented immigrants are:
   a) 50 million, 5 million, and 2 million.
   b) 34 million, 8.8 million, and 2.4 million.
   c) 25 million, 20 million, and 18 million.
   d) 38.3 million, 10.2 million, and 2.7 million.

4. "Latino" or "Hispanic" is one of the racial categories in the U.S. Census, which is taken every 10 years.
   a) true
   b) false

5. Compared to the proportion of immigrants who speak English at home in the U.S. population, the proportion of immigrants in California who speak English at home is
   a) greater.
   b) lesser.
   c) the same.

6. According to this book, the inability of the California legislature to make decisions that benefit the state as a whole is due to
   a) the influence of interest groups.
   b) the two-thirds requirement to raise taxes.
   c) California's size and diversity.
   d) all of the above

7. California's term limits are
   a) 8 years for the governor, 4 years for the Assembly, and 6 years for the state Senate.
   b) 6 years for the governor, 6 years for the Assembly, and 8 years for the state Senate.

c) 8 years for the governor, 12 years for the Assembly, and 12 years for the state Senate.
d) 8 years for the governor, 8 years for the Assembly, and 12 years for the state Senate.

8. Undocumented immigrants will be able to obtain a driver's permit in California as of 2015.
   a) true
   b) false

9. "Majoritarian" as applied to California government means that
   a) the state requires majority rule in all major decisions.
   b) the state does not have a "republican" form of government; it has a "majoritarian" form.
   c) the state makes many important decisions through direct democracy and the initiative process.
   d) the California legislature uses majority rule for all decisions.

10. California's institutions of higher education produce sufficient numbers of graduates for the state's needs in the foreseeable future.
    a) true
    b) false

CRITICAL-THINKING QUESTIONS

1. How distinctive is California compared with other states? Are we really that different from citizens in the rest of the country?
2. California's population differs from that of other states on several levels. What are the two or three that are most significant, and why are they significant?
3. What are the advantages and disadvantages of the "majoritarian" form of government? Of the "republican" form of government?

KEY TERMS

California dream (p. 2)
capital gains tax (p. 10)
consensus (p. 13)
cultural diversity (p. 3)
foreign-born (p. 5)
Latino or Hispanic (p. 5)

majoritarian (p. 3)
public financing (p. 14)
racial and ethnic diversity (p. 5)
recall (p. 3)
redistricting (p. 9)
republican (p. 3)

special interests (p. 11)
supermajority (p. 12)
term limits (p. 11)
top-two primary (p. 9)
two-thirds vote (p. 9)
undocumented immigration (p. 7)

2 The Constitution and the Progressive Legacy

WHAT CALIFORNIA GOVERNMENT DOES AND WHY IT MATTERS

The purpose of a constitution is to define the rules under which political actors and citizens interact with each other to fulfill their goals as individuals, as members of a group, and as a population as a whole. The California Constitution is long and very detailed, with numerous amendments added over the years, dealing with both the fundamental principles and power of government as well as commonplace issues such as the right to fish on government property, English as the state's official language, and grants for stem cell research. Today California has the second highest number of constitutional amendments (over 500 by some counts), behind Alabama, and the second longest state constitution, behind Louisiana.

One distinctive feature of the California Constitution is that it allows the people to enact both constitutional amendments and legislation through a majority vote without going through the legislature. The process through which citizens make legislation at the ballot box is called the initiative. The initiative developed out of a political movement called Progressivism, which opposed the influence of monied special interests in politics and called for political power to be returned to the people. Any individual or group can propose a statute or an amendment to the California Constitution.

However, the initiative process has not always lived up to its progressive ideals. Today, hundreds of millions of dollars are spent by wealthy individuals and special interest groups on campaigns for and against initiatives. In the November 2014 election, almost $200 million was spent by both sides on six propositions. Although the initiative does put legislative power in the hands of the general public, it does not eliminate the influence of money in politics, and—ironically—bypasses the more careful debate and compromises that might take place in the legislature.

As one example, in 2006 California voters cast their ballots on Proposition 87, a high-profile initiative that was also the most costly in history, with over $156 million spent advocating for and against the proposition. The goal of the proposition was to establish a $4 billion program, the primary goal of which was to reduce petroleum consumption by 25 percent, with research and production incentives for alternative energy, alternative-energy vehicles, and energy-efficient technologies, as well as funding for education and training. The program would have been funded by a tax of 1.5 to 6.0 percent (depending on oil price per barrel) on California oil producers. The stakes were high because California is the third largest oil-producing state in the nation. Roughly 37 percent of California's oil at the time was pumped in the state, and another 21 percent came from Alaska. The rest was imported.

Supporters of the proposition contributed $61.9 million (with $49.6 million alone coming from film producer Steve Bing) and opponents contributed $94.4 million (with Chevron Corporation, Aera Energy, and Occidental Oil and Gas contributing $38 million, $32.8 million, and $9.6 million, respectively).[1] The initiative brought out celebrities on both sides, including prominent individuals, companies, and organizations. These included former President Bill Clinton, actor Brad Pitt, and the Coalition for Clean Air in support of the measure, and Governor Arnold Schwarzenegger, Chevron Corporation, and the California Chamber of Commerce in opposition.

The campaign was bitter and acrimonious. Accusations of dirty tactics abounded, and both sides filed lawsuits. Supporters alleged that the opposition's print and television advertisements created the false impression that it was financed by a broad coalition, including educators and public-safety officials, when in fact it was subsidized by the oil industry. Opponents to the measure accused their adversaries of illegally registering several "no" Web sites that, when accessed, redirected viewers to the "Yes-on-87" site. In the end, little came of either lawsuit; however, each helped sharpen and intensify feelings on both sides.

In the end, Proposition 87 failed to pass, getting 45.3 percent of the vote, as voters feared that passage of the initiative would raise gas prices, resulting in a greater demand for foreign oil. It is a prime example of an issue that, rather than being debated by experts and elected officials in the legislature, was appropriated by wealthy individuals and interest groups in the name of direct democracy. In the November 2014 election, two high-profile initiatives pitted consumers against health insurance companies in one case and trial lawyers in a second, but in neither case did the money spent approach the $156 million spent on Prop. 8 in 2006. Such examples abound in California politics.

In Chapter 1, we discussed some of the demographic differences between California and other states. We also mentioned that California's government is institutionally designed to not be able to solve critical state issues. Here are some of the unique features of the state's political process:

- The **sheer size of the state** increases the cost of political campaigns and media cost.

- The **competing networks of interest groups** cause groups to jockey for position and influence.

- The **increasing use of the initiative** significantly impacts state and local governance and policy.

- The **divided executive branch**, composed of nine separately elected officials, each with his or her own area of authority and responsibility, leads to overlapping responsibilities and fragmentation in the execution of state policy.

- The **widespread, almost universal use of nonpartisan elections at the local level of government** eliminates a valuable clue for voters to identify the policy positions of the candidates on the ballot.

Aside from the size of the state and the interest-group network, the other characteristics listed above are a result of the **Progressive movement**, which flourished in California from 1900 to 1917. The leaders of this movement focused on one goal: making government more responsive to the political, social, and economic concerns of the people. Their reforms continue to shape California government and politics in ways that sharply differentiate it from other states. To some, these features hamper the political process and should be changed. To others, they form part of the essence of California—an essence that, were they to be changed, would be destroyed.

The Rules of the Game: California's Constitution

The California Constitution has a long and storied history that can be divided into four stages:

- **The 1849 Constitution**   Written by residents of the territory in anticipation of statehood, this constitution contains many of the basic ideas underlying California's government today.

- **The 1879 Constitution**   Written by a constitutional convention in 1878, this is the basic governing document, with amendments, that is in force today.

- **From 1900 to 1917**   During this period, the Progressives amended the constitution and passed laws to temper the power of special interests and make government responsive to the people's desires and needs. The most prominent reforms of this period were the initiative, referendum, and recall.

- **From 1918 to the present**   Amendment after amendment lengthened the state's constitution, resulting in a document that at one point was almost 100,000 words long. Several commissions proposed substantive changes, but only two, one in the 1960s and the other in the 1990s, saw their proposals realized: the constitution's language was shortened and clarified, but no substantial changes were made to its provisions.

The 1849 Constitution

By 1849, 80,000 unruly gold miners had moved to California, inflating the population of the state enough for the settlers to apply for territorial status and draft a constitution. Admitting California as a free state, however, would have upset the balance between free and slave states that had existed in the Union since 1820, and was therefore delayed. In 1849, newly elected president Zachary Taylor proposed that California draft a constitution and apply directly to Congress for admission as a state, rather than applying first as a territory and later shifting to state status. California citizens elected delegates to a constitutional convention; the delegates met in turn and drew up the proposed constitution in 43 days.

The constitutional convention of 48 elected men met in Monterey in September of 1849, and relied heavily upon a book containing the constitutions of the federal government and some 30 states. Several of the provisions were taken directly from the constitutions of New York and Iowa. The basic provisions of the 1849 Constitution are still in force:

- The framework of the government rests on a separation of powers— executive, legislative, and judicial—interacting through a system of checks and balances, like the federal government.

- Executive power is divided, with the separate election and jurisdiction of the governor, lieutenant governor, comptroller, treasurer, attorney general, surveyor general, and superintendent of public instruction. This division weakens the governor, who cannot appoint—or remove—senior members of his or her own administration. Moreover, each of these statewide officials is a potential competitor for the governor's office, and each can release statements that contradict what the governor is saying.

- An extensive bill of rights begins the constitution.

- The legislature is elected and consists of two houses, one called the Senate, the other the Assembly.

However, there are also notable differences between the 1849 Constitution and the framework that exists today:

- The right to vote at that time was limited to white males 21 years of age or older who had lived in California for at least six months. Another provision denied citizenship to African Americans, Chinese Americans, and Native Americans; they were also prohibited from testifying against whites in court. The legislature could, by a two-thirds vote, enfranchise Native Americans "in such special cases as such proportion of the legislative body may deem just and proper."

- The judiciary was elected, as judges are today, but they were organized into four levels—as Mexico's judiciary was at the time.

- All laws and other provisions were to be published in both English and Spanish, since California was a bilingual state.

In 1850, the federal government passed a series of bills that composed the Compromise of 1850. One bill admitted California to the union as a free state. In Utah and New Mexico, the Compromise established territorial governments and allowed residents to decide whether or not to allow slavery in the state. It settled a dispute over the border between Texas and New Mexico and compensated Texas with $10 million to repay debts to Mexico. Finally, it abolished the slave trade in the District of Columbia and put the Fugitive Slave Act into effect.

California's 1849 Constitution quickly proved to be problematic. Its framers had written it so quickly that they had neglected to include provisions for the financial stability of the new government; within the first five years, California was in deficit. There were few provisions for taxation but no limits on spending, legislative salaries, or the governor's pardon power.[2] Four times between 1859 and 1873, the legislature called for a new constitutional convention to fix obvious defects; each time, too many voters left their ballots blank to achieve the necessary majority to approve the convention.

The 1879 Constitution

The call for a new constitutional convention finally succeeded in 1877, as California suffered from the worst recession in the brief history of the nation. In 1873, a Wall Street panic had spread into a full-fledged economic collapse, and thousands of businesses went bankrupt. Unfortunately, as Kevin Starr writes in *California: A History*, Chinese immigrants "became increasingly the scapegoats for collapsed expectations."[3] The situation had its origins in the expansion of the Central Pacific Railroad. A years-long project to extend the railroad over the Sierra Nevada mountain range began in 1863, when few California-born workers were willing to do the backbreaking work at the price that the construction supervisor for the railroad, Charles Crocker, was willing to pay. Starting in 1865 Crocker began to rely on Chinese workers, who lacked the bargaining power to campaign for higher wages; he eventually employed some 10,000. In 1869 the Union Pacific and Central Pacific railroads met in Utah, completing a track that would cut the journey across the nation to one week.

When the influx of Chinese workers resulted in unemployment for many non-immigrant workers, anti-Chinese sentiment began to grow. In 1871, Los Angeles witnessed a mass lynching of 18 Chinese men, including a boy of 14, after which an Anglo-American mob looted the Chinese section of town. By 1875, the state had seen an influx of over 150,000 migrants from other states, including many who had worked to build the Union Pacific railroad, and by 1877 unemployment rates in San Francisco were high. On July 23 of that year, some 8,000 assembled for a meeting of the Workingmen's Party, and speakers "denounced the capitalist system in general and the railroads in particular . . . , with emphasis on the Chinese labor the railroad had employed."[4]

Fifty-one of the delegates to the 1879 convention belonged to the Workingmen's Party; thus, it effectively enjoyed veto power over any of the decisions on both the convention rules and recommendations for the new constitution, for which a two-thirds majority was necessary. Joe Matthews and Mark Paul call the convention's recommendations "a demonstration of a difficult fact of California political life"—that "supermajorities are dangerous."[5] The Workingmen's Party supported restrictions on corporations and railroads and was strongly opposed to the presence of Chinese workers in California. One of its rallying cries was "The Chinese must go!"[6] The party also opposed the centralization of power for the government and the legislature. (It made an unsuccessful proposition to the convention that California collapse the two houses of the legislature into a unicameral one and abolish the lieutenant governor's office.)

The delegates at the convention adopted a large number of diverse provisions. Among these was the shifting of responsibility to stockholders for the debts of a corporation, and various new rules regarding the railroads: the railroads could not give free passes to those holding political office; they could not raise rates on one line to compensate for reductions made to compete on alternative lines; and they would be regulated by a Railroad Commission.

These provisions added words—almost doubling the constitution's size—and policies that read very much like a series of laws rather than a fundamental framework within which laws could operate. In this way, the California Constitution differs greatly from the federal U.S. Constitution, whose articles and amendments deal strictly with institutional procedures and rules that construct a governmental framework. The Eighteenth Amendment stands as the only experiment in establishing a substantive policy in the U.S. Constitution, prohibiting the manufacture, sale, import, or export of alcohol. It was repealed with the Twenty-First Amendment just 14 years later.

At the time, however, the many specific, substantive policies in the drafted California Constitution were viewed as beneficial, and it was approved by a vote of 54 to 46 percent in May 1879, with 90 percent of those eligible to vote participating. Most of the reform measures were not put into practice right away, as corporate and railroad power continued to dominate the state and sued to block their implementation. These setbacks were temporary, however. In a matter of three decades the broad reforms of the Progressive movement gained passage, weakening the grip of these special interests in the legislature and reshaping the landscape of California politics.

One notable feature of the 1879 Constitution was the procedures it established for amendment. The federal constitution and every state constitution in the United States include procedures for their own amendment, but these procedures vary considerably. The U.S. Constitution is one of the most difficult to amend in the world, requiring a two-thirds majority vote in the House and Senate followed by ratification by three-fourths of the states.[7] This very high hurdle explains in part why the U.S. Constitution has only been amended 27 times since 1789. In contrast, the California Constitution is much easier to amend. See Figure 2.1 for an overview of the different paths through which the constitution can be amended. Convening a constitutional convention is a more dramatic method of reform and has been used rarely. It is not particularly difficult, however, to get 8 percent of voters in the most recent gubernatorial election to sign a petition adding an amendment to the next ballot; the amendment then needs a simple majority vote to pass. This method has been used more than any other to amend the California Constitution.

You can get a sense of the California Constitution and how different it is from the U.S. Constitution by examining California's bill of rights, called the "Declara-

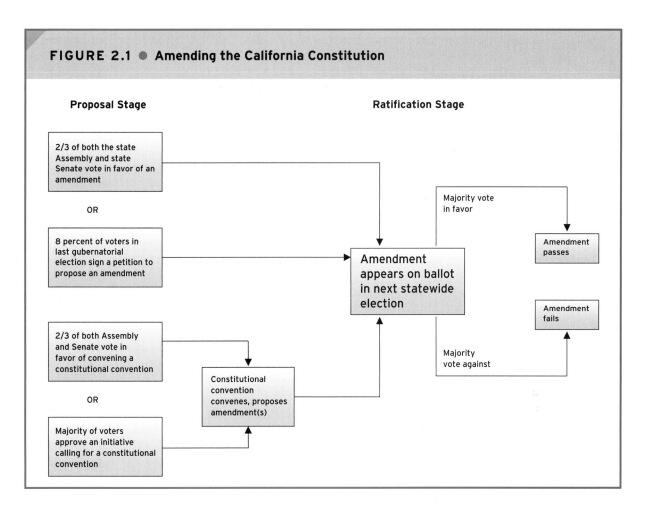

FIGURE 2.1 ● Amending the California Constitution

Proposal Stage

Ratification Stage

2/3 of both the state Assembly and state Senate vote in favor of an amendment

OR

8 percent of voters in last gubernatorial election sign a petition to propose an amendment

2/3 of both Assembly and Senate vote in favor of convening a constitutional convention

OR

Majority of voters approve an initiative calling for a constitutional convention

Constitutional convention convenes, proposes amendment(s)

Amendment appears on ballot in next statewide election

Majority vote in favor

Majority vote against

Amendment passes

Amendment fails

tion of Rights." The federal Bill of Rights consists of the first 10 amendments to the U.S. Constitution, and while other amendments may be passed, the first 10 will remain the Bill of Rights as they were written. California's bill of rights, meanwhile, can be expanded or rewritten as times change, and therefore reflects the political changes and conflicts that have occurred over time, with some of the rights described in much greater specificity than the corresponding federal right. You can see an example of this specificity in the provisions for freedom of speech as they apply to a newspaper. The federal constitution has the familiar First Amendment:

> Congress shall make no law respecting an establishment of religion, or prohibiting the free exercise thereof, or abridging the freedom of speech, or of the press; or the right of the people peaceably to assembly, and to petition the Government for a redress of grievances.

California's corresponding section has both more detail and more specificity, since it has been amended over time.

> SEC. 2. (a) Every person may freely speak, write and publish his or her sentiments on all subjects, being responsible for the abuse of this right. A law may not restrain or abridge liberty of speech or press.

(b) A publisher, editor, reporter, or other person connected with or employed upon a newspaper, magazine, or other periodical publication, or by a press association or wire service, or any person who has been so connected or employed, shall not be adjudged in contempt by a judicial, legislative, or administrative body, or any other body having the power to issue subpoenas, for refusing to disclose the source of any information procured while so connected or employed for publication in a newspaper, magazine, or other periodical publication, or for refusing to disclose any unpublished information obtained or prepared in gathering, receiving, or processing of information for communication to the public. Nor shall a radio or television news reporter or other person connected with or employed by a radio or television station, or any person who has been so connected or employed, be so adjudged in contempt for refusing to disclose the source of any information procured while so connected or employed for news or news commentary purposes on radio or television, or for refusing to disclose any unpublished information obtained or prepared in gathering, receiving, or processing of information for communication to the public.

Note the use of modern language, such as *wire service* and *television*.

From 1900 to 1917: The Progressive Movement

Pressure for political reform did not end with the 1879 Constitution. Beginning at the turn of the twentieth century, the Progressives pursued three goals: attack corporate political influence, eliminate the political corruption that went with such influence, and democratize the political process.[8]

They understood that these goals had to be accomplished before they could address equally pressing but more mundane concerns of the time. They accomplished all of this—and much more. Beginning with the 1911 legislative session, these reformers passed dozens of constitutional amendments and statutes that changed the face of California government and politics.[9] The most prominent of the political reforms were the following:

- **Nonpartisanship**   This is the norm in local elections and means that no party label is affixed to the candidates' names on the ballot. Of the more than 19,000 elected public officials in California, fewer than 300 are elected in partisan races.

- **Primary elections**   Before the institution of primary elections, political parties chose their candidates in party conventions (the stereotypical smoky back room) or caucuses—meetings of party members at the local level. In a primary election, each prospective party nominee has to obtain more votes than any other prospective nominee to run as the party's candidate in the November general election. (This system was changed again in 2010; see next section.)

- **The office block ballot**   This is the ballot that we vote on today, with a "block" for each office and the candidates listed for that office. Before this reform, in some elections, voters cast ballots for their preferred party, not for individual candidates.

- **Direct democracy**   These grassroots processes—the initiative, referendum, and recall—give citizens the ability to exert some control over both the legislative and executive branches. In this way, citizens can rein in the abuse of power by elected officials or ignite officials paralyzed by inaction and partisan bickering. These processes will be examined in detail later in the chapter.

- **The civil service** An essential element of the Progressive reform movement was the implementation of a civil service in which government employees are selected on the basis of merit, replacing the spoils system in which employees are selected based on their personal connections to the party in power. In California, the 1913 Civil Service Act created a Civil Service Commission to eliminate politics and the spoils system among the state's public employees.

During this period, the California Constitution grew substantially as the legislature enacted dozens of constitutional amendments and statutes. In the first three months of 1911 alone, the legislature passed more than 800 statutes and 23 constitutional amendments.

From 1960 to the Present: Late Revisions

In 1963, the legislature created a constitution revision commission as a result of a 1962 initiative. The commission, composed of 50 citizens, 3 state senators, and 3 Assembly members, submitted two major reports with recommended revisions to the state constitution. The legislature incorporated these into 14 constitutional amendments and submitted them to the voters for approval between 1966 and 1976; the voters approved 10. These amendments simplified, shortened, and re-organized the constitution but made few substantive changes to it.

In 1993, the legislature again established a constitution revision commission, which proposed a number of substantial changes, some of which reformers had discussed for generations. For a variety of reasons, including the difficulty of achieving the two-thirds vote in the Assembly and Senate required to place them on the ballot, they were never submitted to the voters.

In 2010, the voters implemented a change to the primary election system that echoed the effort of many Progressive era reforms to further democratize the political process. This change replaced the party primaries with a "top two" primary election, in which the top two candidates from a list of all candidates, regardless of party, proceed to the November runoff. The new system is no longer a party primary; instead it is like a swim or track meet, with preliminary and final races.

Despite numerous amendments, the California Constitution is not well suited to a state that is 25 times larger than it was in 1900. The legislature is the same size, with 40 state senators and 80 Assembly members, but each state Senate district has grown from just over 60,000 persons each to almost 1 million people; legislators are able to offer far less individualized attention to their constituents than they could in an earlier era (see the Who Are Californians feature on the next page). Small amateur groups could utilize the initiative in the early twentieth century, but well-funded interest groups are now uniquely able to take advantage of it. Serious efforts to modernize state government have been few and far between, unfortunately, and when they have occurred, as with the constitutional revision commission of the 1990s, the results have been subject to partisan voting and have not achieved the majorities necessary to send them to the people for a final decision.

Who Draws the Lines in California?

The Constitution of 1879 provided for 80 Assembly and 40 Senate districts based on population, and after each U.S. Census the lines were supposed to be redrawn by the state legislature (to account for births, deaths, and people moving). This procedure was followed until 1910, when conflict between urban and rural areas led to the Reapportionment Act of 1911, which shortchanged the growing urban areas of Los Angeles and San Francisco. In 1926, a constitutional amendment made representation in the California Senate even more unequal. In 1964, this unequal representation was declared unconstitutional by the U.S. Supreme Court (in *Reynolds v. Sims*), leading to new districts of roughly equivalent populations.

In 2008, California voters approved a new constitutional amendment that placed redistricting in the hands of the new Citizens Redistricting Commission. The commission drew new districts that followed a set of nonpartisan rules, such as geographically compact districts that kept existing cities and communities intact.

State Senate Districts, 1883

Population per district

Approx. 29,000

State Senate Districts, 1961

Population per district

- 50,000 or less
- 50,001 – 99,999
- 100,000 – 199,999
- 200,000 – 499,999
- 500,000 – 999,999
- 1,000,000 or more

State Senate Districts, 2011

Population per district

Approx. 950,000

forcriticalanalysis

1. Does the large population size of current Assembly and State Senate districts make it difficult for Californians to truly be represented in the legislature?

2. If the plan adopted by California in 1926 is unconstitutional because representation is unequal, why is it that the representation in the U.S. Senate is not invalid?

SOURCES: Join California, "Election History for the State of California, http://www.joincalifornia.com/; Don A. Allen Sr., Legislative Sourcebook (1965); California Citizens Redistricting Commission, http://wedrawthelines.ca.gov/

The Progressive Movement and Its Impact on California Politics

The development of California's distinctive constitution has been influenced by many different groups over the course of the state's history. One group whose influence is still deeply felt in California politics is the Progressives. The Progressive movement had its roots in the economic and political changes that swept the United States after the Civil War. It was foreshadowed by the Populist movement, which dominated American politics from 1870 to 1896.

Some of the political concerns and much of the moral indignation expressed by the Populists about the changes taking place in the United States were subsequently reflected in the Progressive movement. From the Civil War on, the country rapidly industrialized, and wealth became concentrated in the hands of a new breed of corporate entrepreneurs. *Monopoly* was the word of the day. These corporate giants dictated economic policy, with significant social and political consequences. One giant corporation, the Southern Pacific Railroad, held a monopoly on shipping in California and could charge producers and retailers exorbitant prices. Its vast wealth and power gave it undue influence not only economically but also politically; along with a web of associated interests, it ruled the state to a degree previously unparalleled in the nation. Bribing public officials was not unusual, nor was handpicking candidates for the two major political parties.[10]

The Progressives countered the powerful corporations, specifically the Southern Pacific Railroad, by prosecuting the corrupt politicians who served them. Eventually, this tactic led to a series of regulatory reforms that loosened the choke hold of the railroad, corrupt politicians, and interest groups on state and local politics.

Local Politics

Progressive reforms began at the local level. The battle against the Southern Pacific Railroad and corporate influence in general started in San Francisco in 1906, with the reform movement fighting to rid city government of graft and bribery. President Theodore Roosevelt stepped in to help. Working hand in hand with James D. Phelan, the former mayor of San Francisco, Roosevelt sent in federal agents led by William J. Burns to investigate bribery and corruption charges.[11] Public officials were put on trial for the bribery, bringing to the public's attention the extent of graft and political corruption in municipal government, and 17 supervisors and a number of corporate leaders were indicted.[12] The mayor was forced to resign, and his henchman, Abraham Reuf, who implicated officials of the Southern Pacific Railroad and several utility companies, was convicted and sentenced to 14 years in jail. Although the graft trials largely failed to convict those indicted (Reuf was an exception), they were nonetheless an important step in breaking the power of the Southern Pacific Railroad and its political allies.

In 1906, the Southern Pacific Railroad also dominated local politics in Los Angeles.[13] During this time, a group dedicated to good government, the Non-Partisan Committee of One Hundred, was formed. They selected a reform candidate for mayor who was opposed by the two major parties, labor groups, and the *Los Angeles Times*. While the reform candidate lost his bid for the mayoralty, 17 of 23 reform candidates for other city positions were elected.[14] The nonpartisan reformers were on their way to ridding the city of the Southern Pacific machine.

This cartoon from 1882 depicts the Southern Pacific Railroad as a destructive octopus with farmers, miners, lumber dealers, and other victims of the Railroad's monopoly on shipping entangled in its tentacles. The faces of Mark Hopkins and Leland Stanford, two of the railroad's founders, form the creature's eyes.

THE CURSE OF CALIFORNIA.

State Politics

The 1907 legislative session was one of the most corrupt on record, heavily controlled by the political operatives of the Southern Pacific Railroad. At the end of the session, the editor of the *Fresno Republican*, Chester Rowell, wrote, "If we are fit to govern ourselves, this is the last time we will submit to be governed by the hired bosses of the Southern Pacific Railroad Company."[15]

At the same time, Rowell and Edward Dickson of the *Los Angeles Express* began to organize a statewide movement to attack the Southern Pacific's power. At Dickson's invitation, a group of lawyers, newspaper publishers, and other political reformers met in Los Angeles. They founded the Lincoln Republicans, later to become the League of Lincoln-Roosevelt Republican Clubs, dedicated to ending the control of California politics by the Southern Pacific Railroad and linking themselves to the national Progressive movement.

The Lincoln-Roosevelt League participated in the statewide legislative elections of 1908 and managed to elect a small group of reformers to the legislature. Two years later it fielded a full-party slate, from governor down to local candidates.

STATEHOUSE VICTORY In 1910, Hiram Johnson became the Lincoln-Roosevelt League candidate for governor. He campaigned up and down the state, focusing on one main issue: the Southern Pacific Railroad. He claimed that the company, acting in concert with criminal elements, had corrupted the political process in California. He defined the battle as one between decent, law-abiding citizens and a few corrupt, powerful individuals who were determined to run the state in their own best interests.

Johnson won the election and met with leading national Progressives—Theodore Roosevelt, Robert La Follette, and Lincoln Steffens—to discuss a reform program for California. The new administration in Sacramento set out to eliminate every special interest from the government and to make government solely responsive to the people and Johnson. Through a series of legislative acts and constitutional amendments, they made significant progress in that direction. In 1911, the voters passed the initiative, the referendum, and the recall. These three reforms, widely known as **direct democracy**, placed enormous power and control over government in the hands of the voters. Now citizens could write their laws or amend the constitution through the initiative, approve or reject constitutional amendments through the referendum, and remove corrupt politicians from office through the recall.

In addition to these reforms, a new law set up a railroad commission with power to fix rates beginning in 1911. Other reforms included the direct primary, which gave the power to ordinary citizens to select the candidates of the political parties for national and state offices. Women obtained the right to vote in California in 1911. Legislation was also enacted that limited women to an eight-hour workday, set up a workmen's compensation system, put into practice a weekly pay law, and required employers to inform strikebreakers that they were being hired to replace employees on strike (and therefore might face verbal abuse and physical violence). These reforms were in part a reaction to what were viewed as harsh employment practices by Southern Pacific Railroad.

The Progressives in California made significant headway in limiting the influence of the corporations and the political parties in politics. In its first two years in office, the Johnson administration succeeded in breaking the power of the Southern Pacific Railroad.[16]

LAST HURRAH The national Progressive Party lost its bid to capture the White House in 1912 with Theodore Roosevelt on the ticket for president and Hiram Johnson for vice president. The failure to win an important national office weakened the party by lessening the enthusiasm of its supporters. It also meant that the party had no patronage with which to reward its followers between elections. Electoral failure was just one of several major problems that plagued the Progressives. Several other factors also contributed to the decline of the party: the public grew tired of reform; there was a major falling out among the leadership in California; the Progressives generally opposed World War I, which was supported by the overwhelming majority of the American public once the country got into the war; and the party failed to support reforms that labor so badly wanted.

When the Progressives learned that the Republican Party would not nominate Roosevelt in 1916, they offered him the nomination. Roosevelt declined. At a dinner in San Francisco in July 1916, the California Progressive Party disbanded and Hiram Johnson urged his followers to join either the Republican or the Democratic Party. Later that year Johnson, now a Republican, was elected to the U.S. Senate, where he served for 28 years.

If there was one major flaw in Progressive thinking, it was the belief in the active, informed citizen willing to participate in politics. Progressives believed that given the opportunity, citizens would be happy to support the democratic process and spend whatever time and effort was needed to participate in elections. Since the late 1940s, however, a host of studies have shown that many people neither vote nor pay attention to politics. But the Progressives leave behind the significant legacy of having gained tremendous political power for the people of California, if and when Californians choose to use it.

The Progressive strategies to gain power for the people were appropriate for 1910, when California had 2.4 million people. Since then, California has grown so much and so quickly that its constitution has been unable to catch up: in a state of now 38 million people, reforms that allowed "the people" to propose initiatives and recall public officials cannot now be exercised on a *statewide*[17] level without a great deal of money, organization, and professional help. The last initiative that did *not* use paid, professional signature gatherers was introduced in 1990, and it relied on a paid campaign coordinator. An initiative organized completely by volunteers has not been successful since 1984.

Direct Democracy

The Progressives established civil service reforms, nonpartisan commissions to control key state regulatory functions, nonpartisan elections to cripple local machines, office block voting (a ballot listing all candidates for a given office under the name of that office), and primary elections. Even if these innovations failed to check the power of special interests, they gave voters the power of direct action through the initiative, referendum, and recall. Citizens activate these three mechanisms by circulating petitions to gather a required number of signatures and bring the measure to statewide vote. The number of signatures, as we shall see, varies depending on the mechanism.

Initiative

THE PROCESS Of the three direct voices in government, the **initiative** is the most well known and most frequently used. The process, also known as direct legislation, requires the proponent to obtain a title (e.g., "Public Schools: English as Required Language of Instruction") and summary of the proposed initiative from the state attorney general. Upon obtaining the title and summary, the proponents have 150 days to circulate a petition to gather the required number of signatures to qualify for the ballot—5 percent of voters in the last gubernatorial election for statutes, and 8 percent for constitutional amendments. The secretary of state submits the measure at the next general election held at least 131 days after it qualifies or at any special election held before the next general election. The governor may call a special election for the measure.

Before 1960, initiatives appeared only on the general election ballot, thus limiting their use to the two-year election cycle. From 1960 to 2012, they appeared on the primary, general, and special-election ballots. In 2012 a new law, propelled by the Democratic majority in the legislature, again required that ballot propositions appear only on the general election ballot in November, motivated by the general consensus that the smaller and more conservative primary electorates disadvantage more liberal initiatives.

FREQUENCY OF USE Initiatives have become indispensable to California's political fabric. From 1912 to 2014, over 1,800 initiatives were titled and summarized for circulation. Of this number, 363 qualified for the ballot, 3 were removed by court order, and 123 were approved by the voters—for an overall passage rate of 34 percent. Of the 123 initiatives approved, 40 were constitutional amendments and 10 were constitutional/stationary changes.[18]

Figure 2.2 presents the use of initiative by decade. Note these two points: the increasing frequency of initiatives since 1970, and the varying, but generally low, level of success for the measures that made it to the ballot.

For discussion purposes, we can compress the 100-year history of initiatives into four time periods: 1912–39, 1940–69, 1970–1999, and 2000–14.

1912–39 From the beginning, various individuals and special interests understood that the initiative could be used to forward their special causes. Social and cultural

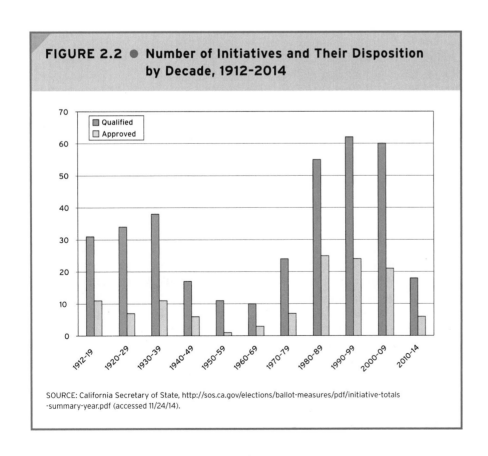

FIGURE 2.2 ● Number of Initiatives and Their Disposition by Decade, 1912-2014

SOURCE: California Secretary of State, http://sos.ca.gov/elections/ballot-measures/pdf/initiative-totals-summary-year.pdf (accessed 11/24/14).

issues, such as outlawing gambling on horse races, professional fighting, prostitution, and land ownership by Asian Americans, drew the highest voter turnout during this period. Labor issues (closed versus open shops) and tax propositions were also volatile issues.

No single issue, however, dominated the initiative process during this period more than the so-called liquor question.[19] These initiatives were among the most controversial, and they drew high voter turnouts. Twelve measures related to liquor control appeared on the ballot between 1914 and 1936, for and against full prohibition and anti-saloon measures, and state regulation versus local control. Voting was consistent throughout this period, with the anti-Prohibition forces generally prevailing on every measure. The issue, however, wouldn't go away; in 1948, after many failures to qualify an initiative, the anti-liquor forces qualified another local option measure, which was rejected by 70 percent of the voters. After this vote, the issue lost its appeal, never to appear on the ballot again.

1940–69 In this time period, use of the initiative declines markedly. Compared to the previous 27 years, a higher percentage of proposed measures failed to gather enough signatures to qualify for the ballot. The subject matter of the initiatives also varied from those of 1912–39. Newer issues came to the forefront: race and civil rights, property taxes, and labor and welfare.

Proposition 14 (1964) was the most prominent of a number of initiatives that dealt with fair housing. The initiative was drafted to nullify the Rumford Fair Housing Act, which prohibited discrimination in the rental, lease, or purchase of housing on the basis of race and national origin. The Rumford Act, supporters of Proposition 14 claimed, interfered with their private property rights. Real estate and homeowners' associations led the efforts in support of the proposition; a coalition of Democratic Party leadership, organized labor, churches, and a variety of other groups led the forces against it. The broader issue of race, specifically regarding treatment of and biases toward African Americans, lingered in the background of the campaign; by all accounts, race was the deciding factor in how people voted. Proposition 14 passed by a 2-to-1 margin in November 1964. Its victory was a major impetus for the Watts riots during the summer of 1965, which lasted six days, resulted in 34 deaths, and damaged almost 1,000 buildings.[20] Over the next two years, Proposition 14 was overturned, first by the California Supreme Court and then by the U.S. Supreme Court, for violating the Fourteenth Amendment.

1970–99 In this period initiatives abounded, with over 1,000 initiatives receiving titles, 141 qualifying for ballot, and 56 approved by the voters. The subjects involved social, cultural, and economic issues, including the death penalty, gun control, busing, the property tax, nuclear power, water resources, air quality, coastal preservation, English as the official language, affirmative action, undocumented immigrants, and gay marriage.

The most controversial initiative of this period was Proposition 13, titled the "People's Initiative to Limit Property Taxation" (1978). Sponsored by longtime antitax activists Howard Jarvis and Paul Gann, Proposition 13 was a reaction to the spiraling appreciation of property throughout the 1970s. In just one year, some properties were reassessed at a value 50 to 100 percent higher, and their owners' tax bills jumped accordingly. Proposition 13 included several provisions, one of which dramatically reduced residential property taxes and another that required a two-thirds supermajority in both houses of the legislature to approve tax increases.

Proposition 13 was a grassroots effort, opposed by nearly every state employee and labor union and most Democratic leaders. The pro side raised $2.2 million, and the con side raised $2 million. On June 6, 1978, nearly two-thirds of California's voters passed the proposition, reducing property tax rates by about 57 percent.

Now, almost 40 years later, Proposition 13 is still hotly debated. Critics argue that it creates tax inequities by treating residential and commercial property as equivalent and assessing similar properties in different ways based solely on when a homeowner bought a house. Supporters argue that pegging property taxes to the value of the property, assessed yearly, exposes homeowners to accelerated yearly property taxes, which leaves them vulnerable to losing their homes.

2000–14 During this period, California voters decided on 78 initiatives in 17 separate elections, 3 of which were special elections, including the special election to recall Governor Gray Davis. Twenty-seven passed, including measures on farm animal confinement practices, redistricting the state legislative boundaries, victims' rights, and parole procedures.

The most controversial and long-lasting ballot issue deals with same-sex marriage, an issue that has been publicly debated for some 35 years. In 1977, the state legislature passed a law stating that marriage was a "personal relation arising out of a civil contract between a man and a woman." This was reaffirmed in 2000 when the voters passed Proposition 22, a statutory—not constitutional—amendment that revised the California Family Code to define marriage formally as between a man and a woman. However, in May 2008, the California Supreme Court ruled Proposition 22 invalid. At about the same time, fearing such a decision, proponents of Proposition 8 ("Eliminates Right of Same-Sex Couples to Marry") had already begun to qualify the initiative for the ballot, relying on a **constitutional amendment**, not a **statute**, to end debate on the issue.

The campaign over Proposition 8 was fiercely contested. In the end, the initiative passed by a margin of 52.3 to 47.7 percent. Both sides raised significant amounts of money: those supporting Proposition 8 contributed $39 million, while those opposing contributed $44 million, making it the second most expensive initiative campaign in state history (behind only Proposition 87 in 2006) and the highest expenditure on a same-sex marriage initiative campaign in the nation. After the election, six lawsuits were filed with the California Supreme Court by same-sex couples and government bodies challenging the constitutionality of Proposition 8. The court consented to hear three of the six jointly, but denied the request to stay the enforcement of Proposition 8. On May 26, 2009, the court ruled that Proposition 8 was valid but allowed existing same-sex marriages to stand (in *Strauss v. Horton*).

Opponents of Proposition 8 then took their fight to federal court, which on August 4, 2010 declared the ban unconstitutional in *Perry v. Schwarzenegger* (now *Perry v. Brown*). This decision was upheld by the Ninth Circuit in February 2012. The supporters of Proposition 8 (but not the state government) then appealed to the U.S. Supreme Court. The Court ruled in *Hollingsworth v. Perry* in June 2013 that the proposition's supporters could not appeal the case; only the state government could defend a proposition approved by the voters, and the state had declined to do so. As a result of this decision, same-sex marriage is legal in California.

How can we account for the increase in initiatives over the past four decades? The simplest explanation is that it is a consequence of several factors, including

The debate over Proposition 8 continued well after the initiative was passed by a popular vote in November 2008. Supporters of same-sex marriage lined the streets of San Francisco in May 2009 in protest of the California Supreme Court's ruling in *Strauss v. Horton* that the Proposition was valid under California law.

the complexity of modern society and the increased willingness to regulate decisions previously left to citizens. Additionally, the legislature went from part to full time in 1968, which had a number of significant effects on California politics: more politicians made a career in the field, more legislation was passed, the budget grew, and decision making and power shifted to Sacramento.

These shifts, coupled with the other Progressive reforms designed to rid the capital of political corruption and an unresponsive legislature—direct primaries, term limits, regulation of campaign contributions, and various tactics to weaken political parties—undermined voters' influence on elected officials. Frustrated by the action or inaction of the legislature, voters have turned to the initiative to get what they want.

In addition to voters, special interests frequently turned to initiatives during this period to promote policies they could not get through the legislature. Increasingly, money has become the only requirement for a successful initiative campaign. As a result, an industry of professional campaign managers and signature gatherers is flourishing. These so-called policy managers identify hot issues and then search for clients who will pay for the privilege of sponsoring the initiative.

Referendum

THE PROCESS A **referendum** allows voters to approve or reject statutes or amendments passed by the state legislature. The process is as follows: the measure may be proposed by presenting to the secretary of state a petition with signatures equal to 5 percent of the voters in the last gubernatorial election. The filing of the signatures must take place within a 90-day period after the enactment of the statute. If the measure qualifies to be on the ballot, the law in question may not take effect until the electorate decides whether it should become a law.

FREQUENCY OF USE The referendum is used infrequently. In fact, it has almost faded from use. Between 1912 and 2014, 49 referenda have appeared on the ballot. Voters rejected 29 laws and approved 20. Of the 14 referenda since 1970, three appeared in 1982 and concerned congressional, state Senate, and state Assembly redistricting. The district boundaries drawn by the Democratic state legislature were condemned by the Republicans as unfair. The voters concurred and rejected all three Democratic laws, forcing new boundaries to be drawn, which, from the Republican point of view, were more reflective of political reality.[21]

Recall

THE PROCESS The **recall** allows voters to determine whether to eject an elected official from office before his or her term expires. Proponents first submit a petition alleging the reason for recall. They then have 150 days to present to the secretary of state a petition with the required number of signatures to qualify for the ballot. If the sitting official is recalled, a successor is elected. Most recalls are of school board or city council members at the local level.

For statewide offices, the number of signatures must be equal to 12 percent of the last vote for the office, with signatures from at least five counties equal to 1 percent of the last vote for the office in the county. For the Senate, Assembly, members of the Board of Equalization, and judges, the number of signatures must be equal to 20 percent of the last vote for the office. Upon receiving the petitions, an election must be held between 60 and 80 days from the date of certification of sufficient signatures.

FREQUENCY OF USE Recalls of statewide offices or the state legislature are rare. There have been eight recall elections out of 118 filings against state officeholders. Seven of the eight were state legislators; Governor Gray Davis in 2003 was the other. Four of the state legislators were expelled from office. The recall was put into use against three state legislators almost immediately after its passage—twice in 1913, against Senator Marshall Black for involvement in a banking scandal, which succeeded, and against Senator James Owen for corruption, which failed. The next year, Senator Edwin Grant, who represented the red-light district in San Francisco, was recalled for opposing prostitution, which succeeded.

Four other state legislators faced a recall vote in 1994 and 1995. The National Rifle Association failed in its attempt to recall Senator David Roberti for his position on gun control legislation. Two Republican members of the Assembly, Doris Allen and Paul Horcher, were voted out of office for supporting Willie Brown for speaker in a battle between the parties for control of the Assembly. And an attempt to recall Democratic Assemblyman Mike Machado for backing Republicans failed.[22]

The most notorious recall, however, was that of Governor Davis. He is the only California governor to have been recalled, although there have been over two dozen previous attempts, including three against Ronald Reagan in the 1960s and one against Pete Wilson in the 1990s. During the 2002 campaign for governor, Davis had claimed that the budget deficit was $18 billion, but a week after his election he revealed it was actually $35 billion. Proponents of the recall immediately accused Davis of misleading voters about the severity of the state's budget crisis during his reelection campaign. Other actions prompting the recall included the governor's efforts to prevent the anti-immigrant Proposition 187 from being appealed to the U.S. Supreme Court and his approval of two gun control measures. The public also held Governor Davis partially responsible for the electricity crisis, during which some people's electricity bills doubled and even tripled. Supporters of the recall also blamed Davis for California's generally weak economy. After Representative Darrell Issa, who hoped to run for governor, funded the signature collection effort with a contribution of $2 million, the recall took off on its own momentum. Because the filing requirements to run as Davis's successor were relatively low, 135 candidates filed to replace him. Arnold Schwarzenegger's candidacy quickly gained the most attention and he easily won the two-part election, in which voters were asked to decide whether Davis should be recalled and to choose his successor. Only 4 of the 135 candidates received more than 1 percent of the vote.

Debating the Merit of Direct Democracy

The debate about the merits of direct democracy has been ongoing since its adoption in the early twentieth century. As we have seen, the initiative has been employed more than referendum or recall and is generally the focus of the debate on the value of direct democracy.

Many scholars believe the initiative blurs the complexity of many issues and reduces them to clichés or sound bites for the voter. Some writers, such as journalists David Broder and Peter Schrag, believe that special interests with deep pockets dominate the initiative process, undermining the efficacy of representative government with its built-in system of checks and balances. Other writers, such as academics Elisabeth R. Gerber and Shaun Bowler, take a broader view, arguing that money plays a vital role in defeating initiatives but not in passing them. They argue that successful initiatives are the product of grassroots movements that have more to do with easily grasped social and economic issues than with well-financed campaigns.

Most who have studied the initiative believe it to be a flawed method of forming public policy. Many initiatives are poorly drafted and are difficult to understand even for judges and legislators. The process is complex, and proponents cannot correct errors once circulation of petitions has begun. The legislature is discouraged from participating in the process at all. Reflecting the strong historic bias of its citizens against the legislature, California is the only state that prohibits the legislature from amending initiatives unless permission is written into the initiative itself. When such permission is given, it usually requires a supermajority of two-thirds of the legislature to approve changes, a level of support difficult if not impossible to obtain on significant amendments. Qualifying initiatives by signature is too easy for a signature-gathering firm and too difficult in the five months allowed for those without one, meaning that a large amount of money is necessary in order to qualify an initiative.

Supporters of the initiative, on the other hand, claim that it is a more effective means of serving the majority in California than the legislative process. Therein lies the catch-22 that largely defines California politics: the legislature is supposedly hamstrung by the zealous use of direct democracy, while direct democracy is supposedly necessary to overcome an unproductive legislature.

A 2013 Public Policy Institute of California (PPIC) poll (see Figure 2.3) showed continued strong support for the initiative process, with 72 percent of likely voters

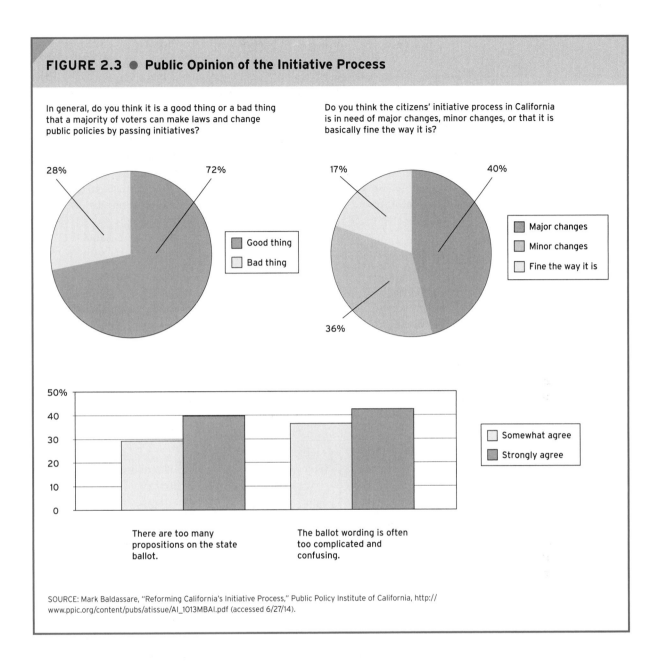

FIGURE 2.3 ● Public Opinion of the Initiative Process

In general, do you think it is a good thing or a bad thing that a majority of voters can make laws and change public policies by passing initiatives?

28%   72%

- Good thing
- Bad thing

Do you think the citizens' initiative process in California is in need of major changes, minor changes, or that it is basically fine the way it is?

17%   40%

36%

- Major changes
- Minor changes
- Fine the way it is

There are too many propositions on the state ballot.

The ballot wording is often too complicated and confusing.

- Somewhat agree
- Strongly agree

SOURCE: Mark Baldassare, "Reforming California's Initiative Process," Public Policy Institute of California, http://www.ppic.org/content/pubs/atissue/AI_1013MBAI.pdf (accessed 6/27/14).

viewing as positive the initiative's power to change public policy, and 60 percent agreeing that public policies made through the initiative are superior to those made by the governor and legislature. Likely voters support several reforms of the initiative process, however: more public disclosure of funding sources on initiatives; giving the legislature and the initiative's sponsors more time to seek a compromise before the initiative goes on the ballot; and increased public engagement, such as a citizens' commission to hold hearings on initiatives and make ballot recommendations. Oregon established such a program in 2011.

California's Constitution: Where Are We Now?

California's constitution has been through three stages—establishment in the mid-1800s, rewriting in 1879, and extensive amendment during the Progressive era. Since then, a fourth, ongoing stage has been defined by political scientists and others, in which numerous suggestions have been made to update the constitutional framework. Most notably the 1996 California Constitutional Revision Commission made many suggestions to strengthen the governor and make state government less susceptible to interest-group influence. These suggestions included:

- Having the governor and lieutenant governor run as a team. Because the governor and lieutenant governor currently are elected separately, their political agendas may diverge.

- Having the other elected members of the executive branch appointed by the governor. The governor currently has no supervisory responsibility over the lieutenant governor, the secretary of state, the treasurer, the controller, attorney general, insurance commissioner, and the state superintendent of public instruction. The lack of supervisory authority significantly weakens the governor as a leader (see Chapter 6).

- Merging the several tax administration agencies. The state currently has three tax administration agencies; merging them would save money (see Chapter 6).

- Lengthening term limits for legislators. In 2012, the term limit for state assembly members was lengthened from 6 years to 12 and for state senators from 8 years to 12, provided the total time in both chambers is limited to 12 years. This is an improvement over the stricter limits enacted in 1990, but the term limits still increase the likelihood that major, complex state legislation will be enacted by inexperienced legislators (see Chapter 4).

Most of these proposals have never come before the voters.

Study Guide

FOR FURTHER READING

Allswang, John M. *The Initiative and Referendum in California, 1898–1998*. Stanford, CA: Stanford University Press, 2000.

Broder, David. *Democracy Derailed: Initiative Campaigns and the Power of Money*. New York: Harcourt, 2000.

California Secretary of State. "Initiative Totals by Summary Year 1912–March 2012." www.sos.ca.gov/elections/ballot-measures/pdf/initiative-totals-summary-year.pdf. Accessed August 3, 2012.

Donovan, Todd, S. Bowler, D. McCuan, and K. Fernandez. "Contending Players and Strategies: Opposition Advantages in Initiative Elections." In *Citizens as Legislators: Direct Democracy in the United States*, edited by S. Bowler, T. Donovan, and C. Tolbert, 133–52. Columbus: Ohio State University Press, 1998.

Gerber, Elisabeth. *The Populist Paradox: Interest Group Influence on the Promise of Direct Legislation*. Princeton, NJ: Princeton University Press, 1999.

Hofstadter, Richard. *The Age of Reform*. New York: Washington Square Press, 1988.

Johnson, Hiram. "First Inaugural Address." January 3, 1913. http://governors.library.ca.gov/addresses/23-hjohnson01.htm. Accessed August 3, 2012.

Matthews, Joe, and Mark Paul. *California Crackup, How Reforms Broke the Golden State and How We Can Fix It*. Berkeley: University of California Press, 2010.

Mowry, George. *The California Progressives*. Chicago: Quadrangle Paperbacks, 1963.

Olin, Spencer C., Jr. *California's Prodigal Sons: Hiram Johnson and the Progressives, 1911–1917*. Berkeley: University of California Press, 1968.

"Policy Forum: Do Ballot Initiatives Undermine Democracy?" Cato Policy Report (July–August 2000): 6–9. www.cato.org/pubs/policy_report/v22n4/initiatives.pdf. Accessed June 20, 2012.

Schrag, Peter. *Paradise Lost: California's Experience, America's Future*. Berkeley: University of California Press, 1998.

Starr, Kevin. *Inventing the Dream: California through the Progressive Era*. New York: Oxford University Press, 1985.

———. *California: A History*. New York: The Modern Library, 2005.

Swisher, Carl Brent. *Motivation and Political Technique in the California Constitutional Convention: 1878–79*. New York: Da Capo Press, 1969.

ON THE WEB

Baldassare, Mark. *At Issue, Reforming California's Initiative Process*. San Francisco: Public Policy Institute of California, 2013. www.ppic.org/main/publication.asp?i=1071. Accessed May 13, 2014.

Baldassare, Mark, Dean Bonner, Sonja Petek, and Jui Shrestha. *The Initiative Process in California*. San Francisco: Public Policy Institute of California, 2013. www.ppic.org/main/publication_show.asp?i=1072. Accessed May 13, 2014.

California Secretary of State. *Ballot Measures*. www.sos.ca.gov/elections/elections_j.htm. Accessed May 13, 2014.

California State Constitution. www.leginfo.ca.gov/const.html. Accessed May 13, 2014. [This site makes the California State Constitution searchable by keyword.]

Center for Governmental Studies. *Democracy by Initiative*. Los Angeles. May 2008. www.cgs.org [search for "Democracy by Initiative"]. Accessed May 14, 2014.

Initiative & Referendum Institute. www.iandrinstitute.org. Accessed May 13, 2014.

Southern Pacific Historical & Technical Society. www.sphts.org. Accessed May 13, 2014.

SUMMARY

I. The history of the constitution comprises four stages.
  A. 1849: basic structure of government established. Includes separation of powers, bicameralism, federalism, and popular election of most state offices.
  B. 1879: a constitutional convention adds nine new articles and 8,000 words to respond to the reform needs of the time.
  C. 1910–17: the Progressive era adds the initiative, referendum, and recall, as well as hundreds of reform laws.
  D. 1960–present: California voters have authorized a few significant reforms.

II. Proposing an amendment to the California constitution is easy.
    A. Amendments can be proposed in three ways:
        1. Through a constitutional convention. The legislature can convene the convention by a two-thirds vote, or it can be convened by a majority vote of the electorate from an initiative. A Bay Area business group tried to collect sufficient signatures for a new constitutional convention in 2009–10 but gave up because professional signature-gathering firms refused to work with the group, feeling that the effort would imperil their future existence.
        2. Amendments may be proposed by collecting signatures through the initiative process.
            a) Signatures totaling 8 percent of the vote in the last gubernatorial election are required, collected over a five-month period.
            b) Most amendments are proposed this way. The cost is approximately $1 million to $2 million, mostly for signature gathering.
        3. The legislature may propose an amendment by a two-thirds vote.
    B. Ratification stage. In each case, the electorate must then ratify the amendment before it goes into the constitution. A majority vote is required.

III. The Progressive reformers had several key goals.
    A. Ending the dominance of big business over the state, especially the Southern Pacific Railroad.
    B. Reforming the corrupt political process.
    C. Removing from office corrupt political officials at the state and local levels of government.
    D. Returning political power to the people.

IV. Progressive laws and constitutional amendments wrought many significant changes.
    A. Ended child labor.
    B. Established a state park system.
    C. Enacted protections for working people.
    D. Established nonpartisan elections.
    E. Instituted primary elections.
    F. Created office block voting.
    G. Set in motion the process of direct democracy—the initiative, referendum, and recall.
    H. Resulted in the vast bulk of the Progressive reforms that are still in operation today.

V. Direct democracy is a vital aspect of California politics.
    A. The initiative is the most popular of the three direct democracy mechanisms.
        1. Proponents need to gather signatures equal to 5 percent of voters in the last gubernatorial election for statutes and 8 percent of the voters for constitutional amendments.
        2. Since 1912, roughly 34 percent of initiatives that have been voted on have passed.
        3. The initiative has increasingly become a mechanism by which special interests or wealthy individuals can pass legislation by circumventing the legislature.
    B. The referendum allows voters to approve or reject statutes or constitutional amendments passed by the legislature.
        1. Proponents need to gather signatures equal to 5 percent of voters in the last gubernatorial election.
        2. The referendum is infrequently used and has appeared on the ballot less than 50 times since 1912.
    C. The recall allows voters to remove a public official from elected office before his or her term is up.
        1. The number of signatures that needs to be gathered depends on the office: 12 percent of the last vote for statewide office from at least five counties equal to 1 percent of the last vote in the county; 20 percent of the last vote for office for Senate, Assembly, and Board of Equalization.
        2. Since 1912, there have been only eight recalls of statewide officials and legislative members.
        3. Governor Gray Davis is the only statewide official to have been recalled.

PRACTICE QUIZ

1. The popular democracy process by which citizens can place a constitutional amendment or statute on the ballot is called a(n)
   a) referendum.
   b) initiative.
   c) recall.
   d) nonpartisan election.

2. The individual who served as governor during much of the Progressive period was
   a) Chester Rowell.
   b) Edward Dickson.
   c) Hiram Johnson.
   d) Samuel P. Huntington.

3. The process by which a certain percentage of those who voted in the last gubernatorial election can sign petitions to vote on a law enacted by the legislature is a(n)
   a) referendum.
   b) initiative.
   c) recall.
   d) nonpartisan election.

4. The process by which an elected official is removed from office before his or her term expires is called a(n)
   a) referendum.
   b) initiative.
   c) recall.
   d) nonpartisan election.

5. Progressive reformers pointed to this company whenever they spoke about machine politics and corporate privilege in Sacramento:
   a) Standard Oil Company
   b) Bank of America
   c) Southern Pacific Railroad
   d) Northern Securities Company

6. The only sitting California governor to be recalled from office was
   a) Ronald Reagan.
   b) Jerry Brown.
   c) Gray Davis.
   d) Pete Wilson.

7. Which of the following direct democracy devices allows voters to approve or reject statutes or amendments passed by the legislature?
   a) referendum
   b) direct primary
   c) initiative
   d) recall

8. In which historical block was the greatest number of initiatives titled?
   a) 1912–39
   b) 1940–69
   c) 1970–99
   d) 2000–14

9. Which of the following is not a Progressive Era reform?
   a) nonpartisan elections
   b) primary elections
   c) the office block vote
   d) party caucuses

10. Which of the following is not a legal way to amend the California constitution?
    a) The legislature can convene a constitutional convention by a two-thirds vote.
    b) The governor can sign into law a proposed amendment passed by the legislature.
    c) The legislature may propose a constitutional amendment by a two-thirds vote.
    d) The electorate can propose a constitutional amendment through the initiative process.

CRITICAL-THINKING QUESTIONS

1. The California Constitution has gone through a series of revisions. Identify the periods of those revisions and discuss the contributions that each made to the state's political structure.
2. Suppose you worked for a coalition of interest groups supporting legislation to increase the state sales tax to fund a state-run health care system. The coalition is frustrated by the lack of action in the legislature. They come to you for advice about the initiative process and the possibility of success. What would you tell them, based on what you've learned in this chapter?
3. Some people argue that direct democracy provides citizens with another way to correct the behavior and deci-sion making of public officials. Others argue that it is merely the instrument of those special interest groups that have enough money to manipulate the political process. Present an argument for each position. Where do you stand in this debate?
4. California is the model Progressive state. The key components of the Progressive agenda, however, greatly weakened the role of political parties in the state. Identify and discuss how some of the reforms of this period have weakened the state's party system. Is this a good or a bad thing? Do you think there are any correlations between weak parties and the increasing use of the initiative process?

KEY TERMS

constitutional amendment (p. 35)
direct democracy (p. 31)
initiative (p. 32)

Progressive movement (p. 21)
recall (p. 37)

referendum (p. 36)
statute (p. 35)

3

Interest Groups and the Media in California

WHAT INTEREST GROUPS DO AND WHY THEY MATTER IN CALIFORNIA POLITICS

Consider the diversity of organizations that try to influence governmental policy or legislation:

- A **student organization** opposes legislation to raise tuition at state universities.
- A **business trade association** supports legislation that would reform the state's workers' compensation insurance system.
- A **telecommunications company** opposes legislation mandating the use of hands-free telephones in cars and trucks.
- A **citizens' group** supports legislation that would impose stricter penalties on people convicted of drunk driving.
- An **association of county governments** opposes legislation that prohibits the placing of certain juvenile offenders into group homes that are located in residential neighborhoods.
- A **public employees' union** supports legislation that prohibits state agencies from contracting with businesses unless the businesses pay their employees the equivalent of a living wage.

Each of these organizations is an interest group. Interest groups have always been part of California's (and the United States') political landscape. They are a product of freedom of association, a First Amendment right under our democratic system of government.

Interest groups are associations of individuals who seek to influence policy decisions in the legislature, the executive branch, and administrative agencies, as well as through direct legislation (the initiative). They are one method, as is voting, for individuals to voice their opinions on issues that concern them.

Interest groups are also called pressure groups, political advocacy groups, special interest groups, and lobbying groups. Because they focus primarily on influencing policy decisions in the legislature, interest groups are often referred to as the **third house**, a term that describes their standing and influence in the legislative process.[1]

In California, interest groups are especially influential because of the state's unique political landscape. As we shall see, open primaries, top-two primary elections, term limits, and nonpartisan elections at the local level have freed candidates from party dependence and pushed candidates toward interest groups for financial backing and help with mobilizing voters. At the same time, interest groups have realized that they can successfully use the initiative process to achieve political goals, and have spared no expense in launching propositions, even when they are in conflict with broad-based citizen interests.

Character of Interest Groups

All Californians are represented by interest groups, whether wittingly or not, such as county and city governments, trade associations, labor unions, professional and religious organizations, educational institutions, and environmental groups. When a government recognizes the right of association, citizens will exercise that right, and groups of all types will form. There is much debate about the influence of interest groups in the political arena, especially about whether the theories of **pluralism** or **elitism** best explain their status and power in the political process.

In pluralist theory, the political system is considered a marketplace in which a multitude of interests compete, no single interest or combination of interests is powerful enough to dominate, and government sits outside as an umpire or referee. Pluralist theory argues that power is dispersed. To achieve success, interests often have to join together to bargain and negotiate with opposition interests, producing, by the end of the process, policy decisions. Pluralist theory acknowledges that some groups are stronger and even more successful than others; however, it also contends that these groups do not necessarily succeed all or a majority of the time—weaker but well-organized groups do succeed sometimes in achieving their goals or checking stronger groups.

Elitist theory acknowledges that there are many interest groups active in the political process, but most of them have minimal power. Power rests in the hands of a few groups, such as large national and multinational corporations, universities, foundations, and public policy institutes, where leaders (elites) set the agenda and determine the policy outcomes of government. Accordingly, when it comes to important policy matters—the economy and noteworthy social policies—elites representing a narrow range of groups determine the basic direction of public policy. Still, elite theory recognizes that less powerful groups, most commonly in coalition with other less powerful groups, are occasionally able to check the proposals of elites. This is especially true when elites can't agree among themselves on policy choices.

But neither of these theories perfectly describes interest groups in California; in practice, California politics is a blend of pluralism and elitism. In each legislative session, there is widespread interest group activity, with literally thousands of interests competing for influence on more than 2,000 bills. Most of these groups, from child care facilities and auto repair shops to environmental organizations, trade unions, and businesses, focus on measures that directly affect their interests. Often these issues are of limited concern to the public at large. In these circumstances, the groups involved in the issue, whether supporting or opposed to it, work to create policy through competition and compromise. Here the pluralism theory fits well. Yet on some broad-based issues, a small number of (elite) groups, such as public employee unions and multinational corporations, influence decision making to favor their own special interests. They are able to exert power on the legislature, the public, and other interest groups because of their economic clout and ability to contribute great sums of money to candidates, independent committees, ballot initiatives, and public relations campaigns. In the end, California politics is a mixture of pluralism and elitism, depending on the issue in question and the stakes presented.

Diversity of Interest Groups

The term *interest group* is all inclusive, covering a wide range of businesses and organizations. The California secretary of state classifies interest groups into 19 categories and indicates the amount spent by each category for lobbying during a two-year legislative session. Table 3.1 lists the figures for the 2011–12 session.

Many organizations openly state in their literature and on their websites that **lobbying** or advocacy is a major part of their activity; this is a principal reason why many individuals and businesses join the group. For example, the California Applicants' Attorneys Association claims to be "the most powerful and most knowledgeable legal voice for the injured workers of California"; the California Labor Federation, AFL-CIO, professes to promote "the interests of working people and their families for the betterment of California communities"; and the California Alliance of Child and Family Services lobbies "on behalf of its member agencies and the children and families they serve."

Table 3.2 lists the top employers of lobbyists. This list has remained relatively stable over the past several years, with 4 or 5 groups moving in and out of the ranks from one year to the next, depending on their agenda in the legislative session. By most standards, the lobbyists for these groups are some of the most successful in Sacramento. Note how the top 10 employers of lobbyists match up with the categories in Table 3.1. The health sector, for instance, is third in total contributions, and the California Hospital Association and Kaiser Foundation Health Plan both make the list.

Individual businesses and educational institutions, however, rarely identify lobbying as one of their activities. This is understandable and perfectly legitimate: lobbying is not a primary reason for the existence of these organizations. They participate in politics to protect their chief interests, profits and education. But they are careful not to call attention to their involvement in politics out of fear that they may alienate customers or tarnish their image. Accordingly, information

TABLE 3.1 ● Lobbying Categories and Spending, 2011–12

Category	Amount ($) (in millions)
1. Government	$95.1
2. Miscellaneous**	95.0
3. Health	70.0
4. Manufacturing, industrial	46.6
5. Finance, insurance	38.2
6. Education	33.6
7. Labor unions	28.9
8. Utilities	28.3
9. Professional, trade	27.8
10. Oil and gas	25.5
11. Transportation	14.3
12. Entertainment, recreation	12.5
13. Real estate	12.2
14. Merchandise, retail	11.4
15. Agriculture	8.5
16. Public employees	7.3
17. Legal	5.6
18. Lodging, restaurants	2.1
19. Political organizations	0.3

**Includes hundreds of interest groups, such as professional and trade associations, environmental organizations, and religious groups.

SOURCE: Data from California Secretary of State, http://cal-access.ss.ca.gov/Lobbying/Employers/list.aspx?view-category (accessed 6/20/14).

about their lobbying activity must be obtained from newspaper accounts and public disclosure documents.

Many businesses do join professional or **trade associations** to give them a voice on issues that affect their industry. "We're the champion of California businesses, large and small," the California Chamber of Commerce proudly asserts on its web site: "For more than 120 years, CalChamber has worked to make California a better place to do business by giving private-sector employers a voice in state politics." Its more than 13,000 member businesses give the chamber tremendous clout and stature. In turn, individual members enjoy several advantages—sharing of cost, strength in numbers, and, perhaps most important, anonymity.

Government also lobbies government. Taxpayer protection groups have come to call these interests—education, health, special districts, local government, state agencies—"the spending lobby" because they are motivated by the desire to maintain or increase their revenue. In 2012, for instance, government was the highest spender among the 19 categories of lobbyist employers registered with the secretary of state.

According to governmental lobbyists, the passage in 1978 of Proposition 13, which limited the property tax revenues to local government, spurred the growth in governmental lobbying and the competition for funds. John P. Quimby, Sr., a former Assemblyman who lobbies for San Bernardino County, told the *Riverside Press*

TABLE 3.2 ● Top Ten Lobbyist Employers, 2011–12

Organization	Cumulative Expenditures
Western States Petroleum Association	$9,972,581
California State Council of Service Employees	9,673,834
California Teachers Association	8,392,908
California Chamber of Commerce	6,656,837
Kaiser Foundation Health Plan Inc.	5,969,645
Chevron Corporation and Subsidiaries	5,664,624
California Hospital Association	5,042,076
California Manufacturing Association	4,548,643
City of Vernon	4,319,069
AT&T	4,305,482

SOURCE: Data from California Secretary of State, http://cal-access.ss.ca.gov/Lobbying/Employers/list.aspx?view-category (accessed 6/20/14).

Enterprise in 1997: "I wish government wasn't for sale like this, but the fact is you have to hustle to get your share. Local governments without lobbyists see the ones with representation doing better so they say, 'We need to get our butts on board and get one [lobbyist] or they're going to steal everything from us.' "[2] Or, to put it another way, government agencies spend taxpayers' money to lobby government for more money to spend on taxpayers.

Proliferation of Interest Groups

In California over the last two decades, the number of interest groups and lobbying expenditures has grown steadily. In 1990, lobbyists represented approximately 1,300 interest groups; in 2000, the number had nearly doubled to 2,552; and in 2012, it had increased to 3,468.[3] During the same period, lobbying expenditures also grew substantially with just a slight dip in 2009–10, as seen in Table 3.3.[4]

California continually ranks first nationally in number of interest groups and amount spent on lobbying activity. California accounts for one-third of all lobbyist activity in the country (but only 12 percent of the country's population). Texas and New York rank second and third behind California in population, and together they spend around 60 percent of what is spent in California on lobbying activities.[5] What Carey McWilliams said about California politics during the 1930s and 1940s still holds true today: "Interests, not people, are represented in Sacramento. Sacramento is the marketplace of California where grape growers and sardine fishermen, morticians and osteopaths bid for allotments of state power."[6]

Several factors have encouraged the proliferation of interest groups:

WEAK POLITICAL PARTIES California has weak parties for a variety of reasons, but largely because of the Progressive reforms of the 1910s. The reforms were directed at the spoils system in government, the control of the political parties over which candidates would represent the party in general elections, and the influence of interest groups in the legislature. To balance these influences, the Progressive

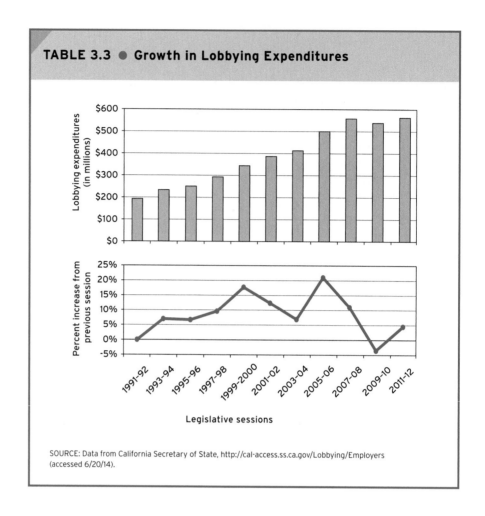

TABLE 3.3 ● Growth in Lobbying Expenditures

SOURCE: Data from California Secretary of State, http://cal-access.ss.ca.gov/Lobbying/Employers (accessed 6/20/14).

reforms granted voters the direct democracy practices of initiative, referendum, and recall. These measures and subsequent reforms—many of which were considered citizen initiatives, such as the direct primary, term limits, redistricting by an independent commission, and top-two open primaries—greatly free officials from party structure and discipline. But politicians still need money, resources, and support to win reelection, and so they have looked to interest groups in lieu of parties for help. In this way, Progressive attempts to curb interest group influence strengthened it instead.

GROWTH OF GOVERNMENT California government has grown substantially over the past half century. Californians, like other Americans, initially were suspicious of government, perceiving it as a force whose powers had to be kept in check to protect individual rights. As time passed, however, citizens began to perceive government as a tool that could be used to solve myriad social and economic problems. The legislature has eagerly taken up the challenge. A byproduct of the expansion of government has been a growth in local levels of government lobbying the state legislature. For example, in 2011–12, counties, cities, special districts, school districts, and public employee unions spent over $95 million, more than any other sector, on lobbying legislation that would affect their interests. (See Table 3.1.)

TERM LIMITS In 1990, California voters approved term limits for all state and legislative offices. Term limits, it was argued, would break the cozy relationship between elected officials and lobbyists. Yet this has not been the case. As legislators with years of institutional memory left office, the legislature became more chaotic and less efficient. This opened the door for the "third house" of special interests to gain influence, as lobbyists had institutional memory that new legislators lacked. Legislators often rely on lobbyists to write intricate legislation and counsel them on the flood of complex issues that come across their desks.[7]

PUBLIC INTEREST GROUPS The growth of **public interest groups**, what some call the New Politics movement, began in the 1970s and continues through today. Examples of such groups are AARP, Sierra Club, and the Foundation for Taxpayers and Consumer Rights. As the textbook *We the People* explains, the public interest lobby sought to distinguish itself from other groups—business groups, in particular—by "purporting to represent the general good rather than its own economic interests." Although these so-called public interest groups claim to represent *only* the public interest, they should be judged critically; they are sometimes facades behind which narrow private interests hide.

Interest-Group Strategies

Today, in California, politics *is* interest groups. Not all interest groups, however, are equal. Some have considerably more clout than others. The success of an interest group depends on several factors: a clear message, group cohesiveness, the alignment of the group's interests with those of other groups and elected officials, an understanding of the political process, technical expertise, and money. As we shall see, money is especially important.

Lobbyists

The people who do the work for interest groups are called lobbyists, and the work they do is called lobbying. Lobbyists are at the forefront of interest-group activity. They coordinate the efforts to secure passage, amendment, or defeat of bills in the legislature and the approval or veto of bills by the governor. Having a good lobbyist is paramount to the success of any group.

There are citizen lobbyists and professional lobbyists. A **citizen lobbyist** is not paid to advocate for a particular issue or set of issues. Citizen lobbyists interact with their representatives to express their personal views on an issue and to attempt to influence legislation on that issue. Professional lobbyists are paid for their services and must register with the secretary of state. They also must submit quarterly disclosure reports detailing for whom they are working, the amount of money earned, and payment such as gifts and honoraria made to public officials they lobby.

There are two categories of professional lobbyists: contract and in-house. **Contract lobbyists** make up 50 percent of all lobbyists in Sacramento; **in-house lobbyists** account for the other half.[8] Contract lobbyists offer their services to the general public; they are advocates for hire and often represent multiple clients on a variety of issues at the same time. In-house lobbyists are employees of a trade, professional, or labor association and represent that group's interest only. Many of these interest groups also use contract lobbyists because the group is involved

Lobbyists and special interests are often seen as the driving force behind politics in California, as illustrated by this cartoon from the Los Angeles Daily News.

in too many issues for its in-house staff to handle, or it may want to use a lobbyist who specializes in a specific subject area such as health insurance. A group may also want to use a lobbyist who has a close relation with a particular legislator or members of a specific committee whose support is vital for the group's success.

LOBBYING THE LEGISLATURE Few issues are just lobbied—that is, discussed with a legislator or his staff during the legislative process. Most issues are managed using a combination of techniques: public relations (marketing), grassroots mobilization, and coalition building.

The first job of the lobbyist is to know the group's objective. Is the goal new legislation? Is it to amend existing law? Or is it to stop another business or interest group from passing new legislation or amending an existing law that may affect the group's interest? The goal may not even be legislation. The group may want to amend current regulatory policy or shape the content of new regulations that will affect its members.

The lobbyist must also identify other groups that may have an interest in the issue and assess whether these groups, as well as legislators, the executive branch, regulators, or the general public, will support or oppose the group's activity. Moreover, lobbyists who can rely on the group's members, especially if they reside in the legislator's district, can more easily influence policy making. The most successful efforts are built around networks of activists who have made it a point to know their elected officials. These relationships can be built in many ways: working on election campaigns, commending a representative in writing for an action he or she has taken, contributing to political campaigns, and connecting in other ways so as to have a positive relationship with these officials.

With this preparation in hand, the lobbyist has a greater chance of success. Of course, several other factors are also important: knowledge of the legislation process, strong communication skills, established relationships, credibility, adaptability to change, and the ability to negotiate.

LOBBYING THE EXECUTIVE BRANCH The techniques used to lobby the executive branch are similar to those used in lobbying the state legislature. There are, however, two main differences between these two branches that make lobbying the executive more challenging. First, unlike most other states, California has a number (seven) of statewide elected administration offices composing the plural executive, making it more difficult to coordinate lobbying, especially when the elected officials of those offices are from different political parties. Second, the executive branch includes more than 85 agencies, 325 state commissions and boards, and 30 educational institutions (see Chapter 6). The agencies write and oversee the implementation of thousands of regulations that have a powerful impact on different sectors of society at different times. The regulations they write and implement are generally very subject-specific, and often very technical. This forces a lobbyist to develop expertise—and relationships—with a number of different agencies.

Campaign Contributions to Candidates

Besides expenditures on lobbying to influence legislative action, interest groups also make campaign contributions, which enable them to become familiar with and gain access to legislators. They do so through **political action committees (PACs)**.

There is a connection between lobbying success and campaign contributions. Those who invest heavily in lobbying generally invest heavily in PAC contributions, and vice versa.[9] Table 3.4 lists the top 10 contributors for the 2011–12 legislative year. The table shows only the amount directly contributed to candidates for the state legislature—the total of which was $120,581,941. This figure does not include what these organizations may have contributed to the Democratic or Republican Party committees ($63,248,773) or ballot initiatives ($517,380,752), which, when totaled, comes to an additional $580,629,525.[10] Campaign contributions enable a lobbyist to gain access to legislators. The lobbyist can then make his or her argument—at which time he or she can provide the legislator with important,

TABLE 3.4 ● Top Ten Contributors to Legislative Candidates, 2011–12

Organization	Amount ($)
California Association of Realtors	$1,279,774
California Teachers Association	833,200
California Dental Association	711,021
Pechanga Band of Luiseno Mission Indians	695,200
AT&T	671,401
California State Council of Laborers	668,800
State Building & Construction Trades Council	603,100
AFSCME District Council 57	545,750
Service Employees Local 1000	528,330
California State Association of Electrical Workers	511,200

SOURCE: National Institute on Money in State Politics, http://beta.followthemoney.org (accessed 6/20/14).

Who Spends Money in California Politics?

Cost of a Seat in the California Legislature, 2011–2012

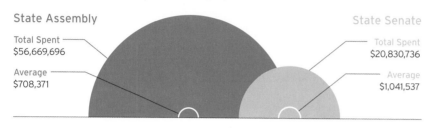

State Assembly

Total Spent
$56,669,696

Average
$708,371

State Senate

Total Spent
$20,830,736

Average
$1,041,537

Highest and Lowest Spenders

$ State Assembly $ State Senate

$0 $5M

$21,142
Steve Fox
(D-Palmdale)

$259,147
Steve Knight
(D-Antelope Valley)

$3,028,308
Richard D. Roth
(D-Riverside)

$4,112,876
Ken Cooley
(D-Rancho Cordova)

Top Individual and Interest Group Contributors, 2012

■ Donations for ballot initiatives   ■ Donations to Democrats   Donations to Republicans

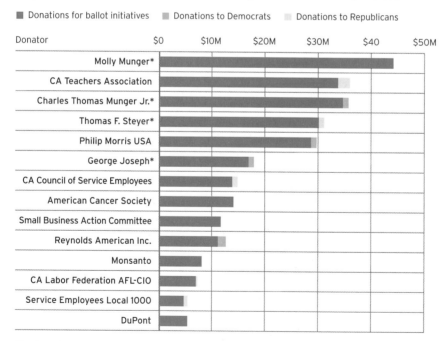

Donor $0 $10M $20M $30M $40 $50M

Molly Munger*

CA Teachers Association

Charles Thomas Munger Jr.*

Thomas F. Steyer*

Philip Morris USA

George Joseph*

CA Council of Service Employees

American Cancer Society

Small Business Action Committee

Reynolds American Inc.

Monsanto

CA Labor Federation AFL-CIO

Service Employees Local 1000

DuPont

*Denotes Individual

SOURCES: Maplight, "The Cost of a Seat in the California State Legislature, http://maplight.org/data-release/data-release
-the-cost-of-a-seat-in-the-california-state-legislature (accessed 4/11/14); National Institute on Money in State Politics,
http://www.followthemoney.org/database/state_overview.phtml?s=CA&y=2012 (accessed 4/11/14).

Every election cycle, interest groups and individual donors spend massive amounts of money in California politics. As the data here show, a large proportion of donations go to support or oppose ballot initiatives rather than to candidates, which suggests how important the initiatives are to law-making in California. But candidates also raise large amounts of money. In the 2012 election cycle, each member of the California State Assembly raised $708,371 on average, which comes to $970 every day over the two-year cycle. Each member of the California State Senate raised $1,041,537 on average, or $1,427 every day.

forcriticalanalysis

1. Should more be done to limit the role of wealthy interest groups and individuals in California politics, or is this sort of campaign spending an important component of political speech?

2. What do you think contributes to the high cost of candidate and ballot measure campaigns in California?

often technical information. To put these numbers in perspective, consider that the average cost of a seat in the California Assembly was $708,000 and in the California Senate was $1 million during the 2011–12 election cycle.

In 2010, the U.S. Supreme Court in *Citizens United v. Federal Election Commission* held that political action committees could raise unlimited funds from individuals, corporations, and unions to support or oppose candidates for office. Though a landmark case nationally, *Citizens United* had little impact on political spending in California because California had allowed such spending before the Supreme Court's ruling.

Interest groups in California also spend large sums of money on initiative campaigns. In fact, as the Who Are Californians feature shows, the top spenders in California politics in the 2011–12 election cycle gave between 86 and 100 percent of their total political expenditures to ballot initiatives. Donations to candidate campaigns were small in comparison.

California's disclosure laws require independent committees to file the same financial reports as candidate committees and ballot measure committees. In a study of independent committees in California from 2005 to 2010, Linda Casey of the National Institute on Money in State Politics demonstrated that independent spending amounted to 9 percent ($228.8 million) of the total amount spent directly on candidates and initiatives ($2.5 billion).

Jesse Unruh, former speaker of the Assembly, once said, "Money is the mother's milk of politics." This adage still holds true today. Most interest groups have PACs and carefully target their campaign contributions. They support individuals in positions of power (e.g., incumbent state officers, party leaders in the legislature, committee chairs, and rising stars). Contributions have little to do with a legislator's or party's political ideology. The only question is this: Can this legislator help me achieve my goals?

CALIFORNIA CORRECTIONAL PEACE OFFICERS ASSOCIATION An example of the dynamics of campaign contributions and lobbying can be seen in the California Correctional Peace Officers Association (CCPOA), one of the most powerful interest groups in Sacramento. It has achieved this status through a combination of aggressive lobbying, large campaign contributions, and skillful public relations. The CCPOA, a union, is one of the biggest contributors to candidates running for statewide and legislative office. Over the past decade, the union has spent nearly $42 million on lobbying and campaign activities,[11] contributing aggressively to the campaigns of its supporters and just as aggressively to defeat those who oppose its agenda. The union is one of the few public employee groups to give generously to both Republicans and Democrats. For example, when Pete Wilson ran for governor in 1990, prison guards gave $1 million to his campaign. Wilson reciprocated with substantial pay increases and stronger sentencing policies. The union made its most significant show of support, however, to Gray Davis. Besides granting him early endorsement in the primary, which guaranteed his selection as the Democratic candidate for governor, it contributed more than $3 million between 1998 and 2002 to his campaign war chest. During the same period, the union gave millions of dollars to members of the legislature, with especially large sums going to the leadership of both parties. Governor Davis responded in kind. Correctional officers' wages were tied to those of highway patrol officers. Retirement benefits, sick leave and overtime provisions, and uniform allowances were greatly increased.

CCPOA also spent heavily—$1.8 million—in support of Jerry Brown's 2010 gubernatorial victory. In March 2012, the legislature and Governor Brown agreed on a new contract, which the union overwhelmingly approved. The contract increased officers' pension contributions, reduced pay in one year by requiring one day of unpaid leave each month, and eliminated a state-funded, $42 million-a-year 401(k)-type plan that correctional officers had received in addition to their pensions. These changes sound like losses. However, as the *San Francisco Chronicle* pointed out, the contract eliminated limitations on accrual of vacation time, currently estimated at more than 33 million hours and with costs to the state calculated at $1 billion.[12]

Governor Brown argued that collective bargaining is about "give and take" and claimed that the deal with the correctional officers was comparable to what other public employee unions received under Governor Schwarzenegger. Moreover, some allege that the union contract is a bargaining chip to gain union support for the governor's prison reform agenda, including closing youth prisons and transferring up to 30,000 low-level offenders from state prisons to local jails. These reforms are intended to save the state millions of dollars. Still, the returns from CCPOA's campaign spending and lobbying suggest that the strategy has paid off handsomely for the union. Today, "California's prison guards are the nation's highest paid, a big reason that spending on the state's prison system has rocketed from less than 4.3 percent of the budget in 1986 to more than 11 percent today."[13]

Grassroots Mobilization

Up until now, we have focused on the influence of interest groups on the state legislature and executive branch. Interest groups, however, flex their muscles in other ways in the electoral process: through get-out-the-vote and initiative (direct legislation) campaigns.

GET OUT THE VOTE Many interest groups engage in get-out-the-vote (GOTV) operations among their members to help a candidate (and political party) or an

The California Correctional Peace Officers Association, the union representing the state's prison guards, is one of the most influential and aggressive lobbies in Sacramento. California's prison guards are now among the highest paid in the country.

issue win at the ballot box. This is especially true during what are perceived as hotly contested elections. In such instances, GOTV can be the most important activity undertaken because there are many examples of an election being won or lost by a handful of votes.

GOTV operations are often considered "outsider strategies"—that is, they take place outside the traditional arena of interest-group activity (the legislature) and they are supported by groups that feel they have a vital stake in the outcome of the election. Examples of this are Hispanics' interest in 1994 in defeating Proposition 187, which declared undocumented people ineligible for public services, and the Protect Marriage Coalition's efforts in 2008 on behalf of Proposition 8, which eliminated same-sex couples' right to marry.

Some interest groups, such as organized labor, religious denominations, and minorities, have a long history of mobilizing their members to vote for or against a candidate or critical issue. Other interest groups, such as gay people, environmentalists, and gender-based groups, have more recently begun to participate in GOTV activities. They mobilize their supporters at the grassroots level through a variety of techniques, including direct mail, door-to-door canvassing, telemarketing, poll watching, pickup, phoning, and assistance. Months of work go into planning the campaign. While the goal is simple—delivering members' votes—the outcome is unpredictable until the final tally of ballots.

INITIATIVES Chapter 2 explored the history of the initiative and the impact of some of those that passed. What was initially considered a tool for citizens to check the actions of elected officials and the influence of interest groups in the legislature is still considered so today. The majority of voters support the use of the initiative because they believe that the public is better suited than elected representatives to decide "important government issues," although many believe that a few narrow economic interests also shape public policy through the initiative process.[14]

Yet, as Elisabeth Gerber shows, this may not be as big of an issue as voters think. Although there are now more initiatives and considerably more money spent on them, groups with different goals use the initiative process differently. On the one hand, narrow (economic) interest groups, whose members join because of their occupation or professional status, rely primarily on the mobilization of money for initiative campaigns. They use these monetary resources and, to a lesser extent, personnel in two ways: "to protect the status quo or to pressure the legislature." When they sponsor initiatives, the measures generally fail. On the other hand, citizen groups, whose members join as free individuals committed to some personal belief or social issue, rely primarily on the mobilization of personnel who "volunteer their personal time and energy . . . to pass new laws by initiative."[15] In the end, the measures citizen groups back succeed at a higher rate than those sponsored by narrow economic interests.

Regulating Interest Groups

Interest-group politics is not new; lobbyists have played a visible and sometimes controversial role in California politics for a long time. The most notorious figure was Arthur Samish, whose influence in the state legislature during the 1930s and 1940s drew national attention. Samish represented the most powerful industries in the state: oil, liquor stores, transportation, breweries, and racing. Samish was not shy about his influence. He once told a grand jury looking into his lobbying activities, "To hell with the governor of California. I'm the governor of the legislature."[16]

Samish's downfall came as a result of two articles in *Collier's* magazine in 1949 about "the man who secretly controls the state."[17] In the article, when asked who had more influence, himself or Samish, Governor Earl Warren responded, "On matters that affect his clients, Artie unquestionably has more power than the governor."[18] Soon after the articles appeared, Governor Warren asked for legislation to regulate lobbyists and require the disclosure of lobbyists' financial activities. The legislature obliged first with the Collier Act and later with the Erwin Act, two of the earliest efforts to regulate lobbying in the state. The legislature also voted to ban Arthur Samish from the capitol building. Somewhat thereafter, Samish was convicted of income tax evasion and sentenced to three years in federal prison, thus ending his career as a Sacramento power broker.

As the preceding discussion has illustrated, interest-group influence has not remained on the sidelines; quite the opposite, in fact. It is not surprising that with the growth of the "lobbying industrial complex" in California, allegations of influence peddling follow and sometimes turn out to be true. For example, Clay Jackson, one of the most influential lobbyists in Sacramento, was accused in the early 1990s of offering large campaign contributions to Senator Alan Robbins in return for the lawmaker's support on legislation benefiting Jackson's clients. The FBI uncovered Robbins's part in the plan, and he agreed to wear a wire to expose Jackson in exchange for a reduced sentence. In the end, Jackson, Robbins, and former state senator Paul Carpenter (who funneled campaign money through a public relations firm for Robbins's personal use) were convicted of engaging in a money-laundering scheme.

Again, in 2014, the Senate was rocked by the indictment of three members—Ron Calderon, Rod Wright, and Leland Yee. Senator Wright was convicted of voter fraud and perjury, and the other two still face trial on federal charges for alleged misdeeds that include accepting money to influence legislation (Senator Calderon) and coordinating weapons sales to help pay down campaign debts (Senator Yee).

Senator Wright appealed the verdict; however, he lost the appeal. He has been sentenced to 90 days in jail and ordered to complete 1500 hours of community service. Each of the accused, however, remains on voluntary pay leave until the courts rule on their case. In the interim, several reform bills have moved forward in the Senate that include stricter limits on gifts that lawmakers can accept and tighter campaign fund-raising and disclosure laws. Whether such laws pass the Senate, or would make an impact if in fact passed, remains to be seen.

These incidents raise questions about the connections among interest groups, money, and power in Sacramento. They reveal how a legal fund-raising system can be used to benefit legislators, especially in an environment in which there is a fine line between campaign contributions and influence over legislators' votes—even when these processes are conducted legally.

This dubious history of influence peddling has prompted numerous efforts at reform. With the passage of the **Political Reform Act (PRA)** of 1974, California lobbyist and interest groups are required to report campaign and lobbying expenditures. At the same time, the PRA shifted the filing of lobbying statements from the state legislature to the independent Fair Political Practice Commission.

Since its passage, the PRA has undergone numerous amendments, the most significant being in 2000 with the passage of Proposition 34. The following rules now govern interest groups and lobbyists:

- A lobbyist or lobbying firm cannot present a gift to a state-elected official or legislative official in aggregate of more than $10 a month. Anyone who is not a registered lobbyist can give up to $250 in gifts in any calendar year.

- A lobbyist cannot contribute to state candidates or officeholders if he or she is registered to lobby that candidate or officeholder's agency. However, the various interest groups that employ lobbyists have no such restrictions.

- Interest groups, individuals, and businesses have specific limits on election contributions to candidates or officeholders. The limits for legislative candidates are $3,200; for all state offices except the governor, $5,300; and for governor, $21,300.

Some public interest groups, such as Common Cause, Clean Money Campaign, and the League of Women Voters, have called for further restrictions on lobbying expenditures and campaign contributions by both individuals and interest groups. Such measures, they argue, would constrain the power of special interests and allow public-policy decisions to reflect the overall interests of society.

Recommendations to restrict the power of interest groups fall into three categories: clean-money elections, contribution restrictions, and conflict-of-interest laws.

Clean-Money Elections

The first category, clean-money elections, would provide public funding to candidates who demonstrate a base of public support by obtaining a qualifying number of voter signatures and a certain number of small contributions and who agree to forgo any other private donations. Such measures would cover all state legislative and statewide offices and have recently been adopted by Maine and Arizona. In California, it would be difficult to get the political parties and most legislators, who are tied to the current funding system, to support the idea. It would also be difficult to convince the public that they should subsidize campaigns for elective office. Over the years, only 35 to 40 percent of California voters have supported public financing of election campaigns.

Contribution Limits

The second category, contribution limits, has been a focal point of campaign reform for some time. Most of the effort has come from citizen groups disgruntled with the current system. Together they have established stricter reporting requirements and limits on campaign contributions and loans to state candidates and political parties. The changes have been accomplished almost wholly through initiatives sponsored by these groups over the past decade—Propositions 63 and 78 in 1993, Proposition 208 in 1996, and Proposition 34 in 2000. These efforts will continue in the future as various groups attempt to rein in the free flow of money into political campaigns.

One of the biggest issues involving campaign finance has been the rise of super PACs. Technically known as independent expenditure-only committees, super PACs may raise unlimited sums of money from corporations, unions, associations, and individuals and then spend unlimited sums to overtly advocate for or against political candidates. Super PACs must, however, report their donors to the Federal Election Commission, and may choose to do so on either a monthly or quarterly basis, as a traditional PAC would. Unlike traditional PACs, super PACs are prohibited from donating money directly to political candidates, though this has not prevented them from exerting enormous influence in elections.

Conflict-of-Interest Laws

The last category, conflict-of-interest laws, covers a multitude of situations. These laws are based on the belief that government officials owe their loyalty to the public, and that personal gain should not be part of the political process. Conflict-of-interest laws prohibit government officials from participating in decisions in which they have a vested interest, such as a business or real estate investment, or in any variety of situations in which they or their family would stand to gain financially.

There are, however, government official–lobbyist activities that technically fall outside of conflict-of-interest laws but may give the impression of conflict-of-interest. For example, the California Senate offers lobbyists who contribute to its charity, the California International Relations Foundation, the opportunity to travel with the lawmakers to various foreign countries.[19] Each donor contributes $2,000 to $3,000, which gives the donor a seat on the foundation's board of directors and the invitation to travel with legislators on trade and cultural trips to foreign countries. Since 2004, there have been 18 trips to places such as Tokyo, Jerusalem, and Rio de Janeiro. The foundation operates out in the open, and it does not underwrite the expenses of either the traveling legislators or the supporters. Critics, however, contend that it creates a conflict-of-interest situation by providing a unique opportunity for supporters to gain the goodwill of and access to legislators. This is especially convenient when the supporter's interest group has a bill pending in the legislature.

The Media

For most Californians, the **media**—news stories, paid political commercials, public debate, direct mail—are the most influential sources of information on the activity of interest groups, the amount of money spent on lobbying and political campaigns, and the increasing frequency and amount of money spent on initiatives. The media keep citizens actively involved in politics.

The term *media* refers to the dispensers of information, including broadcast media (radio and television), print media (newspapers and magazines), and electronic media (the Internet). An individual source is a *medium* (the Latin singular of *media*). Sometimes we speak about mass media but most often the limiting adjective (*mass*) is assumed.

Television

For many years, television has been the medium of choice for obtaining political information for the vast majority of Americans, and Californians are no exception. Although the rise of digital media has challenged television's dominance, TV retains a slight edge.[20] This medium can spread messages quickly, covering a wide variety of topics, including car chases, earthquakes, and the latest political scandal. Television is particularly important for conducting political campaigns in a large state with a diverse population such as California. Yet for all its speed and ability to reach large numbers of viewers, television is a medium that provides little information on government.

Two facts account for this lack of information: (1) California is so big and diverse that it is difficult to cover statewide political and governmental news, and (2) Californians in general are not that interested in state government and policy. These dynamics, along with a fragmented political structure, produce a stark reality—the largest state in the nation, with some of the largest media resources and markets in the nation, provides relatively little political and governmental news, particularly on television news programs.[21] There are few media correspondents in Sacramento. More important, because there is no newspaper distributed statewide, there is no incentive to cover news on a statewide basis.

The nightly news stations compete with one another for viewers. But in reality, the news formats provide little in the way of important political information. The half-hour news format is crammed with commercials, weather reports, entertainment news, sports coverage, and a host of other topics that do little to inform the viewer about the political problems that affect the state and nation. Those topics that are reported with any depth are calculated to achieve ratings and are structured to last over several newscasts.

Each local station has its own version of some type of "action" news team or consumer protection group bringing audiences the latest artificially hyped crisis. From the nature of the issues covered, it is clear that local television, for the most part, has made a concerted effort to treat political news as a secondary issue. Issues related to political parties, government, or interest groups in California don't have the power to reach and energize large populations on a day-to-day basis.

Local television stations focus our attention on issues such as crime in a way that government representatives cannot. Sensational undercover stories are frequently broadcast, such as the financial deceptions practiced by automobile dealers, the unsanitary conditions in local restaurants, and the health risks of cosmetic surgeries. These exposés help identify dishonest practices in our communities, but they are also examples of how the ability to identify important political issues has passed from the political parties to the media. The media place an issue on the agenda, often based more on its sensational appeal than its practical importance, and the next day government representatives are telling the public what must be done to fix the problem. They are reacting to the media's promotion of the issue.

In California, where voters have the ability to put statute and constitutional initiatives on the ballot, local television plays a major role in disseminating information to voters about these issues through extensive advertising campaigns. These messages are drafted and paid for by the interest groups that support the initiatives, and the political parties may or may not play a role in the process. The broadcast media have the power to reach a vast audience, something the parties cannot do on their own.

Newspapers

The number of newspapers across the United States has fallen during the last 25 years, and newspaper circulations have declined in every recent year as well. Newspapers still remain active in identifying political corruption, reporting the workings of state and local government, covering political campaigns, and helping keep the public focused on important political issues. But newspapers in the final analysis are businesses and must be able to generate revenues and profits. To adequately cover state government, reporters and news staff have to be located in Sacramento. At the same time, on-the-spot coverage of county and local government requires a second set of reporters and news staff. The expense is prohibitive, and, over time, newspaper coverage at the state and local levels has noticeably declined. The public is not as fully informed about the activities of its various levels of government as it needs to be. The *Los Angeles Times* and the *Sacramento Bee* cover developments in Sacramento more extensively than other newspapers, but both have become victim to cost pressures and the need to reduce news reporting staffs in the 1990s and 2000s.

The drive for profits has reduced the news reporting capabilities of broadcast and print media, which cover only the big stories at the state government level. Ultimately, this means the public receives little information about the political activities of state and local government. This leads to a public that constantly finds itself surprised by political crises that seem to develop suddenly, such as rising state deficits, electricity shortages, declining state bond ratings, school facilities that are falling apart, and an overwhelmed freeway system. But for all their failings, broadcast and print media still play an important role in the election process and in formulating the political agenda. The media continue to identify the major political issues, report on the political progress of candidates at all levels, question the candidates and officeholders, and edit the replies the public is allowed to hear and read. These powers continue to undermine the role of political parties in California.

With Arnold Schwarzenegger's election as governor in October 2003, the public gained a renewed interest in state politics. People were curious. A few stations that had closed their Sacramento news bureaus announced their reopening. This wasn't surprising: nationally known figures have generally drawn more media attention than regional or local personalities. There was more coverage of Governors Edmund G. Brown, Ronald Reagan, and Jerry Brown, each of whom was a presidential contender, than of Governors Deukmejian, Wilson, and Davis, who were not.[22]

As time passed, however, though the increase in coverage remained, it was due no longer to Schwarzenegger's celebrity but to the state's economic woes: record budget deficits, sinking bond ratings, high unemployment, and staggering foreclosure filings. These concerns still persist today under Governor Jerry Brown. Local government, interest groups (especially public employee unions whose members are impacted by the budget deficits), and the general public have turned to Sacramento for solutions. Economic issues are the big concern, not the political personalities to whom have been thrown the responsibility for resolving these problems.

The Internet

Today the Internet offers instant access to political information and the opportunity to communicate one's views quickly to political leaders, news outlets, interest groups, and other individuals through blogs, Twitter, Tumblr, Facebook, and other social media channels. Many experts see the Internet as a catalyst for enhancing the democratic process. It offers candidates the opportunity to communicate rapidly with supporters and to recruit campaign workers. During the presidential election season, it has proven to be an excellent tool for raising campaign funds. The

Internet offers political parties the opportunity to disseminate their issue positions to millions of potential voters quickly and inexpensively. Whether it will restore some of the power political parties have lost remains to be seen. The Internet is open to all users, and in that environment, political parties will still have lots of competition over control of the political agenda.

Online and digital news are the only forms of news media that have continued to increase their number of users over the past three years. Americans are turning more and more frequently to their tablets and smartphones to obtain news—64 percent of tablet owners and 62 percent of smartphone owners use these devices to get their news on a weekly basis, while 37 percent of tablet owners and 32 percent of smartphone owners use them for news on a daily basis.[23] At the current rate of increase in their usage, these devices will soon surpass television as Americans' preferred source for news.

Politics currently lags behind other domains such as advertising and marketing in its use of social media. At best, political campaigns develop web sites that outline a candidate's or party's position on important issues in hopes that possible supporters will visit the web sites and donate to the campaigns that they represent. However, campaigns are beginning to recognize and harness the power of social media networks and digital media to influence the electorate.

The example of Proposition 32, a 2012 initiative, demonstrates how the strategic implementation of new media campaigns can transform voting behavior. Proposition 32 would have limited the money that unions could spend on lobbying and prohibited them from putting money toward campaign contributions that had been gained through automatic dues deductions from members' paychecks. By the end, the amount spent in the election was great—$75 million against and $60 million for the proposition. Midway through the campaign, with support for the "No on Proposition 32" cohort lagging, union leaders concluded that young voters—those under 30 years old—weren't being influenced by the union television ads because they weren't watching them. Therefore, the unions switched tactics. Employing sophisticated data-mining techniques and research via Facebook, they identified patterns of behavior among younger voters that gave clues about their political beliefs. In turn, they began speaking the language of these voters through their medium of choice, particularly through smartphones and tablets, in an attempt to influence their voting. They sent online messages, ads, and even some direct mail to individuals whom they had targeted through their research. Within a couple of weeks, support for "No on Proposition 32" among young voters rose from 40 percent to 60 percent, and the measure was ultimately defeated in the statewide election.[24]

With the growth of social and digital media, access to California's political and news sources has expanded exponentially. Today, major newspapers provide daily emails that focus on topics of the reader's interest, while research organizations, libraries, and blogs provide political information, background, and research. A list of some of the major sources covering California politics is provided in Table 3.5.

Media and Political Campaigns

Running for office is a very expensive endeavor, and it requires highly focused political messages. Because of these requirements, electronic media are the media of choice to reach large numbers of citizens. The media are also very useful in mobilizing supporters on Election Day. Mobilizing a candidate's base of support

TABLE 3.5 ● Online Sources Covering California Politics

MAJOR NEWSPAPERS

Capitol Weekly (www.capitolweekly.net)
Los Angeles Times (www.latimes.com)
Sacramento Bee (www.sacbee.com)
San Francisco Chronicle (www.sfgate.com)

ORGANIZATIONS

Around the Capitol (www.aroundthecapitol.com)
California Progress Report (www.californiaprogressreport.com)
Calitics (www.calitics.com)
Calbuzz (http://www.calbuzz.com)
California Politics and News (http://capoliticalnews.com)
California Political Review (www.capoliticalreview.com)
CalWatch (www.calwatch.com)
Flashreport (www.flashreport.org)
Fox & Hounds (www.foxandhoundsdaily.com)
Rough & Tumble (www.rtumble.com)

PUBLIC POLICY SITES

Public Policy Institute of California (www.ppic.org)
California Health Care Foundation (www.chcf.org)
California Policy Inbox (http://inbox.berkeley.edu)

UNIVERSITIES

University of California at Berkeley (http://igs.berkeley.edu/)
California State University Bakersfield (www.csub.edu/library/)

MAJOR COLUMNISTS

Joe Garofoli of the *San Francisco Chronicle* (www.sfchronicle.com)
George Skelton of the *Los Angeles Times* (www.latimes.com)
Dan Walters, Daniel Weintraub, and Peter Schrag of the *Sacramento Bee*
  (www.sacbee.com)

is essential to winning elections. Without the media, no effective message is conveyed to the electorate, and consequently no money can be raised to fuel the modern type of media campaign that candidates must use to get elected.

In some cases, the media themselves and their coverage can become a central issue in the campaign, with a candidate running against the media and positioning him- or herself outside the political establishment. During the recall election of 2003, the *Los Angeles Times* ran a story just before the election about inappropriate sexual behavior on the part of Schwarzenegger during his acting days. Many citizens reacted by asserting that the newspaper was taking incumbent Governor Gray Davis's side, not that it was uncovering important information that citizens might want to consider in their voting decisions.[25]

Interest-Group Politics in California:
Where Are We Now?

Interest groups play an important and often dominant role in California politics. The continued growth in the number of groups and their lobbying expenditures attests to this fact. Moreover, if the past decade is any indication, the number of interest groups doing business in Sacramento will continue to grow, and lobbying expenditures will continue to increase. The size and structural deficit of the state budget, weak political parties, mandated term limits, increase in public interest groups, and continued dependence of local governments on Sacramento for financial assistance are all factors that will continue to promote interest-group politics.

Much of the time, these groups are self-regulating, checking one another and forging broad-based coalitions of interests to achieve important policy decisions. Of course, interest groups will always be able to win on narrow issues affecting their members, and the most powerful will generally be the most successful, as long as they can convince a group of legislators to fall in behind them. That's why interest-group disclosure rules, campaign expenditure limits, and other reporting requirements are necessary. They enable us to keep these groups in check. That's the theory, at least.

Today, however, there is a disjunction between theory and practice. Interest groups have undue influence on politics in the state. Without some limit on the amount of money an interest group can spend on lobbying and campaign contributions, the only check on their power may be divided government, whereby one party controls the executive and one controls one or both houses of the legislature, so that no single interest or coalition of interests can ride roughshod over government.

That's the state of affairs in California today. California's politics is not broken, but unless these concerns are addressed, California will continue to hobble along, and interest groups will continue to flourish and prosper at the expense of the general public.

Study Guide

FOR FURTHER READING

Baldassare, Mark. "The California Initiative Process—How Democratic Is It?" Public Policy Institute of California, February 2002.

Boyarsky, Bill. *Jesse Unruh and the Art of Politics*. Berkeley, CA: University of California Press, 2007.

Gerber, Elisabeth R. "Interest Group Influence in the California Initiative Process." Public Policy Institute of California, 1998. www.ppic.org/main/publication.asp?i=49. Accessed August 4, 2012.

McWilliams, Carey. *California: The Great Exception*. Berkeley, CA: University of California Press, 1999.

Michael, Jay, Dan Walters, and Dan Weintraub. *The Third House: Lobbyists, Power, and Money in Sacramento*. Berkeley, CA: Berkeley Public Policy Press, 2000.

Miller, Kenneth P., Thad Kousser, and Frederick Douzets. *The New Political Geography of California*. Berkeley, CA: Berkeley Public Policy Press, 2008.

Rasky, Susan F. "Covering California: The Press Wrestles with Diversity, Complexity, and Change." In *Governing California: Politics, Government, and Public Policy in the Golden State*, Ed. Gerald C. Lubenow and Bruce E. Cain. Berkeley, CA: Institute of Government Studies Press, University of California, 1997, pp. 157–88.

Samish, Arthur H., and Bob Thomas. *The Secret Boss of California*. New York: Crown Publishers, 1971.

ON THE WEB

Around the Capitol: www.aroundthecapitol.com. Accessed August 4, 2012. A portal to California legislative information.

California Alert: http://blogs.sacbee.com/capitolalertlatest/. Accessed September 2, 2014. California and national political news and commentary.

Capitol & California: www.sacbee.com/capitolandcalifornia. Accessed June 22, 2012.

Capitol Weekly: www.capitolweekly.net. Accessed June 22, 2012.

Lobbying activity: http://cal-access.ss.ca.gov/lobbying. Accessed June 22, 2012. The secretary of state's office reports on lobbying in California politics.

SUMMARY

I. Interest groups are at the center of California's campaign and lobbying activities.
   A. Interest groups are associations of individuals who join together for the purpose of influencing governmental or legislative policy. They can be individual businesses, trade and professional associations, or labor unions.
   B. Some believe they play a necessary role in our democratic society, advocating a pluralist theory to explain the power of interest groups.
   C. Others see them as detrimental to our political system, because only a few, elite groups have power.

II. The number of interest groups (and registered lobbyists) has grown substantially in each legislative session since 1990.
   A. In the 2011–12 legislature, interest groups employed over 3400 lobbyists.
   B. In the same legislature, they spent less that $500 million on lobbying activities.

C. Interest groups have proliferated over the past three decades for four reasons: weak political parties, growth of government, term limits, and public interest groups.

III. Lobbyists do the work of interest groups. There are three different categories of lobbyists: citizen lobbyists, contract lobbyists, and in-house lobbyists.
   A. Citizen lobbyists are individuals who have an interest in an issue and want to make their view known to their public official.
   B. Contract lobbyists and in-house lobbyists are professionals who must register with the secretary of state and submit a variety of disclosure statements yearly regarding their activities.

IV. Lobbyists perform a variety of activities to accomplish their goals.
   A. The first job of the lobbyist is to know the interest group's objective.
   B. The lobbyist must also identify other organizations that could support or oppose their goals.

C. Lobbyists may work with a grassroots network of activists in a legislator's district to establish a relationship with a legislator.

D. Lobbying the executive branch is more difficult to coordinate because of the large number of regulatory agencies and commissions within the branch.

V. There is a strong correlation between lobbying expenditures and campaign contributions.

A. Interest groups that invest heavily in lobbying also invest heavily in political campaigns. Interest groups contribute to candidates' and officeholders' campaigns to leverage their influence.

B. The California Correctional Peace Officers Association is a prime example.

VI. Many efforts have been made to regulate the relationship between lobbyists and legislators.

A. The Political Reform Act of 1974 was passed to regulate lobbying practices and requires the disclosure of lobbying financial activity.

B. Proposition 34, the most recent amendment to the act, includes new restrictions:

1. Lobbyists cannot contribute to the campaigns of anyone for whom they are lobbying.

2. Lobbyists are limited in the amount of money they can contribute during any election cycle.

VII. The media are important vehicles for mobilizing and informing voters and candidates' supporters.

A. Television and newspapers have traditionally had the greatest influence on politics.

B. Today the Internet and social media, as well as the increased use of smartphones and tablets, are changing the way political messages are conveyed. Given the current growth in usage of these devices, digital media will surpass all other media as the primary source for political news and campaign management.

C. Little of this mobilization, however, comes from news programs, which generally provide scant political information.

1. Television news programs cover scandals and dishonest practices of politicians and focus viewers' attention on the latest special investigation which indirectly mobilizes citizens.

2. This demonstrates how the power to set the political agenda has passed from the political parties to the media.

PRACTICE QUIZ

1. The term *third house* refers to which of the following entities?
   a) judicial branch
   b) executive branch
   c) interest groups
   d) media

2. Over the past two decades, interest-group expenditures in California have
   a) declined.
   b) increased.
   c) remained relatively the same.
   d) fluctuated from year to year.

3. An individual who offers his or her lobbying services to multiple clients at the same time is called a(n)
   a) contract lobbyist.
   b) "hired gun."
   c) citizen lobbyist.
   d) in-house lobbyist.

4. The principal function of an interest group is to
   a) provide its members with educational and social opportunities.
   b) contribute money to candidates for public office who favor its programs.
   c) attain favorable decisions from government on issues that it supports.
   d) seek to inform the public on the role of interest in the economy.

5. Political action committees (PACs)
   a) have declined in popularity in recent years.
   b) must disclose campaign contributions and expenditures in connection with state and local elections.
   c) may make unlimited contributions to political candidates.
   d) provide candidates with public funding for their campaign.

6. According to the text, all of the following factors are involved in the media's decision not to cover more political and governmental news except:
   a) Californians are not that interested in political and governmental news.
   b) The ratings for political and governmental news are lower than other kinds of news, such as the weather, consumer news, and sports coverage.
   c) So many news programs cover California political and governmental news that there is little for each station to report.

d) Political and governmental news, except during election campaigns, does not lend itself to sensational coverage.

7. Which former speaker of the California Assembly said, "Money is the mother's milk of politics"?
   a) Jesse Unruh
   b) Willie Brown
   c) Antonio Villaraigosa
   d) Fabian Nuñez

8. Over the past two decades, the number of newspapers across the United States has _____, and newspaper circulations have _____ in every recent year as well.
   a) risen, increased
   b) remained the same, increased

   c) risen, declined
   d) fallen, declined

9. Which of the following is *not* a reason for the increase in interest groups in California?
   a) divided government
   b) weakness of political parties
   c) term limits
   d) growth of public interest groups

10. Many experts see digital media as a catalyst for _____ the democratic process.
    a) threatening
    b) enhancing
    c) having little effect on
    d) undermining

CRITICAL-THINKING QUESTIONS

1. Over the past several decades, interest groups have grown and expanded their influence over public-policy decisions in the legislature and at administrative agencies. Identify the reasons for this phenomenon.
2. Interest groups use a variety of techniques to accomplish their goal. Suppose you worked for an interest group that opposed stricter requirements for the recycling of plastic bottles. Outline a campaign to achieve your goal. Justify why you would take the action you propose.
3. Some people argue that interest groups provide citizens with another way to become involved in the political pro-

cess. Others argue that interest groups undermine the political process. Discuss the arguments for both positions. Give your opinion on the controversy.
4. Interest groups play a significant role in the funding of political campaigns. Should more restriction be put on their activity? If you decide that interest groups should be limited or altogether prohibited from contributing to political campaigns, how would this policy affect political campaigns? What would be the outcome of this reform?
5. What are the factors that have led to relatively low levels of coverage of politics and government in California?

KEY TERMS

California Political Reform Act (p. 58)
citizen lobbyist (p. 51)
contract lobbyist (p. 51)
elitism (p. 46)
in-house lobbyist (p. 51)

interest group (p. 45)
lobbying (p. 47)
media (p. 60)
pluralism (p. 46)
political action committee (PAC) (p. 53)

public interest group (p. 51)
third house (p. 46)
trade association (p. 48)

4

Parties and Elections in California

WHAT CALIFORNIA GOVERNMENT DOES AND WHY IT MATTERS

California is a trendsetter in many ways: culturally, economically, and also politically. Since it is the most populous and diverse state in the nation, laws passed in California garner a lot of national attention. Initiatives passed by California voters often set a trend as other states adopt similar ballot measures. This means the voters of California can have an impact way beyond their state border. This is quite a responsibility! In spite of this, California voters are somewhat lackadaisical about voting. A recent study by Nonprofitvote.org ranked the 50 states and Washington, DC, according to the percentage of eligible adults who actually voted in the 2012 presidential election. California ranked 41st—nearly at the bottom! While 76 percent of the eligible voters turned out to vote in Minnesota (ranked number 1), less than 60 percent of Californians voted. This ranking, moreover, was determined during a presidential election, when voter turnout is greatest. During less exciting elections, such as primaries and midterm elections, the turnout rate is much lower. For example, the June 2014 statewide primary election had the lowest turnout rate in California's history, at less than 20 percent. Only 14 percent of eligible voters in Los Angeles, the state's largest county, cast ballots. And in one of the more bizarre results of the June primary, candidate Leland Yee finished third in a field of eight candidates competing for the office of secretary of state, despite having publically withdrawn from the race after being indicted on charges of conspiracy to run guns and political corruption. He received nearly 400,000 votes.

If voting, and particularly the voting choices of Californians, is so important to the American democratic process, why aren't more Californians paying attention to and participating in elections? This chapter will look at the many factors that affect patterns of voting in California.

Political Parties

A political party is an organization of people with roughly similar political or ideological positions who work to win elections in order to gain greater control of the government and change public policy. Political parties perform many valuable functions in a democratic society. One of their most important roles is to mobilize voters at election time. They are directly involved in political campaigns: providing workers, raising money, and identifying important political issues. In theory, parties help bring about consensus on important political issues and serve as two-way communication channels between government and the people. Consequently, most political scientists consider them vital to the health of a democratic state.

California has a **winner-take-all** system of voting in which the candidate receiving the highest number of votes wins the election. Political scientists have long known that such a system promotes two dominant political parties, and, as expected, the Republicans and the Democrats dominate the political process in California. But as you will discover below, California has what is considered a weak political party system, a consequence of the reforms brought about by the Progressive movement, which took a considerable amount of power away from organized political parties.

The Progressive Impact on Political Parties

The Progressive movement viewed political parties as corrupt organizations operating in concert with big corporations to control and manipulate the political system for their own benefit. Spencer Olin describes the attitude of Progressives toward political parties:

> Accompanying their democratic faith in the wisdom of the individual voter was a distrust of formal party organizations, which were viewed as the media of special-interest power. . . . Furthermore, it was argued by progressives that science and efficient management would solve the problems of government; parties were irrelevant and unnecessary.[1]

The Progressives attacked the power of the political parties with reforms such as party primaries. **Primary elections** are used to select the party candidate who will run for office against candidates of opposing parties in the **general election**. Before primaries, party leaders typically selected their candidates in proverbial "smoke-filled rooms," outside of public view. Primaries were designed to allow voters, not parties, to select candidates for office. The primary system also opened up the opportunity to run for office to anyone capable of meeting the basic qualifications, which included age and residency requirements. Historically the party leadership and their corporate allies had selected candidates and subsequently manipulated them while they held office; with these reforms the people could participate in a whole new class of elections, forcing candidates to direct their political messages and loyalty to the average voter.

The Progressives also introduced a new type of ballot, the **office block ballot**. This type of ballot made it difficult to vote the straight party ticket, a method popular in many other states where ballots listed all the candidates running for each office by party. The use of the office block ballot in California discourages such behavior by listing each office separately.

Another Progressive reform was the introduction of nonpartisan elections, which further weakened parties by preventing party designations from appearing on the ballot for most local contests (city councils, board of supervisors, school boards, and judges). Instead, voters were given only the current occupational status of the candidate, and thus could no longer use their party loyalties to make voting decisions on Election Day at the county and city level. The Progressives wanted the electorate to research the candidates by reading up on them or attending forums.

Political scientists believe that the weakening of political parties through nonpartisan elections at the county and city levels has an impact on voters. Despite the hopes of the Progressives, most voters do not devote a lot of time to conducting research on each candidate to determine how to cast their vote. County and city races are typically low profile, so forbidding party labels on ballots further diminishes already limited information to voters. However, we do know that voters who identify with a political party view the party affiliation of candidates as important and rely on it to make their voting decisions. As Schaffner, Streb, and Wright describe it, "party identification is a, or even the, central component of voter decision making. As an effective attachment, it motivates individuals to participate as a display of party support."[2] Therefore, nonpartisan elections may have lower turnout rates than partisan ones.

The Democratic and Republican Parties in California

Currently, California is considered a very Democratic state. Democratic candidates running for the presidency are fairly confident that they will win the popular vote in California, and they visit our state not to sway voters but to hold expensive fund-raisers. Republican candidates don't spend too much time campaigning in California, as they are certain they will lose the popular vote—although, like Democrats, they do visit to collect campaign contributions. For over 20 years, our state has had two Democratic U.S. senators and the Democratic Party has controlled the state legislature.

But California has not always been in the Democratic camp. From 1952 to 1988, Republican presidential candidates won every presidential vote in California except for one (Democrat Lyndon Johnson defeated Republican Barry Goldwater in 1964). Richard Nixon and Ronald Reagan were both hugely popular in California: Nixon represented California in both the U.S. House and Senate before being elected president, and Reagan served two terms as governor of California before serving in the White House.

What caused the Republican Party to lose support? Many experts believe that demographic changes in the state help explain the ascendancy of the Democratic Party. White voters, an important part of the Republican Party coalition, are declining in numbers; as of March 2014, whites constitute just 39 percent of California's population. The state's young and ethnically diverse voters prefer the Democratic

Party. Non-whites now amount to a majority in the state, and these voters have not supported some of the more strident anti-immigrant policies touted by Republican candidates. Conservative, right-wing Republicans do not do well in statewide elections: California voters largely prefer centrist leaders who advocate moderate policies. (See the Who Are Californians feature for more information on California's party affiliation over time.)

Third Parties in California

The American political system, which is a federal system, delegates power to three levels of government: national, state, and local. One of the powers that states retain is to determine how political parties may organize and gain access to the ballot. By dominating the legislature in California, Republicans and Democrats have not made it easy for third parties to qualify for the ballot, and consequently the two parties dominate California politics. Third parties then are defined as any party other than Republican or Democrat.

Traditionally, third-party candidates do not win in a winner-take-all system, a fact that both major parties emphasize to warn voters against throwing their votes away. However, a significant percentage of voters continue to vote for third-party candidates anyway.

There are two ways that political parties can qualify to get on the ballot in California. The first method is by registration; the second is by petition. Both methods are based on a percentage of those persons who voted in the preceding gubernatorial election. In the election held in November 2014, 5,324,649 persons turned out to vote. To qualify a new party by the registration method, the law requires that 53,246 persons or 1 percent of those who voted in the 2014 gubernatorial election officially register with the new party. The law also requires that voters complete and mail their registration by the 154th day preceding the upcoming primary. The petition method is even more difficult and tedious. It requires that a new political party petition to be included in the upcoming primary, and collect signatures equal to 10 percent of those who voted in the last gubernatorial election. Currently, that number stands at over 1 million signatures. Qualifying as a new political party clearly is not an easy task and requires time, personnel, expertise, and resources. In 2014, California had seven qualified parties (see Box 4.1): the American Independent Party, the Americans Elect Party, the Democratic Party, the Green Party, the Libertarian Party, the Peace and Freedom Party, and the Republican Party.

So what is the role of third parties in politics, particularly in California? One theory is that third parties act as spoilers, drawing enough votes from one or the other of the two major parties to alter the election outcome. Third parties also help focus public attention on important political issues. Once an issue attracts enough public attention, it will be taken over by one or both of the two major political parties. Sometimes, third parties can motivate people who do not usually vote to turn up at the polls because the third-party candidate better represents their views than the established Democratic or Republican candidates.

Party Affiliation of California Voters

A plurality of California voters identify with the Democratic Party. As of October 2014, about 43 percent of voters are registered with the Democratic Party

When Did California Become Democratic?

Democratic Share of the Presidential Vote, 1948–2012

When the difference is positive, the Democratic candidate received a higher percentage of the vote in California than nationally. When the difference is negative, the Democratic candidate received a smaller percentage of the vote in California than nationally. Thus large positive values suggest California is more Democratic than the country as a whole.

■ California ▨ National

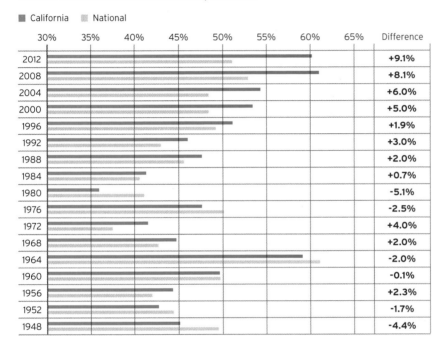

Year	Difference
2012	+9.1%
2008	+8.1%
2004	+6.0%
2000	+5.0%
1996	+1.9%
1992	+3.0%
1988	+2.0%
1984	+0.7%
1980	-5.1%
1976	-2.5%
1972	+4.0%
1968	+2.0%
1964	-2.0%
1960	-0.1%
1956	+2.3%
1952	-1.7%
1948	-4.4%

Political Party Registration

● Democratic   ○ Republican   ◉ Decline to state

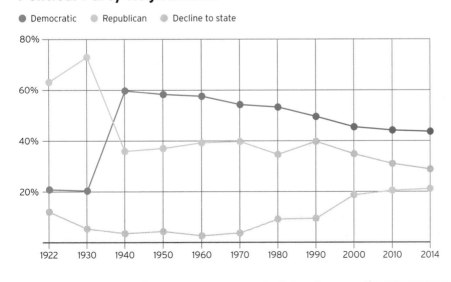

The Democratic Party dominates California politics, including all statewide executive offices, both U.S. Senate seats, and large proportions of the delegation to the U.S. House of Representatives and to the two chambers of the California State Legislature. In addition, Democrats dominate voter registration rolls. Yet, California was once similarly dominated by Republicans. During the last 25 years, Democrats have retained an edge in voter registration but have dipped below the 50 percent mark, losing increasing numbers of citizens to the "Decline to state" category.

SOURCE: California Secretary of State, http://www.sos.ca.gov (accessed 4/11/14).

forcriticalanalysis

1. Why is California so heavily dominated by the Democratic Party? To what degree is this domination related to the population shifts discussed in Chapter 1, and to what degree is this a reflection of national trends?

2. Recent years have seen a dramatic increase in the number of Californians choosing to register as "Decline to state," rather than choosing to identify with either the Democratic or Republican Party. Why do you think this is happening, and do you think it matters?

compared to 28 percent affiliated with the Republican Party. A substantial 23 percent of voters have **no party preference**, and 5 percent identify with one of the minor third parties. Party affiliation is fairly easy to determine because voters are asked to declare **political party affiliation** when registering to vote (one of the options, however, is no party preference).

As Figure 4.1 illustrates, since 1998, registration in the two major political parties has declined. The percentage of voters registering with the Democratic Party fell by over 3 percentage points, while registrations with the Republican Party fell by over 7 percentage points. The most dramatic change has been among those who have no political party preference (also referred to as independent voters). This group has nearly doubled its size over the past 20 years; more than one in five voters now claim no party preference when they register to vote.

Now let us look at political-party affiliation and some demographic factors. Figure 4.2 presents the results of a California statewide survey conducted in September 2014 that asked respondents about their party affiliation, age, gender, race, educational level, and place of birth. The results suggest that nearly 45 percent of all young, middle-aged, and older Californians prefer the Democratic Party. A recent California Field Poll (2011) found that the Republican Party is becoming the party of senior citizens. Currently, those 50 years of age or older make up 54 percent of the party, and this number is growing annually as the population ages. Many are questioning what the Republican Party of the future will look like in California with the passing of these older Republicans. Will the party be able to survive this demographic trend?

We also observe gender differences in party affiliation, with more women affiliating with the Democratic Party and slightly more men than women registering as independents. The Democratic Party has more support than the Republican Party regardless of educational level. Race is also a key predictor of party identification, with Latinos preferring the Democratic Party at a much higher rate than whites (58 percent compared to 38 percent).

Some of these demographic trends suggest that politics in our state will change in the future. Older white males' proportionate decline in the population will continue to have an impact on the Republican Party as it loses a large segment of its support.

Another important demographic change is the increasing Latino population. Data from the Census Bureau demonstrate that from 2000 to 2010 the Latino population grew by nearly 28 percent to 14 million, whereas the white population declined more than 5 percent to just under 15 million. Currently, Latinos favor the Democratic Party over the Republican Party by sizable percentages, and there is no reason to expect this to change in the future. Thus many are predicting an even stronger Democratic Party presence in the state in the future.

THE RED AND THE BLUE IN CALIFORNIA You may recall that most television programs focusing on the 2012 presidential election color-coded maps of the United States to represent the states that voted Republican as red and those states that voted Democratic as blue. The map nicely illustrated the national split between urban areas and rural, agricultural, and suburban areas: the West Coast and most of the Northeast as well as major urban areas of the United States were blue and the South, agricultural regions, and the Great Plains states were red.

As the map in Figure 4.3 illustrates, the same geographic split appears within the state of California, between the coastal counties and the inland counties. Most of the Democratic counties are coastal and encompass major urban areas, whereas most of the Republican counties are inland and rural.

As reported by the *Los Angeles Times:*

Over the last decade, Republican influence has grown more concentrated in conservative inland California—largely the Central Valley and Inland Empire but also

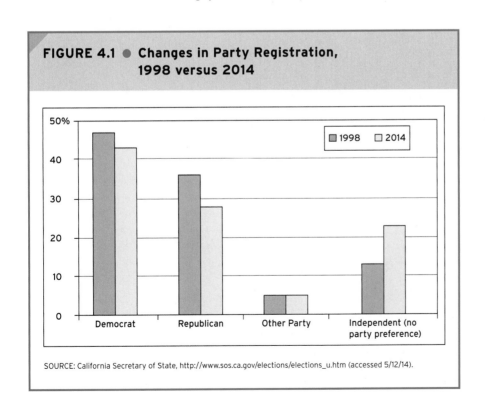

FIGURE 4.1 ● Changes in Party Registration, 1998 versus 2014

SOURCE: California Secretary of State, http://www.sos.ca.gov/elections/elections_u.htm (accessed 5/12/14).

FIGURE 4.2 ● Party Registration by Demographic, 2014

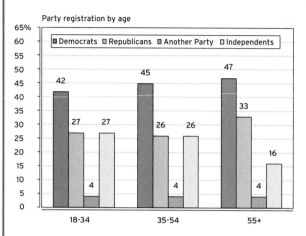

Party registration by age

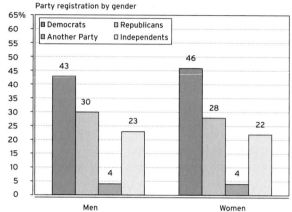

Party registration by gender

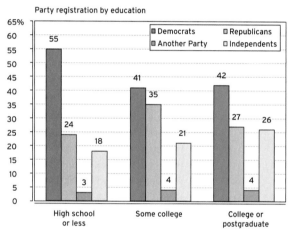

Party registration by education

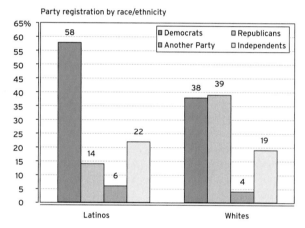

Party registration by race/ethnicity

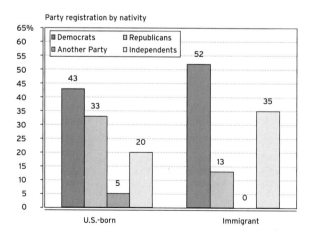

Party registration by nativity

SOURCE: Public Policy Institute of California, September 2014 survey of approximately 1,300 adult Californians.

the Antelope Valley, the Sierra and rural north. . . . At the same time Democrats have strengthened their domination of counties along California's coastline, building overwhelming advantages in the San Francisco and Los Angeles areas as Latino voters have expanded the party's base. And from San Diego's beachfront suburbs to the Central Coast, Democrats have eroded Republican support among moderates, especially women.[3]

Overall, the Democratic Party has an electoral advantage in California; nearly 70 percent of the state's population resides in Democratic-leaning coastal regions. Republicans have an uphill battle winning statewide elections and are more likely to succeed if they nominate ideologically moderate candidates who are able to win the support of Democratic voters. The fact that the urban and coastal population centers are largely Democratic and moderate to liberal, coupled with the tendency of the majority of independent voters to lean toward the Democratic Party, suggests that California will remain a distinctly blue state. This is not to imply, however, that all populated coastal regions are the same politically and ideologically. As the next section illustrates, there are some interesting variations.

California's Local Political Cultures from Left to Right

Political culture is difficult to define and quantify. However, we can offer at least a few statistics to show how three of the state's most populous counties differ in terms of political partisanship, political ideology, political activism, political tolerance, and voting tendencies on important issues. Table 4.1 compares and contrasts the City and County of San Francisco, Los Angeles County, and San Diego County on these selected indicators of local political culture.

POLITICAL PARTY REGISTRATION As of October 2014, registered Democrats outnumbered Republicans in San Francisco by eight to one and by more than two to one in Los Angeles County. In San Diego County, however, Republicans and Democrats were nearly equal at 33 and 35 percent, respectively.

POLITICAL IDEOLOGY Based on community surveys conducted in late 2000, about one in five San Franciscans identify themselves politically as "very liberal" and only 4 percent as "very conservative." In both Los Angeles County and San Diego County, conservatives outnumber liberals by about two to one.[4]

POLITICAL PROTEST AND VOTER TURNOUT Those same surveys show that San Franciscans are much more inclined to engage in political protest than are their counterparts in the southland. Specifically, 47 percent of San Francisco citizens scored "high" on a nationally normed political protest activity index, as compared with only 30 percent in both Los Angeles and San Diego counties. In terms of more conventional forms of political participation, however, San Diego County's citizens are on top, with higher voter turnout rates than San Franciscans and Angelenos in both the November 4, 2008, general election and the November 2, 2010, general election. The November 6, 2012, general election saw both San Diego and San Francisco with near equal turnout rates, with Los Angeles lagging behind. In

FIGURE 4.3 ● Percent Difference between Democratic and Republican Registration by County, 2012 Presidential Election

Dominant political party affiliation
☐ Democratic advantage
☐ Republican advantage

SOURCE: California Secretary of State, October 22, 2012, www.sos.ca.gov

TABLE 4.1 ● Regional Political Cultures: Three California Counties Compared from Left to Right

Indicator	San Francisco (%)	Los Angeles (%)	San Diego (%)
1. Democrats (2014)	56%	51%	35%
2. Republicans (2014)	8	21	33
3. Very liberal (2000)	21	8	6
4. Very conservative (2000)	4	15	14
5. High protest activity (2000)	47	30	30
6. Voter turnout (Nov. 4, 2014)	38	23	33
7. Voter turnout (Nov. 6, 2012)	57	52	56
8. Yes on Proposition 13 (1978)	47	67	60
9. Yes on Proposition 187 (1994)	29	56	68
10. Yes on Proposition 209 (1996)	29	45	63
11. Yes on Proposition 8 (2008)	25	50	54
12. Yes on Proposition 30 (2012)	77	60	46
13. Yes on Proposition 34 (2012)	70	54	45
14. Yes on Proposition 47 (2014)	79	63	55
15. Vote Brown for governor (2014)	88	66	50
16. Vote Kashkari for governor (2014)	13	34	50
17. Vote Obama for president (2012)	83	69	51

SOURCE: Indicators 1–2, 6–17: California Secretary of State, various official statements of vote. Indicators 3–5: Analysis of sample survey data obtained from the Social Capital Benchmark Survey 2000.

November 2014 voter turnout dipped overall, as this was a non-presidential election year, but a similar turnout pattern held: San Francisco voters turned out at a slightly higher rate than San Diego voters with the turnout rate in Los Angeles substantially lower.

SUPPORT FOR PROPOSITION 13 Proposition 13, the 1978 initiative that rolled back property tax rates and limited the government's ability to raise local property taxes in the future, regarded by some observers "as one of the most significant political events in California's history,"[5] won by a landslide vote nearly everywhere throughout the state, including a 67 percent vote in favor in Los Angeles County and a 60 percent vote in favor in San Diego County. In San Francisco, however, it mustered only 47 percent, not even a majority.

POLITICAL TOLERANCE AND SUPPORT FOR RACIAL AND CULTURAL DIVERSITY Table 4.1 reports county voting results on six different statewide ballot propositions over the period 1994–2014. All six can be viewed as indicators of political tolerance and support for racial and cultural diversity.

- Proposition 187 was a 1994 initiative constitutional amendment that made undocumented immigrants ineligible for various public social services. The state's voters approved it by a wide margin, with 56 percent voting yes in Los

Angeles County and 68 percent in San Diego County. Only 29 percent voted for it in San Francisco.

- Proposition 209 was a 1996 initiative constitutional amendment that prohibited state and local government agencies from giving preferential treatment to any individual or group on the basis of race, sex, color, ethnicity, or national origin. Widely viewed by friends and foes alike as an attack on affirmative action, this measure also passed in the statewide vote, with 63 percent support in San Diego County. It received only 45 percent in Los Angeles County, however, and a mere 29 percent in San Francisco.

- Proposition 8 was a 2008 initiative constitutional amendment that eliminated the right of same-sex couples to marry. Backers of the proposition placed it on the ballot as a direct challenge to the California Supreme Court's ruling in May 2008 affirming the constitutionality of same-sex marriage. The measure was approved 52 to 48 percent in the statewide vote. Only 25 percent of San Francisco County's voters voted yes, however, compared with 50 percent in Los Angeles County and 54 percent in San Diego County.

- Proposition 30 was a 2012 initiative constitutional amendment that would temporarily raise taxes to fund education. Personal income taxes would increase on those earning over $250,000 for seven years and the sales tax would increase by 0.25 cents for four years. This increased state revenue would be used to fund education at the K–12, community college, and university levels, which otherwise faced budget cuts. Teacher unions and Governor Brown campaigned aggressively for the passage of this initiative. Failure of the proposition would result in extensive budget cuts to the already struggling public school and university systems. Proposition 30 was approved statewide by a vote of 54 to 46 percent. Over three-quarters of San Francisco voters approved of the measure, as did 60 percent of Los Angeles County voters. In San Diego, however, only 46 percent voted yes.

- Proposition 34 was a 2012 initiative statute asking voters to approve the repeal of the death penalty and replace it with life imprisonment without the possibility of parole. This measure would apply retroactively to those inmates currently on death row. The measure failed to pass, with a statewide vote of only 47 percent. Contrary to the statewide vote, 70 percent of voters in San Francisco and 54 percent of voters in Los Angeles voted in favor of this measure. In San Diego County, only 45 percent voted yes.

- Proposition 47 was a 2014 initiative that would reform the state's "three strikes" law. This law resulted in harsh prison sentences for those convicted of a third offense, with the "third strike" for many being a non-violent crime. Research has found that the "three strikes" law has disproportionately affected minority populations; over 45 percent of those serving life sentences under this law are African Americans.[6] Under the law as reformed by the initiative, those convicted of certain drug and property crimes would receive a misdemeanor sentence instead of a felony sentence if they had no prior convictions for serious or violent crimes such as rape, murder, or child molestation. Additionally, this measure would allow offenders currently serving felony sentences for non-violent crimes to petition to have their felony sentences reduced to misdemeanor sentences. The measure passed with a statewide vote of 59 percent. It passed 79 percent to 21 percent in San Francisco and 63 percent to 37 percent in Los Angeles County. In San Diego County it passed by only 55 percent to 45 percent.

THE PRESIDENTIAL ELECTION OF 2012 In the November 6, 2012, presidential election, voters preferred President Barack Obama over former Massachusetts governor Mitt Romney by 59 to 38 percent. San Francisco County overwhelmingly voted for President Obama with a resounding 83 percent; voters in Los Angeles County supported him at 69 percent, and San Diego County at 51 percent.

THE GUBERNATORIAL ELECTION OF 2014 In the 2014 race for governor, the winner, Democrat Jerry Brown, easily beat Republican Neel Kashkari by 75 percent in San Francisco and 32 percent in Los Angeles County. In San Diego County, however, Kashkari beat Brown by 241 votes.

TO SUM UP The statistics in Table 4.1 demonstrate that political life varies dramatically in California from region to region. If you happen to reside in San Francisco, you live in one of the nation's most liberal, tolerant, and activist political cultures.[7] The political environment in San Diego County, on the other hand, is more conservative, less tolerant, and more passive. Los Angeles County falls somewhere between these two. These three counties reflect the range of political cultural differences that exist across the state. You can easily see why local representatives in the state legislature fight so much and so fiercely and have a very hard time agreeing on anything.

Elections in California

The Battle over the Primary

The past decade has seen considerable controversy and upheaval and a number of court challenges regarding the type of primary system used in California. In primary elections, voters select their party's nominee in the general election. In the United States, there are three general types of primary-election systems, and states have the authority to determine the system under which they will operate.

- **Closed primary system** Only voters who declare a party affiliation when they register to vote are permitted to vote in their party's primary election. Each party has its own ballot, listing the names of the candidates from their party competing to be the party's candidate in the general election. Voters receive the ballot of the party for which they are registered. Voters who decline to state a party affiliation when they register are not eligible to receive a party ballot; only party members can elect the party's nominees. Approximately 25 states use this system.

- **Open primary system** Registered voters, regardless of their party affiliation, can vote in the party primary of their choice on primary election day. For example, a registered Democrat can decide if he or she would like to vote in the Republican Party primary and request that ballot. The choice of party ballot on primary election day does not affect the voter's permanent party affiliation. Approximately 20 states operate under this system.

- **Blanket primary system**   One ballot lists all candidates from all of the parties. All registered voters, including those not affiliated with any party, are permitted to vote, and all voters receive the same ballot. For instance, a voter who is not affiliated with a party may vote for a Democrat to run as the nominee for governor and a Republican to run as the nominee for the U.S. Senate. Under this system, voters who are not affiliated with a party help to choose that party's nominees. Alaska, Louisiana, Washington State, and California all use this primary system.

California operated under the closed primary system until the passage of Proposition 198 in 1996. Proposition 198 instituted a blanket primary system in which all voters received a single ballot containing the names of all candidates from all parties. California held two blanket primaries—in June 1998 and March 2000—before the U.S. Supreme Court (in the case of *California Democratic Party v. Jones*) invalidated Proposition 198. The Court ruled that, based on the First Amendment's guarantee of freedom of association, California's political parties have the right to exclude nonparty members from voting in party primaries. In an effort to include the growing number of nonaffiliated voters, California adopted a **modified closed primary system**. Beginning with the March 2002 primary election, political parties still had their own ballots but now had the option of adopting a party rule that would allow unaffiliated voters to vote in their party primary. If an unaffiliated voter was not allowed to request a party's ballot, he or she was given a ballot containing only the names of candidates for nonpartisan races and ballot measures.

Proponents of the blanket primary were not satisfied with the modified closed primary system, arguing that the blanket primary system is more inclusive and would result in more moderate candidates running in primary elections, thus producing more competitive races. The logic is that if independent, ideologically moderate voters participate in the primary election, they will bring a counterbalance to the more extreme and ideological views of traditional primary party voters, the party loyalists. Primary candidates would, therefore, need to moderate their positions to attract the votes of moderate, independent voters. So, in June 2010, voters once more passed a proposition that changed California's primary-election system.

Proposition 14 mandates a form of a blanket primary system known as the "top-two vote getters" system. This primary system is used for state legislative and congressional seats as well as for statewide offices, such as governor and attorney general. All registered voters, even those stating no party preference, receive a ballot listing all candidates from all qualified political parties. The two candidates with the most votes for each office are then in a runoff in November's general election. An interesting feature of this new primary election system is the possibility that the top two candidates can belong to the same political party. (This system does not apply to candidates running for U.S. president, country central committees, or local offices. Presidential primaries continue to use closed or semi-closed primaries.)

The June 5, 2012, primary election was the first statewide election held under this new system, and the results were quite interesting. Of the 53 primary elections for U.S. House seats, 8 of these races resulted in top two candidates from the same party; the general election featured 6 contests pitting two Democrats against each other and 2 contests pitting Republicans against each other. Of the 20 primary contests for the California Senate, 5 resulted in November matchups between two members of the same party (all Democrats); the state Assembly contests included 15 in which Democrats went head to head and 6 involving two Republicans. This trend continued for the June 2014 primary with 25 same-party runoffs: 7 same-party contests for the U.S. House, 6 for the California Senate, and 12 for the state Assembly.

For statewide races only, this new primary system also allows candidates to designate whether they have a political party preference and how it should be stated on the ballot. According to California law, "a candidate for nomination to a voter-nominated office shall have his or her party preference, or lack of party preference, stated on the ballot, but the party preference designation is selected solely by the candidate." This means that candidates can state the party with which they identify or they can state that they don't have a party preference. In this age of voter frustration directed at party politics and legislative gridlock, electing to have the ballot state "Party Preference: None" appears to be a strategy adopted by some candidates. This is what happened in a race for a hotly contested congressional seat in Ventura County in 2012. The redrawing of the state's congressional district boundaries created a new swing district in the area. A swing district is one in which there are near equal numbers of Republican and Democratic voters and a significant number of independent voters—who often decide the winner. This new district consisted of 41 percent Democrats, 35 percent Republicans, and 19 percent independent

California's top-two primary system can result in competitive general election contests between candidates of the same party. Here, Democrats Ro Khanna (left) and incumbent Representative Mike Honda, both running for the 17th congressional district in California, shake hands after a televised debate. Honda beat Khanna by a very slim margin.

voters. There were four Democrats, one Republican, and one independent running in this primary. The "independent" candidate was actually a Republican who switched her party registration to no party preference just before filing her papers to run, hoping to win the support of enough independent and moderate voters to be one of the top two winners. A number of candidates have used this strategy, hoping voters won't remember or even know that they have been party loyalists before the campaign. Unfortunately for this candidate, the only Republican on the ballot and the better-known Democrat captured the top two positions and competed against each other in the November general election.

Will this new primary system have the intended impact of encouraging more moderate candidates to run in primaries and ensuring their success? Louisiana and Washington operate under similar primary systems, and analyses of their election outcomes found that these states have not seen more moderate candidates elected. However, some argue that blanket primaries can boost voter turnout by 3 to 6 percent by attracting voters with no party preference. The June 2014 primary election in California did not meet these expectations.

Presidential Primaries: Maximizing California's Clout?

Until 2000, California held its presidential primaries in June of election years, one of the last states to cast its votes for the parties' nominees. States holding earlier primaries and caucuses often determined the presidential nominees before Californians had a chance to go to the polls. To have more influence in the nomination process, California changed its presidential primary election date to early March. Many believed it fitting that the most populous state should have an early primary date. This earlier primary date did not give California voters more clout in the presidential nomination process, however, as other states moved their primaries to even earlier dates. So for the 2008 presidential primaries, California changed the date once again, to February 5, the earliest permissible date under national party rules.

Many political analysts and journalists heralded the early February presidential primary date. But did this move really have the intended impact, as reflected in a hopeful 2007 *Los Angeles Times* article titled "Earlier Primary Gives California a Major Voice"? Many who had argued for the 2008 presidential primary in early February believed that candidates would have to campaign early and hard in the Golden State and win support from a racially and ethnically diverse population, especially the growing number of Latino voters. To win voters' support, issues important to Californians would need to be addressed, and all this would result in California's greater prominence in presidential campaign politics. Or so the theory went.

One of the unanticipated consequences of California's adoption of an early primary date was that a number of states with long-standing early primaries set their election dates even earlier, not wanting to be overshadowed by the most populous state in the nation. Twenty-three other states also moved their primaries to February 5, resulting in something akin to a national primary. California's dream of being in the electoral limelight quickly faded.

Another consequence of the early February presidential primary was additional cost for the state, as the primaries for statewide offices continued to be held in June. The June 2008 primary election for statewide offices cost the state and counties $100 million and resulted in a historically low voting turnout rate of less than

25 percent of the registered voters. Including the November 2008 general election, California voters were asked to vote in three elections in less than 10 months. Now California's presidential primary is once again back to the June date. However, the June 2012 California primary (which included primaries for presidential and statewide candidates) saw a record low turnout of only 25 percent of eligible voters. Some believe that the frequent date changes for primary elections contribute to California's less than spectacular voting turnout rates by confusing voters.

Initiative Campaigns: Direct Democracy or Tool of Special Interests?

One legacy of California's early-twentieth-century reform movement is the **ballot initiative** process. Californians can completely bypass the state legislature and their elected representatives and place proposed policies on the ballot for direct vote by the people. As the name suggests, the electorate *initiates* initiatives. Most people think of the initiative process as direct democracy in action—concerned citizens circulating petitions to qualify their issue for the ballot and then holding an election for the public to state its preference for or against the proposed policy. In reality, only a small number of ballot initiatives emerge as a result of grassroots efforts. Initiatives are largely a political tool used by special-interest groups to achieve their policy goals. Depending on the issue, interest groups sometimes find it politically expedient to bypass the legislature altogether, believing they have a better chance of achieving their policy goals if they take the issue directly to the voters.

For example, many members of the California legislature would find it politically unwise to introduce legislation to legalize marijuana, abolish the death penalty, or raise taxes. Positions on these issues are sure to outrage some voters, making reelection more difficult. That is why these types of issues find their way onto our ballots as initiatives or referendums. Likewise, legislation that would curb the power of special interests, interests that make sizable campaign contributions to legislators, also are unlikely to be dealt with by our elected representatives. Recently, some local ballot measures have passed that reduce retirement benefits for public employees. If an elected official introduced this type of proposal, he or she would be targeted by unions representing public employees for re-election defeat. So, for many of these types of issues, interest groups realize the most productive route is to go directly to the voters via the initiative process. In addition, citizen groups have found the initiative process to be the only avenue for policy change in the areas of legislative term limits, nonpartisan redistricting, and the blanket primary system. These changes would never have been proposed or approved by legislators, whose power and that of their political party would be curbed.

Since 1912, the first year initiatives were permitted, over 350 statewide initiatives have appeared on the California ballot. These ballot initiatives have dealt with a wide range of issues, such as legalization of marijuana, campaign finance reform, same-sex marriage, taxation policy, legalization of gambling casinos, the establishment of a state lottery, environmental regulations, affirmative action policy, the criminal justice system, and labor issues. Of these hundreds of initiatives, only about one-third have been approved by the voters. In the past three decades, there has been a dramatic surge in the number of initiatives that have been proposed and that have qualified for the ballot. Many surmise that the reason for this increase is that special interests have become more sophisticated in their use of the initiative process to achieve their policy goals.

QUALIFYING FOR THE BALLOT To qualify for the ballot, the state requires over 500,000 signatures of registered voters for initiatives creating new laws (statutes) and over 800,000 signatures for propositions that aim to amend the state constitution. Signatures are gathered on petitions, which are then submitted to the secretary of state's office for verification. Collecting hundreds of thousands of signatures of registered voters is a daunting task. Rarely is this a grassroots movement in which ordinary citizens fan out across the state, knock on doors, and stand in front of supermarkets, asking strangers to support their initiative by signing a petition. More common is the hiring of professional signature gatherers, such as political consulting firms that hire individuals to go to college campuses, supermarkets, malls, and other places where voters congregate. They are paid an average of $1.50 for every signature they acquire. This means that it costs over $750,000 just to collect the signatures to qualify a proposition for the ballot.

CAMPAIGNING To wage a successful campaign either in support of or in opposition to a more controversial initiative, one needs ample political resources, particularly money. Not only must a statewide initiative campaign hire political consultants, but it must also plan and implement a sustainable media campaign. Such campaigns are very costly because of California's size and expensive media markets. Therefore, it is not surprising that the more high-profile and controversial initiative campaigns cost tens of millions of dollars. In 2008 slightly over $80 million was spent on the highly controversial initiative Proposition 8, a constitutional amendment to eliminate same-sex marriage in California. Proposition 8 was put on the ballot in response to the state Supreme Court's May 2008 ruling (in a 4-to-3 decision) declaring that the state constitution protects a fundamental "right to marry" that extends equally to same-sex couples. Both sides of the issue collected near equal contributions, with the majority of the contributions in support of Proposition 8 coming from members of the Mormon Church throughout the United States.[8] As expensive as Proposition 8 was, it did not break the record for the most expensive initiative campaign. In 2006 both sides spent more than $150 million on Proposition 87, the alternative energy initiative, which was soundly defeated by a 55 percent vote. Breaking that spending record was a series of initiatives in 2008 (Propositions 94–97) that sought to expand the number of Native American casinos in the state. According to a recent report by the *Washington Post*, the two sides spent over $170 million on those campaigns.[9] This was, by far, the most expensive proposition campaign not only in California history but in U.S. history.

It should be noted that spending more money than the opposing side does not always guarantee victory. Case in point: Proponents of Proposition 34, an initiative to repeal the death penalty on the November 2012 ballot, spent over $8 million on the yes campaign, whereas the opposition spent only a paltry $400,000 to defeat the measure.

Political savvy is another important resource. The chances of winning an initiative campaign increase if one understands how the game is played. For example, the naming of the proposition can increase its chance of passage. In the November 1996 election, Proposition 209, officially titled "Prohibition against Discrimination or Preferential Treatment by State and Other Public Entities," appeared on the ballot. Its supporters referred to the proposition as the "California Civil Rights Initiative." Considering these titles alone, it would be difficult to imagine this proposition failing; in these progressive times, it is fair to say that most voters are opposed to discrimination and are supportive of civil rights. In reality, however, Proposition 209 was not what most would consider a civil rights statute. The proposition proposed to eliminate affirmative action programs in California for women and minorities in public employment, education (college admissions, tutoring, and outreach programs), and contracting. But the clever naming worked: Proposition 209 passed and is now state law.

CRITICISMS OF DIRECT DEMOCRACY Critics of the initiative process believe that too many complicated issues are presented to the voters as ballot propositions. In some recent elections, voters have had to vote for candidates for federal, state, county, and city elective offices as well as cast their votes for over a dozen important state propositions and numerous county and city measures.

Some argue that many of the issues that appear as ballot initiatives are best suited for debate and deliberation by our elected representatives and should not be decided by misleading television ads aimed at the public. Sometimes the propositions are very confusing in name and in substance, and some question whether we are asking too much of the electorate to wade through all this information. Another problem with the initiative process is that the constitutionality of many propositions approved by the voters is later challenged. It takes years for the courts to render a decision, and it is not uncommon for the courts to declare the law based on the passage of the proposition to be unconstitutional, null, and void. Not only does this complicate the process, it also frustrates the public to see the courts invalidate its will.

The legislature understands some of the problems associated with the initiative process and has created state commissions to investigate and reform the process. Some suggested reforms aim to prohibit the use of paid signature gatherers whom only the well-funded interest groups can afford; to increase the number of signatures required, with the goal of reducing the number of initiatives; to restrict the types of issues that can appear as ballot initiatives; and to review the constitutionality of initiatives prior to placing them on the ballot. Recently, the legislature enacted two bills reforming the initiative process. These bills provide for a 30-day public review period that commences when the initiative is first proposed. Reformers hope that public input during this time will result in constructive modifications to propositions before they appear on the ballot, and that such input may motivate supporters of the proposed initiative to work with lawmakers to find a legislative solution to the issue. Additionally, the new reforms require that the Secretary of State post online and continuously update the top ten donors contributing to both sides of an initiative. This provision creates more transparency by addressing the issue of exactly who is contributing big money in support of or in opposition to an initiative.

The 2003 Gubernatorial Recall Election: A Perfect Political Storm

On October 7, 2003, Governor Gray Davis made history. Only 11 months after he successfully won his re-election bid, he was recalled from office. He was the first and only governor in the state of California and the second governor in the nation's history to be recalled. The recall movement and election of Arnold Schwarzenegger was in every sense dramatic, historic, and stunning.

Davis was reelected in November 2002, thanks in part to a very weak challenger, even though just before the election a majority of voters disapproved of his overall performance as governor.[10] Voters held Governor Davis responsible for the 2000–01 energy crisis during which Californians were forced to reduce their energy consumption and pay more for their electricity, experiencing or being threatened by blackouts. News reports focused on this issue for many months, which had a negative impact on Davis's popularity. Compounding the problem was a dramatic decrease in state revenues. The governor had to announce that the state was short $23.6 billion and that the 2003–04 budget shortfall would rise to nearly $35 billion. The state legislature could not produce a budget on time and voters were very uneasy about the economic future of the state. Davis entered his second term as a wounded, unpopular governor, viewed as distant, too beholden to special interests, and ineffectual.

Darrell Issa, a multimillionaire Republican member of Congress from the San Diego area, was a dominant force in the movement to recall Davis. He injected nearly $2 million into the recall effort and had hopes of running for governor if the recall succeeded. Nearly 1.5 million voter signatures were collected on recall petitions, meeting the state requirement for an October 2003 recall election. Unfortunately for Representative Issa's hopes of capturing the governorship, a well-known, charismatic, moderate Republican anti-politician, antiestablishment actor/businessman appeared on the scene: Arnold Schwarzenegger. In the summer of 2003, Schwarzenegger announced his candidacy and immediately became the front-runner among Republican candidates, making national and international headlines with his decision to run.[11] Politically, it was a perfect storm: a weak and unpopular governor, an unhappy electorate, and an internationally known celebrity. On the day of the election, 9.4 million Californians cast ballots, 11 percent more than the turnout in Davis's 2002 re-election. Fifty-five percent voted to remove Davis from office, and Schwarzenegger was elected governor in his place with 48.6 percent of the vote. Schwarzenegger's adoption of moderate positions—pro-choice on abortion, moderate on the environment, and cooperative with the Democratically controlled state legislature—placed him in sync with voters, resulting in his re-election victory in 2006.

The 2008 Election: Demographic and Ideological Shifts

The 2008 election was somewhat unusual, even by California standards. A very popular, young, charismatic candidate, Barack Obama, topped the ticket as the Democratic candidate for the presidency, winning 61 percent of the popular vote compared to John McCain's 37 percent, the biggest margin in the state of California since 1964.

The *Los Angeles Times*, in an article aptly titled "State's Shifting Political Landscape," described the election results:

> Those unpredictable decisions by voters, however, were accompaniments to the election's main theme: the demographic and ideological shifts that have delivered the state into Democratic hands and demonstrated anew the tough road ahead for the Republican minority.[12]

The Democratic Party was hopeful that it could continue to win the support and allegiance of the overwhelming number of voters who had cast their votes for Obama, including 83 percent of first-time voters. Seventy-six percent of those 18–29 years of age voted for Obama compared to only 48 percent of those 65 and older. However, some analysts were not confident that future elections would see high percentages of young voters turning out to vote or substantial increases in support for the Democratic Party.

By November 2, 2010, the evidence was in. The lead headline from Scott Fahey's Elections 2010 blog from Southern California Public Radio read, "Low youth voter turnout hurts Democrats." As he described it, "in California, one of every five voters in 2008 was between the ages of 18 and 29, compared with about 1 in 10 on Tuesday." California reflected the overall national trend with fewer young, liberal, and black voters casting votes in the November 2010 general election.

The 2010 General Election

While the nation witnessed a historic "shellacking" of the Democratic Party, as President Obama called it, with an unprecedented loss of Democrat-held seats in Congress, Californians voted to the beat of a different drummer. All of the Democratic candidates running for statewide elective office won and nearly all won by respectable margins. The *Los Angeles Times*, in an analysis of the vote based on exit poll data, concluded that the strength of the Latino vote was a key factor in the success of Democratic candidates. Latino voters made up 22 percent of the California voter pool, a record tally that sunk the election hopes of many Republicans.

THE GOVERNOR'S RACE The costliest statewide race in the nation's history pitted novice politician and billionaire Meg Whitman against political insider Jerry Brown. Whitman spent a record-breaking $160 million on her general election campaign (see Table 4.2 later in the chapter), with over $140 million from her own personal wealth. Of this total, she poured nearly $110 million into TV and radio advertising. Californians quickly became aware of her candidacy, and voters easily recognized her name. In contrast, Jerry Brown, who had served two terms as governor (1975–83), had been mayor of Oakland (1999–2007), and most recently had served as state attorney general, spent only $25 million on his campaign. In the end, Brown won by a very comfortable margin, 54 percent to 41 percent. Furthermore, Brown's cost per vote was only $1.24, whereas Whitman spent a whopping $51.82 per vote!

THE U.S. SENATE RACE Barbara Boxer, a liberal Democrat running for her fourth term in the U.S. Senate, had a tough re-election challenge, the toughest of her political career. Boxer, a career politician, ran against outsider and novice campaigner Carly Fiorina, a Republican and former CEO of Hewlett-Packard (HP). Typically, incumbents such as Boxer, running for re-election in a state where their political party dominates, have a relatively easy time keeping their seat. The situation was different this time around. California's economy was in shambles, Boxer's popularity had been declining, and Fiorina was a formidable opponent. In the end, Boxer prevailed, winning re-election with 52 percent of the vote compared to Fiorina's 43 percent. Many pundits believe that Fiorina's failure to moderate her position on social issues (she was ardently anti-abortion and anti-illegal immigration), along with Boxer's stinging ads highlighting the layoff of 30,000 HP workers under Fiorina's stewardship, was responsible for Fiorina's loss.

PROPOSITION 20: REDISTRICTING CONGRESSIONAL DISTRICTS VS. PROPOSITION 27: ELIMINATING THE STATE REDISTRICTING COMMISSION Propositions 20 and 27 were actually competing initiatives. Proposition 20 is an extension of Proposition 11, which passed in November 2008. Proposition 11 created the 14-member Citizens Redistricting Commission that would be in charge of drawing the boundaries of state Assembly and state Senate districts after each U.S. Census. November 2010's Proposition 20 asked voters to remove the authority for congressional redistricting from the legislature and give this power to the newly created Citizens Redistricting Commission. The commission would then be responsible for drawing congressional district lines as well as continuing to exercise the power to draw state Assembly and state Senate district boundaries. The competing initiative, Proposition 27, on the other hand, would have eliminated the Citizens Redistricting Commission and returned to the legislature the power to draw state district boundaries (essentially repealing Proposition 11). California voters soundly endorsed the Citizens Redistricting Commission (defeating Proposition 27 with a 59 percent vote against it) and gave the Commission the power to determine congressional districts as well (Proposition 25 passed with a 61 percent vote in favor).

PROPOSITION 25: SIMPLE MAJORITY VOTE TO PASS BUDGET Proposition 25 changed the legislative vote requirement from two-thirds to a simple majority required to pass the budget. In addition, all members of the legislature must permanently forfeit reimbursement for salary and expenses for every day the budget is late. California had not passed a state budget by the mandatory June 15 deadline in 23 years. Budget negotiations in 2010 extended 100 days past the deadline, just close enough to Election Day for it to be fresh in voters' minds. Californians passed Proposition 25, with a 55 percent affirmative vote. Supporters of this initiative were labor unions (especially teachers who received layoff notices when the budget was not passed on time), the League of Women Voters, groups representing retirees, and others who were able to devote resources to the "Yes on Prop 25" campaign. Since passage of this proposition, the state budget has been passed on time.

The 2012 Primary Election

The June 2012 primary was an interesting one. Usually, the major contest in the primary during a presidential election year is between the candidates competing for their party's nomination for the presidential race. But, as typically happens when states hold their primary late in the political season, Mitt Romney already had won enough delegates to secure his party's nomination, and President Obama had no Democratic challenger and was, by default, his party's nominee. Perhaps this explains why only one in three registered voters participated in this election with one of the lowest turnout rates in Los Angeles County, at less than 22 percent. As mandated by the passage of Proposition 14, this was the first statewide blanket primary using the new top two candidates system. It was also the first election since the adoption of the newly drawn congressional and state legislative districts. The ballot looked different; all voters regardless of party affiliation were given the same ballot; the results were calculated differently; and some candidates found themselves running in new or very different districts. A very interesting election, indeed.

The 2012 General Election:
More Demographic and Ideological Shifts

THE PRESIDENTIAL RACE The outcome of the November 2012 presidential election looked similar to the 2008 presidential election, with young and minority voters favoring President Obama and older and white voters supporting Romney. Statewide, President Obama won 59 percent of the vote, slightly less than the 61 percent he won in 2008. He received 71 percent of the votes cast by 18- to 29-year-old Californians, which is close to the 76 percent he received in 2008. Of those 65 years of age and older, 48 percent voted for Obama, the same percentage as did in 2008. Other notable demographic results were based on race, marital status, and place of residence. While only 45 percent of whites supported Obama, 79 percent of Asian Americans and 72 percent of Latinos voted for him. Marital status also made a difference in vote choice, with Obama receiving 67 percent of the votes of unmarried Californians and 51 percent of married voters. Voters living in urban areas voted to reelect the president by 65 percent compared to rural voters at 50 percent.

The 2012 election was interesting in terms of voter turnout rates. Although 5 percent fewer people voted in 2012 than in 2008, more young voters turned out to vote in 2012. The youth vote accounted for 20 percent of all votes cast in 2008 and 28 percent of all votes in 2012. That is a 40 percent increase in turnout among 18- to 29-year-old voters. Nationwide, there was a very slight increase in the youth vote, which grew from 17 percent in 2008 to 19 percent in 2012. What accounted for this dramatic increase in the turnout of young California voters?

According to Peter Levine, California's new online voter registration system (described later in this chapter), made available shortly before the 2012 election, registered nearly 700,000 new voters, many of whom were young people.[13] Also, Proposition 30 (the initiative to fund higher education) was a salient issue for young voters. If the measure did not pass, college students were facing another round of tuition increases, crowded classes, and cuts in enrollment to the California State University and University of California systems. This combination of an accessible online voter registration system and an important initiative impacting higher education motivated young voters.

CONGRESSIONAL RACES As mandated by the U.S. Constitution, all House members serve two-year terms in office. California has 53 House members, and in the November 2012 election, 11 new members were elected, the most new members in 20 years. Democrats won 38 of the 53 seats, and the number of seats held by Latinos also increased. These changes were a result of the recent remapping of House districts and changing demographics. A number of incumbent House members retired when their districts were redrawn after the 2010 Census, and some found themselves in competitive districts where their re-election was not assured. Prior to the 2012 election, only 1 House seat had changed between the parties during the last five Congressional elections. In 2012, Democratic candidates won 4 more House seats than they had in 2012. A second factor related to the strong showing by Democratic candidates is the growing number and clout of Latino voters, especially in southern California. As reported in the *Los Angeles Times*, "Voters in Riverside and San Bernardino counties elected three Democrats to Congress—two Latinos and a gay Asian American—after having sent only two Democrats to Washington in the last four decades."[14]

CALIFORNIA LEGISLATIVE RACES The headline in the *Los Angeles Times* on November 8, 2012, read, "Blue reign in Sacramento: Democrats' historic gains position them for unchecked power." Prior to the November 6 election Democrats had controlled both the state Assembly and the state Senate. Amazingly, the election not only allowed the Democratic Party to maintain its majority status but also its electoral successes gave it *supermajority* status. Having a supermajority means that there are enough Democratic votes in each chamber to raise taxes without needing any votes from Republicans. The last time a party had supermajority power was in 1933 when the Republicans were in charge. The Democrats last had this power in 1883. This supermajority status was short-lived—three Democratic state senators were suspended in March 2014 after being indicted on felony criminal charges.

PROPOSITIONS There were 11 measures on the November 2012 ballot. Voters were asked to weigh in on a number of issues ranging from increased taxes to funding for educational programs to the repeal of the death penalty. A record-breaking amount of money was spent on these campaigns. George Skelton, a *Los Angeles Times* columnist, wrote, "It's almost unfathomable that $372 million was spent to promote or attack the 11 measures. To put it in perspective, that amount of money could pay for the annual tuitions of 31,000 undergrads at the University of California. The top 20 donors provided 69 percent of all initiative funding."[15] What follows is a description of some of the more high-profile measures.

- **Proposition 30: Taxes to Fund Education versus Proposition 38: Tax to Fund Education and Early Childhood Programs**   These two competing propositions dealt with ways to raise revenue to fund education. Proposition 30, backed by the governor, would temporarily raise the state sales tax for 4 years and increase taxes on the wealthy for 7 years. Proposition 38 would raise taxes on earnings for all Californians for 12 years. Since these were competing measures, if both passed, the one receiving the most votes would prevail. Proposition 30 passed with 55 percent of the vote. Proposition 38 received only 28 percent of the vote even though its sponsor, Molly Munger, spent $44 million of her own money on the measure. In addition, an outside political group from Arizona spent over $11 million to defeat both Propositions 30 and 38.

- **Proposition 34: Death Penalty**   This initiative statute would repeal the death penalty and replace it with life in prison without possibility of parole. Those currently on death row would have their sentences commuted to life imprisonment. Proponents of this measure spent over $8 million. Opponents spent a small fraction of that amount. The measure was defeated with a 52 percent "no" vote.

- **Proposition 36: Three Strikes Law: Repeat Felony Offenders**   This measure would revise the existing Three Strikes law to impose life sentences only when the offender is convicted of a new violent felony. Those previously convicted under this law for nonviolent felonies may have their sentences reviewed. The measure easily passed with 69 percent of the vote.

- **Proposition 37: Genetically Engineered Foods Labeling**   This proposition would require the labeling of food that is made from plants or animals containing genetically altered material. Agroscience opponents such as

DuPont, Dow Agro, and Monsanto spent over $15 million to defeat this measure. The proposition failed, receiving only 48 percent of the vote.

The 2014 Election

Nationally, the contest between Democrats and Republicans over control of the U.S. Senate was the most important issue of the 2014 midterm elections. If the Republican Party gained 6 Senate seats, they would then control both chambers of Congress. The Democratic Party hoped to maintain control of the Senate but faced an uphill battle in a number of important U.S. Senate contests. The Republican Party prevailed and both chambers of Congress are now controlled by the Republican Party. In California, however, 2014 was a rather subdued election year, evidenced by the fact that fewer than three in ten voters participated in this election. California's two U.S. senators were not up for reelection, the governor's race was not very competitive, and only a few ballot initiatives engaged in media campaigns.

THE GOVERNOR'S RACE Governor Jerry Brown, a popular incumbent, was reelected by a comfortable margin. His opponent, Neel Kashkari, never stood much of a chance to win. Unlike Brown's 2010 challenger, Meg Whitman (who raised over $176 million, see Table 4.2), Kashkari was virtually unknown to the public and was seriously underfunded. Six weeks prior to the election his campaign had less than $700,000 to spend compared to Governor Brown's nearly $24 million. Brown agreed to only one 60 minute televised debate, which did not enjoy a large audience and did little to boost Kashkari's popularity. Kashkari's weeklong stint as an undercover homeless person in Fresno also failed to generate support for his campaign. Kashkari even gave away $25 cash cards to the first 100 people who showed up at one of his campaign events (most likely violating the state's election code that prohibits candidates from giving gifts to win votes). Brown beat Kashkari 54 percent to 41 percent and was reelected to serve a historic fourth and final term as governor.

PROPOSITIONS Six propositions appeared on the ballot, comparatively few by California standards. Below is a description of the initiatives.

- **Propositions 1 and 2: Water Bond and State Budget**   These two measures were publicized as companion initiatives ("Save Water, Save Money") and had virtually no opposition. These propositions dealt with the water crisis in California and stricter enforcement of the state's "rainy day" surplus money fund. Both propositions passed overwhelmingly with 67 percent and 69 percent of the vote respectively.

- **Proposition 45: Healthcare Insurance Rate Changes**   This measure would require the state Insurance Commissioner to review any proposed health care insurance rate increases for individual and small group plans. Proponents argued that healthcare insurance rates should be reviewed using a similar process that currently applies to automobile and homeowner's insurance. Opponents argued that this proposition was unnecessary and would result in costly bureaucratic delays, considering that California already has an independent commission whose mandate is to control healthcare rates. Most televised ads that promoted voting "No" and the "No on 45" campaign were supported by medical insurance companies and medical associations. The proposition failed with 60 percent voting "no."

- **Proposition 46: Drug and Alcohol Testing of Doctors; Medical Negligence Lawsuits**   This contentious measure would require drug and alcohol testing of doctors, mandate that doctors consult a statewide prescription drug database before prescribing certain controlled substances, and increase the cap on medical negligence from $250,000 to over $1 million to account for inflation. Supporters argued that this measure prevents "doctor shopping" by patients who want to obtain multiple narcotics prescriptions and that medical negligence damages need to be readjusted for inflation. Opponents argued that the cost of increased malpractice insurance would reduce access to medical services in rural areas and to other underserved populations because doctors, clinics, and hospitals could not afford the increased malpractice insurance rates. They also believed that the expansion of the statewide prescription drug database would be costly and possibly threaten personal privacy. Opponents which included the California Medical Association, hospitals, clinics, and organized labor outspent the "Yes on 46" side by more than 10 to 1. This measure failed by an even wider margin, with 67 percent voting against this proposition.

- **Proposition 47: Criminal Sentences; Misdemeanor Penalties**   As described earlier in this chapter, crimes such as drug possession, shoplifting, petty theft, and forgery would qualify as misdemeanor, not felony, crimes under this measure, resulting in lesser penalties for those with no prior convictions for serious, violent crimes. As reported in the *Los Angeles Times*, it is believed that 20 percent of criminals would face more lenient sentences and more than 7,000 current inmates could petition the courts to reduce their sentences.[16] Most law enforcement organizations were opposed to this measure, arguing that thousands of dangerous criminals will be released from prison and that our criminal justice system would be overwhelmed with petitions for reduced sentences. However, pre-election polling found the public to be overwhelmingly in favor of this measure. The proposition passed with 59 percent of the vote.

- **Proposition 48: Indian Gaming Compacts**   This measure would allow a band of Native Americans to build an off-reservation casino. Tribes that already have casinos were against this measure and raised nearly $7 million to defeat it. Proponents raised less than $500,000. The measure failed with 61 percent of voters not wanting to expand casinos to non-tribal lands.

Campaigning in California

California politics presents many challenges to those seeking elective office or the passage of a ballot measure. First, the immense size of the state means that statewide propositions, candidates running for statewide office, and those running for the U.S. Senate and the presidency must plan campaigns that reach voters throughout the entire state. In fact, California has 13 distinct media markets, making it very expensive to communicate to its 38 million residents about politics. Second,

California's population is very diverse, with many ethnicities, racial groups, cultures, professions, occupations, and interests represented. Successful campaigns must find ways to effectively communicate their platform and messages to all of the 18 million registered voters in the state. And third, California has passed a number of political campaign reform acts in an attempt to regulate campaign spending and to provide public information on contributions and expenditures. These laws have proved beneficial to some and not as helpful to others.

Whatever the challenges of campaigning in California, one thing is certain: California's campaign politics are watched by the nation. California is a campaign trendsetter.

Money and Politics: California Style

As the record-breaking spending in the campaigns of 2010 demonstrated, campaigning in California requires money, and lots of it. In fact, California is one of the most expensive states in which to conduct a political campaign. Table 4.2 illustrates how the candidates in the 2010 governor's race spent nearly $200 million, making it the most expensive governor's race in U.S. history.

Running for governor is not the only campaign that is costly. Running for the California legislature is also very expensive. Citing a Pew Center on the States study, Osorio notes that California is the costliest state in which to win a state Senate seat ($938,522). The least expensive state is North Dakota at $5,713. In Arizona it costs $36,696; in Wisconsin, $140,287; and in North Carolina, $234,031.[17] The prohibitive cost of campaigning in California restricts who can realistically run for office, another factor contributing to the state's governance challenges. Incumbents far outspend challengers, and incumbents' spending has increased over time while spending by challengers has not. On average, challengers spend only a fraction of what incumbents spend. This discrepancy helps to explain the high re-election rates of those elected to the California legislature. Some competitive races for the California legislature cost in excess of $1 million.

The following are some reasons that California campaigns are so expensive:

MEDIA-DOMINATED CAMPAIGNS Because of the size of the state and its 13 different **media markets**, candidates must run **media-dominated campaigns**, spending enormous amounts of money producing political ads and buying the broadcast time to air them. During the 2003 gubernatorial recall election, it cost approximately $2 million a week to run political ads statewide.[18] In the 2006 governor's race, Schwarzenegger's campaign alone spent $9 million on TV ads in the short time span between July 1 and September 30. As is shown in Table 4.2, an astounding $138 million was spent in the November 2010 governor's race just on TV, cable, and radio airtime and production. This cost is in addition to the $57 million spent on the media during the primary campaign. As one media consultant described it, "There's a lot to be said for traditional politicking, kissing babies and shaking hands, but you have to get on TV to reach voters."[19]

POLITICAL CONSULTANTS Professional campaign managers and various **political consultants**—media consultants, pollsters, fund-raisers, direct-mail experts, and voter mobilization professionals—cost money. Because of California's love for direct democracy, especially the initiative process, many well-known political consultants

TABLE 4.2 ● Spending in California's Gubernatorial Election: How the Money Was Spent, 2010

Expenditure	Whitman ($)	Brown ($)
Television and radio advertising	$106,930,505.28	$21,259,408.00
Campaign consultants	11,693,547.95	167,200.00
Campaign literature and mailings	10,582,303.93	2,532,801.36
Campaign workers' salaries	5,918,110.80	157,870.01
Radio airtime and production costs	5,472,228.17	0
TV or cable airtime and production costs	4,139,919.07	182,103.12
Information technology costs (Internet, email)	3,177,977.76	23,345.51
Office expenses	2,321,340.46	132,023.40
Meetings and appearances	1,772,342.56	0
Polling and survey research	1,410,893.36	93,728.30
Staff/spouse travel, lodging, and meals	1,260,616.12	2,618.30
Fund-raising events	1,241,158.66	70,626.38
Candidate travel, lodging, and meals	950,890.17	12,071.76
Professional services (legal, accounting)	880,044.13	39,310.00
Postage, delivery, and messenger services	668,059.56	2,117.00
Campaign paraphernalia/miscellaneous	633,946.72	65,129.65
Phone banks	549,904.75	0
Contribution	252,500.00	0
Print ads	153,440.00	0
Voter registration	66,710.00	0
Civic donations	16,383.00	0
Returned contributions	0	99,364.14
Candidate filing/ballot fees	0	3,579.74
TOTAL	**160,092,822.45**	**24,843,296.67**

SOURCE: Campaign Watch, http://californiawatch.org/dailyreport/how-whitman-spent-160-million-6292, November 2, 2010.

have established offices in California. There is money to be made in California politics, and candidates and supporters of ballot initiatives know that to win elections you must hire the costly services of top-notch political consultants.

WEAK POLITICAL PARTIES California has comparatively **weak political parties**. The Progressive reform movement of Governor Hiram Johnson implemented many rules that reduced the organizational strength and clout of political parties within the state, as described earlier. Because of the weak party system in California, the party organizations are minimally involved in organizing and conducting the campaigns of candidates running for office. In addition, California has a relatively large number of registered voters who decline to affiliate with any political party and consider themselves politically independent. These unaffiliated, independent voters compose one quarter of all registered voters. The combination of weak party structure and less party attachment means that candidates themselves have to work harder—raise and spend more money—to reach these voters.

Campaign Finance Reform in California

To create more transparency in the electoral process and make public the flow of money in political campaigns, several **campaign finance reform** laws have been enacted in California over the past 100 years. Brief descriptions of the most recent laws follow.

1974: POLITICAL REFORM ACT In 1974 a group of reform-minded Californians crafted a statewide proposition that would require the most detailed campaign finance reporting in the nation. Proposition 9 appeared on the ballot during the Watergate scandal and passed with an overwhelming majority of votes. This act created the Political Reform Division within the office of the secretary of state to administer and oversee key provisions of the law. A new independent state agency, the Fair Political Practices Commission, also was created for the purposes of interpreting and enforcing the act.

1988: PROPOSITION 73 In 1988 California voters overwhelmingly passed Proposition 73, which limited contributions to legislative and statewide candidates to $1,000 per donor, including individuals, labor unions, and corporations. A federal judge struck it down in 1990.

1996: PROPOSITION 208 Voters approved Proposition 208 by a 61 percent vote in 1996. Contributions to candidates from individuals, political parties, committees, corporations, unions, and political action committees (PACs) were limited. Spending limits also were imposed on candidates, although these were voluntary. Candidates who abide by the spending limits are allowed to collect larger contributions, whereas candidates who do not have lower contribution limits. Proposition 208 was being challenged in the courts when Proposition 34 was proposed and passed.

2000: PROPOSITION 34 Proposition 34 was placed on the ballot by the legislature. Spending limits were substantially increased, as were contribution limits. For example, under Proposition 208, individuals were permitted to contribute $1,000 to gubernatorial candidates—$500 if the candidate decided not to abide by the voluntary spending limits. Proposition 34 increased individual contributions to $21,200. Many reform-minded organizations that had supported Proposition 208, such as the League of Women Voters and Common Cause, were opposed to Proposition 34. They saw Proposition 34 as an attempt by the legislature to replace the more stringent Proposition 208 then under review in the courts. Nevertheless, in November 2000, Proposition 34 passed with close to 60 percent of the popular vote and has replaced the provisions of Proposition 208.

Although it could be argued that Proposition 34 has resulted in less control of campaign financing, California does receive high marks when it comes to laws requiring public disclosure of campaign contributions and expenditures. The Campaign Disclosure Project conducted by UCLA in 2008 studied the campaign disclosure laws in all 50 states and ranked the states accordingly. California received a grade of A for its disclosure laws and ranked second in the nation; Washington State ranked first.

Voting in California

Of California's nearly 39 million residents, approximately 24 million are eligible to vote. Seventy-five percent of those eligible (18 million) are registered. To register to vote in the state of California you must meet the following criteria:

- You will be 18 years of age on or before Election Day.
- You are a citizen of the United States.
- You are a resident of California.
- You are not in prison or on parole for a felony conviction.
- You have not been judged by a court to be mentally incompetent to register and vote.

How You Can Register to Vote

Registering to vote is a simple process. Here are the options for doing so:

- **Obtain a Voter Registration form** from any U.S. post office or library. Forms are usually available on counters. Fill out the preaddressed, stamped form and mail it in.

While Latinos in California currently vote at a significantly lower rate than whites, the Latino population is poised to exert great influence over California's electoral outcomes as it increases in size and clout. For example, the Latino vote helped secure passage of Proposition 30 in 2012, which raised taxes to help fund public education and other programs.

- **Visit a branch of the California Department of Motor Vehicles**. The National Voter Registration Act of 1993 (also known as "**Motor Voter**") permits persons conducting business at a DMV office to register to vote or to update their voter registration information. Since 1995 over 12.5 million people have registered or reregistered in conformance with this law.

- **Register online**. Go to the secretary of state's website and use the new online voter registration system (registertovote.ca.gov). The process is very simple and can be completed entirely online if you have a California driver's license or identification card. Because voter registration applications must be signed by the individual, the online system retrieves your signature from your driver license or ID card and electronically transfers it to your online registration application. This new system has proven to be extremely popular: of the record 1.4 million newly registered voters for 2012, over half of them registered online. California is one of only 15 states that offer electronic voter registration.

You will need to reregister to vote if:

- you move

- you change your name

- you change your political party affiliation

You must register at least 15 days before an election.

Who Votes in California?

There are demographic differences between those adults who are very likely to vote and those who vote infrequently or are not registered to vote. Table 4.3 clearly illustrates this. Of the individuals who are very likely to vote, sixty-two percent are white, 17 percent are Latino, 11 percent are Asian American, and 7 percent are African American. Likely voters live in urban areas, are older, college educated, U.S. born, and earn higher incomes. Over the decades the composition of the eligible voting population has changed to where we have more minority voters. But overall the same pattern has held: whites vote at a higher rate. Three factors help explain this discrepancy:

- **Eligibility**   A significant proportion of the Latino and Asian populations are not eligible to vote because they are not citizens.

- **Youth**   The Latino and Asian populations are both younger, and younger people are much less likely to vote than are older people.

- **Education**   The probability of voting increases significantly for those with college or advanced degrees.

Research shows that if you control for these three factors, Latinos vote at rates comparable to whites.[20] The 2012 presidential election saw a decline in voter turnout. In 2008, 59 percent of eligible Californians turned out to vote. In 2012, nearly 2 million fewer

TABLE 4.3 ● California's Likely Voters

	Percentage of registered voters likely to vote in California's next statewide election (%)
Race/Ethnicity	
White	62%
Latino	17
Asian	11
Black	7
Other/Multirace	3
Region	
Los Angeles County	24
San Francisco Bay Area	22
Orange/San Diego Counties	19
Central Valley	16
Inland Empire	10
Other	9
Age	
18 to 34	21
35 to 54	37
55 and older	42
Education	
No college	19
Some college	41
College graduate	40
Nativity	
U.S.-born	83
Immigrant	17

SOURCE: "Likely voters" are registered voters meeting criteria on interest in politics, attention to issues, voting behavior, and intention to vote. Nine PPIC Statewide Surveys, September 2012 to July 2013, including 11,347 likely voters, 2,955 infrequent voters, and 2,992 unregistered adults. From Just the Facts: California's Likely Voters, PPIC, 2013, http://www.ppic.org/main/popup.asp?u=../content/images/Table_LikelyVoters.png&t=Table%20-%20Likely%20Voters.

adults voted, for a turnout rate of 56 percent. As Figure 4.4 illustrates, the 2008 presidential election had the highest turnout rate since 1972. In analyzing voting statistics over the decades, political scientists have found that an exciting political race with charismatic candidates has the potential to encourage more citizens to vote. The 2008 presidential election was an example of this.

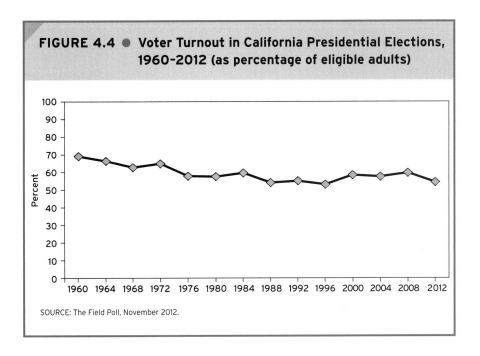

FIGURE 4.4 ● Voter Turnout in California Presidential Elections, 1960–2012 (as percentage of eligible adults)

SOURCE: The Field Poll, November 2012.

THE EVER-EXPANDING GROUP OF VOTERS: VOTING BY MAIL California now has very liberal **vote-by-mail** laws. Before 1978, voters could only receive a mail ballot if they signed a sworn statement stating that they would be away from their home precincts on Election Day or that they were infirm or bedridden and physically unable to cast a vote in person. All this changed in 1978 when California eliminated the requirement that voters present a valid excuse in order to vote absentee. Now, mail ballots are available to any voter who wants one. You are permitted to request a mail ballot for a particular election, or you may request permanent vote-by-mail status, meaning that a mail ballot is sent automatically to your home before each election.

From 1962 to 1978, the percentage of those voting by mail in primary and general elections averaged slightly under 4 percent of all votes cast. After the change in the law, voting by mail increased substantially. Of the over 10 million votes cast in November 2012, 51 percent were cast by mail ballots. Compared to the rest of the country, California's approach is fairly distinctive: 29 states allow voting by mail without an approved excuse, but only 3 other states allow for permanent voting by mail.

EARLY VOTING There is a special type of voter in California: the early voter. In fact, in the November 2012 general election, over half of all voters were early voters. There are several ways Californians can vote early (casting their votes before official Election Day). Most early voters voluntarily request vote-by-mail ballots. Virtually all of these voters are classified as "permanent vote-by-mail" voters, which means they have requested to automatically receive a vote-by-mail ballot for every election. Otherwise, one needs to request such a ballot for each election. These ballots must be received by the county registrar's office no later than Election Day, often making it necessary to mail in the completed ballot at least a few days before this deadline. In fact, a number of voters fill out and mail their ballots weeks before Election Day because state law permits voting as early as twenty-nine days before an election. A number of sparsely populated rural precincts in California, where staffing a traditional polling place makes little sense, have moved entirely to mail-in ballots for all voters. And in an attempt to lighten the volume of voters on Election Day, some counties have permitted "early voting," in which voters can go to various publicized locations (such as shopping malls, registrars' offices, and civic centers) to cast their votes as early as 29 days before an election. Nationally, states' approach to early voting is varied: Early voting, requiring no special excuse, is permitted by 31 other states and prohibited in 15 states.

Many view these developments as positive changes, believing that making voting more convenient will increase participation in this important civic activity. However, as with many reforms, there are unintended consequences. One major consequence is that early voting has had a direct impact on campaign strategy. Traditionally, political campaigns approach the weekend before the election as their last opportunity to communicate with voters. Candidates spend an enormous amount of money in the last days of their campaigns trying to convince voters to vote for them or their initiative, or at least not to vote for their opponent or opposing side, bombarding viewers with TV ads and messages. By this point in the election cycle, however, nearly half of California voters have most likely already voted by mail or at an early-voting location. So candidates must now spend money earlier in the campaign cycle to reach these early voters before they cast their votes. As an example, state Senator Tom McClintock lost a race for state controller by less than one-half of a percentage point because he did not have enough money to buy TV ads until the final days of the campaign. Many absentee voters had already mailed in their ballots and did not see his campaign ads until after they had cast their vote. Earlier campaigning means more expensive campaigning in a state that is already prohibitively expensive.

HOW YOU CAN VOTE BY MAIL To apply for a mail ballot you may use the application form contained in the sample ballot mailed to your home before the election, or you may apply in writing to your county elections official. Ballots can be returned by mail or in person to a polling place or elections office within your county on Election Day.

What Reforms Are Needed?

It is fascinating to observe electoral politics in California. We live in a state where ballot initiatives are frequently used to make law, bypassing our duly elected representatives and the deliberative process of the legislature. In recent elections voters have been asked to weigh in on important policy matters such as same-sex marriage, abortion and parental notification, renewable energy, legalization of marijuana, the state budget process, tax issues, and the process by which state and congressional districts boundaries are determined. Many people question whether the initiative process is the best way to make public policy.

Although the recall, referendum, and initiative originally were established as Progressive reforms, during the past few decades these tools of direct democracy have been taken over by special-interest groups. Some believe that reforms are needed to make it more difficult to recall an elected official or to bypass the legislative branch through the initiative process. Suggested reforms have included the prohibition of paid signature gatherers, judicial review of the proposed initiative before placement on the ballot, and a higher requirement for the number of signatures needed to qualify a recall or initiative for the ballot. For a recall to qualify for the ballot, California law requires the number of signatures to equal 12 percent of the votes cast in the last gubernatorial election. Other states require 25 to 40 percent. While progress has been made with the reforms recently signed into law, many serious issues with the initiative process remain.

Candidates and initiative campaigns spend enormous amounts of money in hopes of electoral victory. Proposition 34, the campaign finance initiative passed in 2000, substantially increased spending and contribution limits. California's limits on contributions to gubernatorial candidates are far more liberal than federal limits on contributions to presidential candidates. In fact, Californians can contribute more than 10 times the amount to gubernatorial candidates than they are permitted to contribute to presidential candidates ($25,900 versus $2,500). Many fear that these high limits will lead to spiraling campaign costs in a state where it is already expensive to campaign. The amounts of money spent in the 2010 governor's race seem to indicate that these fears are becoming reality.

Study Guide

FOR FURTHER READING

Bostock, Mike, and Shan Carter. "Over the Decades, How States Have Shifted." FiveThirtyEight, www.nytimes.com /interactive/2012/10/15/us/politics/swing-history.html ?_r=0. Accessed December 3, 2014.

Cain, B. "The California Recall." Interview, Brookings Institution, October 8, 2003.

Cain, Bruce E., and Elisabeth R. Gerber. *Voting at the Political Fault Line: California's Experiment with the Blanket Primary.* Berkeley: University of California Press, 2002.

California Fair Political Practices Commission. "Proposition 34." www.fppc.ca.gov. Accessed December 3, 2014.

California Secretary of State's History of Political Reform Division, www.sos.ca.gov/elections. Accessed December 3, 2014.

Douzet, Frédérick, Thad Kousser, and Kenneth P. Miller, eds. *The New Political Geography of California.* Berkeley: Berkeley Public Policy Press, 2008.

Lubenow, Gerald C., ed. *California Votes: The 2002 Governor's Race and the Recall That Made History.* Berkeley: Berkeley Public Policy Press, 2003.

Peterson, Pete. "Why Californians Don't Vote." Business Insider. www.businessinsider.com/why-californians-dont-vote -2014-6. Accessed June 24, 2014.

Rarick, E. *California Votes: The 2010 Governor's Race.* Berkeley: Institute of Governmental Studies, 2012.

Rasky, Susan. Introduction to "An Antipolitician, Anti-establishment Groundswell Elected the Candidate of Change." In *California Votes: The 2002 Governor's Race and the Recall That Made History,* edited by G. Lubenow. Berkeley: Berkeley Public Policy Press, 2003.

UCLA School of Law, Center for Governmental Studies, and the California Voter Foundation. "Grading State Disclosure 2008: A Comprehensive, Comparative Study of Candidate Campaign Finance Disclosure Laws and Practices in the 50 States." 2008. http://campaigndisclosure.org /gradingstate. Accessed October 16, 2014.

ON THE WEB

California Elections and Voter Information: www.sos.ca.gov /elections. Accessed December 3, 2014. The California Secretary of State offers a comprehensive guide to California elections, including information on how to register to vote.

California General Election Results: http://vote.sos.ca.gov. Accessed December 3, 2014. Detailed breakdowns of California election results.

The California Voter Foundation: http://calvoter.org. Accessed July 25, 2012.

Fair Political Practices Commission: www.fppc.ca.gov. Accessed December 3, 2014.

Join California: www.joincalifornia.com. Accessed December 3, 2014.

SUMMARY

I. Introduction.
   A. California as a political trendsetter.
      1. Impact on other states.
      2. Low voter participation.

II. Political parties.
   A. Functions of parties.
   B. Progressives' impact on parties was sizable.
      1. They disliked corrupt parties.
      2. They weakened the power of parties.
   C. Two dominant parties: Democratic and Republican.
   D. Third parties struggle to compete.
      1. There are five certified minor parties.
      2. Third parties can impact the political agenda.

III. Party affiliation of California voters varies by region and demographics.
   A. The Democratic Party represents a plurality of voters.
   B. There has been an increase in the number of independents ("decline to state").
   C. Demographics and party affiliation.
      1. Whites tend to vote Republican; Latinos tend to vote Democratic.
      2. Younger and middle-aged voters compose the highest percentage of independents.
      3. Women tend to prefer the Democratic Party, as do non–U.S.-born citizens.
   D. Blue and red in California.
      1. Coastal and urban areas tend to be Democratic.
      2. Inland and rural areas tend to be Republican.

IV. Elections in California.
   A. There have been many changes in the primary system.
      1. Closed primary until Proposition 198 in 1996.
      2. Blanket primary 1998–2000. In *California Democratic Party v. Jones* (2002), California Supreme Court ruled blanket primary unconstitutional.
      3. Modified closed primary system, 2002–10: "decline to state" voters permitted to vote in party primaries if party grants permission.
      4. Proposition 14, passed in 2010, replaced modified closed primary system with another version of blanket primary.
   B. Presidential primaries.
      1. Changes in date of primaries.
      2. 2008 presidential primary: February date. Increase in clout for state unrealized.
      3. 2012 presidential primary: Moved back to June.

C. Initiative campaigns.
   1. Tool of special interests or grassroots movements.
   2. 1912–2014: over 350 ballot initiatives.
   3. How to qualify an initiative for ballot.
      a) Over 500,000 signatures of registered voters needed for initiative, and over 800,000 for constitutional amendment.
      b) Costs and other political resources needed to be successful.
   4. Criticisms of direct democracy.
      a) Critics say that issues presented as ballot propositions are often too complicated or confusing, and should be decided through legislative deliberation rather than a popular vote.
      b) Recent reforms have provided for a 30-day public review process for all proposed initiatives as well as more transparency regarding donations to initiative campaigns.
D. 2003 gubernatorial recall election.
   1. Major players.
   2. Issues.
E. 2006 election: Schwarzenegger's re-election. Unpopular governor beats weak challenger.
F. 2008 election: ideological and demographic shift to Democratic side. Long-term or situational?
G. 2010 election: most expensive governor's race in history. Brown, former governor, beats wealthy billionaire. Initiatives pass that will have an important impact on state budget process and political representation and party politics.
H. 2012 election: results similar to 2008 but more of a Democratic shift. Democratic Party gains supermajority status in state legislature (loses it in 2014). Young voters' turnout increases but overall turnout declines. New online voter registration system. Proposition 30 passes, increasing the state sales tax and taxes on the wealthy to fund education.
I. 2014 election: non-competitive governor's race, as incumbent Brown easily beats underfunded challenger Neel Kashkari. For the more controversial ballot measures (Propositions 45, 46, and 48), the well-funded "no" campaigns were successful as the proponents were absent from the airwaves.

V. Campaigning in California is expensive.
   A. Money and politics.
      1. Record-breaking spending.
         a) Wealthy candidates.
         b) Personal fortunes.

2. Media-dominated campaigns.
3. Political consultants.
4. Weak political parties.
B. Campaign finance reform.
　1. 1974: Proposition 9, Political Reform Act.
　　a) Created Political Reform Division.
　　b) Established Fair Political Practices Commission.
　2. 1988: Proposition 73 passes, limiting contributions; declared unconstitutional in 1990.
　3. 1996: Proposition 208 passes, limiting contributions.
　4. 2000: Proposition 34 passes, increased spending and contribution limits. Invalidates Proposition 208.
　5. 2008: study of fifty states; California gets A grade for campaign-finance disclosure laws.

VI. Voting in California.
A. Population of 39 million, 18 million registered voters.
B. How to register to vote:
　1. Obtain a voter registration form from any post office or library.
　2. Visit the California DMV.
　3. Register online.
C. Who votes?
　1. Whites overrepresented in voting population; Latinos and Asians underrepresented; African Americans vote in equal proportion to their percentage of population. Reasons: youth, eligibility, education.
　2. Voter turnout rates 1960–2012. November 2008: highest turnout since 1972.
　3. Vote by mail: over 50 percent of all registered voters.

VII. Reforms may be necessary.
A. Is initiative process best way to make policy?
B. Need for campaign-finance reform to limit contributions and candidate spending.

PRACTICE QUIZ

1. In the 2012 general election, 18- to 29-year-olds voted at a higher rate than they did in 2008.
a) true
b) false

2. In running for the state legislature, incumbents and challengers spend nearly the same amount of money on their political campaigns.
a) true
b) false

3. Political campaigns are so expensive in California because
a) campaigns need to hire political consultants.
b) campaigns need to spend a substantial amount of money on media advertising.
c) political parties are not very involved in the planning and running of campaigns.
d) all of the above

4. Special-interest groups often use the initiative process to achieve their policy objectives.
a) true
b) false

5. Which of the following is *not* true about Proposition 34, which deals with campaign finance?
a) The League of Women Voters and Common Cause supported Proposition 34.
b) Proposition 34 increased allowable individual contributions to candidates to $21,200.
c) Proposition 34 has resulted in less control on campaign financing.
d) Proposition 34 replaced the stricter campaign finance law enacted through Proposition 208.

6. Of California's 38 million people, approximately how many are registered to vote?
a) 30 million
b) 25 million
c) 5 million
d) 18 million

7. Democrats are the plurality party in California.
a) true
b) false

8. The number of voters who decline to state a party affiliation at the time they register is declining.
a) true
b) false

9. Most of the Democratic counties encompass major urban areas, whereas most of the Republican counties are more rural in nature.
a) true
b) false

10. California presently operates under which of the following primary election systems?
a) open primary
b) blanket primary
c) modified closed primary
d) fully closed primary

CRITICAL-THINKING QUESTIONS

1 How might the cost of campaigning be reduced in California? Because incumbents spend much more money than challengers, what reforms might level the playing field of campaign politics?

2. What do you think have been the successes and failures of campaign finance laws in California? Do you think that additional reforms are needed? Why or why not?

3. How do you think the increase in unaffiliated voters and the increase in mail voters will affect campaigns and elections in the future?

4. Why do you think so many states follow California's lead in the areas of ballot propositions and recall efforts? Do you think this is a good or bad development? Explain why.

KEY TERMS

ballot initiative (p. 85)
blanket primary (p. 82)
campaign finance reform (p. 97)
closed primary (p. 81)
general election (p. 70)
media-dominated campaign (p. 95)
media market (p. 95)

modified closed primary (p. 82)
Motor Voter (p. 99)
no party preference (p. 74)
office block ballot (p. 71)
open primary (p. 81)
political consultant (p. 95)

political culture (p. 77)
political party affiliation (p. 74)
primary elections (p. 70)
vote-by-mail ballot (p. 101)
weak political parties (p. 96)
winner-take-all (p. 70)

5

The California Legislature

WHAT CALIFORNIA GOVERNMENT DOES AND WHY IT MATTERS

Californians give little if any thought to their legislature. We have a general sense that it is made up of a group of elected individuals who write laws but beyond that, our knowledge is limited.

Our lack of knowledge is related to the minimal coverage that legislatures receive in the media. The media find it difficult to cover institutions with multiple members who are doing many different things and have no single voice. They find it much easier to focus on a chief executive who has a press office to provide news-ready stories. Moreover, media coverage of state politics is minimal. Although most people get their news from television, no Los Angeles television station before the election of Governor Schwarzenegger had a Sacramento bureau. But even the interest in a movie-star governor did not carry over to the legislature, and since the arrival of Jerry Brown, who makes only a minimal effort to feed the news establishment, media interest in Sacramento has sharply declined. The last out-of-town TV news bureau in Sacramento closed in 2013.

Accompanying our lack of knowledge is the general belief that the legislature does not work well. According to the Field Poll, in May 2010, only 16 percent of Californians approved of the job that the state legislature was doing (72 percent disapproved). Our dissatisfaction with the legislative process stems in part from a lack of understanding of how it works, but it has several other sources as well.

First, Americans dislike and distrust politics in general. They also like harmony and are turned off by conflict between the governor and the legislature and between parties. Since the legislature is the most observable political arena, conflict here is more obvious.

Second, the dysfunction that so often characterizes state government negatively affects attitudes towards the legislature. While the legislature is not the principal cause of this state of affairs, term limits and voting rules lead to gridlock and elevated partisan conflict, which makes it difficult for the legislature to function well.

Third, while voters want their legislators to work together, the same citizens want their individual interests forcefully represented against competing ones. We have conflicting expectations of legislatures, and legislators' attempts to balance these expectations often contribute to our dissatisfaction. The quote often attributed to the nineteenth-century German statesman Otto von Bismarck has a point in suggesting that respect for the making of laws, like the making of sausages, decreases with our knowledge of how they are made.

Finally, the occasional bad behavior of individual legislators brings the entire institution into disrepute. During the spring of 2014 three Democratic senators facing criminal charges were suspended by their colleagues. This was followed by a dip in the public's evaluation of the legislature.

This kind of dissatisfaction is typical in California. However, starting in 2010 and accelerating from 2012 to the spring of 2014, the popularity of the legislature increased to such a degree that more people approved than disapproved of the job it was doing, before sliding slightly back as a result of the scandals in the Senate.[1]

Several factors contributed to the legislature's jump in reputation: redistricting by a nonpartisan commission, new primary election rules, and changes in term limits, each of which will be discussed later in this chapter. But perhaps most important, a Democrat was elected governor and the Democrats gained a two-thirds majority in each legislative house, greatly reducing both gridlock and conflict. It was not that the Democrats and Republicans began to work together, but rather that the Republicans became marginalized. At the same time the public's approval of the U.S. Congress, in which power is closely divided and gridlock common, dropped to an historic low of 9 percent in November of 2013, rising slightly in 2014 to 15 percent.[2]

In spite of Californians' distrust of and lack of interest in their legislature, the impact of that body on their lives—and yours—is significant. In the 2013-14 session alone the legislature considered (and in some cases passed) legislation dealing with plastic grocery bags, women donating their eggs for research, driving under the influence of drugs, texting while driving, pension reform, and prohibiting public agencies from requesting the social media passwords of their employees or job applicants. In addition, the legislature funds all the agencies of state government including parks, the Highway Patrol, and universities.

Legislatures, although poorly understood, play a critical role in our government. The framers of the national constitution, fearing a powerful executive, gave Congress the most significant and most explicit powers, including control over taxation and spending and the writing of all laws. The fact that the president gets the most attention in the media today and that some congressional powers have gravitated to the executive branch does not negate the fact that Congress remains a very powerful body.

Most state legislatures, including the one in California, have been modeled on the U.S. Congress in structure, process, and function. California has a **bicameral** (two-house) legislature consisting of the 40-member Senate (sometimes called the upper house) and the 80-member Assembly. Like Congress, members of both bodies represent geographically determined districts and are elected in winner-take-all elections. As in Congress, bills become law by being approved by both houses and signed by the chief executive. The bulk of the work of each house is done in committees. Each house is organized by party, and party leaders determine committee membership. Despite these similarities, significant differences—such as the role of seniority in committee assignments—do exist, and will be explained in more detail later in the chapter.

The recent history of the California legislature has been remarkable in its extremes. In the 1960s, under the leadership of Assembly Speaker Jesse Unruh, the legislature was transformed from an often corrupt, amateur body to a well-paid, well-staffed professional organization regarded by many as the best state legislature in the country. Then in 1990 the voters of California passed **Proposition 140**, imposing term limits on the legislature. Although this did not change the basic structure of the legislature, it did change the collective knowledge, effectiveness, and power of the legislature by reducing the time that legislators were permitted to serve to 14 years, and by reducing the size of the staff that makes legislative work possible.

In 2012 this was slightly modified when voters passed Proposition 28 which further reduced the time that legislators could serve to 12 years. However unlike previously when members were limited to 6 years in the Assembly and 8 in the Senate, these years can all be served in one house. The principal impact should be to increase the effectiveness of the Assembly by giving members and leaders more time to become knowledgeable in their jobs.

Functions

Legislatures have two principal functions: **representation** and policy making. The tensions between these functions make it difficult for a legislature to perform as effectively as citizens might wish.

Representation

The legislature is the principal representative institution in our society, although the executive branch and interest groups also lay claim to this function. It is the duty of legislators (also called members, representatives, assemblypersons, or senators) to represent the voters and other residents (collectively known as **constituents**) within their districts, as well as the dominant district interests. This is easier said than done. In the first place, the term *representation* has many meanings. Here we will simplify it to mean that our representative is our counterpart in Sacramento and that he or she will do what we would do if we were there, especially when it comes to influencing legislation or voting. Of course, there are many more constituents than there are legislators, and rarely do all people see things the same way. Some are wealthy and educated; others, destitute. Some see government as the means to solve society's problems; others see it as the main problem with society.

Furthermore, representatives face many different and difficult issues—same-sex marriage, lower taxes versus improved services, new highways versus preservation of neighborhoods, higher spending on prisons versus lower college tuition. How one faces these issues depends in part on the way in which one understands the goal of representation: is it to give constituents what they want or what they need?

Political scientists talk about two poles of representation style: the delegate who tries to find out what constituents want and act according to their wishes, and the trustee who believes he or she has been chosen to act based on his or her own best judgment. Delegates most often try to provide what constituents want, whereas trustees are more inclined to provide for their districts' needs as they perceive them. Both types of representation are difficult to achieve in practice. It is often impossible to know what constituents want because they do not communicate with their representatives very well. It is no easier to determine district needs, which are often diverse, conflicting, and influenced by ideology or other subjective factors.

In theory, a representative should act based on the wants and needs of each member of his or her district equally. But in practice, certain groups carry more influence than others. For instance, some legislators identify closely with a particular group, such as women, small business owners, or immigrants, and view themselves as representatives of that group. (See the Who Are Californians feature for more information on the different groups of voters in California.) In addition, some groups are better organized than others and are particularly adept at gaining the representative's attention. These would include chambers of commerce, large employers, labor unions, and environmental organizations. Large campaign contributors do not give their donations without expecting something in return, so the legislator is unable to ignore them. Ultimately it is the constituents who have the vote, which should force representatives to pay attention to the needs of the entire district, but even this principle has been weakened in recent years due to big money, gerrymandered districts, and term limits. Rarely do voters have a realistic chance of keeping favored representatives in power or "throwing the rascals out."

In addition to representing our policy views, representatives try to look out for us when we have specific problems with government whether it's not getting a disability check, being treated unfairly by an inspector, worrying that a new highway will be built through our property, or opposing the sale of liquor near our kids' school. This ombudsman function is called "constituency service" or "casework," and it involves intervening with the bureaucracy to solve specific problems. Representatives also try to get favorable treatment for economic interests in their districts—when a restaurant owner wants a liquor license that he or she believes is being unfairly denied, for instance, or when a construction company wants to build more buildings at the local state university. Representatives will also take stands on issues that are largely symbolic but still important to their constituents, such as flag burning or prayer in schools.

Who Votes in California?

Gender

■ Male ▪ Female = 10% of eligible voters

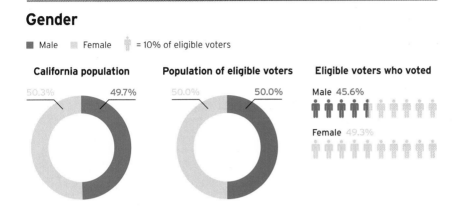

California population
50.3% 49.7%

Population of eligible voters
50.0% 50.0%

Eligible voters who voted
Male 45.6%
Female 49.3%

The active voting population in California is not a reflection of the general population demographics. Compared to their proportion of the population, white non-Latinos and older voters are overrepresented among active voters. Despite the large size of the Latino population, they are a relatively small share of the electorate.

Race

■ White ■ Latino ■ African American ▪ Asian American ▪ = 10% of eligible voters

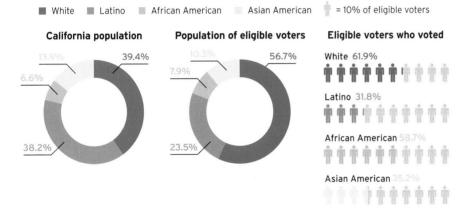

California population
13.9% 39.4%
6.6%
38.2%

Population of eligible voters
10.3% 56.7%
7.9%
23.5%

Eligible voters who voted
White 61.9%
Latino 31.8%
African American 58.7%
Asian American 35.2%

forcriticalanalysis

1. What do you think might account for the differences in turnout rates among different groups in California? Why is turnout among whites and blacks so much higher than among Latinos and Asians? Why is turnout among older voters higher than among young voters?

2. Looking ahead, what impact will the shifting electorate have on California politics, when the percentage of Latinos in the population increases and the percentage of whites decreases, as described in Chapter 1?

Age

▪ Youth (under 18) ■ Young Adults (18–29) ■ Older Adults ▪ = 10% of eligible voters

California population
31.3% 17.9%
50.8%

Population of eligible voters
73.0% 27.0%

Eligible voters who voted
Young Adults 43.7%
Older Adults 61.9%

SOURCE: U.S. Census Bureau, Current Population Survey, November 2012, and CNN Exit Polls (http://www.cnn.com/election/2012/results/state/CA/president). Projections from California Department of Finance Population Projections.

Another important part of representation is being available to constituents. People want to see their representative, and representatives accordingly spend much of their time in their districts attending functions, speaking to groups about the activities of government, distributing commendations and certificates, and listening to constituents. Constituents and representatives of organized groups also visit with them in Sacramento. See Box 5.1 for information on contacting your state representatives.

Policy Making

Representatives come together to make policy, most obviously through the complex process of making laws, which involves writing bills, holding committee hearings, conducting legislative debates, and adding amendments. These steps will be described in more detail later in the chapter.

Policy making also involves ensuring that legislation is carried out by the bureaucracy as the legislature intended and looking out for potential problems in the implementation of policy. This function, called oversight, is carried out through a variety of means, including legislative hearings, staff follow-up on constituents' concerns, budgetary hearings, and confirmation hearings. Legislators do not have much appetite for holding hearings that might make a governor of their own party uncomfortable, but any scandal involving a public agency almost automatically triggers such hearings. In recent years the legislature has held hearings on construction flaws in the new Bay Bridge, costly failures in computer upgrades in the Employment Development Department and the DMV, and the unnecessarily cumbersome college transfer process. Congressional oversight hearings at the federal level gain far more attention. California Representative Darrell Issa, who chairs the U.S. House Committee on Oversight, has been very effective in using his position to embarrass the Obama administration on a wide range of policies.

Members and Districts

Unlike Congress, in which each state has two seats in the Senate regardless of population, both houses of the California legislature are apportioned by population. The state is divided into 80 Assembly districts and 40 state Senate districts. In each of these districts a single representative is elected by local voters, which means that these representatives will give serious attention to local interests. As former speaker of the U.S. House of Representatives Tip O'Neill once said, "All politics is local." Our legislative system is designed to favor local interests (and interests with money), and these interests often take precedence over statewide interests.

Legislative elections are **winner-take-all** elections, which means that minor or third parties are generally excluded from the legislature even if they have substantial support statewide. Without a majority of votes in any one district, they cannot place a representative in Sacramento.

Most members with previous elective experience have served on school boards, city councils, or county boards of supervisors. Many are self-selected. Others are tapped to run for office by party leaders or interests who see them as viable and friendly to their policies.

Legislators have offices in both Sacramento and their districts. Mail, email, and phone messages are answered from both places. In the districts they listen to the concerns of their constituents and tell them about government activities, policy, and politics (e.g., try to explain what life is like in the capital). In Sacramento they interact with those constituents who travel to the capital as well as with representatives of interest groups. In addition, they work on framing policy, primarily in committees. Legislators often spend Monday through midday Thursday in Sacramento and return to their districts for the remainder of the week; however, this varies with the time of the year, and special events often bring them back to their districts. It is essential to keep a high profile in the district to discourage potential

Legislators often try to maintain visibility among constituents by making public appearances in their home districts. For example, State Senator Ted Lieu, representative for Senate District 28 encompassing part of Los Angeles County, participated in the West Hollywood Gay Pride Parade in June 2014.

election opponents. Being accused of ignoring their districts could be fatal in an election.

Elections

Every member of the California Senate and Assembly must be elected by the voters from a single geographic district. Assembly members serve two-year terms while senators serve for four years.

The process through which candidates are elected changed significantly in 2010 with the passage of Proposition 14. Prior to 2010, the primary elections were structured to select one candidate from each party to run in the general election. Candidates ran as Republicans, Democrats, or as representatives of a third party in separate contests against members of their own party only. Voters could choose one of those contests in which to vote. The winners faced off against each other in the general election in November. In districts where the voters were overwhelmingly of one party—typical of many California districts—the real contest was in the primary, and election was all but assured to the candidate of the majority party. Many believed that this resulted in the election of extremist legislators beholden only to the majority of the voters in their party, not to the majority of the voters in their district.

Proposition 14 provides for a single open primary in which all candidates run and all voters take part. Voters vote in the primary or preliminary election for the candidate of their choice for each office from a single list of all candidates, and the top two candidates go on to the November election regardless of party. Candidates need not state their party identification on the ballot. The expectation is that, even if both of the winning candidates are in the same party, the more moderate candidate will win the general election by appealing to voters in the minority parties (see Chapter 4). If there are only two candidates in the first election, they will have to run against each other for a second time. While this may seem redundant, the electorate in November is almost always larger (and therefore less Republican) than in June, which can affect the outcome of the election. In 2012, the 65th Assembly District in Orange County provided an excellent example of an incumbent challenged by a single opponent—in this case, a Republican challenged by a Democrat. When they ran against each other in June, the Republican incumbent won with over 58 percent of the vote. In the runoff in November, the Democratic challenger won with about 52 percent of the vote, helping the Democrats gain a two-thirds majority in the Assembly. Contributing to this victory was a significant increase in turnout: about 50,000 people voted in June while over 120,000 voted in November.

Two other key features of California politics have a significant influence on who gets elected. First, the large size of each district means that campaigns are expensive and fundraising is necessary. Second, the manner in which district boundaries are drawn impacts the role of political parties and the strength of incumbents.

Fund-raising

Campaigns can easily cost millions of dollars (see Chapter 4) and campaign expenditures are likely to be much higher in the future given the Supreme Court ruling in *Citizens United* (see Chapter 3), which rejected corporate spending limits, and given that the California Citizens Redistricting Commission has created more competitive legislative districts. Fund-raising is one of the most significant obstacles to winning an election. The nature of California and the size of the districts make election victories unlikely through old-fashioned precinct work. Use of TV and radio advertising is also impractical in the larger media markets because of cost. Most candidates have campaign consultants and engage in polling and targeted distribution of literature.

Districting

Because of the relatively small size of the state legislature, its districts are among the largest in the country. Senate districts have over 950,000 constituents, and Assembly districts over 475,000. (For comparison, U.S. House districts in California have approximately 715,000 constituents.) Historically, district lines were drawn by the legislature, often leading to charges of **gerrymandering**. This term dates to the early 1800s, when Massachusetts governor Elbridge Gerry oversaw a redistricting that benefited his party and resulted in district lines that resembled, in a famous cartoon of the day, a salamander. *To gerrymander* means to draw district lines in a manner that favors one party over another, generally by packing most of the opponent's voters into a few districts and spreading the remainder thinly over the remaining districts. The courts have generally accepted this practice, saying only that districts must be equal in population and must not be drawn to diminish the voting strength of any minority.

Redistricting is done following each census and until 2012 had to pass both houses and be signed by the governor, like any other piece of legislation. However, after the 2000 census, despite Democratic control of both houses and the governor's office, the party did not create more gerrymandered Democratic districts. Instead, endeavoring (successfully) to avoid a lawsuit, they approved a set of maps known as the "incumbency protection plan," which maintained safe seats for both parties. Thus, the power of voters to hold their legislators accountable was diminished, as incumbents throughout the state were unlikely to lose a future election.

Most action, therefore, took place in the primaries, though incumbents rarely faced a serious challenge there following the advent of term limits. Knowing that an incumbent assemblyperson would be out of office in no more than four years, the astute challenger waited for that vacancy to occur rather than engaging in an expensive, divisive challenge. Term limits had the unintended consequence of inhibiting voters from "throwing the rascals out." The legislature was more immune from direct electoral challenge than ever before.

Since 2012, the situation that created safe districts with highly partisan incumbents has significantly changed. As a result of their continued frustration with the legislature, the voters approved two measures, Proposition 11 in November 2008 (followed by Proposition 20 in 2010) and Proposition 14 in June 2010, that have had an impact on who gets elected to the legislature.

The consequences of Proposition 14, the open primary law described above, have been overwhelmingly overshadowed by those of Propositions 11 and 20, both redistricting initiatives that unexpectedly resulted in a two-thirds Democratic majority in both houses. Proposition 11 took the task of drawing legislative districts away from the legislature and replaced it with a 15-person Citizens Redistricting Commission. This commission created districts with a closer partisan balance.

The expectation was that Proposition 11 would result in fewer safe seats and in the election of moderate legislators more willing to engage in bipartisan compromise. It will take several election cycles before these results can be assessed, because the large Democratic majorities currently in the state legislature make bipartisan compromise largely unnecessary. However some observers believe that the smaller Republican minority is less moderate and less inclined to compromise, while the larger Democratic majority is more moderate.

Even though this two-thirds majority in the Senate was weakened by the suspension of three Democratic members, the Democrats still can carry out business with little regard for their Republican colleagues. Thus, gridlock has been reduced, and the public's regard for the legislature has become correspondingly more favorable.

Still, the supermajority of Democrats has not proven to be radical; they have not raised taxes or implemented draconian new regulations. This partially stems from the fact that they have to work with a moderate Democratic governor, who would probably **veto** such measures. More important, many of these new Democratic legislators are from marginal seats (such as the 65th in Orange County and 32nd in Bakersfield) and are reluctant to take bold action that might endanger their chances of re-election. A new chapter in California politics has begun, and no one knows how exactly it will be written.

Organization

The process of policy making is complex, involving many steps and many actors. Over time, both the Senate and Assembly have, for reasons both practical and political, adopted principles of organization that structure how the legislature works.

Leadership

The leader of the Assembly is the **speaker**, and he or she has a remarkable array of powers (although these are now diminished because of term limits on members of the Assembly). In an attempt to increase the power of the speaker by lengthening his or her time in the position, in 2003 and 2009 the Democrats elected a first-term legislator to the speakership (in 2014 they elected a member in her second term). The Assembly speaker's powers are considerably more extensive than the Speaker of the U.S. House of Representatives. Beginning with control over parking spaces and offices, these powers include almost complete control over establishing **committees**, assigning members to serve on them, and removing members if the speaker chooses. Because the bulk of legislative work is done in committees, members depend on the speaker to provide them with a meaningful role in the legislature. The speaker can also assign floor leadership of high-profile or popular bills to the legislators of her choice, enhancing these legislators' reputations both within and outside the Assembly.

The speaker acts as presiding officer when the full Assembly meets and thereby controls debate; when not presiding, he or she designates the person who does. The speaker also appoints the majority floor leader, who assists in running legislative sessions. It is difficult to overstate the power of the speaker, which can move bills, help supporters, and hurt opponents. Speakers can raise money as well, which in turn allows them to solidify support. Members find it advantageous to cooperate with the speaker. The speaker is elected by the entire membership of the Assembly, but in most cases the outcome is determined in advance by the majority party caucus, which consists of all of the members of the majority party meeting together. Only when the majority is split does the full Assembly vote become significant.

The minority caucus elects the Assembly minority leader, who is the public voice of the minority party and who works with the speaker to determine minority party assignments on committees. The speaker, however, has the final say.

The other important element of the leadership is the **Assembly Rules Committee**, which is made up of nine members, four elected by each party's caucus plus a chair appointed by the speaker. The committee's responsibilities include hiring staff, assigning bills to committees, and reviewing legislative rules. Rarely does this committee operate independently of the speaker's wishes.

The organization of the Senate is similar, but the leader, the **president pro tempore**, does not have the absolute power of the Assembly speaker. Many of the speaker's powers in the Assembly rest with the Rules Committee in the Senate. Yet in recent years the president pro tempore—most notably John Burton—has become the most influential legislator in Sacramento, largely because of the impact of term limits. Assembly members currently have a maximum of 6 years of experience, and their leaders may have only 1 or 2 years. Senators have often served in the Assembly first, and their time in the Senate can last up to 8 years. Senate leaders may have accrued 10 to 12 years of experience in Sacramento before assuming leadership. John Burton, who was the last of his breed, had far more experience than that, including experience in the U.S. Congress.

This pattern is changing thanks to the passage of Proposition 28 in June 2012. Legislators elected in 2012 and after may now serve no more than a total of 12 years in the state legislature, but those years can be spent entirely in one house or in a combination of both houses. Thus, a person elected to a leadership position in a second term can remain in that position for up to 8 years beyond that term, greatly increasing his or her knowledge and effectiveness. This will provide the members of the Assembly with the opportunity to attain the same level of experience as their counterparts in the Senate.

Committees

The bulk of legislative work is done in **committees**. Committees allow for greater specialization, greater expertise of those involved, and greater attention to detail. In 2013–14 there were 30 standing or permanent committees in the Assembly and 23 in the Senate (see Table 5.1). Each member sits on several standing committees. In addition to standing committees, there are many select committees that exist to study specific issues, and joint committees to look at issues that concern both houses. Members may serve on a dozen or more of these less important committees.

Committees are at the heart of groups of players often referred to as **issue networks**. These networks consist of committee members and **staff**, senior members of the respective executive branch agency, and interest groups concerned with issues in a committee's jurisdiction. The bulk of policy details are worked out in

TABLE 5.1 ● Standing Committees of the California Legislature, 2013–14

State Senate

Agriculture
Appropriations
Banking and Financial Institutions
Budget and Fiscal Review
Business, Professions and Economic Development
Education
Elections and Constitutional Amendments
Energy, Utilities, and Communications
Environmental Quality
Governance and Finance
Governmental Organization
Health

Human Services
Insurance
Judiciary
Labor and Industrial Relations
Legislative Ethics
Natural Resources and Water
Public Employment and Retirement
Public Safety
Rules
Transportation and Housing
Veterans Affairs

Assembly

Accountability and Administrative Review
Aging and Long-Term Care
Agriculture
Appropriations
Arts, Entertainment, Sports, Tourism, and
    Internet Media
Banking and Finance
Budget
Business, Professions, and Consumer Protection
Education
Elections and Redistricting
Environmental Safety and Toxic Materials
Governmental Organization
Health
Higher Education
Housing and Community Development

Human Services
Insurance
Jobs, Economic Development, and the Economy
Judiciary
Labor and Employment
Local Government
Natural Resources
Public Employees, Retirement and Social Security
Public Safety
Revenue and Taxation
Rules
Transportation
Utilities and Commerce
Veterans Affairs
Water, Parks, and Wildlife

these networks. Lobbyists and bureaucrats tend to be specialists who spend their entire careers in a single subject area. It would be unusual for someone who has spent a career in transportation to move to education. Previously, legislators would spend their careers in specific issue areas as well. Term limits have changed that, or rather have shortened the length of careers. While policy is still worked out within these networks, power has shifted to those with greater permanency, experience, and expertise—namely, lobbyists and bureaucrats. The less experienced and less knowledgeable legislator is now more dependent than before on these individuals for policy details. Experienced staff can help, but often staff members are no more experienced than legislators.

Staff

Without staff, the legislature cannot effectively do its job. Staff is crucial in both the policy-making and representative functions of the legislature. All legislators have staff in both their Sacramento and district offices to help with constituency contacts, including casework, scheduling appearances, and answering mail and phone calls from constituents. In addition, committees have staff, called consultants, to help with the policy work of that committee, and consultants are critical components of the issue networks. Some of the best consultants will take their hard-earned experience and move on to become lobbyists, for whom the pay is often far higher and the job more secure. Each legislator is allotted an office budget for staffing. Legislators are permitted additional staff depending on whether they occupy a committee leadership role and on the generosity of the party leadership. In addition, the house leaders and caucuses have staff that may number more than 150 for the majority. This staff helps with bill analysis for individual members and public relations for both individual members and the party.

There are over 2,000 legislative aides. It is not unusual for majority legislators to have 13 or 14 staff members. Minority members may have only 4 or 5. While most aides are modestly paid, some—especially highly valued committee consultants—make over $150,000 a year. The total personnel budget for legislative workers in 2009 was $129.3 million. The median salary for a staff member in the Assembly was about $51,000 and in the Senate, $61,000. These aides often work alongside members of the prestigious Assembly and Senate Fellows program and many college interns.

There are three important and well-regarded groups of staff who are nonpartisan and work for the entire legislature. The first is the Legislative Analyst's Office, which analyzes budget proposals and the fiscal impact of ballot propositions. The second is the Legislative Counsel, which helps write bills, analyze ballot propositions, and provide legal advice. The third is the State Auditor's Office, which handles management and fiscal audits of the executive branch.

Before Proposition 140 passed in 1990, the staff of the California legislature was considered the best in the nation. However, the proposition required a staff cut of 40 percent and resulted in layoffs and the departure of many of the best staffers, especially the experts on which the committees relied. Staff is still a significant factor in the legislature, and over the years, it has inched back toward its previous size.

Legislative Process

There are three types of items that may pass the legislature: bills, which if successful become laws; constitutional amendments, which require a two-thirds vote of both houses and a referendum by the voters; and resolutions, which are largely symbolic expressions of opinion. The remainder of this section is concerned primarily with bills.

Bills are introduced only by legislators, even if the content was originally proposed by someone as politically important as the governor. Indeed, bills are often written by someone other than the person who introduces them. Many bills may be written by, or in conjunction with, lobbyists, and the nonpartisan Legislative Counsel's office may help in drafting language. An individual senator may introduce no more than 65 bills in a two-year session, whereas Assembly members may introduce only 30. Legislators may have a variety of motives for introducing a bill, such as impressing constituents or paying off a political favor, and most go nowhere. In the 2011–12 legislative session, 1,866 bills passed the legislature and reached the governor's desk. He signed 1,621 of them and vetoed 245, some of which were strongly supported by his allies. In the 2013–14 legislative session, 2,766 bills were introduced in the Senate and 1,467 in the Assembly for a total of 4,233. Of these, 1970 reached the governor's desk and 1,731 became law.[3] This is far fewer than was common 20 years ago. In 1989 and 1990, for example, 3,174 new laws were enacted.

Once bills are introduced, the rules committee of the appropriate house assigns the bill to a standing committee or even two committees, depending on its content. The bill is also numbered and printed. Committees cannot act on a bill until it has been in print for 30 days, to allow comment from interested parties. Committees hold hearings, scrutinize the language carefully to make sure that it clearly and accurately states what members intend, add amendments, and pass or reject bills. An absolute majority of the committee must vote favorably to report a bill out. If a bill is reported out of committee, it goes to the floor for discussion by the entire house. Amendments may be added at this time, and require only a majority vote. Bill passage requires an absolute majority (41 in the Assembly, 21 in the Senate). Once a bill has passed one house, it goes to the other house for similar consideration. Bills must pass both houses with identical language before they are forwarded to the governor for his or her signature. If the governor vetoes a bill, a two-thirds vote in each house is required to override the veto. This rarely happens.

Most bills pass through each house with different wording. In this case one house may acquiesce to the wording of the other house or a conference committee will be established to work out the differences. A conference committee is a joint committee consisting of three members from each body. Assembly members are appointed by the speaker, and Senate members are appointed by the Senate Rules Committee. They suggest compromise language that must pass both houses. If this attempt fails, two additional attempts may be made before the bill is put to rest. See Figure 5.1 for an illustration of how a bill becomes a law in the California legislature.

SHORTCUTS While this is the textbook approach, much legislation is able to bypass some of these steps, especially near the end of a legislative session when bills tumble over one another and deals are made in back rooms in a rush to adjourn. Many bills reappear as amendments to other bills, garnering even less public attention than in the normal process. At this time, the influence of party leaders is greater because they are able to grease the skids for compromises and logrolling. **Logrolling** is vote trading, the process by which members exchange votes—"You vote for my bill, and I will vote for yours." A common end-of-session legislative tactic is to hijack a bill and then "**gut and amend**" it. A bill that may have been presumed dead suddenly reappears, dealing with an entirely different topic. In an editorial denouncing the practice, the *Sacramento Bee* describes how it works:

> A bill on air pollution morphs into a bill on immigration. A bill on college tuition becomes a bill on shark fins. In the last three weeks of the 2011 session, legislators

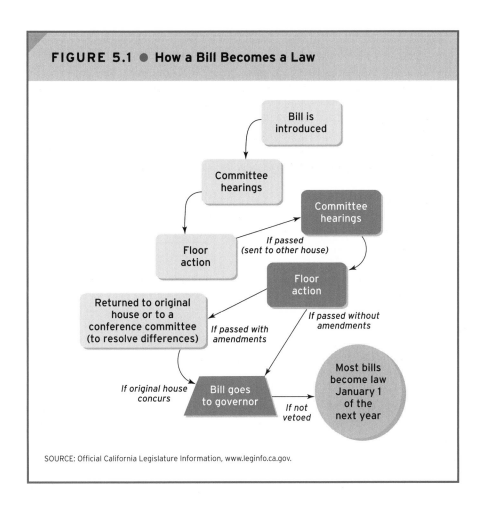

FIGURE 5.1 ● How a Bill Becomes a Law

Bill is introduced

Committee hearings

Floor action

If passed (sent to other house)

Committee hearings

Floor action

If passed without amendments

Returned to original house or to a conference committee (to resolve differences)

If passed with amendments

If original house concurs

Bill goes to governor

If not vetoed

Most bills become law January 1 of the next year

SOURCE: Official California Legislature Information, www.leginfo.ca.gov.

gutted and amended 48 bills, passing 22 of them. Gov. Jerry Brown signed 19 of them.[4]

Efforts to reform this procedure by requiring bills to be in print for several days before coming up for a vote have gained no traction.

End-of-session periods in Sacramento reflect quintessential American politics: a system that favors insiders, corporations, and big money. While this goes on throughout the year, these backroom strategies work best when time is compressed and the media and other outsiders cannot follow what is going on or cannot do anything about it.

At the end of the session there is intense pressure to get things done. As noted earlier, 1,970 bills passed in 2013–14 and many others were in play. Insiders and lobbyists focus their attention on a single bill or a small number of bills that are important to their clients. Large corporations and other interest groups hire full-time lobbyists and lawyers, sometimes a full platoon of them, to follow their important bills, develop strategy, and take the necessary actions to ensure the desired outcome, all of which can be written off as business expenses.

These insiders work out deals behind the proverbial closed doors, and provisions to bills are added and removed at the last minute. Often the junior members voting on the floor have no idea of what they are voting on.

Before the legislature was term-limited, members were extremely well-versed about their policy interests and had long memories about what tricks lobbyists and other legislators had tried to pull in previous sessions. This meant that it was more difficult to make unnoticed changes in legislation to benefit a special interest. There is no such institutional memory now among legislators. Experience and skills rest mostly with lobbyists and agency representatives.

Differences from U.S. Congress

While the California legislature is modeled closely on the national legislature, there are important differences that, collectively, make the California legislature a weaker body.

Term Limits

Unlike members of Congress, who can serve as long as they are reelected, California legislators are limited to a total of 12 years, which can be served in one or both houses. Term limits enacted by the passage of Proposition 140 in 1990 limited members to three 2-year terms in the Assembly and two 4-year terms in the Senate for a maximum total of 14 years. Proposition 28 instituted the current 12-year limit.

There were numerous reasons for the success of Proposition 140. First, it was a reaction to the highly effective Assembly Speaker Willie Brown, a flamboyant African-American politician from San Francisco who was immensely unpopular with conservative voters. Second, it was an effect of public aversion to **gridlock** and divided government (generated by partisan conflict between the Republican governor and the Democratic legislature). Third, voters were protesting against the large fund-raising efforts of incumbents. Fourth, it was a reflection of the national trend against entrenched incumbents. Finally, it was the product of a belief among some Republicans that term limits could overthrow the Democratic majority. However, these term limits did not end divided government, gridlock, or large fund-raising and only briefly suspended the Democratic majority and in only one house, the 1994 Assembly. The proposition did reduce the ability of the legislature to act effectively. It is too early to know if Proposition 28 will ultimately make the legislature more effective.

Item Veto

In Washington, D.C., the president has to sign or reject bills passed by Congress in their entirety. He cannot approve parts that he likes and reject those he dislikes. In California, as in most states, the governor has a **line-item veto** on appropriations, including those in the budget. This power allows the governor to reduce or eliminate a specific spending item, although he or she cannot increase items. This means that the legislature cannot force the governor's hand by including an item that he opposes in a larger bill that he mostly supports.

Apportionment and District Size

Both houses of the California legislature are **apportioned** by population; in Congress, the Constitution allots two senators to each state, regardless of size. California has a population about equal to the populations of the 22 smallest states combined. While these states have 44 senators between them, California has the same number of senators as the smallest of these states, Wyoming. In fact there are four states that have fewer residents than each of California's 53 congressional districts.

Because California is so populous (about 38 million people) and because its legislature is relatively small, its legislative districts are among the largest in the nation. Senate districts have over 950,000 constituents, while Assembly districts contain over 475,000 residents. Compare this to New Hampshire, with a population of about 1.3 million and with 400 members in its lower house, which results in one representative for about every 3,000 residents. While New Hampshire's representatives are very accessible and elections are not expensive, most representatives do not wield very much influence in their very large chamber. California senators, unlike any other U.S. legislative body, represent more constituents than members of Congress and more than the U.S. senators of seven states. This means that they are considerably less accessible than their counterparts in other states and that their elections are considerably more expensive.

The fact that both legislative houses are apportioned by population has led some informed observers to suggest that a unicameral legislature of 120 members would make more sense. This would result in smaller districts and increased accessibility to legislators.

Media Visibility

In Washington, D.C., the media interpret the national government's actions by focusing on the president, who consequently dominates the news. The comments of members of Congress are generally used to give more depth to a presidential story. Most often, these are party leaders, committee chairs, or the occasional legislator who has managed to make a name for him- or herself on a given issue.

The same is true in California's capital, but the statewide media, especially television, rarely cover news in Sacramento. Only the four party leaders receive air time, and because they hold their positions for so few years, the public has difficulty keeping track of who they are. Speaker of the U.S. House of Representatives John Boehner is practically a household name, but California Assembly Speaker Toni Atkins is not. Consequently, most of what happens in Sacramento occurs out of the spotlight.

Court Appointments

Some of the greatest legislative battles in Congress have occurred during the Senate's hearings to confirm judicial appointments, especially to the Supreme Court. In contrast, many judges in California are elected. Those who are appointed by the governor are approved by the Commission on Judicial Appointments. The Senate does get to approve many other gubernatorial appointments to executive positions and regulatory boards and commissions, including the governing boards of both the California State University and the University of California. In both the U.S.

Senate and California Senate, legislators have rejected recent nominees over policy differences.

Filibusters

In the U.S. Senate—a body that is not apportioned on the basis of one person, one vote—41 members potentially representing slightly more than 33 million people, can block the passage of most legislation through use of the filibuster. California has no such provision. Indeed, in most cases the majority rules. The principal exceptions are tax increases and constitutional amendments, which require a two-thirds vote.

Initiatives

Unlike the U.S. Constitution, the California Constitution provides several means of taking issues directly to the voters. Most significant is the initiative. This is important in the legislative context because those who are thwarted in their attempts to get legislation passed can always threaten to take it—or an even more extreme version of it—to the voters. This tactic is often used to persuade legislators to vote for measures that they would otherwise oppose and significantly weakens the legislature.

Seniority

In the U.S. Congress, seniority is used as an informal rule in appointing members to committees and choosing each committee's majority and minority leaders; once members are appointed to their committee positions, they are almost never removed. In the California legislature, both the appointment and removal power resides with the Assembly speaker and Senate majority leadership, with seniority playing a much smaller role. Both the speaker and the Senate majority leadership in 2007 and 2008 removed members of both parties from committee leadership roles for disagreeing with them over various issues.

Challenges Facing the California Legislature

When voters pay attention to the legislature, complaints and criticism of its actions often result. At times these objections are on target, at times not. State government tends to be perceived as dysfunctional, and the legislature is an easy target. It is easy to be repulsed by the contentious process of arriving at legislative agreements. Moreover, individual members often run for the legislature by running against it, emphasizing the legislature's shortcomings and foibles in order to play up their own importance to the legislature.

Scandal also gets the public's attention. In 2014 three senators were suspended for misbehavior: Rod Wright (D-Inglewood) was convicted of lying about living in his district in a 2008 race, and Ron Calderon (D-Montebello) and Leland Yee (D-San Francisco) were caught taking bribes in FBI sting operations. Yee was also charged with international gunrunning, not a typical legislative misdeed. In addition, Senator Tom Berryhill (R-Twain Harte) and his brother, a former assemblyman, were fined for improper handling of campaign funds. The misbehavior of any one of the 120 legislators is often amplified out of proportion and reflects badly on the whole institution. To have several legislators in the news at the same time for their improper behavior is especially damaging.

Among the most common criticisms of the legislature are the following:

Money

In the California legislature, as is the case throughout American politics, money carries a great deal of clout. Elections are expensive, and the money for elections comes from many sources, including the candidate's personal wealth, small contributions from many individuals, and larger contributions from business, unions, and other special interests. Large contributions are generally given to ensure support for a particular interest. Although legislators claim that their vote cannot be bought and that contributors are buying access and nothing else, that claim is difficult to support. Moreover, simply having access that the ordinary voter does not have is a significant advantage. We have the best legislature that money can buy, and short of moving to public financing of campaigns—an idea rejected by the voters in June 2010—those with money will always have an advantage over those who do not. With increasing social inequality and more money available to big industries and a few very wealthy individuals (and less available to the rest of us), and with the Supreme Court having loosened the restrictions on campaign spending, this advantage is growing.

Money is usually distributed to those who support the position of a given interest or to those who might be swayed by an offer of monetary support. It also goes to party leaders, who then distribute it to other legislators or candidates to solidify their support both within their party and against the other party. Indeed, the amassing of a large war chest contributed to the distrust and dislike of Speaker Willie Brown and led to the passing of Proposition 140, setting term limits. However, term-limited legislators, having little background in fund-raising, have become more dependent than their predecessors on large donations from special interests. Jesse Unruh once said, "If you can't take their money, eat their food, drink their booze . . . and then vote against them, you don't belong here."[5] On this basis, there are probably more legislators now than before that "don't belong here."

Term Limits Lead to a Lack of Knowledge and Experience

It was believed historically that term limits would remove a remote professional class of legislators and bring in a new breed with closer ties to their districts. The ballot argument said that term limits "would remove the grip that vested interests have over the legislature" and create a "government of citizens representing their fellow citizens."[6] The expectations for this proposition were too high, and the results were unfortunate.

Legislative politics works best as an ongoing game among a relatively stable group of experienced players. Many of the aphorisms about politics, such as "Politics makes strange bedfellows" and "Don't burn your bridges," are based on ongoing relationships played out over a period of years. With a short, fixed term limit, the players change too rapidly for legislators to learn whom they can trust, with whom they can work, and whom they should avoid. This knowledge would facilitate cooperation across party lines as legislators would come to learn that not all good is on their side of the aisle and not all evil on the other side. In a short six years, legislators cannot learn that well; the players change too rapidly. The people who can work out effective compromises seldom emerge, and even if capable negotiators materialized, they would not know with whom to work.

Nor can effective leadership emerge in a term limit as short as six years. In recent years, to give leaders more time in office, the Assembly Democrats have often chosen freshmen legislators as committee chairs and as speaker. But a freshman legislator, no matter how talented, cannot effectively lead a large collegial body.

Nor in six short years is there time to develop expertise in process or subject matter, the ordinary skills of a legislator. This dilemma was summed up by a lobbyist:

> I feel sorry for the first-term members who faced the energy crisis. They don't know who's smart; they don't know who knows what they're doing; they don't know the policy; they don't know the politics. And they are faced with a crisis.[7]

Real power has shifted from the legislature to the permanent establishment—the bureaucracy and interest groups. Members in these institutions may spend a career in Sacramento outlasting five sets of Assembly members.

Much as they were dissatisfied with the legislature, it is doubtful that the voters wanted to shift power to either of those two groups by approving term limits. In June 2012 voters made a change in term limits, which on balance may shift *some* power back to the legislature. Proposition 28 reduced the time a legislator could serve in Sacramento from 14 years (6 in the Assembly and 8 in the Senate) to 12 years, but now those years can all be served in one house. This will give each house more stability and should result in the selection of leaders with greater experience. It is likely that senators will be less experienced in general, but whatever is lost in that body will be gained by the much greater experience that Assembly members will be able to gain before being forced to leave.

The result could be a more knowledgeable and effective legislature that is at least marginally better able to deal with lobbyists and bureaucrats. But we have not yet reached this point. Only those legislators elected in 2012 and after will operate under the new term limits, and change is not likely to be significant until after 2018. The speaker elected in 2014, Toni Atkins, entered the Assembly in 2010 and will be termed out at the end of 2016. Up until now, leaders have been elected based on the word of earlier party leaders or on their reputation prior to joining the legislature. In 2016 or early 2017, after Speaker Atkins is termed out, the class of 2012 will have had 4 years of experience working together and 8 more years ahead of them. They will not need to choose a freshman to lead, they will know more about each other, and they will be able to vote for a leader with whom they are familiar. A real contest for the speakership will probably take place, rather than the rubber stamp of a handpicked candidate.

If there has been a positive aspect to term limits, it is the increased diversity of the legislature. The percentage of Latino legislators rose from 6 percent in 1990 to 25 percent in 2009, before declining to 22 percent in 2012. The percentage of women increased from 17.5 percent in 1990 to 32 percent in 2008 before dropping to 27 percent in early 2014. The current speaker of the Assembly Toni Atkins is the first open lesbian to hold that office (and the first speaker from San Diego). She was immediately preceded by John Pérez, an openly gay Latino, and before that by Karen Bass, an African American woman. Members of non-white ethnic

Toni Atkins (center) was sworn in as speaker of the Assembly in May 2014, accompanied by her spouse (left). Atkins exemplifies the increasing diversity of the California legislature as the first open lesbian to serve as speaker.

groups and women regularly occupy positions in the Democratic leadership of both houses.[8]

Partisanship

Many believe that **partisanship** has increased in the legislature in recent years. This trend is often attributed to safe districts, where representatives were elected who couldn't lose in a general election and who were responsive only to their party's majority, which determines the primary election outcome and which is more extreme than the average voter. Safe districts, according to the common interpretation, resulted in increased partisanship and legislators who were less willing to compromise.

As usual, the issue is more complex than this, although the new, more competitive general elections beginning in 2010 might result in the election of more moderates. The problem is not that there are strong partisans in the legislature—this has always been so. But in recent years, the quality of public discourse has become less civil, and the participants have come to have less regard for their opponents and less willingness to work with them. Part of this incivility is a reflection of the increasing homogeneity and polarization of the national parties and their leaders. Term limits may play a role as well. Recognizing that they will not have to live with and deal with their opponents for years into the future, legislators make less effort to develop civil working relationships with them.

But legislators should be partisan. We elect representatives on a partisan basis. If we vote for Republicans rather than Democrats, then the Republicans should deliver on their partisan promises. Even those who rail against partisanship still want their interests to be forcefully proposed and protected.

Some of the greatest legislatures in the world, such as the British Parliament, are fiercely partisan and yet manage to govern. The difference is that in those bodies, the majority is permitted to rule. In our system, which permits a minority veto on taxation, bipartisan cooperation is essential; when it is not forthcoming, the system functions badly. If the California legislature appeared to function better in 2013–14 it was not because of a reduction in partisanship, but because the Democrats' overwhelming majority made cross-party cooperation largely unnecessary.

Gridlock, Minority Rule, and Lack of Accountability

While California does not have the filibuster that thwarts majority rule in the U.S. Senate, it does have two major checks on effective majority governance. One is that the legislature and the governor are elected separately and may represent different parties. The second is that a **two-thirds vote** is required to raise taxes (and before 2010 was required to pass a budget), necessitating, in the absence of an overwhelming one-party majority, that the two parties work together to produce realistic fiscal policy.

Perhaps no other provision of governance has contributed more to the dysfunctional state of California and the **lack of accountability** that characterizes the legislature than this provision. Californians may elect a majority in the legislature and even a governor of the same party, but unless that party controls two-thirds of each house, it cannot control fiscal policy. Voters blame the majority party for gridlock when in fact the control rests with the minority party, a political dynamic known as **minority rule**. This provision is even more restrictive than the filibuster, which can only work with 40 percent of the U.S. Senate actively backing it; California fiscal policy is held hostage to a one-third minority sitting on its collective hands, ensuring gridlock. As Peter Schrag describes it:

> More than any other structural flaw, it [the two-thirds rule] diffused accountability and brought on much of the budgetary gridlock that California became notorious for in the 1980s and early 1990s.[9]

This structural flaw has been in place for several decades and in recent years the minority party has relied on it to refuse to compromise on the most critical issue before the state: the need for adequate and stable sources of revenue. The increased levels of partisanship combined with the power of the minority to block taxation measures have led to harmful gridlock.

Even Jerry Brown, a political moderate, a skilled negotiator, and one of the most experienced individuals to serve as governor, has been unable to find negotiating partners in the legislature's minority leadership. If he were governing amid the political culture of the 1970s, when he first served, he would be very successful. According to a long-time associate of the governor, Jodie Evans, "He is aghast. He reports on some of his conversations like he couldn't believe the narrowness or lack of comprehending by public officials. . . . He said, 'Some of my old tools are not going to work.'"[10] Brown himself says that the Republicans have a "perverse fidelity to each point in the Republican gospel."[11] These points are reinforced in the party caucuses.

The Republicans, of course, see it differently. Senator Bob Dutton states, "He's all talk and no go. He throws a few scraps out there . . . let's demonize the Republicans, and that's supposed to fix a problem?"[12] *Los Angeles Times* columnist George Skelton writes, "The entire legislative system has been corrupted by Democrats' fear of angering labor unions and Republicans' subservience to a few anti-tax opportunists and entertainers."[13] But while the governor has shown a willingness to oppose the unions (an important Democratic constituency) on pensions and organizing child care workers, the Republicans seem unwilling to agree to increasing revenues.

The situation began to change with the passage of Proposition 25 in 2010 which permitted enacting budgets with a simple majority vote. Budgetary gridlock tapered off further after the Democrats' overwhelming electoral victory in 2012 and the passage of Proposition 30 that same year, which raised taxes and lessened the need for further immediate tax increases. Together these greatly lessened the need for Republican cooperation for legislative action. Although the Democrats lost their two-thirds margin in the Senate in 2014 with the suspension of three senators, with overwhelming majorities, the Democrats could still largely ignore the minority. However, when Governor Brown decided to put a "rainy day fund" constitutional measure on the ballot for November of 2014 (ACA 4), he needed and—in a rare demonstration of bipartisanship—gained Republican support. Brown also secured bipartisan support for a $7.5 billion water bond for the same election. Both measures passed by healthy margins.

Initiatives

A further complication to effective policy making in California is the initiative, which is often used to bypass the legislative process. If an interest group believes that it can get an initiative proposition on the ballot with a populist appeal, then it has little incentive to submit legislation for careful consideration by committees in each house of the legislature or to engage in legislative bargaining. Moreover, initiatives have passed that have weakened the legislature or weakened the legislature's ability to make responsible policy. Proposition 140, which instituted term limits, greatly weakened the ability of the legislature to function effectively by ensuring that there are rarely any experienced legislators in Sacramento. Propositions 13 (1978) and 98 (1988) each limited legislators' ability to make responsible fiscal policy, the first by limiting the use of a stable tax tool (property taxes), the second by locking up a huge chunk of the available funds for a single purpose—education. In 2014, modest changes were made to the initiative process through the passage of SB 1253, providing a public review period for initiatives (see Chapter 4). Of most significance to the legislative process is the bill's provision that after 25 percent of the needed signatures for an initiative proposition are obtained, the Senate and Assembly must hold a joint hearing on the issue. These hearings could possibly result in compromise legislation that would make the initiative unnecessary.

We will probably see many more propositions: it is easier to sway a majority of the voters than a majority of the legislature, and there are increasingly large amounts of money available for initiative campaigns.

Californians have done a lot of damage to effective legislative governance through the initiative process. Voters feel dissatisfied with the legislature and consequently, though not intentionally, pass propositions that result in the legislature working less effectively. That makes voters more dissatisfied, and they vote for more propositions. Since 2008 there has been a modest reversal in this trend and at the moment the state government is functioning more effectively.

California Legislature: Where Are We Now?

The legislature serves two principal functions: policy making and representation. The different requirements of these two functions create tensions. Legislators are also pressured by the needs versus the wants of the district, state versus local interests, and the demands of interest groups, campaign contributors, party leaders, and the governor. California is a large state with many competing wants and needs. Legislative districts are among the largest anywhere. These factors turn the making of policy into a complex and often unseemly process, a process moved by humans who will always be imperfect. Even before term limits, the once highly regarded legislature passed some bad legislation and left problems unaddressed.

Yet the legislature could work better than it does. It is valid to ask if the legislature is the creator or the victim of this impaired system. In large part, problems of inefficacy been generated by outside forces. Term limits, big money for campaigns and elections, and the two-thirds vote requirement for passing tax legislation are the most notable outside factors. The declining level of civility in the legislature is a reflection of the impact of term limits and of the increasing political polarization in the nation. It is also caused in part by the safe districts created by the 2001 legislative redistricting, a process carried out for the most part in the legislature. Legislators representing safe districts do not have to pay attention to moderate elements in their party or voters from the opposition party. But individuals are responsible for their own behavior. Regardless of outside forces, individual legislators of goodwill could make a difference.

Since 2008 a series of changes have taken place (mostly via the initiative process, ironically) that appear to have strengthened the legislative process and reduced gridlock, at least for the time being.

- **Proposition 11 (November 2008), Proposition 20 (November 2010), and Proposition 27 (November 2010, defeated):** Proposition 11 took redistricting of the legislature away from the legislature and put it in the hands of a Citizens Redistricting Commission. It passed by only 50.9 percent of the vote. It was strengthened by the passage by 61 percent of Proposition 20, which extended the jurisdiction of the commission to congressional districts, and the corresponding defeat by 59.5 percent of Proposition 27, which would have eliminated the commission. As a result of the commission's most recent redistricting, districts became more evenly balanced, and Democrats gained a two-thirds margin in both legislative houses.

- **Proposition 14 (June 2010):** Proposition 14 created the open primary system, with the expectation that more moderate legislators would be elected. It is too early to tell if that result was accomplished (and whatever impact this has is overshadowed by the impact of Proposition 11 et al.), but in 19 districts two members of the same party ended up winning the primary election and running against each other in the general election. This kind of primary system offers an opportunity for minority party members to help select the more moderate of the opposing candidates.

- **Proposition 25 (November 2010):** The requirement for a two-thirds majority to pass the annual budget was eliminated by this measure. This has substantially reduced the influence of the minority, whose involvement in this fiscal measure was required every year.

- **Proposition 28 (June 2012):** This proposition reduced the term limits in the legislature from 14 to 12 years, but allowed members to serve all that time in a single house. This will allow legislators to gain more experience, especially in the Assembly, and presumably greater knowledge and effectiveness. It is too early to make that judgment.

- **Proposition 30 (November 2012):** Proposition 30 increased taxes, giving the state greater fiscal stability and reducing the need for the minority party's help in passing tax legislation at the moment.

The two-thirds Democratic majority did not reappear in 2014. During this off-year election, Republicans were more likely to vote than Democrats, meaning that some marginal districts switched to the Republicans.

It is too early to make a long-term assessment of the impacts of these propositions on the legislature. The skilled moderate leadership of Governor Brown is an important factor in the current situation. He will be around for one more term at most. The power of big money and the threat of dominating interests are always there to skew the process.

Given the sour national mood, the diverse nature of the state, and an electorate that is itself divided, positive change cannot be ensured. Moreover, the public has little understanding of legislative functions or the legislative process, making further positive change through the initiative process unlikely. Draconian measures, such as a part-time legislature, have been suggested. As the cartoonist Walt Kelly's character Pogo said, "We have met the enemy and he is us."

But not always. We should be thankful for the current hiatus in gridlock that has permitted the legislature to address the many issues that face our state.

Study Guide

FOR FURTHER READING

Cain, Bruce E., and Roger G. Noll, eds. *Constitutional Reform in California: Making State Government More Effective and Responsive*. Berkeley: Institute of Governmental Studies Press, 1995.

California Journal and State Net. *Roster and Government Guide*. Sacramento: California Journal, 2004.

de Sá, Karen. "How Our Laws in California Are Really Made." *San Jose Mercury News*, July 10, 2010. www.mercurynews.com/politics-government/ci_15452125. Accessed August 11, 2014

Institute of Governmental Affairs. "IGS Goes to Sacramento to Assess Ten Years of Term Limits." *Public Affairs Reports* 42, no. 3 (Fall 2001).

Mathews, Joe, and Mark Paul. *California Crackup: How Reform Broke the Golden State and How We Can Fix It*. Berkeley: University of California Press, 2010.

Muir, William K., Jr. *Legislature: California's School for Politics*. Chicago: University of Chicago Press, 1982.

Schrag, Peter. *California: America's High-Stakes Experiment*. Berkeley: University of California Press, 2006.

———. *Paradise Lost: California's Experience, America's Future*. New York: New Press, 1998.

Wilson, E. Dotson. *California's Legislature*. Sacramento: Office of the Chief Clerk, California State Assembly, 2000.

ON THE WEB

California State Assembly Democratic Caucus: www.asmdc.org. Accessed August 11, 2014

California State Assembly Republican Caucus: http://republican.assembly.ca.gov/. Accessed August 11, 2014

California Choices: http://californiachoices.org. Accessed August 11, 2014.

California State Senate: http://senate.ca.gov/. Accessed August 11, 2014.

California State Assembly: http://assembly.ca.gov/. Accessed August 11, 2014

California Legislative Analyst's Office: www.lao.ca.gov/. Accessed August 12, 2014. The LAO is a nonpartisan fiscal and policy adviser to the legislature.

Capitol and California: www.sacbee.com/capitolandcalifornia. Accessed August 11, 2014.

Legislative Counsel: http://www.leginfo.ca.gov/. Accessed August 11, 2014. The Legislative Counsel of California's official site, maintained by law.

Rough & Tumble: www.rtumble.com. Accessed August 11, 2014. Daily summary of California news.

Senate Democrats: http://democrats.senate.ca.gov/. Accessed August 11, 2014. Senate Republicans: http://cssrc.us/. Accessed August 11,2014.

University of California, Berkeley, Institute of Governmental Studies Library: http://igs.berkeley.edu/library. Accessed August 11, 2014.

SUMMARY

I. Legislatures are not well understood, but are critical to a democratic form of government. Indeed, a working legislature is practically the definition of a democratic government.

II. The California legislature is, for the most part, modeled on the U.S. Congress.
   A. It is bicameral.
   B. Members are elected from single-member, geographically based districts.
   C. Unlike the U.S. Congress, both houses are based on population.

III. Legislators must both represent their constituents and make policy.
   A. These two items are not always compatible.
   B. In representing their districts, members must decide whether to follow the wants or the needs of their constituents and whether to follow directions from the district or use their own best judgment.
   C. Poor communication from constituents makes these actions difficult.
   D. Legislators have offices both in Sacramento and in their districts.

IV. Members of the California Senate and Assembly are elected through an open primary followed by a general election. Two key features of California politics influence who gets elected:
   A. Candidates must engage in extensive fundraising to increase their chances of getting elected.
   B. Redistricting following each census has a significant impact on who is elected. For example, redistricting by a Citizens Redistricting Commission in 2012 resulted in a Democratic supermajority in the legislature.

V. The leader of the Assembly is the speaker; the leader of the Senate is the president pro tempore.
   A. Each is elected by all of the members in that body, but the majority party caucus usually determines the outcome.
   B. The speaker controls most of the resources and is very powerful.
   C. The speaker and the president pro tempore are term-limited.
   D. The president pro tempore shares powers with the Senate Rules Committee.

VI. The bulk of legislative work is done in committees.
   A. Bills are read and amended here.
   B. Committees are made up of a group of individuals—lobbyists, staffers, members, and bureaucrats—who make and control policy in a given substantive area.

VII. Professional staff members make the legislature possible.
   A. Some of them work in districts, some in members' offices, some for committees, and some for the leadership.
   B. The best-paid staff members are usually subject-matter experts working for committees.

VIII. The legislative process has several steps.
   A. Bills are first introduced by members and sent to committees.
   B. Bills must pass the floors of both houses (with identical wording) before they are sent to the governor for his signature.

C. If the governor vetoes a bill, it takes a two-thirds vote in each house to override it.

D. Budget, appropriation, and tax bills also require a two-thirds vote, giving the minority party immense power in the legislature and making it difficult for the majority party to govern.

IX. The state legislature is different from the U.S. Congress.
A. Members are term limited.
B. The governor has line-item veto (he can cut or eliminate any item in a budget bill, while still approving the entire bill).
C. Both houses are based on population.
D. Very little media attention is given to the California legislature.
E. Judges in California are elected, so the legislature does not have a role in their approval.

F. The legislature does not have a filibuster, unlike the U.S. Senate. However, the two-thirds requirement for increasing taxes has a similar impact in thwarting the majority.
G. California also has the initiative process, which allows the legislative process to be bypassed, most often by interests with deep pockets.

X. The effectiveness of the California legislature is limited
A. by the power of big money.
B. by term limits and lack of experience.
C. by increasing partisanship.
D. by the two-thirds-vote rule, which keeps the majority party from governing and makes accountability difficult.
E. by the initiative, which is often used to bypass the legislative process.

PRACTICE QUIZ

1. A line-item veto allows
   a) the governor to reject any single item in an appropriations or budget bill.
   b) the speaker or the president pro tempore to pull any single item from the agenda.
   c) a single member to block a single piece of legislation by signing a written objection.
   d) a petition by a group of 10 legislators to block any single piece of legislation.

2. Proposition 140
   a) limits the time that legislators can serve in Sacramento.
   b) limits the legislature from raising property taxes.
   c) sets aside 40 percent of the budget for education purposes.
   d) requires the speaker to assign staff to the minority party.

3. The legislature is composed of
   a) 80 members in the Senate and 40 in the Assembly.
   b) 120 members in a single body.
   c) 60 members in each body.
   d) 80 members in the Assembly and 40 in the Senate.

4. A two-thirds vote is needed to pass
   a) appropriation bills.
   b) budget bills.
   c) tax bills.
   d) all of the above.

5. Partisanship in the legislature
   a) has declined because of apportionment.
   b) has declined because of the blanket primary now in effect.
   c) has led to greater ease in getting budgets improved.
   d) has increased in recent years.

6. The powers of the speaker of the California Assembly include all of the following *except*
   a) the power to assign parking spaces.
   b) the power to assign office space.
   c) the power to assign members to committees but not to remove them during the current term.
   d) the power to assign a member to a committee against both the member's wishes and the wishes and needs of his or her constituency.

7. Proposition 140 resulted in all of the following *except*
   a) an increase in office budgets.
   b) the establishment of term limits.
   c) a reduction of committee staff and personal staff.
   d) layoffs of some of the most knowledgeable staff experts from committees.

8. The legislative process is biased in favor of
   a) issues favored by the public.
   b) the status quo.
   c) change that interest groups favor.
   d) legislation proposed by the governor, who can introduce a limited number of bills directly to both houses, bypassing some of the steps of the legislative process.

9. California has some of the largest legislative districts in the nation. This means that
   a) elections in California tend to be expensive.
   b) citizen access to legislators is unusually good because legislators need to face the voters so often.

c) staff levels are unusually high to handle the volume of business from constituents.
d) California has an unusually large number of legislators.

10. Term limits have resulted in which the following:
   a) an increase in expertise among legislators, who have only a few years to make a name for themselves.
   b) an increase in citizen legislators, people with little or no political experience who are able to run because seats are open.
   c) an increase in staff members, who are needed to help legislators with little experience.
   d) a decline in the knowledge needed to pass good-quality legislation.

CRITICAL-THINKING QUESTIONS

1. Should a legislator vote for what his or her constituents want or what his or her constituents need?
2. Who should apportion the legislature?
3. What criteria should be used to apportion a legislature?
4. Should a legislator take orders from constituents or use his or her own best judgment, even if it is unpopular?
5. How much access should lobbyists have to legislators?
6. When should a legislature have rules that allow a minority to block legislation?

KEY TERMS

apportionment (p. 123)
Assembly Rules Committee (p. 117)
bicameralism (p. 109)
committees (p. 116)
constituents (p. 109)
gerrymander (p. 115)
gridlock (p. 122)
"gut and amend" (p. 120)

issue networks (p. 117)
lack of accountability (p. 128)
line-item veto (p. 122)
logrolling (p. 120)
minority rule (p. 128)
partisanship (p. 127)
president pro tempore (p. 117)

Proposition 140/term limits (p. 109)
representation (p. 109)
speaker (p. 116)
staff (p. 117)
two-thirds vote (p. 128)
veto (p. 116)
winner-take-all (p. 113)

6

The Governor and the Executive Branch

WHAT CALIFORNIA GOVERNMENT DOES AND WHY IT MATTERS

Consider the following activities in the executive branch of our state government:

- Governor Brown, who had a reputation for being tightfisted in 2012, convinced overwhelming numbers of voters to approve Proposition 30, an initiative raising taxes for five years, by personally campaigning up and down the state.

- Governor Brown's administration initiated an investigation of Caltrans after receiving reports of shoddy work on the new segment of the Bay Bridge and learning that Caltrans had transferred or ended the contracts of the "whistle-blowing" project managers.

- Governor Brown continued to pursue his vision of building a high-speed rail line connecting Los Angeles and San Francisco in spite of declining public support and opposition within his own party.

- After twice vetoing similar bills, the governor signed into law a bill requiring motorists to give bicyclists three feet of clearance when passing from behind.

- Caltrans decided to replace high occupancy vehicle lanes with toll lanes on an Orange County "freeway" over the objections of local governments and agencies.

- Through tough bargaining, Attorney General Kamala Harris negotiated a better settlement for California homeowners from a group of banks charged with fore-closure abuse than other states' attorneys general were able to achieve.

If you think you know little about the executive branch of California, you are not alone. The media rarely pay much attention to state government, and in 2013 the last out-of-town TV bureau in Sacramento closed. California government operates largely out of the public view. The governor's reputation is based mainly on his interactions with the legislature, which have often been contentious—and therefore newsworthy—in recent years. Barring major scandal, the governor's actions as the executive head of a huge bureaucracy are off the press's radar. Few reporters would be able to locate Caltrans or the Natural Resources Agency either physically or on an organization chart. Most of California's 200,000-plus state employees are known to the public only as friends and neighbors.

When Governor Brown came into office in 2011, it was not uncommon to hear that the state was "ungovernable." Now, government is said to be working well, and many credit Brown's widely acknowledged political skills with helping to increase the state's productivity. However, the government's recent successes are due not only to Brown's abilities, but also to the overwhelming Democratic majorities in the California legislature as well as recent changes in the state constitution that have made it possible to pass budgets on a majority vote. When Brown had to deal with a larger Republican minority in the legislature, and when a two-thirds vote was required to pass a budget, he was less successful.

If California government is viewed positively at this time, much of the credit is due to the party profile of the legislature and to an improving economy. The governor, who is often the victim of his circumstances and blamed when things go wrong, can also be the beneficiary of better times.

The Invisible Governor?

While the governor is the most visible political figure in the state, his visibility pales in comparison to that of the president of the United States. There are a number of reasons for this lack of visibility. We depend on the media for most of what we know about our government, and for the most part the media in California are not interested in state politics or governance. The media, after all, are a business, responding to the desires of their consumers and advertisers. For many Californians, and thus for the media, Sacramento does not capture much attention: it is a long way from the major population centers of the state, and what happens there just does not captivate an audience the way a good car chase does. The media have found that their business model works best by focusing on well-known or riveting personalities, and the governor is often perceived as boring. With the exception of U.S. senators, long-serving, high-visibility politicians are rare in California's term-limited government.

The president's job is divided analytically into two roles: **head of government** and **head of state**. So, too, is the governor's job, but while the head-of-government role is similar in both cases, the head-of-state role is vastly different. It is that role that gives the president most of his visibility.

The role of the head of government is to govern—that is, to develop policy, get it passed through the legislature, and implement it via the bureaucracy. The governor's approach to these various tasks is often divisive. Think of the prime minister of Great Britain, who not only develops policy, gets it passed, and implements it, but actually appears on the floor of Parliament to answer questions, often shouted, from his own and opposition parties. In contrast, the queen is the head of state in Great Britain. Her role is highly visible, ceremonial, and important for bringing people together. She cuts ribbons, attends public events, greets foreign visitors, rides in parades, and goes on foreign tours to promote British businesses. In fact, this is her major role. Most of the time when you see the president between campaigns, he is inhabiting his role as head of state: welcoming the troops home, attending funerals, dedicating buildings, posing for pictures with foreign dignitaries, consoling victims of tornados or hurricanes, and making major or minor public announcements. Being head of state is largely a symbolic, positive, and noncontroversial role offering lots of photo ops for the media. In this role the president represents the entire nation, acting for all of us.

The governor does not have this range of opportunities for public visibility, or, if he or she does, the events are so insignificant that not many people care. Few dignitaries of note visit Sacramento, and the press simply does not warm to filming the governor talking to teachers or highway patrolmen. Because he was a showman able to generate his own buzz, Governor Schwarzenegger made as much as he could of the head-of-state role; Governor Brown simply has no interest in it. Indeed, Governor Brown has offered the following advice to President Obama: "Minimize the fanfare and speechifying. Speaking a lot doesn't produce a lot."[1] Nothing else so clearly characterizes the difference between the chief executive of the United States and the chief executive of one of the most important states in the union as this difference in visibility.

There are important similarities between the two positions as well; most notably, both are offices with limited powers, as hard as it is for the public to understand that the most powerful political leader of the most powerful nation on earth is restricted in his authority. And no matter how important a state, it is not run by the governor any more than the president runs the nation. Our nation's founders feared a strong executive, having experienced such rule under a king and under capricious colonial governors. Consequently, they created a system in which the powers of all institutions were strictly limited, and in which the powers of the executive were secondary to those of the legislature.

The governor does have important **formal powers**, in some cases more than the president, but, according to Richard Neustadt, as with the president, the governor's power is mostly the power to persuade.[2] His power to command and direct in any way he chooses is seriously limited.

As with the president, people have many incomplete, incorrect, and conflicting views about the governor. Tom Cronin and Michael Genovese compiled a list of what they call the paradoxes of the presidency:

- We want the president to be an effective politician while being above politics.

- We want him to be a common person and an extraordinary person at the same time.

- We want him to be powerful but not too powerful.[3]

While Governor Brown usually prefers to stay out of the media spotlight, he lobbied vigorously and visibly for Proposition 30 in 2012. Here, Brown and his wife, Anne Gust Brown (who acts as the governor's top aide), present petitions to put the tax hike initiative on the 2012 ballot to employees at the Sacramento Registrar of Voters office.

In sum, we want the president to be all things at all times, and, of course, this is not possible.

The governor is not burdened with as much symbolic baggage as the president, yet many misperceptions carry over to this office as well. These misperceptions are amplified by the fact that people think that they understand the office. After all, it is an executive office, a position with which all of us who work in organizations have some familiarity. But the governorship is a *political* executive office, in an organization that often does not have a single, identifiable chain of command and which does not respond well, if at all, to direct orders.

Our greatest misperception is attributing more power to the governor than he or she has. The governor does not control the legislature, and has trouble making policy without the cooperation, or at least acquiescence, of legislators who may have little reason to support the governor. He or she can win legislative cooperation only through persuasion—perhaps hardball persuasion, but persuasion nonetheless.

Within the executive branch, it is possible for the governor to exert influence more directly. But the executive branch is large and in many cases very remote from the governor. How does the governor get a Caltrans engineer in San Diego or a park ranger in Marin County to follow his wishes? Equally problematic is the insulation of much of the executive branch from direct gubernatorial influence. The executive branch includes several independently elected executives known collectively as the plural executive, often from the opposing party of the governor, and all looking out for their own political ambitions. Some organizations, such as the University of California, are governed by boards that can be influenced only by appointments, budgetary threats, or strongly voiced public opinion.

Moreover, we often elect governors who are not especially knowledgeable about government agencies, Sacramento politics, or the many interests in our large and diverse state. For example, Arnold Schwarzenegger held no political office before being elected governor, and the unsuccessful 2010 Republican candidate for governor, Meg Whitman, did not even vote for many years. More important than formal powers are political skills and an ability to bargain, a long political memory, and friends and allies in important positions. A good economy, an absence of natural disasters, and luck can also be important.

Schwarzenegger's initial popularity was rare in California politics, even exceeding the popularity of Ronald Reagan. By sheer dint of personality and the threat to go to the public with initiatives, he managed a series of impressive victories in the early days of his tenure. His success did not last. He overreached himself, and he antagonized the members of his own party with his moderate positions on many issues. His attempt to pass four initiatives in a special—and costly—election in November 2005 was a disaster. Near the end of his time in office, his approval ratings had reached a low of 23 percent in a Public Policy Institute of California poll.[4]

Jerry Brown is the polar opposite of Arnold Schwarzenegger. He is one of the most knowledgeable governors that California has ever had. He loves the details of policy making, knows the intricacies of governing, and does not crave or need the limelight. He knows how to bargain and make deals. In 2011, at the start of his third term, he was faced with a bad economy, huge revenue shortfalls, and an opposition party that would not bargain on revenue issues. But things turned around with the emergence of favorable political and economic situations. Republican opposition became irrelevant after new redistricting and primary laws provided the Democrats with overwhelming majorities in both houses of the legislature, and the passage of Proposition 25 allowed budgets to pass the legislature on a simple majority vote. Along with the improved economy and the passage of tax-raising Proposition 30—thanks in large part to the governor's political acumen and skills—governing suddenly became much easier.

Formal Powers of the Governor

The formal powers of the governor, while limited, are still significant. The governor has powers—the most important of which is the **line-item veto**—that are denied to the president. The true value of these powers, however, is as vantage points on which the governor bases his **informal powers** or powers to persuade. (See Box 6.1 for a summary of the governor's formal and informal powers.) A governor who expects to use only his formal powers to govern will not accomplish much. He must leverage those powers to persuade other political actors to support his goals. For instance, using his appointment power, he can try to persuade an important legislator to support his budget by promising to appoint one of the legislator's supporters to an important state commission.

The state constitution vests supreme executive power in the governor, a phrase that conveys both more and less than it seems. Less, because the governor's office is an office of limited powers in which nothing is supreme. More, because executives often push established constitutional limits. However, given a supportive legislature that views most executive requests positively—as is true currently—most of the executive's goals can be reached.

Appointments

Making appointments is one of the governor's most significant powers. The governor appoints four distinct groups of individuals: his **personal staff**, heads of major administrative divisions, some judges, and members of a number of **boards and commissions**. Some of these appointments require confirmation by other bodies, while others do not. Some appointees work at the governor's pleasure, while others serve for fixed terms. Some are answerable directly to the governor, and others are several steps removed or protected from his intervention. Over the course of his administration, a governor can make more than 2,500 appointments. At the start of his term about 500 positions will be filled.

The governor's personal staff consists of about 100 individuals who craft policy recommendations, work with the legislature, or make the governor's life possible—providing structure, packaging him, and presenting him to the public. Governors hire, fire, and move these individuals about at will. No confirmation is required.

Next closest to the governor are the members of his **cabinet**. The governor determines who will serve in the cabinet and what role, if any, the cabinet will play in policy development. The heads of the **superagencies** of state government (large organizations similar to federal departments, which contain a number of related bureaus) are in the cabinet, as are the director of finance and others whose presence the governor finds useful and appropriate. These positions require confirmation by the Senate, but the governor can fire them as he wishes.

The governor also appoints the heads of the major bureaus or departments, which are mostly located within the superagencies. These individuals have the

The governor has important formal and informal powers, among which are:

FORMAL POWERS

Organizing and managing the executive branch, including appointing many top executives

Taking independent executive actions

Serving as commander in chief of the National Guard

Appointing people to head executive agencies, to independent boards and commissions, and to the judiciary

Drawing up the budget

Making legislative recommendations

Vetoing legislation

Employing line-item vetoes of budget and appropriation items

Granting of clemency, including pardons and reprieves

INFORMAL POWERS

Bargaining with legislators and other independent power sources

Having access to the public to make his case

Developing a vision or agenda for the state

Raising money for political campaigns

responsibility of overseeing the organizations that do the real work of government and the more than 200,000 state employees in those agencies.

In addition, the governor appoints members to more than 325 boards and commissions, important and unimportant, visible and invisible. Once appointed, individuals do not have to answer to the governor, although the governor can apply political pressure, including threatening to cut the budget of the institution that the individual administers.

Stating that "the state's bureaucracy is a labyrinth of disjointed boards, commissions, agencies and departments,"[5] Governor Brown in 2012 proposed a restructuring and consolidation of agencies, having eliminated 25 boards and commissions the previous year. There is no political payoff in this. Few outside of the government will notice. But it is important and illustrative of Brown's attention to policy detail.

Independent Executive Actions

The governor's powers are constitutionally restricted by the legislature, but in some cases he is able to act independently of it. Independent executive actions are permitted by the constitution or under laws passed by the legislature. They are most significant in times of an emergency.

Few laws passed by the legislature are self-implementing; most require positive action on the part of the administration. This process of implementation involves clarification of the law (e.g., what does the language used by the legislature imply?)

and the assembling of finances and an administrative structure to allow action to take place. All of this requires prioritization and fund requests by the governor's appointees or the governor himself. This allows the governor considerable influence; using the line-item veto or failing to request adequate funds, for example, can effectively kill a program. Governor Brown has used these powers several times, in one instance eliminating both the California Postsecondary Education Commission and the duplicative office of the secretary of education, neither of which he found useful.

Commander in Chief

The governor is the commander in chief of the California National Guard. This role is of little significance until times of civil disorder or natural disaster, when the governor has the power to call out the guard, though not to direct its actions.

Organizing and Managing the Executive Branch

The governor is empowered to organize and manage the executive branch. *Organize* means he can make a number of administrative appointments. *Manage* means that many of these appointees must report to the governor, at least indirectly, and he can remove them from office. Again, the limits of this power should be recognized.

First, the functions of the state government are not boundless. Much of the money that it collects is passed on to local government and school districts to spend.

Second, the rest of the elected executive branch, most notably the attorney general, limits the governor's actions, and some state employees report to these elected officials—5,000 to the attorney general alone.

Third, some of the appointments made by the governor are to boards that can, and do, act independently of the governor. These appointments may be for fixed terms. The best known of these independent boards is the Regents of the University of California. This 26-member board consists of 7 ex officio members (members, including the governor, who sit on the board because they occupy another office); one student; and 18 members appointed by the governor for 12-year terms—terms that are longer than his. Control over this board, if he wishes to exert it, is possible only through new appointments, the loyalty of previously appointed members, and persuasion.

Fourth, the governor must make appointments to agencies about which he knows little, often appointing individuals about whom he knows little. Information coming out of these agencies is limited, so the governor is often in the dark about what is happening until something goes terribly wrong and it appears in the press.

The controversy over Caltrans' management of the rebuilding of the eastern span of the Bay Bridge provides a case in point. In 2006, Caltrans, perhaps the most visible of California's government agencies, hired a Chinese company with limited bridge-building experience to build key elements of the new span. According to the *Sacramento Bee*, numerous flaws and cost overruns followed, leading to questions of whether the bridge will meet its planned 150-year lifespan. Project engineers and inspectors who raised questions about the quality of the work were transferred or removed from the job when their contracts expired in an attempt to keep the issues quiet and to expedite the project. The governor's public stance has been that "stuff happens" (or words to that effect), but his administration initiated legislative investigations, including one by an external agency, into the entire operation and culture of Caltrans. Had it not been for aggressive reporting by northern California newspapers on the issue, the governor might never have acted to address long-standing issues within Caltrans.[6]

Budget

Perhaps the governor's most significant power is that of preparing the budget, coupled with his power to exercise a line-item veto of budget provisions. At the federal level, the president presents Congress with a budget proposal—but it is only a proposal; the House of Representatives has constitutional authority over fiscal matters. The California Constitution gives the power of preparing the budget to the governor. This means that all budget requests from executive branch agencies must pass through the governor. It is at this point that the governor has life and death power over a program and can have a critical impact on the policy that a program implements. The actual work on this process of preparing the budget is done by the Department of Finance.

The budget is prepared and sent to the legislature by January 10, with revisions following later in the spring (called the May Revise) as the financial picture becomes clearer. The governor then has the job of getting the budget approved by the legislature. Until 2012, a supermajority of two-thirds was required to approve a budget; now only a simple majority in both houses of the legislature is required. Although a supermajority vote is no longer needed to pass a budget, it is still required to raise new revenues. Because budgets may not have adequate revenues, and because the Democrats have now lost their brief supermajority, the support of the minority party is important. Obtaining this support may require some expensive trade-offs with recalcitrant legislators who withhold their support until they receive an offer they cannot refuse.

There are in effect five major players in the budget game—the governor and the leaders of both parties in both houses of the legislature. The need for one or two marginal votes, should that occur, may introduce even more major players. Because of his role at both ends of the budgetary process, and because one person needs to broker the deal, the governor usually has the key role. But even he can be held hostage by stubborn legislators. Although in recent years Republican legislators have been adamant in opposing any and all tax increases, the passage of the tax-raising Proposition 30 along with the improving economy has marginalized their influence. While neither the Republican Schwarzenegger nor the Democrat Brown has been able to persuade the two parties to work together to shape revenue legislation, the Democratic majorities in the legislature make bipartisan cooperation largely unnecessary at present.

Veto and Line-Item Veto

The second most significant power of the governor is the veto. Just as in Congress, all bills passed by the legislature can be vetoed by the governor. The legislature passes about 1,000 bills each year and, since 1967, the governor has vetoed 13 percent of them on average. Governor Schwarzenegger vetoed about 26 percent of the bills that came to him, while Governor Brown on average has vetoed 12.6 percent of the bills sent to him.[7] The veto can be overridden by a two-thirds majority of each house of the legislature, but that has happened only seven times since 1946 (and four of those were against Jerry Brown in the 1970s). The most recent veto override attempt was on a 2012 bill that would have permitted local governments to take over the management of some state parks to keep them open during the fiscal crisis.

Equally important, and unlike the national government, the governor has a line-item veto which permits him to reduce or delete any appropriation in a spending bill. Consequently, legislators cannot force the governor to accept funding for a program that he does not like by burying it inside a large spending bill that he must sign. The governor cannot add items, but the ability to reduce or eliminate the favorite programs of legislators is a powerful tool. It is a key item in the governor's box of bargaining tools, and one that no other player has (although it is impossible to tell how often governors use it).

In recent years line-item vetoes have been minor, often correcting technical errors. However, they have also been used to kill programs that the governor feels are unnecessary or ineffective, such as Brown's 2011 veto of funding for the California Postsecondary Education Commission, a body that provided policy advice to the governor on the three branches of higher education. In the state budget for 2014–15, Governor Brown used the line-item veto only 10 times for a total in cuts of $37.9 million (out of a budget of $156 billion).[8] Large majorities in the legislative houses that support the governor make the line-item veto less necessary.

Legislative Powers

Much of the success of the governor depends on his ability to persuade the legislature to go along with his programs. This is a difficult task because legislators owe him little. He does not help elect them. They represent smaller and different constituencies, often looking out for local rather than statewide issues. They are on different career paths with different time constraints. Because they are term limited, they are relatively inexperienced in bargaining and do not have a long-term commitment to the Sacramento governing process. Their next jobs may be in the private sector, perhaps as lobbyists. If so, they may be more interested in pleasing potential employers (special interests) than in cooperating with the governor.

The governor's ability to persuade legislators depends on his political skills as well as many factors beyond his control, including the partisan makeup of the legislature and the political and economic environment. Although much of this influence depends on the governor's informal powers and the use of his other formal powers, he does have several specific powers that are directed primarily toward influencing the legislature, including preparing the budget, vetoing bills or provisions of bills, and making legislative recommendations.

Rather than having to twist arms to get the support of legislators for his programs, Governor Brown is in the enviable—nearly unique—position of having to persuade the Democratic legislature not to overreach and antagonize the electorate by passing too much legislation, spending too much money, or attempting to raise taxes.[9]

Legislative Recommendations

At the beginning of a legislative session, as required by the constitution, the governor presents a State of the State speech to the legislature. This speech may be short or long, general or specific. It is normally not covered in detail by the media, unlike the president's State of the Union speech. Whether or not the State of the State contains the governor's legislative program, most governors have such a program that addresses the problems of the state as they see them and that they hope to get passed through the legislature.

The governor cannot introduce legislation but can persuade allies to introduce his specific proposals. As the most prominent political figure in the state, he is in a position to press for action on these proposals. His success once again depends on a variety of factors, including his political skills. Because of his star power, Governor Schwarzenegger had greater access to the public through the media and, more than most governors, could bring outside pressure to bear on the legislature through public appearances. But Schwarzenegger's governorship is widely considered to have been filled with wasted opportunities, partly because of his support for ill-advised initiatives. Jerry Brown prefers to work on the inside, using his significant personal political skills. But he too needed public support for tax increases, and his successful public appearances to lobby for Proposition 30 may have had more impact simply because previously they had been so rare. Former State Librarian Kevin Starr feels that the governor's reputation is enhanced by "everything he chooses not to say"—by staying, for the most part, out of the press.[10]

Judicial Powers

The governor has the power to grant pardons and commute or shorten sentences for state crimes. He can also reverse parole decisions or delay a death sentence. While these are significant powers, governors tend to use them with extreme care and caution, because appearing "soft on crime" can have serious political consequences. Among other judicial powers of the governor is the power to nominate justices to the Supreme and appellate courts, as well as the power to appoint other judges if positions are opened by retirement or resignation.

Public Roles of the Governor

While the governor's role as head of state does not provide as much access to the public as the president enjoys, he still is occasionally seen cutting a ribbon, bestowing an honor upon some citizen, leading an international trade delegation, or, most often, signing a bill into law. These and other ceremonial and symbolic appearances may have little policy content, but they keep the governor in the public eye. While far less visible than the president, governors do not underestimate these appearances, which remind people that the governor is on the job, that he does care about their concerns, and that, in case of a disaster, the governor and the resources of the state will be available.

Occasionally issues arise of such overwhelming importance—the budget crises are prime examples—that the media are willing to give the governor significant air time. On other occasions the governor can stage policy-related events, such as showing up at a school to emphasize his education policies (or to mask his actual opposition to certain education policies). Finally, disasters such as earthquakes, droughts, and fires require the governor to be publically active, and during these crises the media will broadcast every statement he makes.

The governor also moves into the public spotlight during elections, and not only when he is campaigning for re-election. California governors often think they have a chance to become president, considering that governors of far less populous or attention-getting states have been elected. When governors sense a chance for the presidency, they try to get in the national media as much as possible. Jerry Brown ran for president twice during his first two terms in office (and once afterward), to the detriment of his performance as governor.

Governors also campaign for political allies, including candidates for president or loyal Assembly members. They may also take an active role in an initiative or referendum campaign, either to bolster the chances of an initiative that they support or to gain more public attention. In spite of his mixed success in this arena, Governor Schwarzenegger continued to be involved right through the elections of 2010, endorsing the successful Proposition 14 in June and leading the successful effort in November to defeat Proposition 23, which would have suspended an air pollution control law (AB 32). Governor Brown's campaign for Proposition 30, which greatly enhanced his political reputation and helped put the state on a firmer financial footing, provides a critically important recent example. In 2014 Governor Brown also campaigned vigorously and successfully for Proposition 1, the water bond, and Proposition 2, the Rainy Day Budget Stabilization Fund Act.

The governor's extensive fund-raising appearances may also gain significant public attention. This attention is useful because it indicates to the opposition that the governor has a formidable war chest and convinces the party faithful that the governor is out there stumping on their behalf.

Jerry Brown as Governor

Jerry Brown is the son of Pat Brown, one of California's most popular governors, who in the 1960s helped develop the education system and infrastructure that made California the envy of the nation. In 1974, seven years after his father left office, Jerry Brown was elected governor for two consecutive terms. He earned a reputation as a fiscal conservative as well as a visionary and bold politician willing to ignore the wishes of his allies. He was also a frequent candidate for the Democratic Party nomination for president (in 1976, 1980, and 1992).

As a visionary, Brown was often parodied as "Governor Moonbeam," promoting, for example, the establishment of a space academy and purchase of a communications satellite for the state. His advocacy of fiscal restraints (which reflected his personal lifestyle) did not go over well in a state that still remembered his father, who had presided over an era of seemingly unlimited promise.

After his first two terms of office ended in 1983, Brown, still in his early 40s, was adrift. During the next 16 years, he studied Buddhism, ran for president (again), and chaired the California Democratic Party. In 1999 he reestablished his career as an elected official by starting at the local level as mayor of the economically troubled city of Oakland, and he held the position of attorney general from 2007 to 2011. In the 2010 governor's race, the state voters had the opportunity to select between Brown, an experienced if unpredictable Democratic politician, and Meg Whitman, a billionaire Republican Internet entrepreneur. The voters chose political experience over business acumen. Whitman had little political experience but a lot of money, and her self-financed campaign was the most expensive in California history. Brown spent far less and won by emphasizing his political experience and ability to work with the opposition Republicans.

Jerry Brown's predecessor in office, Arnold Schwarzenegger, was elected in the October 2003 recall of Governor Gray Davis. Davis was recalled due in part to the state's inadequate response to a manipulated energy crisis, legislative budgetary stalemates, fund-raising scandals, and his own remoteness. Hoping for change, the voters turned to an inexperienced but flamboyant movie actor who stood out in a weak field of possible replacements.

Most of the Schwarzenegger years in office were characterized by extreme state budget deficits that the governor and legislature were unable to close on a long-term basis. There were annual standoffs lasting for months with Republicans unwilling to raise taxes and revenues under any circumstances. In the end, the Schwarzenegger governorship failed to resolve the crises in California politics.

Although Brown is perhaps the most experienced nonincumbent elected to governor in California, his first years in office were not easy. From his predecessor, Brown inherited a budget deficit of $25 billion as well as an established pattern of constructing budgets largely with smoke and mirrors. His greatest early accomplishments were initiating the process of cutting the structural deficit while offering budgets that were far more honest than those of recent years. He had to do this with no support from Republican legislators, and he was forced to make deep cuts in popular government programs, including cuts to higher education, which angered many Democrats.

By late 2012, Brown had cut 5,500 positions from government, convinced the e-commerce web site Amazon to pay state sales tax, "realigned" many services back to the local level, and eliminated local redevelopment agencies. Former Senate president pro tempore John Burton concluded that Brown "did as good as he could do with the cards that were dealt him."[11]

Governor Brown has been an active proponent of high-speed rail in California throughout his time in office. In 2012, he celebrated the passage of the bill authorizing initial construction at Los Angeles's Union Station, the proposed terminus of the rail line. The expensive rail project was a point of contention during Brown's campaign for re-election in 2014.

Who Are California's Governors?

Since the creation of the office with the 1849 Constitution, 38 men have served as governor of California (39 if Jerry Brown is counted twice, as he is the only governor to serve nonconsecutive terms). This table lists the last ten governors of the state and various facts about them. Notice that despite the Democratic dominance of the state since the 1980s (see Chapter 4), Californians have often elected Republican governors.

Governor	Term	Party	Education	Religion	Family
Jerry Brown	2011–	Democrat	Law Degree, Law Degree	Catholic	Marriage(s)
Arnold Schwarzenegger	2003–2010	Republican	Bachelor of Arts	Catholic	Marriage(s), Children (4)
Gray Davis	1999–2003	Democrat	Bachelor of Arts, Law Degree	Catholic	Marriage(s)
Pete Wilson	1991–1998	Republican	Bachelor of Arts, Law Degree	Catholic	Marriage(s), Children (2)
George Deukmejian	1983–1990	Republican	Bachelor of Arts, Law Degree	Episcopalian	Marriage(s), Children (3)
Jerry Brown	1975–1982	Democrat	Bachelor of Arts, Law Degree	Catholic	Bachelor
Ronald Reagan	1966–1974	Republican	Bachelor of Arts	Presbyterian	Marriage(s) (2), Children (5)
Pat Brown	1959–1966	Democrat	Law Degree	Catholic	Marriage(s), Children (4)
Goodwin Knight	1954–1959	Republican	Bachelor of Arts	Methodist	Marriage(s) (2), Children (1)
Earl Warren*	1943–1953	Republican, Democrat	Bachelor of Arts, Law Degree	Methodist	Marriage(s), Children (6)

*Warren ran as a Republican and a Democrat in 1946, winning the nomination of both parties.

SOURCE: The Governor's Gallery, governors.library.ca.gov (accessed 4/11/14).

Category Key

Party	
	Republican
	Democrat

Education	
	Bachelor of Arts
	Law Degree

Religion	
	Catholic
	Episcopalian
	Methodist
	Mormon
	Presbyterian

Family	
	Marriage(s)
	Bachelor
	Children

forcriticalanalysis

1. All ten governors in this table are white, non-Latino men, but in other ways they are diverse. What notable differences do you see in terms of the backgrounds of California's most recent governors?

2. Do you think California will ever elect a non-white or non-male governor? Based on the demographic trends you saw in Chapter 1, when do you think this will happen? Do you think it matters?

In the 2012 election Brown was dealt a decidedly better hand. The election resulted in the passage of the tax-raising Proposition 30 and overwhelming Democratic majorities in both legislative houses. Along with an improved economy and the elimination of the supermajority vote requirement for passing a budget, these results set a far more positive tone for state politics. Overnight, gridlock became a thing of the past; rather than encouraging the legislature to act, the governor had to caution Democrats about overreaching—advice that they appeared to take to heart. Journalists who a few years before had viewed California as a disaster area began talking about Jerry Brown's "political reboot," "turnaround," and "revenge."[12] He has been described as "the most interesting politician in America";[13] indeed he is an unusual combination of the intellectual and the practical. If he were younger he would be a strong contender for the Democratic nomination for president in 2016. He remains a strong supporter of such future-oriented programs as high-speed rail and making California a leader in green energy and technology.

But the problems of California, especially the fiscal problems, have not disappeared. Although Brown engineered a change from a $25 billion budget deficit to a $4.5 billion surplus, the Proposition 30 tax increase is temporary. Substantial long-term debts remain, along with vexing issues concerning water, transportation, income inequality, and infrastructure deficiencies. Because the California Constitution still requires a two-thirds vote on tax measures, the minority party has a veto so long as the majority does not enjoy a supermajority; without the minority's support, creating an adequate and stable source of revenue will not happen.

No single individual is to blame for the long-standing political stalemate in California, and no single individual, not even Jerry Brown, can take credit for the current positive situation. However, the highly unusual supermajorities that the Democrats gained in 2012 and the large majorities that they still enjoy have made a difference. These legislators generally support the governor's program and pass bills that he is happy to sign. The popularity of both the governor and the legislature remain high, and the possibility of an electoral backlash is remote. As long as this continues, Governor Brown will be successful.

See the Who Are Californians feature on the previous page for more information on California's recent governors.

Structure of the Executive Branch

The executive branch of California has several significant divisions: the governor's personal staff, the appointed cabinet and other department heads, the other elected officials of the executive branch (the plural executive), appointed boards and commissions, and more than 300,000 state employees, divided into more than 85 agencies and 30 educational institutions. Not all of these agencies and employees are under the control of the governor. Figure 6.1 provides a graphic representation of the executive branch.

Personal Staff

Closest to the governor is his personal staff. The members of this staff include schedulers, speechwriters, and press officers. In addition, some staff members

FIGURE 6.1 ● Executive Branch of the California State Government

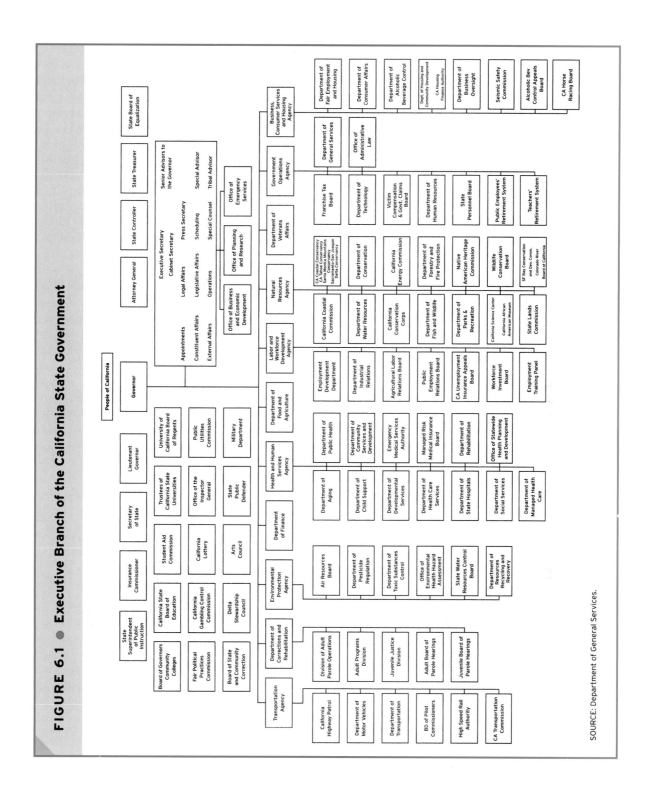

SOURCE: Department of General Services.

oversee the appointments process and the general development of policy, and act as liaisons with the legislature. They structure the governor's day, develop statements for the press and the public, arrange relations with various groups, and set up appearances throughout the state. Members of this staff are expendable, and they tend to be young and transient. Their positions depend on staying in the governor's good graces.

Governor Brown, preferring a flatter administrative structure, has not appointed a chief of staff. His principal (unpaid) aide, with the title "special counsel," is his wife Anne Gust Brown, a former lawyer with Gap, Inc. She is credited with strong political and personal skills and with softening many of the rough edges that Brown demonstrated during his first stint as governor in the 1970s.

The Cabinet and Agency Heads

The governor uses his cabinet as he sees fit. It has no official policy function as a body but can be used to help formulate policy. The cabinet is often more a symbolic body than an integral structure of governing. The executive branch is divided into seven superagencies, and the heads of these agencies, called secretaries, are generally in the cabinet. These are State and Consumer Services; Youth and Adult Corrections; Environmental Protection; Health and Human Services; Labor and Workforce Development; Business, Transportation, and Housing; and Resources. These superagencies contain most of the agencies of the state. It is the individual agencies, not the umbrella superagencies, that carry out functions, and they may act independently of the superagency secretaries. The governor appoints these agency heads, although he often does not have a free choice. He needs to appoint someone with expertise in the area, and sometimes the qualifications are spelled out in law. These agencies and superagencies are called *line agencies*, the term used to describe organizations with their own statutory authority to carry out functions and provide services.

In addition, the governor has several staff advisory agencies, including the Department of Finance, the Office of Planning and Research, and the Department of Personnel Administration. Perhaps the most important of these is the Department of Finance, which prepares the governor's budget.

The Plural Elected Executive

One of the most notable features of California government is the number of statewide *elected* administrative offices. There are seven of these positions, plus the Board of Equalization, which oversees the administration of property, sales, and excise taxes (see Box 6.2). This means that there are eight independent bases of power that do not report to the governor or need to adhere to his wishes. This differs from other states that have a single elected leader who appoints lesser state executives. While this distribution of power may limit the governor's freedom to make or implement policy, most of these positions do not deal with substantial policy issues. The attorney general is usually the only real policy competitor (and is sometimes an electoral competitor as well).

THE LIEUTENANT GOVERNOR The lieutenant governor exists to replace the governor if he or she becomes incapacitated. He also acts in the governor's absence

In addition to the selected duties listed below, all these officeholders sit ex officio on various state boards.

Governor: Organizes the executive branch, prepares the budget and legislation, signs or vetoes bills.

Lieutenant Governor: Replaces the governor if he or she is out of the state, incapacitated, or leaves office for any reason.

Attorney General: Enforces laws, oversees and assists district attorneys.

Secretary of State: Holds elections and oversees the records and archives of the state.

Treasurer: Manages state money.

Insurance Commissioner: Regulates insurance companies.

Controller: Monitors collection of taxes, provides fiscal controls for receipts and payments.

Superintendent of Public Instruction: Administers the state role in public education, sits on the state board of education.

Board of Equalization: Oversees the assessment and administration of property taxes, the collection and distribution of sales taxes, and the collection of excise taxes. The controller is a member of this body.

from the state. Since he is occasionally from a different party, this provides occasions for great mischief. He can also preside over the Senate, breaking tie votes. Perhaps more than others, this position captures the imagination of those who would restructure government, either by eliminating the office or linking the election of the lieutenant governor to that of the governor, as is the case in other states such as Illinois. The lieutenant governor serves on several important boards, including the governing boards of both the University of California and the California State University system. The current lieutenant governor is Gavin Newsom, the former mayor of San Francisco and a rising star in the Democratic Party. The office does not provide much visibility, however.

THE ATTORNEY GENERAL The attorney general oversees the department of justice, which employs more than 5,000 persons and is responsible for ensuring that the laws are enforced. She is free to determine which areas will receive the most attention and resources, and she has oversight responsibilities for local district attorneys and county sheriffs. She is legal counsel to the state and defends the state in lawsuits. She has no obligation to cooperate with the governor and is often viewed as a rival. In 2004 the governor ordered the attorney general to intercede with the state Supreme Court to stop gay marriages in San Francisco. The governor had no statutory basis for giving such an order, and although the attorney general ultimately followed the order, he did it on his own authority. This office is very powerful, and incumbents often see themselves as leading candidates for governor. Although few have successfully made this transition, Jerry Brown used this office to launch his successful campaign for governor in 2010. The attorney general is able to set her own agenda, which may run counter to the governor's agenda. She can use her substantial powers to counter or even embarrass the governor.

The current attorney general is Kamala Harris, another rising Democratic star. Unlike the lieutenant governor, however, she has been able to grab the headlines on several occasions with settlements against major corporations. Most notable have been settlements with mortgage banks that resulted in much larger anticipated payouts to Californians than had originally been proposed.

THE SECRETARY OF STATE The secretary of state's office oversees the records and archives of the state. It is also responsible for holding elections, including publishing election pamphlets, certifying initiative petitions, keeping records, and publishing election results.

THE CONTROLLER The controller is the fiscal officer for the state and oversees the state's money and the collection of taxes. The controller sits on a large number of boards, including the very important Board of Equalization and Franchise Tax Board.

THE TREASURER The treasurer manages the state's money after it comes in and before it is spent. He manages the investment of this money and the sale of bonds.

THE SUPERINTENDENT OF PUBLIC INSTRUCTION The superintendent is the chief administrator of the Department of Education. Unlike the other elected statewide officers, the superintendent is elected on a nonpartisan basis. Education administration is a confusing policy area; the superintendent shares power with an appointed board of education. This arrangement ensures controversy and was even more confusing before Governor Brown eliminated the parallel position of the appointed secretary of education in 2011.

THE INSURANCE COMMISSIONER The insurance commissioner's office was made elective by Proposition 103 in 1988, the only position of the plural executive created by an initiative. The commissioner regulates the insurance industry, and Proposition 103 passed because the public felt that the appointed commissioner was not doing his job. It is not clear that making this an elective post has improved matters, because most of the contributions to the campaigns for this position come from the insurance industry.

In addition to these positions, voters elect by district four members to the Board of Equalization, which oversees the assessment and administration of property taxes, although much of the work is done at the county level. The Board also oversees collection and distribution of sales taxes and the collection of excise taxes. Income taxes are handled by a different nonelected body, the Franchise Tax Board.

Agencies and the Bureaucracy

Most of the work of California state government is carried out by more than 200,000 state employees (not counting employees in higher education) housed in over 85 agencies (see Box 6.3). Most of these agencies are located within the seven superagencies, and most are invisible to the general public, which sustains

---

BOX 6.3 ● How Many State Employees Are There?

How many people are employed by the state of California? We actually don't know, in part because the state is not well managed and its computer systems are out of date. The state also lacks a consistent definition of an employee. Some employees are full-time and have civil service protection. Others are full-time and temporary. Others are part-time with long-term contracts. Still others are part-time and temporary, although some of them work for the state for years. (Further complicating the situation, some are non-state employees who are employed under state contracts.) Many who are definitely not counted as state employees work for local government but with state funding.

Compared with other states, California has relatively few employees. The U.S. Census Bureau data show that in 2012, California had 1,049 full-time equivalent* state employees per 100,000 residents. This was the fourth lowest in the country. The average in the 50 states was 1,729 per 100,000 employees. Most of the states that are most "efficient" are larger states, suggesting that economies of scale for larger states will yield fewer employees to do similar amounts of work.

The Census Bureau estimates that in 2012, California employed 326,000 full-time employees and 156,000 part-time employees in the following sectors:

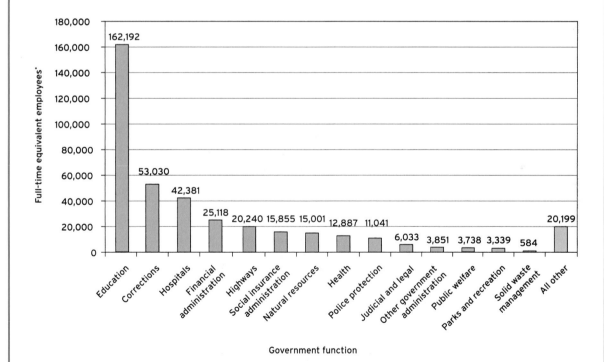

* Full-time equivalence counts part-time employees by adding up the amount of work they do and dividing it by a full-time workload (so one part-time worker who works 60 percent of full-time and a second who works 40 percent of full-time would count as one full-time employee).

SOURCE: U.S. Census Bureau, http://www.census.gov/govs/apes/ (accessed 6/19/14).

---

the impression that state government runs by itself. A few agencies, such as the California Highway Patrol and Caltrans, are well known if not well understood. Others, such as the Office of Small Business Development or the Department of Aging, rarely make it into the news or the public consciousness. Few Californians could name anyone in the executive branch up to and including department heads; few governors could name more than a handful. Many of these individuals are professional experts on policy subjects, quietly doing their jobs.

Most California employees have civil service protection. Many are also represented by unions. A few of these unions, notably the CCPOA (discussed in Chapter 3), are very powerful and politically well connected to the point at which the wishes and desires of the union are more likely to become state policy than the wishes and desires of the governor, the head of the Department of Corrections, or the administration of the department.

There are more than 325 state boards and commissions. Positions on these boards are filled by the governor subject to approval of another body, most often a legislative body. These boards and commissions include the Air Resources Board, the Public Utilities Commission, and the Gambling Control Commission. Probably the most visible are the Board of Regents of the University of California and the Trustees of the California State University, which together are responsible for more than 100,000 employees. On the other hand, boards such as the Board of Chiropractic Examiners and the Apprenticeship Council are probably known only to those with a direct interest in that area. Most members serve for fixed terms, some as long as 12 years, and, once appointed, do not have to respond to the governor's wishes.

California Executive Branch: Where Are We Now?

In recent years several tentative steps have been taken toward tackling the biggest long-term structural problems facing the state and providing the governor with a greater capacity to lead. First, Proposition 25 removed the two-thirds vote requirement to pass a budget. Although this loses some of its force because revenues cannot be similarly raised, its impact has been greater than expected. Even in the absence of a supermajority, Governor Brown has been able to largely ignore Republican legislators and work out legislative deals with the more accommodating Democrats. (This may come back to haunt the Democrats someday, should the Republicans control all parts of the state government with the ability to cut programs at will.)

Second, Proposition 11, approved in November 2008, took the power to draw the state legislative districts from the legislature and gave it to a citizens' commission. This commission created new districts that have a closer partisan balance and which initially pitted some incumbents of the same party against one another. The hope was to gain a legislature willing to cooperate and compromise both internally and with the governor. The result was different than expected: the overwhelming Democratic majorities that resulted made cooperation and compromise between parties largely unnecessary.

Along similar lines, Proposition 14, approved in June 2010, created a system of preliminary and final elections for the party primary (see Chapter 4). Again, the ambition was to create a less partisan legislature. As a result of these two measures, the reduced number of Republicans appear to be no less conservative than before, but many of the Democrats, elected from marginal districts, are more moderate than expected. Even during the supermajority period, for instance, there was no push to raise taxes, as might be expected from a majority Democratic legislature.

While these changes have resulted, unfortunately, in a marginalized minority party, they have also given rise to an executive branch that is more effective, productive, and popular with the electorate.

However, nothing has been done about fixing the distortions caused by Proposition 13, the 1978 proposition that limited property tax increases, and the series of initiatives that have locked in certain parts of the budget and made creating a stable and adequate revenue stream close to impossible. California's revenues are far more volatile than those of other states, and Californians' willingness to govern by initiative remains undaunted.

Study Guide

FOR FURTHER READING

Cain, Bruce E., and Roger G. Noll, eds. *Constitutional Reform in California: Making State Government More Effective and Responsive*. Berkeley, CA: Institute of Governmental Studies Press, 1995.

California Performance Review. *Prescription for Change, Report of the California Performance Review*. Vols. I–IV. Sacramento: California Performance Review, 2004. http://cpr.ca.gov/#cpr. Accessed June 30, 2012.

Gerston, Larry N., and Terry Christensen. *Recall! California's Political Earthquake*. Armonk, NY: M. E. Sharpe, 2004.

Lubenow, Gerald C., ed. *Governing California: Politics, Government, and Public Policy in the Golden State*. 2nd ed. Berkeley: Institute of Governmental Studies Press, University of California, 2006.

Mathews, Joe. *The People's Machine: Arnold Schwarzenegger and the Rise of Blockbuster Democracy*. New York: Public Affairs Press, 2006.

Schrag, Peter. *California: America's High-Stakes Experiment*. Berkeley: University of California Press, 2006.

———. *Paradise Lost: California's Experience, America's Future*. New York: New Press, 1998.

Simmons, Charlene Wear. *To Faithfully Execute the Law: California Executive Branch Agencies 1959–2003*. Sacramento: California Research Bureau, California State Library, 2004.

ON THE WEB

California Choices: www.californiachoices.org. Accessed August 1, 2014.

California Department of Finance: www.dof.ca.gov. Accessed June 30, 2014.

California State Library: www.library.ca.gov. Accessed July 31, 2014.

Center for Governmental Studies, Los Angeles: www.cgs.org. Accessed August 1, 2014.

Governor of California: www.gov.ca.gov. Accessed August 1, 2014. The official site of the Office of the Governor, where you can find background information and up-to-date news and even e-mail the governor.

Public Policy Institute of California: www.ppic.org. Accessed August 1, 2014.

Rough & Tumble: www.rtumble.com. Accessed August 1, 2014. Daily summary of California news.

University of California, Berkeley, Institute of Governmental Studies Library: http://igs.berkeley.edu/library/. Accessed August 1, 2014.

SUMMARY

I. The office of the governor is modeled on that of the U.S. president. There are significant differences between the two offices, mostly having to do with visibility.

II. Each job has two analytical roles.
   A. Head of state, which is largely ceremonial, symbolizing the unity of the state or country. In this role, the governor or president makes public appearances doing activities that bring people together. The president, in this role, is on TV almost every evening. The governor has less opportunity to play this role, and even when he does, the state TV stations seem uninterested.
   B. Head of government, which involves making policy and trying to get it passed by the legislature and implemented by the executive branch. That role is partisan and divisive. It is also an almost invisible role, especially on the implementation side.

III. The formal powers of the office are greater for the governor than for the president.
   A. The governor's formal powers include making appointments and organizing the executive branch; independent executive actions that are permitted by law; being commander in chief; proposing the budget; making legislative recommendations; and exercising the veto, including the line-item veto.
   B. The governor has powers similar to the president's in domestic policy but also can use the line-item veto, which gives him or her more control over the political process of constructing the budget.
   C. California has an initiative process that a popular governor can use to pressure the legislature into action.

IV. The governor's public roles as head of state include cutting ribbons, signing bills, and observing natural disasters. Non–head-of-state public roles include campaigning and fund-raising, and advocating for initiatives.

V. Like the presidency, the office of governor is one of limited powers, which are restricted by the legislature, the judiciary, the plural elected executive, and the permanent executive branch.

VI. The structure of the state government includes the following:
   A. The governor's personal staff.
   B. The governor's cabinet, which includes the heads of major departments (superagencies).
   C. The plural elected executive, which includes the lieutenant governor, the attorney general, the secretary of state, the controller, the treasurer, the superintendent of public education, the insurance commissioner, and the state board of equalization.
   D. The 85 or more agencies that make up these departments.
   E. More than 325 boards and commissions, including the Public Utilities Commission and the Regents of the University of California.

VII. California employs the equivalent of more than 300,000 full-time employees to staff the government, including 100,000 in higher education not under the direct control of the governor.

PRACTICE QUIZ

1. Which of the following is *not* part of the plural executive?
   a) the chancellor of the California State University
   b) the secretary of state
   c) the attorney general
   d) the controller

2. Which of these powers does the governor have that the president does not have?
   a) legislative veto
   b) line-item veto
   c) power to declare war
   d) power to appoint judges

3. Which of the following activities of the governor would be considered part of his role as head of government?
   a) proposing a budget
   b) vetoing legislation
   c) proposing new air quality standards
   d) all of the above

4. Which of the following group of employees are under administrative control and report ultimately to the governor?
   a) legislative aides
   b) supreme court clerks

c) highway patrol
d) professors at California State University, Fullerton

5. How many state boards and commissions are there?
   a) fewer than 50
   b) between 50 and 150
   c) between 150 and 250
   d) between 250 and 350

6. The California governor is "invisible" under normal conditions for all of the following reasons *except*:
   a) California's governors appear in events where they are visible to the public, but for the most part, there is little public interest in those events.
   b) For almost every recent governor, there has been little media interest in Sacramento.
   c) The governor splits his or her power with other state executives, who are also trying to attract the media.
   d) The governor's star power is only of interest to those who like superhero movies.

7. The governor manages the executive branch, but this power is limited by all of the following *except*:
   a) There are so many appointees of the governor, many of whom belong to agencies the governor doesn't know much about.
   b) Some of California government is outside the power of the governor to supervise, such as the University of California and California State University.
   c) The boards and commissions whose members the governor appoints are mostly, except in extreme cases, outside of his power.

d) The attorney general must approve appointments to many boards and commissions, and that appointment power is difficult to obtain.

8. The line-item veto allows the governor to adjust any appropriations item up or down, including reducing it to zero.
   a) true
   b) false

9. All of the following are true of the governor's appointments to the cabinet *except*:
   a) Most cabinet appointments are routine, given to the governor's political supporters and campaign contributors.
   b) The cabinet as a whole has no official policy function, unless the governor wants to give it a role.
   c) Some cabinet and subcabinet positions require an appointment of someone with qualifications that are spelled out in law.
   d) The superagency heads are usually considered part of the governor's cabinet.

10. The job of the lieutenant governor, one columnist wrote not entirely in jest, consists of getting up in the morning, checking that the governor is still alive, and then making arrangements for lunch!
    a) This statement is probably true.
    b) This statement is probably false.

CRITICAL-THINKING QUESTIONS

1. Is the state government too large?
2. Does the plural elected executive contribute to effective or efficient government?
3. What is the value of having independent boards such as the Regents of the University of California that employ large numbers of people?
4. Which is more important for governing: the formal or informal powers of the governor? Think about this question in terms of "necessary" versus "sufficient" powers.

KEY TERMS

At this point you should have a general understanding of the following concepts and terms:

boards and commissions (p. 139)
cabinet (p. 139)
formal powers (p. 137)

head of government (p. 136)
head of state (p. 136)
informal powers (p. 139)

line-item veto (p. 139)
personal staff (p. 139)
superagencies (p. 139)

7

The California Judiciary

WHAT THE CALIFORNIA JUDICIARY DOES AND WHY IT MATTERS

State courts are an integral and necessary component of state government. They ensure that a state's citizenry is guaranteed due process of law and that the other branches and levels of government within the state uphold state statutes, codes, and the provisions in the state constitution. Therefore, judges play a much larger role than simply punishing criminals or imposing fines on a polluting company. Courts make decisions that are often political and sometimes very controversial, with the potential to affect more individuals than just those directly involved in the cases. Court rulings can have far-reaching consequences that not only ignite political debate but also have an iterative effect. This is especially true in California, where politics can be very contentious and the state witnesses a high rate of litigation. And while some cases that come before the California courts gain a significant amount of statewide and national media attention, many cases that remain under the radar still have an impact on citizens' daily lives.

California court decisions on immigration policy, for example, have the potential to influence national debates on immigration reform and are particularly salient in a state with a high population of undocumented immigrants. Questions of state policy regarding undocumented immigrants who entered the United States as children were tested in the case of Sergio Garcia, who came with his family to California only months after his first birthday. Garcia and his family moved back to Mexico when he was nine years old, but they returned to the United States eight years later, in 1994. This time, Garcia's father attained lawful permanent resident status for himself and filed a petition seeking the same for his family. But, due to limits on the number of visas distributed each year, Garcia graduated from high school, college, and law school while still undocumented. After obtaining his law degree, Mr. Garcia passed the California Bar Examination and applied for admission to the bar, at which point his undocumented status came under scrutiny from the Committee of Bar Examiners. The committee asked the California Supreme Court to determine whether state law or public policy banned Garcia's admittance. The court ruled that it did not, and held that the intent of the legislature and the governor clearly indicated that Garcia's status should not be an impediment to his application.[1] Garcia's case illustrates well the complexity of contemporary immigration issues in the United States. It also serves as a good example of what it means to be an undocumented person versus a person with legal immigration status.

Structure of the California Judicial System

To understand the role that courts play in California politics, consider the following: from 2012 through 2013, approximately 7,700,000 cases were filed in California **superior courts** (trial courts of general jurisdiction).[2] Of these, over 80 percent were criminal in nature (crimes against the state or society, e.g., failing to pay state taxes or stealing a car) and the remaining 20 percent were civil cases (disputes between individuals). Each one of these almost eight million cases had to be handled individually by the appropriate state court in one way or another until it was resolved. To put this into context, let's consider the number of people living in the state. According to the U.S. Census Bureau, California's population was estimated at 38,332,521 as of July 2013, which puts the case-to-person ratio at 1 to 5.

To adjudicate both criminal cases and civil cases, California courts comprise three levels: superior courts (trial courts), Courts of Appeal, and the California Supreme Court.

The Lower Courts

Superior courts adjudicate cases that involve violations of state and local criminal and civil law. These are the trial courts of California. When cases come before the superior courts, a jury or judge reviews the facts of the case and determines guilt or innocence in a criminal proceeding. If it is a civil case, the jury or judge determines which side presents the best case and awards damages accordingly. There are 58 state trial courts (one in each county), with approximately 2,000 judicial officers presiding. This number includes judges, commissioners, and referees. The superior courts are the busiest courts of the state court system.

The California Courts of Appeal are intermediate courts with **appellate jurisdiction**; those who lose their cases at the superior court can appeal first to the California Courts of Appeal. The purpose of this intermediate appellate court is to review the trial or the superior court records for error. The California Courts of Appeal are divided into six districts across the state; 105 justices preside over these courts. These judges sit on three-judge panels to review cases.[3]

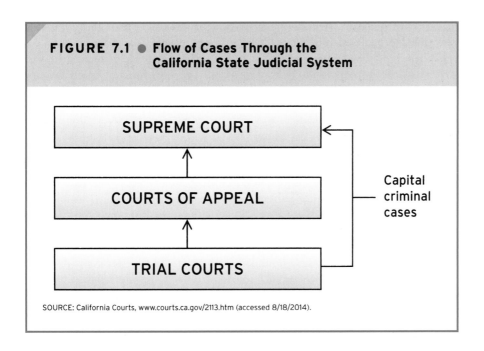

FIGURE 7.1 ● Flow of Cases Through the California State Judicial System

SUPREME COURT

COURTS OF APPEAL

TRIAL COURTS

Capital criminal cases

SOURCE: California Courts, www.courts.ca.gov/2113.htm (accessed 8/18/2014).

The Supreme Court

The California Supreme Court is the highest court in the state. Like the California Courts of Appeal, it is an appellate court that reviews decisions for reversible error, submitted by losing parties in the lower courts. When a party to a case is unhappy with the ruling of the California Courts of Appeal, the next step is to appeal to the California Supreme Court. In California, the Supreme Court has what is known as **judicial discretion**. Discretion allows the justices on the state Supreme Court to decide which cases they wish to review. Therefore, appeals filed with the California Supreme Court are not automatically reviewed. This is the only court in California with discretionary authority. Discretion is valuable because it provides the high court with a tool to moderate its workload. However, this discretion is not absolute: all death-penalty sentences are automatically appealed and go directly to the California Supreme Court for review (see Figure 7.1). The Supreme Court is also required to hear disciplinary cases involving judges or attorneys. Four out of the seven justices must agree in order for a party to win the case. The Supreme Court includes one chief justice and six associate justices (see Table 7.1).

While the Supreme Court may seem remote, it often makes decisions that have an impact on Californians' daily lives. For example, on June 21, 2010, the California Supreme Court announced its ruling in *Kleffman v. Vonage Holdings Corp.* At issue in this case was the legality of commercial electronic advertising. Craig E. Kleffman sued Vonage on the basis that its use of multiple domain names to advertise its products and services through unsolicited emails (or spam) violated provisions in the California state code. The California high court ruled unanimously that "sending commercial email advertisements from multiple domain names for the purpose of bypassing spam filters is not unlawful under [the state code]." This recent ruling serves to illustrate the importance of the California judiciary; in this case, the Court's decision results in Californians receiving more spam email.

When individual citizens or groups of citizens believe that private entities or government have trampled on state law or on their civil liberties or civil rights, they turn to the courts. The judges serving on California's courts must decide if the state's laws or the rights of Californians have been violated.

Jurisdiction

Both criminal and **civil courts** in California are limited as to the cases and controversies they handle because of jurisdiction. Jurisdiction refers to the kind of law handled by a court. For example, there are criminal courts that deal with violations of state and local laws, and there are civil courts that hear cases involving disputes between individuals or classes of individuals. Civil courts may rule on cases involving breach of contract, tort liability, and wrongful-death suits, to name a few. Jurisdiction also refers to geographic boundaries. There are 58 superior court divisions in California, with at least one branch in each county. Cases are assigned to these courts depending on where the parties in civil suits reside or where alleged crimes have been committed in criminal cases.

It is easier for an individual to go to criminal court—just drive over the speed limit and get caught—than to civil court. Civil courts have rules about the types of cases they can hear. In civil disputes, parties must also have what is known as "standing to sue." To bring a case to court, an individual must suffer personal and real injury. Typically, an individual cannot sue on behalf of someone else. As well as requiring standing, California courts, like the federal courts, will not handle collusive suits. Collusive suits are lawsuits in which both parties want a similar or the same outcome. Our legal system is an adversarial one, in which it is presumed that parties want opposite outcomes, and when one party wins, the other loses.

Access to the Court

The California Constitution and its statutes provide rights to the people of California regarding access to the courts. For example, Californians have:

- the right to sue for money owed and for other relief.
- the right to defend oneself against a lawsuit.
- the right to be presumed innocent if charged with a crime.
- the right to defend oneself against all criminal charges.
- the right to a public and speedy trial by jury if charged with a misdemeanor or a felony.
- the right to an attorney at public expense if one is charged with a felony or misdemeanor and cannot afford an attorney.

These rights apply to citizens of the state and noncitizens alike. They do not mitigate against concerns about quality of legal representation for indigent persons. The lack of resources in some local court jurisdictions, especially in smaller localities, and the impact of the current budget crisis on the state's judiciary as a whole will affect access to the courts.

Federalism and the California Courts: The Case of Medical Marijuana

The California court system must occasionally negotiate discrepancies between federal law and state law in a particular policy area. For example, California's laws permitting medicinal marijuana use are at odds with federal laws that classify marijuana as a controlled substance. In 1996, through use of the initiative, voters in California approved Proposition 215, the Compassionate Use Act (CUA). This act provides for the medical use of marijuana for seriously ill persons. It requires that a physician recommend that a patient's health would benefit from using marijuana to alleviate symptoms of serious illness. In addition, the act also shields patients and their caregivers from criminal prosecution for cultivating or possessing marijuana for use approved under the act.

Confusion ensued shortly after the act was implemented. First, there were many (successful) attempts at expanding the scope of the law. Second, the state law came directly into conflict with federal law which makes the cultivation, possession, sale, and consumption of marijuana illegal.

Seven years after the CUA was passed, Governor Gray Davis signed Senate Bill 420, the Medical Marijuana Program Act (MMPA), into law. The MMPA was designed to flesh out the parameters of the CUA. Among other things, the MMPA sought to create collective cooperatives in the state where marijuana could be cultivated and sold to qualified patients and caregivers. The cooperatives would be regulated by state and local agencies, and the patients and caregivers would be issued identification cards that would help law enforcement more easily determine whether persons were covered by the CUA and, therefore, not subject to criminal prosecution under state law. The MMPA also allows for persons who can be classified as cooperatives, caregivers, or patients to raise a defense if they are charged with violating state laws involving the cultivation, possession, sale, or consumption of medical marijuana.

The MMPA had immediate implications regarding federalism. Although both the CUA and the MMPA are technically "good law" (meaning they are still current and enforceable), various attempts have been made by the national government to exercise preemption—a practice in which the government claims to have authority over a particular policy area when it comes to legislation, thus preempting state and local regulations. In 2005, for example, the U.S. Supreme Court reviewed the case *Gonzales v. Raich*. At issue was whether Congress's power to regulate the manufacture and possession of marijuana under the Controlled Substances Act (21 U.S.C. §§ 801) allowed the national government to preempt California's laws governing the medicinal use of marijuana. The Supreme Court

California's U.S. attorneys assigned to judicial districts in California, including Laura Duffy, have taken a hard-line stance against commercial marijuana activity in the state, which is illegal under federal law.

ruled in a 6-to-3 decision that the Commerce Power gives Congress the authority to regulate and to punish the manufacture and cultivation of marijuana despite California law allowing for compassionate use. The dissenting Supreme Court justices argued that to preempt these laws was a violation of federalism and that, because the issue involved purely local or *intrastate*, rather than interstate, commerce, the state law should prevail.

Since this ruling in 2005, many local governments have seized the opportunity to create new zoning ordinances to limit the expansion of marijuana dispensaries. In fact, one tactic commonly used by local governments to close down dispensaries involves calling the U.S. attorney's office. The U.S. attorney has the authority to order these shops to discontinue their operations under the threat of having their property forfeited or seized, as well as other criminal sanctions under federal law.

Despite the U.S. Supreme Court's ruling in *Gonzales v. Raich*, California courts have continued to try medical marijuana cases according to state law. For example, a 2009 case, *People v. Colvin*, involved a co-owner (William Frank Colvin) of two nonprofit medical marijuana dispensaries, Holistic I (in Santa Monica) and Holistic 2 (in Hollywood). The dispensaries are registered with the city of Los Angeles and have been incorporated for several years. In addition, they are often reviewed by local law enforcement to ensure that they meet the requirements and restrictions of the MMPA. Like other similar dispensaries, and in compliance with to the MMPA, Holistic 1 and 2 grow some of their marijuana on site but also belong to a cooperative that includes growers in Los Angeles and Humboldt. In March 2009, Colvin was less than a block from Holistic 2 en route to Holistic 1. He was stopped by police, taken into custody, and charged with violating state laws for possession of cocaine, sale or transportation of marijuana, and possession of marijuana. He was carrying an identification card for medicinal use and showed it to the arresting officer at the time. He also presented evidence to the trial court that he was registered to run the Holistic dispensaries.

The trial court judge agreed that Colvin's dispensaries seemed to be in compliance with both the CUA and the MMPA, which are still California law despite the *Raich* decision. Colvin's attorneys argued that he was only transporting the marijuana (one pound) from one dispensary to another. However, the trial court judge disagreed and ruled that the MMPA did not cover the transportation of marijuana. Colvin was found guilty of all three charges, placed on probation, and given community service. Colvin appealed this conviction, and the Court of Appeal determined that the transportation of marijuana from one dispensary to another fell within the scope of the MMPA, reversing the trial court's decision with respect to two of Colvin's convictions (transportation and possession; the cocaine conviction was not appealed).

However, both parties to a case have the right to appeal, and the state appealed the decision of the Court of Appeal. The California Supreme Court had to determine whether it would take the case and rule on its merits or if it would choose not to hear the case and allow the Court of Appeal decision to stand (remain in effect). In May 2012, the California Supreme Court denied review, noting that medicinal marijuana remains an issue that has important implications for local, state, and federal law. It also cited the many cases that continue to be filed in the courts dealing with this policy issue. It is an interesting case study in the principle of federalism, particularly in those circumstances in which state and national law clearly conflict over a very controversial issue.[4]

In January 2014, the U.S. Court of Appeals for the Ninth Circuit disposed of a number of cases involving medical marijuana use. In their "unpublished" memorandum, the court wrote that states have no special protection from federal law when it comes to use, including medicinal, of marijuana.[5] One month later, the Ninth Circuit disposed of the case *Sacramento Nonprofit Collective v. Holder*. Here, the plaintiffs argued that, given the fact that nine western states permit the use of marijuana for medicinal purposes, it should be recognized as a fundamental right. The court chose to dismiss the case in favor of the federal government. In fact, it dismissed with prejudice: the plaintiffs in this legal action are prohibited from ever bringing the case back to the court.[6]

Judicial Selection

California's court system is the largest in the nation. Serving on the bench requires (1) qualifications and (2) having been selected to serve. The qualifications for judges are the same for the three court levels. Potential judges in California must have at least 10 years of experience practicing law in the state of California or service as a judge of a court of record.

The selection process for judges serving on the California Supreme Court and California Courts of Appeal is the same. Judges are initially nominated by the governor to serve on the appellate bench and then approved by the Commission on Judicial Appointments. The Commission on Judicial Appointments consists of the chief justice of the Supreme Court, the attorney general, and a presiding judge on the California Courts of Appeal. In addition, all nominees for California's appellate courts are reviewed by the State Bar of California's Commission on Judicial Nominees Evaluation. This body evaluates the nominees by conducting thorough background checks on their qualifications as judges and as citizens. The governor may use the commission's decision as a source of information when making his or her selections but is not bound by the commission's findings. After a judge's appointment is confirmed, the judge holds office until the next **retention election**. To remain on the appellate courts in California, judges must win their retention elections. These elections are noncompetitive; the voters are simply asked whether the judge should remain on the appellate bench. If a judge does not receive a majority of affirmative votes, he or she is removed and the governor will appoint a new judge.

Likewise, judges serving on California's superior courts must face nonpartisan retention elections. However, their electoral process is different from the retention elections of sitting Supreme Court and Courts of Appeal judges. While appellate court judges run uncontested, simply against their own records, judges serving on California's superior courts can be challenged in their retention races. In addition, superior courts may have open seat races from time to time. These occur when a judge decides to retire close to an election. Finally, if an incumbent is up for retention and has no challengers, he may simply be declared re-elected; thus, no retention election is held.

Governors take advantage of opportunities to appoint judges to the courts by placing qualified jurists on the bench whose political beliefs most closely resemble their own. From time to time, a governor may be quite transparent about his or her preferences for those serving on the state Supreme Court. In the 1980s, former governor George Deukmejian spoke out to the press and public about his desire to put more conservatives on the state Supreme Court because the liberals serving on the bench at the time were making decisions he vehemently disliked. In addition, governors may have other political goals for the bench. They may, for example, seek to place more women and minorities on the Supreme Court so that it is more representative of the state's diverse population. Today's Supreme Court is diverse in regard to gender, race, and ethnicity: as of early 2015, three of the justices will be women and four will be people of color. (See the Who Are Californians feature for more on the diversity of California's justices.)

However, the court is not so diverse ideologically. Four of the seven justices seated on the court were appointed by Republican governors.[7] Generally, Republicans are more conservative than Democrats on issues of ideological preference, such as civil rights or civil liberties. For example, a liberal judge is more likely to uphold laws that involve regulating business than a conservative judge. This expectation, that ideology or party identification translates into differences in judicial decision making, is even more important when we consider issues such as affirmative action, voting rights, freedom of expression, and capital punishment. Because the decisions of the California Supreme Court are binding on all persons residing in the state, the composition and dominating political ideology of the state's high court can be very important.

We may start to see some ideological shifts in the Court. Justice Joyce L. Kennard left the bench in April 2014 and Justice Marvin R. Baxter announced on June 18, 2014, that he would also be retiring, providing Governor Brown, a Democrat, with the opportunity to appoint two new judges who will likely be more liberal than their predecessors. On July 22, 2014, the governor announced his nomination of Mariano-Florentino Cuéllar to replace Justice Baxter, and the California Commission on Judicial Appointments unanimously confirmed the nomination. Cuéllar will take office on January 5, 2015 as the first Latino immigrant

In April 2014, the members of the California State Supreme Court were (from left to right) Carol A. Corrigan, Joyce L. Kennard, Kathryn M. Werdegar, Chief Justice Tani Cantil-Sakauye, Ming W. Chin, Marvin R. Baxter, and Goodwin Liu. Justice Kennard retired from the bench in early April 2014. Justice Baxter will retire in early January 2015, to be replaced by Mariano-Florentino Cuéllar.

Who Are California's Judges?

Since 2006, the Judicial Council of California has produced an annual report with information about the demographic characteristics of the state's justices and judges. Over time, increasing proportions of the judiciary have been women and people of color, although the proportions do not yet reflect the general population. The ethnoracial composition of the California bar (lawyers who are qualified to practice law in California) is heavily white at 79.3 percent (7.7 percent Asian/Pacific Islander, 4.2 percent Latino, 2.7 percent black); the bar is 39.4 percent female.

Justices and Judges in California, 2013

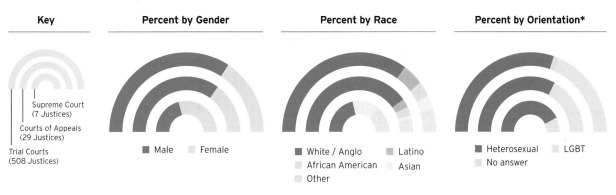

Key

Supreme Court
(7 Justices)

Courts of Appeals
(29 Justices)

Trial Courts
(508 Justices)

Percent by Gender
- Male
- Female

Percent by Race
- White / Anglo
- African American
- Other
- Latino
- Asian

Percent by Orientation*
- Heterosexual
- No answer
- LGBT

*37.2% of judicial officers did not provide information on sexual orientation/gender identity.

Gubernatorial Appointments, 1975–present

- Female
- Latino
- African American
- Asian
- Democratic governor

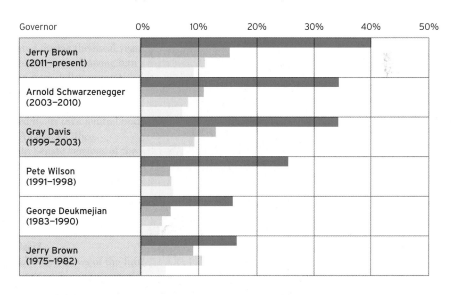

forcriticalanalysis

1. Is it important for the judiciary to reflect the diversity of the California population? Why or why not?

2. Besides gender, ethnicity, race, and sexual orientation/ gender identity, what other dimensions of diversity are important to consider and why?

SOURCE: Judicial Council of California, "2013 Court Statistics Report: Statewide Caseload Trends," http://www.courts.ca.gov/documents/2013-Court-Statistics-Report.pdf (accessed 4/11/14).

Tani Gorre Cantil-Sakauye, Chief Justice, appointed by Governor Arnold
    Schwarzenegger in 2010
Kathryn M. Werdegar, appointed by Governor Pete Wilson in 1994
Ming W. Chin, appointed by Governor Pete Wilson in 1996
Carol A. Corrigan, appointed by Governor Arnold Schwarzenegger in 2005
Goodwin Liu, appointed by Governor Edmund G. Brown in 2011
Mariano-Florentino Cuéllar, appointed by Governor Edmund G. Brown in 2014

appointed to the California Supreme Court.[8] Governor Brown has decided to bring additional diversity to the bench by appointing an African American attorney, Leondra Kruger, to replace Justice Kennard. Ms. Kruger was previously a deputy attorney general in President Obama's administration. If confirmed, Kruger would be the first African American to hold a seat on the Court since 2005.[9]

Judicial Elections

Unlike the federal judiciary, which consists of appointed judges who serve life terms with good behavior, many states, including California, have some form of election system for selecting their judges. Federal judges are appointed to allow for **judicial independence**. Theoretically, appointed judges are less likely to be influenced by politics in their decision making because they do not have to rely on the electorate to maintain their positions on the bench. Most states, however, have adopted some kind of election system for selecting or retaining their judges in order to secure **judicial accountability**. Elections allow voters to select members of the courts and remove them for decisions contrary to the public's preferences.

Justices Werdegar, Liu, and Cuéllar faced elections in November 2014, and all successfully retained their seats on the bench. Over 70 percent of California voters supported Werdegar's retention, while Liu and Cuéllar received approximately 67 percent of all votes. Although the voters rarely pay much attention to competitive judicial races or retention elections, there have been instances when judges have lost their seats on the bench because of voters' perceptions about judicial rulings. In the November 1986 election, six justices serving on the California Supreme Court were seeking retention. Governor George Deukmejian spoke out against the retention of three of the six judges for their rulings on death-penalty cases and was especially critical of Rose Bird, the chief justice of the California Supreme Court at the time. While she served on the Court, Bird participated in 61 death-penalty cases and voted every time to vacate the death sentence—an especially notable choice during a time of widespread public support among Californians for the death penalty. In fact, her appointment as chief justice occured the same year that the death penalty was reinstated by a legislative override of a gubernatorial veto. One year later (1978), an initiative was adopted that expanded the number of special circumstances allowed for death-penalty cases. While she had many supporters, her decision making went against the tide of moneyed interests and those supportive of capital punishment.[10]

Governor Deukmejian warned Bird and two associate justices, Cruz Reynoso and Joseph Grodin, that he would oppose their retention elections if they did not change their rulings in death-penalty appeals and uphold the death-penalty sentences. Numerous interest groups and political action committees joined the governor's campaign against Rose Bird and her two colleagues. Political advertisements against the retention of Bird, Grodin, and Reynoso aired on radio and television. In response, Chief Justice Rose Bird produced a television ad explaining her decision-making record. Her explanations did not satisfy voters, however, and on November 4, 1996, Bird, Grodin, and Reynoso lost their seats on the California Supreme Court. Shortly thereafter, Governor Deukmejian appointed three justices to replace them, including Malcolm Lucas, who was nicknamed "Maximum Malcolm" for his rulings that sentenced convicted criminals to the maximum penalties, including death.

Despite the low visibility of judicial elections, these elections have many political scientists and jurists concerned, particularly over the amount of money being spent by candidates in judicial elections. A 1995 study of contested elections in Los Angeles County Superior Court reported that campaign spending by trial court judges had risen a great deal in the years between 1976 and 1994. In 1976, the median cost of a judicial campaign for a Los Angeles County Superior Court seat was approximately $3,000. By 1994, the median had skyrocketed to $70,000. Incumbents running for re-election spent, on average, $20,000 more than the median challenger, or $95,000 in 1994. Compare that to the $1,000 median campaign expenditure of an incumbent in 1976.

The Civil Justice Association of California (CJAC), a group of citizens, taxpayers, and professionals, reviewed campaign contributions to the California judiciary from 1997 to 2000 and found the following:

- From 1997 to 2000, contributions to candidates in contested superior court elections totaled over $3 million for four counties.

- In a single race in Sacramento County, over $1 million was raised.

- Attorneys are the largest contributors to most judicial races.

- Two Supreme Court justices seeking retention in 1998—in uncontested elections—received contributions of $887,000 and $710,000.

The escalation of campaign spending in judicial elections is controversial because it usually requires judicial candidates to seek funding support from outside sources. Like candidates seeking election to state legislative or executive offices, judges now receive and even solicit financial support from organized interests. This phenomenon has even spilled over into retention elections for the state Supreme Court, even though these elections are noncompetitive. Judges must solicit campaign contributions to retain their seats on the bench. Contributors often include trial lawyers' associations and other special interests. This connection has raised concern: financial contributions by interest groups to a judge's campaign increase the potential for influence over judicial decision making. The original intent by lawmakers in instituting elections for judicial candidates was to ensure judicial accountability to voters, not to the more narrow preferences of an organized interest group. This concern has mobilized a national movement for reform. One of the most active advocates is former associate justice of the U.S. Supreme Court Sandra Day O'Connor. Retired Justice O'Connor has been a vocal critic of state judicial elections because of the amounts that judicial candidates are soliciting and spending and because of the public perception that money buys influence.

Most people consider the judiciary the least political of all branches of government, yet the increased spending in competitive and noncompetitive elections for judgeships compromises this assumption. Even judges are expressing concern. In 2001, an opinion survey, "Justice at Stake Campaign," revealed that 53 percent of California judges are dissatisfied with the current climate of judicial campaigning in the state. Over 80 percent of the judges surveyed believed that voters knew little about candidates for the bench and were electing judges based on criteria other than qualifications for office. The majority of judges polled agreed that reform of campaign financing for judicial elections is necessary and that public financing of these elections would be an appropriate alternative.

In response to stories in the media, including a series of articles published in the *Los Angeles Times*, and the concerns of the public, judges, public officials, and others, the Judicial Campaign Task Force for Impartial Courts was established in 2007. It consists of 14 members appointed by former California Supreme Court Chief Justice Ronald M. George, and it investigates several issues, including the structure of California judicial elections as well as the filing, reporting, and accessibility of judicial campaign contributions and spending. The findings to date of this commission were reported in a 408-page volume in December 2009.[11] Many problems were noted with respect to judicial campaigns and elections, most notably the amount of money spent by candidates for judicial elections and, ironically, the poor quality or low level of information disseminated by judicial candidates to the public. The commission is not finished with its work, and additional reports are expected. The following reforms have so far been successfully implemented:

- Judicial candidates are prohibited from making statements that commit or appear to commit them with respect to cases, controversies, or issues that could come before the courts.

- Judicial candidates may not knowingly misrepresent certain facts including the identity, qualifications, or present position of themselves or an opponent.

- Any contributions to or expenditures of $100 or more by judicial candidates must be itemized. Judicial candidates for superior court may file a candidate statement to be included in the voter's pamphlet. These statements are very expensive, however, and the cost is prohibitive for most candidates.

There is one further caveat that should be mentioned. Whenever limits or rules are placed on campaign spending, the rights of freedom of expression and freedom of association guaranteed by both the California and U.S. Constitutions may be abridged. Campaigning for political office is guaranteed by the right to speak freely, and in today's political contests, it is becoming increasingly expensive. Therefore, it is almost impossible to impose limits on campaign spending. So judges running for retention on the California Supreme Court or running to serve on the state's trial courts must exercise their own restraint—not an easy task if your opponent or opposing forces are spending a lot of money to keep you off the bench. Added to this are concerns about the impact of the U.S. Supreme Court's 2010 ruling in *Citizens United v. FEC*. This decision allowed corporations and unions substantial freedom to spend money during elections through "independent expenditures." As long as corporations and unions do not coordinate their campaign advertising expenditures with candidates, they can spend practically without limits.

Removing Judges from the Bench

As we have already discussed in this chapter, voters may remove judges from the bench during an election. In addition, there are other means for removing judges in the case of public concern regarding judicial misconduct or judicial competency.

- **Impeachment**   California's judges may be impeached by the Assembly and convicted by a two-thirds majority of the state Senate.

- **Recall election**   Like the governor, California judges are subject to recall election petitioned by voters.

- **Regulatory commission investigation**   The Commission on Judicial Performance may, after investigation of complaints regarding misconduct or incapacity, punish, censure, or remove a judge from office.

Contemporary Issues in the Judiciary

Change in the Court

The retirements of Justices Kennard and Baxter will have an effect on the composition of the Court. More importantly, the new justices appointed by Governor Brown could influence the Court's patterns of decision making. The California Supreme Court has had a conservative majority for a significant period of time, and Governor Brown will likely appoint justices who are more liberal than their predecessors. This will shift the ideological direction of the state high court from conservative majority to at least moderate if not liberal. Of course, we will not know the full impact of this change on the bench until the new justices begin participating in cases.

Legislative Redistricting

Every term, judges serving on the California bench across all court levels (trial, intermediate appellate, and Supreme) are confronted with cases that require them to make political decisions or decisions that have political consequences. One example of this is political redistricting. The redrawing of electoral districts is always a political process. Political parties seek either to maintain or to increase their odds of getting candidates re-elected through the redrawing of district lines. It is very common for redistricting plans to end up contested in the courts by political parties, elected officials, candidates seeking political office, or organized special interests.

Since the 1980s, the California courts have been involved in many cases and controversies regarding redistricting. Perhaps the most controversial occurred in 2005 when Governor Schwarzenegger and others proposed an initiative, Proposition 77, that would reform redistricting procedures in the state. Rather than having legislators redraw district lines after each census, the responsibility would be given to a panel of three retired judges (selected by legislative officials). This ballot measure was contested in the California Courts of Appeal before it even appeared on the ballot. Those opposed to the measure argued that judges should not have the power to redraw or create new political districts. Although there was some success with procedural challenges to the initiative in the courts of appeal, attempts to block the initiative from the ballot finally failed, and in November 2005 the voters vetoed the measure by a margin of approximately 19 percent, prohibiting retired judges from redrawing the state's electoral district lines.

Judicial Review and the Statewide Initiative

Another issue of concern regarding the judiciary in California is the relationship between direct democracy and judicial review. California is one of 26 states in the United States that allow citizens to propose and enact their own legislation through the initiative. Like any piece of legislation coming out of the state legislature, the initiative is subject to judicial interpretation and review. When the initiative is used to enact controversial policies—such as anti–affirmative action laws, a temporary tax to fund education, the decriminalization of marijuana, or term limits for elected officials—it is usually debated in the press and often contested in the courts. In fact, the constitutional validity of each of the initiatives mentioned above has been challenged in at least one court of law. The outcomes of these court cases have been varied. But most central to the controversy is the ability of state court judges, like judges on federal courts, to conduct judicial review. When state judges have the power to overturn laws enacted by the people as well as laws composed by state legislators, the tension between lawmaking and law reviewing is heightened.

Is this tension all that important? Many scholars and many voters would argue that it is. In fact, the common opinion among the electorate in California is that the initiative as an alternative policy-making tool has become an exercise in futility, precisely because of legal intervention. The consensus among California voters is that once an initiative passes at the ballot box, it ends up in a court of law. In truth, courts are reactive bodies. Judges must wait until a case comes to their courtrooms to make a legal decision. So why do so many initiatives end up in the California courts? The answer is simply politics. California is a very diverse state, and our diversity can be measured in a number of ways. We are diverse in race and ethnicity, we are diverse in culture, we are diverse economically, we are even diverse in terrain and climate. Given so many dimensions of diversity, there is no dearth of conflict in our state regarding which political problems are important and which solutions to these problems should be adopted. Hence California courts also function as an arena for the continuation of political debate.

For example, there has been significant political backlash throughout the nation since the previously mentioned U.S. Supreme Court ruling in *Citizens United*

(2010). Interest groups have mobilized in numerous states to overturn this decision. The California legislature also took action by attempting to place an advisory question on the 2014 ballot. The question would have effectively asked voters if they wanted to advise Congress to adopt a constitutional amendment overturning the *Citizens United* decision. Unlike the initiative or referendum, this ballot measure, known as Proposition 49, would not amend or create a new statutory or state constitutional law. It would have no authority except to relay the opinions of voters. The state Supreme Court determined on August 11, 2014, that Proposition 49 had to be removed from the 2014 ballot pending further court review. This review did not take place in time for the question to be reinstated on the 2014 ballot, but the measure may appear in another form in the future. It will all depend on what the Court decides.[12]

Caseload

While the caseload for all court levels in California has recently begun to decline after increasing over a period of several years, it remains very high when compared with other state court caseloads. And while the superior courts and appellate courts have managed this load fairly efficiently, there are legitimate concerns about the system's ability to continue to do so, given the state's continued fiscal crisis. As noted earlier, from 2012 to 2013, approximately 7.7 million cases were filed in California superior courts (trial courts of general jurisdiction).[13] California, like many other states, has modified its laws to allow juveniles to be tried as adults in some criminal cases. Although the intent of this law may have been to let juveniles know that California has little tolerance for certain types of crime, regardless of the defendant's age, the effect has been to shift cases from the courts of judges who deal exclusively with juveniles to the already overburdened courts handling crimes involving adults. In addition, victims' rights legislation, which has elevated some misdemeanors (nonserious crimes) to felonies (serious crimes), increases not only the severity of the penalties for the accused but also the workload for the courts. California's three-strikes law, originally enacted to punish repeat offenders, has had a similar impact. Keep in mind that these are just a few examples.

To be sure, most of the civil cases filed in California's civil courts will be resolved through negotiation between the parties and their attorneys. For example, in 2012–2013, 79 percent of unlimited jurisdiction civil cases were resolved without trial, while 92 percent of limited jurisdiction civil cases were disposed of before trial.[14] The courts are still involved, however, in processing the paperwork and dealing with the other administrative issues each civil case may involve.

Similarly, most of the criminal cases in the state's criminal courts will be resolved through plea bargaining, despite what we see in film or on television. Full court trials for the prosecution of high-profile crimes, like that of Conrad Murray, the personal physician found guilty in 2011 of involuntary manslaughter of his patient, singer Michael Jackson, are rare. A plea bargain is the norm. Even so, the courts are still involved in the process. Even if a criminal case never goes beyond the formal filing of charges against a defendant, judges are part of a plea bargain. As a referee, the judge's job is to determine if the plea bargain is appropriate and if the defendant entered into the plea bargain knowingly. If the judge decides that the terms of the plea bargain are inappropriate, that the defendant's ability to comprehend the terms of the plea was compromised, or that the plea was not entered into voluntarily, then a new plea may have to be negotiated or the case may actually go to trial. Regardless, a single case involves many people in the criminal courts, from clerks to administrators and, of course, a judge.

Despite this incredible workload, California's criminal courts typically resolve cases involving felonies within 12 months. Civil cases are also resolved fairly quickly; on average, over 75 percent of civil cases filed in a given year are resolved within a year. Most recently, California superior courts reported disposing of all civil cases within the 2012–2013 fiscal year, including a backlog from prior years.

While these are impressive figures, problems remain. The lack of resources in some local court jurisdictions, especially in smaller localities, and the impact of the current budget crisis on the state's judiciary as a whole affect access to the courts and can compromise the quality of legal representation for indigent persons.

California Courts: Where Are We Now?

A number of issues currently confront California's courts. As discussed earlier, chief among these issues is the court system's ability to manage an increasing caseload as the state continues to face a tenuous fiscal situation. Courts are subject to constraints similar to those that affect state agencies. It is fairly easy to argue that the greatest of these constraints, aside from jurisdiction, is the state's economy and budget. Most recently, the court system in California has found itself constrained by the extraordinary challenges of the state's budget. Chapter 8 discusses the budgetary process and its political implications in greater detail, but here we can examine the impact of this budgetary crisis on the courts.

Taken at face value, a discussion about budgets and courts may not appear all that interesting. However, when Governor Brown signed the budget on June 27, 2012, it included $6 billion of automatic cuts—hundreds of millions to the court system—severely affecting both day-to-day operations and future construction plans. It is important to note that these cuts come on top of other actions that have been taken to reduce the size of court administration throughout the state. Because most courts are located at the local level, counties and municipalities have taken the brunt of these budget cuts. Responses to the ramifications of these cuts have included threatened strikes by state court administrative personnel and the elimination of some innovative, albeit controversial, programs at the local level. One such program focuses on nonviolent misdemeanor crimes by juvenile offenders in the Los Angeles area. This program is part of a relatively recent legal movement known as "problem-solving justice," or the good courts movement. It served as an alternative to traditional, more punitive, forms of addressing juvenile low-level crime. The nontraditional court served more than 100,000 children each year, but has been shut down by the county due to budget cuts.[15]

In addition, Chief Justice Tani Gorre Cantil-Sakauye has had to respond to some criticisms by organized interests and other parties about wasteful spending on projects and the growth of the state's Administrative Office of the Courts (AOC). The Alliance of California Judges, established in 2009, has been pressuring the chief justice and the judicial council to respond to past and present budget cuts more proactively and to pay closer attention to wasteful spending, predicting (accurately) that, like his predecessors, Governor Brown would include more cuts to the state courts' budgets in the new fiscal year. More specifically, this organization targeted the now defunct electronic Court Case Management System. According to the *Courthouse News Service*, "even as trial courts were closing, the [Judicial] Council voted repeatedly, with only one or two dissenting votes, to continue pouring hundreds of millions into that now failed IT project. That money came primarily from trial court funds." The same article claims that over half a billion dollars was spent before the Court Management Case System was terminated.[16]

On top of this, Chief Justice Cantil-Sakauye released a report "prepared by a committee of state judges" in late May 2012 criticizing the AOC for understating the number of its employees and for paying "hundreds" of its personnel six-figure salaries. The report noted that this growth in both size and salaries paid was taking place during a hiring freeze. The investigation concluded, among other things, that the AOC had circumvented the hiring freeze and had violated some of its own personnel rules; it recommended significant cuts to the staff and organizational consolidation to allow for more oversight and, presumably, more efficiency.[17]

Finally, reforming judicial campaigns in the state is also a critical agenda item. Some attempts at reform, such as campaign finance reporting, have been implemented and have not been found unconstitutional. However, when voters amended the state constitution in 1986 to prohibit political parties from endorsing judges who run in nonpartisan elections, the California Supreme Court found the initiative unconstitutional because it violated Californians' rights to freedom of expression and freedom of association. Obviously, judges have a lot of say when it comes to these reforms, and it is up to the individual judge to decide how much is too much when it comes to campaign spending.

Study Guide

FOR FURTHER READING

American Judicature Society (AJS). "Judicial Selection in the States." www.judicialselection.us. Accessed August 16, 2012.

Bonneau, Christopher W., and Melinda Gann Hall. *In Defense of Judicial Elections*. New York: Routledge Press, 2009. This book is a critique of previous empirical studies of judicial elections. Bonneau and Hall argue that elections as a selection method for judges are actually beneficial to democratic society.

Bonneau, Chris W., and Damon Cann. "Campaign Spending, Diminishing Marginal Returns, and Campaign Finance Restrictions in Judicial Elections." *Journal of Politics* 73 (October 2011): 1267–1280.

Hall, Melinda Gann, and Chris W. Bonneau. "Attack Advertising, the *White* Decision, and Voter Participation in State Supreme Court Elections." *Political Research Quarterly* 66 (March 2013): 115–126.

Streb, Matthew J., and Brian Frederick. "When Money Can't Encourage Participation: Campaign Spending and Rolloff in Low Visibility Judicial Elections." *Political Behavior* 33 (2011): 665–684.

California Courts. *Guide to California Courts*. www.courtinfo.ca.gov/courts. Accessed September 27, 2012.

Civil Justice Association of California. "Campaign Contributions to the California Judiciary 1997–2000." http://cjac.org/assets/finalrept2000.pdf. Accessed August 16, 2012.

Streb, Matthew J., ed. *Running for Judge: The Rising Political, Financial and Legal Stakes of Judicial Elections*. New York:

New York University Press, 2007. This edited book is a collection of contemporary research conducted by professors who study state courts and judicial elections. Each chapter examines current issues and controversies that are confronted by state courts and state court judges.

ON THE WEB

California Courts: www.courts.ca.gov. Accessed August 14, 2014. This is the official web site of the California court system.

Institute for the Advancement of the American Legal System: http://iaals.du.edu/. Accessed August 14, 2014.

The American Judicature Society (AJS): www.ajs.org. Accessed August 16, 2012. The AJS is a nonpartisan organization made up of legal professionals and citizens. It seeks to provide a better understanding of the judiciary and the justice system to the public.

The California Supreme Court Historical Society (CSCHS): http://cschs.org. Accessed August 16, 2012. CSCHS catalogs and archives information about the history of the California Supreme Court.

The National Center for State Courts (NCSC): http://ncsconline.org. Accessed August 16, 2012. NCSC is an organization that provides services for court administrators, practitioners, and others interested in state courts. The web site includes information, data sets, and articles about state courts and court-related topics.

SUMMARY

I. Structure of the California courts
   A. Court rulings can impact all Californians, such as the recent rulings on undocumented immigrants.
   B. Superior courts are the trial courts of the California court system. They are courts of "first instance" and triers of fact. The California Courts of Appeal are intermediate appellate courts. They are divided into six districts across the state. All cases except for death-penalty cases are first appealed to the California Courts of Appeal.
   C. The Supreme Court is the highest court in the state. It is composed of seven justices and, like the Courts of Appeal, is an appellate court—that is, it reviews

cases that were first heard in lower state courts such as the Courts of Appeal or a superior court.
   D. Jurisdiction limits the types of cases that civil courts and criminal courts can hear. Criminal courts deal with violations of state and local laws, and civil courts hear cases involving disputes between individuals or classes of individuals.
   E. Access to California courts is widely available. However, there is concern about the cost of litigation and legal representation.
   F. Federalism and California courts
      1. Legal challenges to Proposition 215, the Compassionate Use Act (CUA), illustrate the

tension between state and federal government. California permits the use of medical marijuana under certain conditions, but the federal government does not. There have been continuous attempts by federal law enforcement to close marijuana dispensaries that would otherwise be operating legally under the CUA.

2. Local governments are also adopting ordinances to regulate or even prohibit dispensaries from operating in their communities. At times, local governments will use federal law enforcement to assist them with closing dispensaries.

3. The California courts currently have a number of cases across all levels examining this policy.

II. Judicial selection

A. Methods of selection for the California courts include nonpartisan elections for superior court and merit selection for appellate courts.

B. The California courts are diverse in terms of gender, race, and ideology. Justice Joyce L. Kennard left the bench in April 2014, and Justice Marvin R. Baxter announced on June 18, 2014 that he would also be retiring from the bench. These retirements provided Governor Brown, a Democrat, with the opportunity to appoint two new judges who will very likely be more liberal than their predecessors.

C. There are two competing theories regarding judicial selection—appointment and election. Those who favor judicial independence argue that appointment is a better method for selecting judges because it insulates judges from politics. Conversely, those who favor accountability argue that election as a method of selection is essential in a democracy and that judicial elections allow citizens to hold judges accountable for their decision making, similar to the way other elected officials are held accountable for their actions in office.

D. Recent controversies about judicial campaigning and campaign finance have led to some high-profile jurists (for example, retired U.S. Supreme Court associate justice Sandra Day O'Connor) and others to call for reforms. The most radical reforms proposed would eliminate judicial elections entirely. The increasing cost of judicial campaigns, which are low-saliency and low-turnout elections, have many members of the bar and legal community concerned.

E. Methods of removal from the bench include recall elections and impeachment. In addition, because all judges in California face some sort of election (direct or retention), voters may choose to vote for another judicial candidate or they may choose to vote against retaining an appellate court judge.

III. Contemporary issues in the judiciary

A. The retirements of Justices Kennard and Baxter will have an effect on the composition of the court. More importantly, the new justices appointed by Governor Brown could influence the court's patterns of decision making.

B. Judges serving across all court levels are confronted with cases that require them to make political decisions, including cases involving legislative redistricting.

C. State judges have the power to overturn laws enacted by the people through the initiative as well as laws composed by state legislators. There is a very strong likelihood that contested initiatives will end up in the courts, and the courts serve as an arena for continued political debate.

D. California courts have a very high caseload, though they remain fairly efficient and are able to dispose of a significant percentage of their criminal and civil caseload at all court levels.

PRACTICE QUIZ

1. All death-penalty sentences are automatically appealed directly to the California Supreme Court for review.
   a) true
   b) false

2. The California Supreme Court is similar to the U.S. Supreme Court in that it has nine justices.
   a) true
   b) false

3. Most civil cases in California are resolved before going to trial.
   a) true
   b) false

4. Voters in California are highly informed about the candidates running in judicial elections.
   a) true
   b) false

5. Initiatives passed in California are not subject to either judicial interpretation or judicial review.
   a) true
   b) false ⟵circled

6. In recent years, campaign spending in judicial elections
   a) has increased. ⟵circled
   b) has decreased.
   c) has remained the same.
   d) cannot be determined.

7. Chief Justice Rose Bird and Associate Justices Cruz Reynoso and Joseph Grodin were voted out by citizens who were angry about the judges' decisions concerning
   a) same-sex marriage.
   b) the death penalty. ⟵circled
   c) Proposition 13.
   d) term limits.

8. Judges selected by the governor to serve on the Supreme Court and the Courts of Appeal in California must be approved by
   a) the state legislature.
   b) the attorney general.

c) the Commission on Judicial Appointments. ⟵circled
d) none of the above

9. Superior courts in California adjudicate the following types of actions:
   a) civil and criminal cases. ⟵circled
   b) only civil cases.
   c) only criminal cases.
   d) only appeals.

10. One method of removing judges in the state of California is
   a) removal by the governor.
   b) censure by the state legislature.
   c) agreement between the speaker of the Assembly and the attorney general.
   d) a recall election. ⟵circled

CRITICAL-THINKING QUESTIONS

1. Given the concern on the part of lawmakers and the public over the role of money in judicial elections, what kinds of reforms might be implemented that would still allow for accountability? Is it possible to keep money and special interests out of judicial elections?
2. What factors do you believe are responsible for the tremendous criminal caseload in the California superior courts?
3. Is judicial independence important for state court judges?
4. What kinds of checks have been placed on the California judiciary? How do the other branches and political actors hold the state courts accountable?

KEY TERMS

appellate jurisdiction (p. 160)
civil courts (p. 162)
judicial accountability (p. 168)

judicial discretion (p. 161)
judicial independence (p. 168)

retention election (p. 165)
superior courts (p. 160)

8 The State Budget and Budgetary Limitations

WHAT CALIFORNIA GOVERNMENT DOES AND WHY IT MATTERS

Why does student tuition keep rising? The answer to rising student tuition is actually simple. Higher education is a major category of the state budget, the third or fourth largest in most years, and charts circulating in Sacramento made it look as if students until recently paid relatively low tuition and fees by national standards. The charts came from the Legislative Analyst's Office and from the California Postsecondary Education Commission (CPEC), a research agency created by the legislature to be independent of the three systems of higher education. Everyone involved in higher education policy saw these charts: the governor's department of finance, the legislative committees and their staff, the bureaucracy, and one of this book's authors, a member of the California State University (CSU) statewide academic senate for several years. After seeing these charts, legislators on the hunt for an extra several hundred million dollars to cut from the budget felt fairly justified in saying, "Well, the students are paying relatively little by U.S. standards; just increase the university's fees to cover the difference."

And that was the process that occurred, year after year, for about a decade. Then in 2011, in a budget-saving move, Governor Brown abolished CPEC. Meanwhile, CSU's fees had moved from the bottom to the middle of the list, and the University of California (UC), which had started higher on the list, had moved up. The five-year increase from 2008-09 to 2013-14 in average tuition for four-year public colleges in California (both UC and CSU) was 57 percent, a rate exceeded by only four states.[1] In the CSU system, "**student success fees**" substituted for tuition increases when the latter became politically controversial and tuition was frozen in 2012. Student success fees are fees added to tuition that range from $200 to $600 per year, approved by the students on campus, and used for faculty hiring, adding course sections, and technology expenditures. In 2014, after student protests, the state budget prohibited additional student success fees.[2]

Ultimately, over the four years from 2008 to 2012, higher education lost $2.8 billion in funding, about 22 percent of its total. Some of this has been replaced by success fee and tuition increases, but even with the increased money available to the state in 2014, existing state agencies are not being restored to the higher budget levels that existed in the 1990s and early 2000s. The state simply has other priorities. UC and CSU received an extra $125 and $142 million each from the state surpluses in 2013-14 and 2014-15, but these increases are a far cry from the cuts administered in the previous decade. In July 2014, CSU cut the number of incoming students by half, from 20,000 to 10,000, as a result of the state's failure to increase its budget sufficiently for 2014-15.

Students aren't the only citizens heavily impacted by California's budget woes. With a budget of over $155 billion, plus $98 billion in federal funds, California represents one of the largest economies in the world. Its projected *deficit* in recent years has been larger than the entire budgets of all but the 10 largest states. Over 2.5 million workers in California—1 out of 6—work for the federal, state, or local governments, and some of the rest are indirectly funded by the public sector.[3]

It is therefore unsurprising that the process to approve the budget, which controls the livelihood of so many people, is controversial. The public itself is split—most Californians are opposed to spending cuts in public programs as well as increases in taxes or fees. They are also distrustful of state government and disapprove of the job their politicians are doing. One political party in the state legislature—the Republicans—won't increase taxes under any circumstances; indeed, some Republicans consider the entire budget so illegitimate that they won't vote for it under any realistic set of circumstances (one didn't vote for a budget for over a decade). The legislature came within one vote of increasing the sales tax in 2002, but that vote was impossible to procure. The amount and intensity of political controversy over the state budget, a document that embodies the values and decisions of the citizens, its legislature, and its leaders, is truly remarkable.

Passing the budget is at the center, both in difficulty and in scope, of what the state government does each year. Since the passage of Proposition 13 in 1978, the state government has received less revenue and that revenue has become more volatile, rising and falling with the economy. The state constitution mandates that the legislature pass the budget by June 15. Since 1990, the legislature has met this deadline only eight times. Two of those were budget surplus years, when it is always easier to pass a budget. Four others have occurred since the passage of Proposition 25 in 2011, which requires only a majority vote to pass the budget and penalizes legislators by cutting their salaries when the budget is overdue.

How Is the Budget Formed?

The process of forming a budget has four steps. Most governments today follow a similar process—proposal by the executive branch, enactment by the legislature, approval by the governor, and implementation by the executive branch. Note that the preparation, enactment, and implementation of the budget for a single fiscal year takes almost three calendar years. See Box 8.1 for a summary of the budget process and Box 8.2 for the constitutional requirements for California's budget.

Executive Proposal

Each fall, state agencies send their budget proposals to the governor through the state **Department of Finance**. The governor formulates a proposal and sends it to the legislature in January. In late spring, he revises the proposal in what is called the "**May revise**."

Before 1922, agencies proposed their budgets directly to the legislature; there was no **unified budget** proposed by the governor or anyone else. Instead, "budgeting was the domain of interest groups, department heads, and ranking committee members."[4] In 1911, upon finding little or no justification for the amounts contained in the appropriations bills sent to him, Progressive governor Hiram Johnson created the Board of Control to advise him on the fiscal justification for each appropriation.

In 1922, California adopted its own version of new federal legislation that had been passed the previous year, thus *unifying* the budget process. The legislation called for a consolidated administration proposal in the form of a **governor's budget** that must be balanced, contain justifications for the amounts proposed, and be accompanied by bills introduced by legislative leaders in each house, thus providing a starting point for the negotiations and decisions each year. The existence of a governor's budget was an improvement over the situation before 1900, when "government structures . . . hid more than they revealed to the public."[5]

Legislative Adoption

The legislature adopts a balanced budget based on the governor's proposal. As of 2011, both the Assembly and the state Senate must adopt the budget by a majority of the entire membership. The Assembly and Senate budget committees and their subcommittees hold hearings on the budget bills during which they receive testimony and input from individuals and groups, including the affected departments and agencies, the Department of Finance, the **Legislative Analyst's Office**, committee staff, and interest groups.

The Legislative Analyst's Office provides nonpartisan and independent review of the entire budget, including alternative ways to accomplish the same goals and objectives. Former legislative analyst Elizabeth Hill has been called the Budget Nun because "her fiscal reports are incorruptible. They're the bible. The one source of truth. . . . She's the most influential non-elected official in the Capitol."[6] The current legislative analyst, Mac Taylor, was appointed in 2008 and has 30 years of experience in the Legislative Analyst's Office.

Before 2011, a **Budget Conference Committee** was appointed to work out the differences between the Assembly and Senate budget bills. Since the passage of Proposition 25 in 2010, however, a majority vote is now the sole requirement

BOX 8.1 ● California's Budget Process

CALENDAR YEAR 1

JULY–SEPTEMBER

- Agencies prepare requests and make proposals.
- Requests sent to Department of Finance.

OCTOBER–DECEMBER

- Department of Finance reviews requests and consults governor.

CALENDAR YEAR 2

JANUARY–MARCH

- California Constitution requires governor to send a balanced budget to the legislature by January 10.
- Governor's budget proposal is introduced in both houses as identical budget bills.
- Legislative Analyst's Office prepares extensive analysis.
- Budget hearings held in both houses.

APRIL–JUNE

- May: Governor sends revised and updated projections of revenues and expenditures to legislature (the May revise).
- June 15: California Constitution requires legislature to pass (by a majority vote) a balanced budget by this date. As of 2010, all members of the legislature permanently forfeit salary and expenses every day until the budget is passed.
- Governor signs budget, using item veto, if desired, to lower any appropriation items. Legislature can override by a two-thirds vote.

JULY–SEPTEMBER

- July 1: California's fiscal year begins. This is the first quarter. (The federal fiscal year, in contrast, begins October 1.)

OCTOBER–DECEMBER

- Second quarter of California's fiscal year.

CALENDAR YEAR 3

JANUARY–MARCH

- Third quarter of California's fiscal year.

APRIL–JUNE

- Fourth quarter of California's fiscal year.

to pass the budget; the endless compromising with the Republican Party that used to occupy Sacramento through the summers of the 1990s and 2000s is over. The "Big 5" group, consisting of the governor, Assembly speaker, Senate president pro tempore, and Assembly and Senate minority leaders, used to be instrumental under the old two-thirds requirement in soliciting a few Republican votes to pass the budget. Their influence in the budget process is now irrelevant, or at least it has been in the first four years under the new system. From 2011 to 2014, the budget was passed by June 15, the official deadline in Proposition 25; if legislators miss this deadline, they lose their salaries on every day that the budget is late.

Raising a tax, however, still requires a two-thirds vote of both the Assembly and the state Senate. While the Democrats achieved majorities of over two-thirds in both the Assembly and Senate in 2012, the voters approved Jerry Brown's initiative proposal on the November 2012 ballot, Proposition 30, to raise the state sales and income taxes in the same year. Because of this new source of revenue, Governor Brown strongly urged the legislature not to pass any additional tax increases in 2013. The two-thirds supermajority disappeared in early 2014 after three Democratic state senators were suspended for their involvement in various scandals.

Gubernatorial Action

The governor may use the **line-item veto** to lower any line-item appropriation in the budget, including lowering it to zero. The legislature may override the governor's veto by a two-thirds majority in each of the two houses and replace the lowered number with its own amount, although doing so is rare. Because of the line-item veto, the final budget is usually very close to the governor's May revise proposal.

Implementation

Agencies implement the budget as passed, with the fiscal year beginning July 1. The Department of Finance states explicitly that agencies and departments are expected to operate within their budgets and comply with any provisions enacted by the legislature: "The general expectation is that state agencies comply with the legislative intent."[7] There is some flexibility in implementation, but, compared to other states, the governor's flexibility is limited, as we shall see.

Other Groups Involved in the Budget Process

In addition to the governor and legislature, the agencies mentioned earlier—the Department of Finance on the executive side and the Legislative Analyst's Office on the legislative side—are closely involved in the process, as are two other groups:

- The courts have sometimes ruled on the constitutionality of particular budget actions, particularly on proposed administrative actions to be taken when the legislature has been late submitting a budget. They have also had to decide on the constitutionality of various budget provisions, such as the limits on property taxes established by Proposition 13 in 1978.

- **Moody's, Fitch Ratings, and Standard & Poor's** rate the ability of the states to repay their bond issues. The rating is one of several factors that influence the cost of selling a bond issue. The lower the credit rating, the higher the interest rate that must be paid to induce investors to purchase the bonds. In 2003, Moody's rating of California's bonds was the lowest rating given for any state. Nothing symbolizes the state's continuing inability to reconcile its desire for high services with its desire to pay low taxes than the fact that its bond rating continues to be in the bottom two or three among all states. The 2014 ratings, however, have come up to the A level, meaning the state has demonstrated a strong capacity to meet financial commitments and "high" credit quality (as opposed to "very high" or "highest"), due to the recent rise in state revenues.[8]

What Is in the Budget?

Every state budget contains the following information:

- economic assumptions—how the economy should respond during the forthcoming fiscal year, and what that response means for revenues and expenditures
- revenues expected in the various categories
- expenditures appropriated by department and program

Revenues

The **general fund** includes all state revenues that are *not* federal funds, special funds, or bond funds. (See Box 8.4 later in the chapter for more on federal funds.) The state budget is usually assumed to consist of either just the general fund or

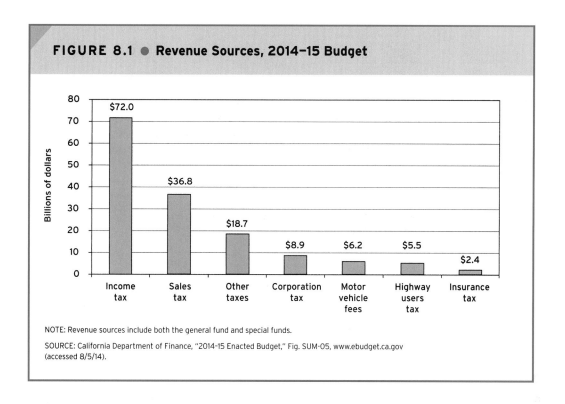

FIGURE 8.1 ● Revenue Sources, 2014–15 Budget

NOTE: Revenue sources include both the general fund and special funds.

SOURCE: California Department of Finance, "2014–15 Enacted Budget," Fig. SUM-05, www.ebudget.ca.gov (accessed 8/5/14).

the general fund plus special funds and bond funds. The general fund receives over 90 percent of its $100 billion-plus revenues from the sales tax, income tax, and corporate taxes and consists of all state money that is not allocated to a special fund or a bond fund. **Special funds** are funds that are allocated for a specific purpose: thus there is a beverage container recycling fund, a fish and game fund, and almost 500 more, totaling some $44 billion in the 2014–15 budget. Each has a specific source of income and a specific use for which the fund is designated. **Bond funds** come from bonds that are repaid over spans of a few years to a few decades, but some of them substitute for current expenditures. During the 1980s and 1990s, the CSU (as well as, presumably, other agencies) was told by the Department of Finance not to spend money upgrading and maintaining its buildings—once they deteriorated to a certain level, bond funds could be used to refurbish them (in case you were wondering why your college buildings are in such sad shape).

Looking at all sources of revenue, both general funds and special funds, we see the revenue sources are as follows, according to the 2014–15 enacted budget (see Figure 8.1).

PERSONAL INCOME TAX California's **personal income tax** ranges from 0 to 12.3 percent of income, with a substantial credit per child or dependent. The income tax is considered highly **progressive**, with the top 10 percent of taxpayers paying 74.2 percent of the income tax in 2010. The wealthiest 1 percent paid 40.9 percent of the income tax in the same year.[9] This is one of the most progressive personal income taxes in the nation. (See the Who Are Californians feature on the next page.) Regular income (salaries and wages) does not vary that much from

Who Pays Taxes?

California has a very progressive income tax system: those with low incomes are taxed at a low rate, while those earning high incomes are taxed at a high rate. With the passage of Proposition 30 in November 2012, California rose to the top of the list in terms of the highest bracket of state income tax: 13.3 percent on $1 million or more. Personal deductions are low, and federal taxes are not deductible.

Tax Rates for Selected States, 2014

▼ Lowest tax rate   ▲ Highest tax rate   ▼ Lowest tax bracket   ▲ Highest tax bracket

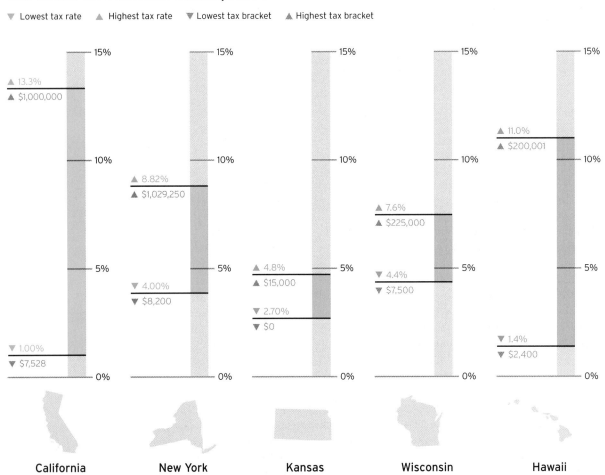

| California | New York | Kansas | Wisconsin | Hawaii |

California: ▲ 13.3% ▲ $1,000,000 ▼ 1.00% ▼ $7,528

New York: ▲ 8.82% ▲ $1,029,250 ▼ 4.00% ▼ $8,200

Kansas: ▲ 4.8% ▲ $15,000 ▼ 2.70% ▼ $0

Wisconsin: ▲ 7.6% ▲ $225,000 ▼ 4.4% ▼ $7,500

Hawaii: ▲ 11.0% ▲ $200,001 ▼ 1.4% ▼ $2,400

forcriticalanalysis

1. Do you agree with the way California structures its income taxes? Should there be more or fewer brackets? Higher or lower rates? Higher or lower exemptions?

2. Comparing California's taxes to those from other states, what do these rates say about California's political culture?

SOURCE: Federation of Tax Administrators, http://www.taxadmin.org/fta/rate/ind_inc.pdf (accessed 4/11/14).

year to year, but **capital gains** income (income from selling stock that has appreciated in value, for example) varies considerably from one year to the next, making revenues from the income tax fluctuate a great deal. Proposition 30 established three new brackets for taxpayers who make more than $250,000 per year: at 10.3, 11.3, and 12.3 percent of income. The new brackets are temporary, lasting from 2012 to 2018. They make the California state income tax even more progressive than it is at present, reflecting the income level of the state (higher than the nation's; see Chapter 1).

SALES TAX The baseline state **sales tax** is 7.5 percent. Counties or taxing districts are allowed to add between 0.13 and 0.5 percent per local district for local services. In some areas there is more than one district tax in effect. The average sales tax in California is 7.75 percent. The minimum in any area is 7.5 percent. The maximum is in Pico Rivera and South Gate, two cities in Los Angeles County, at about 10 percent. Economists consider the sales tax **regressive**—that is, as individual or household income increases, the proportion of income paid through the tax decreases, because lower-income households spend a higher proportion of their incomes on consumption goods that are taxed compared with higher income households. In California, the state refunds 1.25 percent of its share to the local city and county; this feature has led many cities to search for businesses that are both clean industries and have a high sales volume (thus increasing sales-tax revenue) such as **big-box shopping centers and automobile dealerships**. The process has been called the "**fiscalization of land use**."

A state sales tax has existed in California since 1933, with the rate raised on average every five years. In 2013, Proposition 30 temporarily raised the state sales tax one-quarter of 1 percent. The increase expires in 2016.

The sales tax was developed over 50 years ago and is based on an older conception of the economy consisting mostly of goods that are manufactured, bought, and sold. The modern economy is over half services, but these are not taxed in California.

In many states, at least some services are taxed. Having a broader base on the sales tax would enable the rate to be lowered from its current high level, but finding a two-thirds majority in the legislature to pass a tax reform act is close to impossible. Even in 2013, when the Democratic Party had a two-thirds majority in both the Assembly and the state Senate, the Democrats were unwilling and not unified enough to modernize the tax code.

PROPERTY TAX All owners of property pay California's property tax, limited under Proposition 13 to 1 percent of the assessed value in 1975 or the value of a more recent sale. Once acquired, increases in valuation and thus annual tax increases are limited to 2 percent or the amount of inflation, whichever is smaller. Proposition 13 passed overwhelmingly in 1978 and contains provisions requiring special majorities greater than 50 percent for legislators and voters to raise taxes. Proposition 13 rolled back property taxes in California by more than half, and the state has endeavored to make up the difference ever since. Local property tax revenue available for cities, counties, and school districts has been substantially reduced. As a result, all local government entities are more reliant on the state for revenue, and decision-making power has substantially shifted, in the eyes of virtually all observers, from the local level to the state level.

California's public schools have suffered since the passage of Proposition 13 decreased local property tax revenues and effectively transferred the responsibility for funding school districts from the local to the state level. Overcrowded classrooms have been one result of this shift.

School districts are an excellent example of the effects of this shift. Whereas California once had some of the best-quality and best-funded schools in the nation, its expenditures per pupil have fallen in comparison to the rest of the nation. Its staff-per-student ratio is now 70 percent of the average for other states. Its student achievement levels lag behind the rest of the nation, and a greater proportion of high-income families send their children to private schools compared to the pre-1978 period. At the same time, teacher salaries are relatively high to accommodate the cost of living and housing prices, and to attract good-quality recruits to the profession.

Compared to other states, the overall tax structure depends more on taxes that are volatile, rising and falling with the economy (income tax, sales tax), and less on taxes that don't vary with the economy (e.g., the property tax) because of the Proposition 13 limits. The average state obtains 29 percent of its total state and local tax funds from the property tax, but because of Proposition 13's limits, California obtains only 22 percent. (See Box 8.3 for a more detailed explanation and assessment of Proposition 13.)

CORPORATION TAX The corporation tax is levied on corporate profits and provides about 6 percent of state revenues. The corporation tax structure is cited favorably by *Governing* magazine in its appraisal of the state's tax system as "tough on the creation of tax-dodge subsidiaries, and the law covers a firm's property and assets, not just its sales."[10] The 2012 Franchise Tax Board Annual Report states that in 2011, out of the 734,315 corporations that reported their incomes, almost 43 percent either lost money or broke even. The 1.6 percent that earned $1 million or more paid about 85 percent of the total tax, while the top 1,322 corporations earning $10 million or more paid 71 percent of the total.[11]

INDIAN CASINOS Governor Schwarzenegger attempted to increase the amount of revenue received for the general fund from Indian gambling operations in California. In 2005–06, the state received only $27 million for the general fund of the $301 million from the tribal–state gambling compacts negotiated by the

BOX 8.3 ● What Exactly Is Proposition 13?

What is it? Proposition 13, passed overwhelmingly by the voters in June 1978, had the following provisions:

- All property taxes were rolled back to a maximum of 1 percent of the value of the property in 1975-76.

- The value of the property, and thus the tax paid, was allowed to increase by the rate of inflation, but the inflation rate was capped at 2 percent per year.

- When ownership changed, property would be revalued at the current market value.

- No new property taxes could be imposed, either by the state or by local governments.

- Any "special taxes" could be imposed only by a two-thirds margin of the voters in the particular area (the state legislature was already under a two-thirds approval rule for raising taxes, a rule in force since 1933).

- All property taxes collected were to be distributed "according to law," and because no law existed, the legislature had to create them.

THE EFFECTS OF PROPOSITION 13

Proposition 13 immediately affected local governments. Before 1978, local governments and agencies each established their own property tax rate, designed to produce sufficient revenues to accomplish the particular function of the agency. Now, each agency's property tax rate was irrelevant; the state would decide "according to law" how much money to apportion to each local jurisdiction. The total property tax collected decreased by over half. The state, however, had a $5 billion surplus, which helped bridge the gap in funds for several years.

The single biggest change set in motion by Proposition 13 is that the state assumed considerable authority over issues formerly handled by local government.[a] Local governments used to set the local tax rate to produce sufficient funds for public services necessary to the locality. Instead, those decisions are now made by the state, and "clearly, the property tax is now really a state tax."[b]

Another consequence stems from the provision that requires a two-thirds vote of the local area to impose or raise a tax. Many localities have seen election results of 60 to 66 percent in favor, just short of the required two-thirds, and have been powerless to initiate local projects, such as acquiring land for parks. Bond issues for the repair and construction of school facilities, however, were authorized by Proposition 39 in 2000 to require the approval of only 55 percent of local voters.

One of the most important consequences is called "the fiscalization of land use"—that is, the tendency of local governments not only to evaluate land use changes in terms of how much money will be brought to the local government but to make decisions on that basis. Because localities receive a share of the state sales tax, land use changes that produce a lot of sales tax revenues are preferred. Many cities favor big-box shopping centers and auto malls over housing developments, and rely increasingly on development fees and other ways to obtain revenue not available through the property tax.

Finally, we have seen the development of many "arcane" financing techniques, those so intricate that no one understands them except the few who developed them. These are also designed to help obtain revenues and replace property taxes.

(continued)

governor and ratified by the legislature. In 2008–09, the governor's budget projected $430 million in revenues, but much less was actually received. More recent budgets have no information on Indian gambling revenues, as they are so small as to be insignificant (less than one-tenth of one percent) in a budget of more than $100 billion.

Why Do Revenues Vary So Much?

California's budget rises and falls each year, soaring when the economy is healthy and plunging in even the mildest recessions. Here is why:

- Revenues from the sales tax and the personal income tax depend directly on how the state economy performs each year.

- Compared to other states, the budget relies more on the personal income tax, the capital gains portion of which soars when stock options are cashed out, than on the property tax, limited in 1978 by Proposition 13 and roughly constant every year.

How Well Does the Tax System Function?

The tax system seems to be functioning poorly. Little has changed since *Governing* magazine published "The Way We Tax" in 2003, comparing tax policy in all 50 states. The report gave California one star out of four in the category "Adequacy of Revenue," two out of four in "Fairness to Taxpayers," and two out of four in "Management of System."[12] Only Tennessee received a lower overall rating, and four other states were tied with California.

A more recent study of tax administration, conducted by the Council on State Taxation (COST) and published in December 2013, ranked California's tax administration in 49th place, tied with Louisiana, and graded it a D−, citing errors such as permitting the same people to serve on the boards at different levels of tax appeal and allowing officials unqualified in tax administration onto those boards.[13] Some of the problem areas include:

- The "highly progressive and volatile" income tax depends too much on capital gains being taxed at the same level as regular income. Thus tax revenues soared along with the stock market in 2000 and 2013–14, but typically these revenues fall just as quickly. In 2008, for example, the forecast for the income tax dropped 13 percent in just six months due to the downturn in the economy.

- Although the state income tax is highly progressive, both the sales tax and the entire tax system are regressive, meaning that those at the bottom of the income distribution pay a higher proportion of their income as taxes to the state than those at the top.[14]

- The sales tax focuses on goods that are sold, reflecting the manufacturing economy in place when the tax was developed. But the modern economy has shifted toward services, which are not taxed—for example, a doctor's office visit or the labor charge when your automobile is fixed. Broadening the base of the sales tax would enable the high rate (compared to other states) to be lowered.

- Ballot measures have imposed rigid spending demands (discussed in the section "Budgetary Limitations" later in this chapter).

- Tax administration is split among the Franchise Tax Board, the Board of Equalization, and the Employment Development Department, widely considered an inefficient arrangement.

Is California Overtaxed?

THE CONSERVATIVE VIEW Conservatives think California is overtaxed. The California Taxpayers Association makes the case that "the extraordinary level of taxation in California can provide more than enough in tax revenue to fund police and fire services, education for our children, and public works projects and health and welfare services for California's poor."[15] Taxes are so high, in their view, that the state is no longer economically competitive with other states. The Washington, D.C.–based Tax Foundation, which calculates the total tax burden, including taxes paid out of state (for vacation property, for example), found California's state and local tax burden for fiscal year 2011 to be the fourth highest in the nation.[16]

THE LIBERAL VIEW Liberals often argue not that California's taxes are low, but that they are moderate in comparison with California's income, ranked 15th to 20th among the states. The California Budget Project, for example, stated in 2014 that California was a "moderate" tax state, ranking 20th among the 50 states "with respect to total 'own source' revenues raised by state and local governments." California ranked 11th in the percentage of state taxes compared with personal income in the state in 2010–11. Personal and corporate income tax collections are relatively high in California, but the tobacco and alcoholic beverage taxes are relatively low.[17]

THE REALITY California is a relatively rich state. Its household and median family incomes are some $8,000 higher than the U.S. averages. The income and sales tax rates are among the higher tax rates of all American states, although there are numerous exemptions that bring the total tax rate lower.

The critical challenge to California's tax structure is not that taxes are high but that it is outmoded. It reflects the economy of the 1950s and Proposition 13 decisions made in the 1970s. The property tax collects less money proportionally than other wealthy states because of Proposition 13. The sales tax is based on the purchase of goods (with food exempted), not on services. Lower- and middle-class families with children are largely exempted from the personal income tax. The bottom line is that, like so many areas of the state's governmental structure, California's tax structure needs to be reformed. Without tax reform, California

Local governments in California often try to attract car dealerships because of the considerable sales tax revenue the dealerships generate. In 2012, for example, former mayor of Los Angeles Antonio Villaraigosa eliminated the city's business tax on car dealerships as an incentive for dealerships to develop in the city.

will continue to be a battleground for both liberals and conservatives, with conservatives seeking to lower the highest rates, and liberals seeking exemptions for the poor and middle class.

Conservative groups rate California's business climate as one of the worst of any state due to the high levels of taxes; the taxation of capital gains at regular tax rates; and the number of regulations and permits affecting citizens' ability to establish, run, and expand a business.[18] Nevertheless, many large corporations are located in California, particularly in Silicon Valley (the area between San Francisco and San Jose) because of the wealth of skilled talent in the area's labor market.

One question is whether California's level of taxes as a whole reduces the growth the state would otherwise experience. An analysis of the growth rates of nine states with a high rate of personal income taxation compared to the nine states that lack any personal income tax indicates that there is no conclusive relationship. In fact, the states that grow the most seem to be those with high rates of population growth, and several of the non-income tax states have economic resources (such as oil, which obviates the need for a state income tax) not available to other states.[19]

Expenditures

Figure 8.2 depicts the 2014–15 state budget, including the general fund, special funds, and bond funds.

Figure 8.2 indicates that the largest spending category is health and human services, at $49 billion for 2014–15 and about 31 percent of the entire budget.

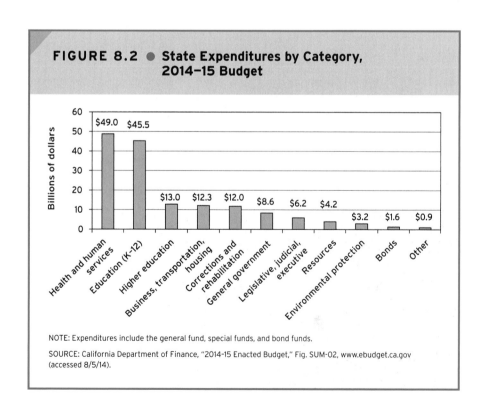

FIGURE 8.2 ● State Expenditures by Category, 2014–15 Budget

NOTE: Expenditures include the general fund, special funds, and bond funds.

SOURCE: California Department of Finance, "2014-15 Enacted Budget," Fig. SUM-02, www.ebudget.ca.gov (accessed 8/5/14).

This category includes the state (but not the federal) contribution for Medi-Cal, California's Medicaid program, which provides health coverage for the poor as well as senior citizens in nursing homes; the public health system; Healthy Families, California's state children's health insurance program; welfare, including Temporary Assistance for Needy Families; and the state contribution to food stamps and the Women, Infants, and Children (WIC) supplemental food program, among many others.

The second largest expenditure category in Figure 8.2 is elementary and secondary education, at $45.5 billion and 29 percent of total expenditures. There has been a long, gradual upward trend in the proportion of the budget devoted to education, although there was a slight decline in the last several fiscal years because of declining state revenues. With the passage of Proposition 13 in 1978, a gradually increasing proportion of the state general fund has been spent on K–12 education. The money in this category supplements property tax revenues for education, collected by each county.

Higher education is the third largest category at $13 billion and 8 percent of total expenditures. Higher education includes funding for the community college system (112 campuses, 2.1 million students), the CSU system (23 campuses, 447,000 students), and the UC system (10 campuses, 5 medical centers, 3 national labs, 233,000 students).

Since 1980–81 there has been a trend downward in the proportion of the budget devoted to higher education. In recent years, state funding for higher education was cut severely. A report from the Public Policy Institute of California demonstrates that funding for higher education composed above 17 percent of the state budget as recently as 1975, but since then the proportion has declined to between 11 and 13 percent.[20] Another report, from the Center on Budget and Policy Priorities in Washington, D.C., compares the states in their spending per student cuts and tuition increases from FY 2008 to 2013.[21] All but two of the states cut their expenditures per student during this time period, and California is in the middle of the pack with a 29.5 percent cut. But California's percentage tuition increase, at 72 percent for the same time period, is the second largest among the states. The recent budget augmentations from Governor Jerry Brown have barely started to make up for the billions that were cut from higher education in the 2000s.

The fourth largest category is business, transportation, and housing, at $12.3 billion or 7.9 percent of the state budget. This area includes Caltrans, which maintains the state's roads; the Department of Motor Vehicles (DMV); and the departments that regulate corporations, alcoholic beverages, real estate, managed health care, and high-speed rail, among others. (The high-speed rail area includes only a few million dollars for state positions to manage the high-speed rail authority; if the high-speed railroad is actually implemented, billions in construction funds will come from the federal government and bond issues.) Most programs in the business, transportation, and housing category are largely funded by special funds and taxes, not by the general fund.

The "corrections and rehabilitation" category provides funding for state prisons and youth authorities. At $12 billion and 8 percent of the budget, this category increased steadily from 1980–81 through the mid-1990s as the public demanded three-strike laws and similar measures. It has since leveled off.

Figure 8.2 contains several other smaller categories: general government administration, the "legislative, executive, judicial" category, the natural resources category (e.g., state parks), and areas covering state expenditures for the environment. "Bonds" is a new category for 2014–15 to cover repayments for state bonds taken out to meet earlier budget crises. The last category is "other," which covers everything else.

Budgetary Limitations

Through the use of initiatives California voters have not only passed bond issues but have also limited what the state government can do in some very significant areas. Many of these initiatives, such as Propositions 99, 111, 49, and 71, have placed money into various "special funds." Here are the most significant:[22]

- **Proposition 13 (1978)** cut property taxes to 1 percent of the assessed valuation of the property in 1975 and allows reassessment only when the property is sold. If justified by inflation, the tax can rise a maximum of 2 percent in between assessments.

- **Proposition 62 (1986)** requires a vote of the electorate on all taxes that might be used to replace revenues lost under Proposition 13.

- **Proposition 98 (1988)** requires that at least 40 percent of the general fund be devoted to K–14 education, including community colleges; annual increases are to be at least equal to the increase in school enrollment and the cost of living.

- **Proposition 99 (1988)** mandated a 25-cent tax on cigarettes, with the proceeds to be spent on antismoking campaigns and medical research.

- **Proposition 111 (1990)** increased the gas tax and trucking fees; the proceeds must be spent on transportation projects.

- **Proposition 5 (1998)** mandated that the state negotiate a compact to allow tribal casinos in California.

- **Proposition 42 (2002)** requires that the sales tax on gasoline be devoted to transportation-related projects.

- **Proposition 49 (2002)**, supported by then-potential Republican candidate for governor Arnold Schwarzenegger, requires that several hundred million dollars be spent on after-school programs.

- **Proposition 71 (2004)** authorizes the sale of $3 billion in bonds to fund stem-cell research in the state.

- **Propositions 1A, 1B, 1C, 1D, 1E, and 84 (2006)** authorize over $40 billion in bonds to be spent on infrastructure improvements in the state. The interest on these bonds is paid from the budget each year.

- **Proposition 1A (2008)**, the "Safe, Reliable High-Speed Passenger Train Bond Act for the 21st Century," authorizes the sale of $9.9 billion in bonds to build a high-speed train connecting San Diego, Los Angeles, Bakersfield, San Francisco, and Sacramento. The interest paid for the bonds, when sold, will be $600 million per year out of the general fund.

Of these, the two that have had the most effect are Propositions 13 and 98. Proposition 13 has made the state budget more reliant on taxes that vary with the economy and less reliant on sources of income that don't vary with the economy, particularly the property tax. Proposition 98 dictated that a certain proportion of the budget, almost half when higher education is included, must be devoted to one policy area.

Because the initiative requires only a majority vote, it is relatively easy to authorize expenditures through the initiative compared with doing so through the legislature. California has become a state in which it is easy to lower taxes/budget items through the legislature or to authorize expenditures through the initiative, but it has become increasingly difficult to raise the funds to pay for basic state functions, such as higher education, health, and others. Voters in recent public opinion surveys find most items in the budget to be popular (except "welfare") but they strongly resist paying extra for any of them.

Recent California Budgets and the Budget Process

In recent years, California lawmakers and the governor have closed the budget gap with the standard techniques used in other states—incremental tax or fee increases; cuts in education, health, and social services, the largest portions of the budget; and borrowing through bond issues that are repaid over a 5- to 10-year period to cover a portion of the yearly deficit. The capital gains tax produced extra funds for the 2013–14 and 2014–15 budgets, making the process easier, although Governor Jerry Brown strongly resisted legislators' push to make agencies that had been cut substantially in the previous decade "whole" again. Governor Brown also insisted that the state begin repaying the funds borrowed during the last decade to close budget gaps.

California Forward, a bipartisan group aimed at fixing some of California's perennial budget process problems, stated in 2008 that

> the current budget process is largely a relic of the mid-20th century, with the focus on how much to increase spending (or how much to cut), rather than the value that public services bring to Californians over time. These annual budget decisions often either push California's fiscal systems toward long-term solvency or away from it. The ongoing and chronic imbalance between revenues and expenditures is one indicator of system failure. Changing how budget process decisions are made could enable public leaders to deal with the more intractable and complex problems involving the revenue system and the state-local relationship.[23]

They identify, as we have, the key problems of budgeting:

> The costs of operating state programs are growing faster than the revenue base that supports them. The revenue system is highly sensitive to changes in the economy, producing significant volatility. The single-year budgeting horizon encourages short-term fixes, rather than long-term solutions. The budget does not take a strategic

BOX 8.4 ● Federal Funds

The 2014-15 budget includes a projected $98 billion in **federal funds**, about 50 percent of which is intended for use in the health and human services category. Most of this is for Medi-Cal, California's Medicaid program (medical care for the poor). Another quarter of the total is for labor and workforce development, mostly federal funds to supplement the Unemployment Insurance program. Another large portion is for education. None of the $98 billion includes the additional $250 billion the federal government spends in California on wages and benefits for California-based federal employees, Social Security payments, Medicare payments to doctors, hospitals, and other providers (for those 65 and over, and some of those with disabilities), procurement contracts (defense and others), grants to universities and nonprofits, and so forth.[a]

Federal dollars are important to states during economic downturns, when states often cut back their budgets to meet balanced budget requirements. Federal money for unemployment insurance and stimulus packages typically increases substantially during recessions. Federal money received in California increased from $52.9 billion in 2006-07, just before the great recession of 2008-09, to $91.5 billion in 2010-11, according to the California Budget Project.[b]

The most recent reports from the state controller's office indicate that cities in California received about 5 percent of their total income in 2011-12 from federal funds, and counties received some 21 percent, about $10 billion. Counties receive more because in California they are responsible for administering state and national health and welfare programs.[c]

Does California receive more from the feds than it paid in taxes? In spite of the large amounts discussed above, the answer is "no," because no wealthy state gets back more from the federal government than it pays in taxes. Federal funds, in general, redistribute money from wealthier states to poorer ones.

[a]Legislative Analyst's Office, "An Overview of Federal Funding in California," Sacramento: Legislative Analyst's Office, (2011).
[b]California Budget Project, "How are Federal Dollars Spent in California?" Sacramento: California Budget Project (November 2011), http://www.cbp.org/publications/fed_taxesbudget_land.html (accessed 7/30/2014).
[c]Controller's Office, State of California. 2014a. "Cities Annual Report." Sacramento: Controller's Office (2014), April 23, www.sco.ca.gov/ard_locrep_annual_financial.html (accessed 7/29/14). Controller's Office, State of California, "Counties Annual Report," Sacramento: Controller's Office (January 28, 2014), www.sco.ca.gov/ard_locrep_annual_financial.html (accessed 7/29/14).

approach to ensure a return on public investments and there is a lack of public and legislative review of how money is spent.[24]

Many commentators noted the cumulative effect of the fees and caps that have been proposed more and more frequently in recent years.[25] Traditionally, California tried to supply sufficient services for all, on the principle that "if you're eligible, we'll serve you." The community colleges guarantee, for example, that any high school graduate can go to college. That principle has been shifting, though. The Schwarzenegger budget for 2004–05 in particular had caps on the number of individuals who could be served in various programs; immigrants in Medi-Cal and the program that supplies drugs for those with HIV/AIDS were both capped at the level of January 1, 2004. California's fees for students attending CSU and community colleges used to be among the lowest in the nation, but have increased substantially in recent years. Measures are often proposed as emergency measures, but few emergency measures have been repealed in the past.

In short, the lowered expectation for services has become particularly apparent in the Schwarzenegger and Jerry Brown eras, but has been in the background for the last decade or more.

The California Budgetary Process: Where Are We Now?

We are more optimistic in 2014 about California's fiscal prospects than we have been in the past. Governor Jerry Brown insisted in his first two years that California live within the means that the voters have provided, and in the next two years, he and John Pérez, former Speaker of the Assembly, insisted that the budget surpluses from the capital gains tax be used to provide the state with a rainy-day fund (Prop. 44 on the November 2014 ballot) and to repay some of the bonds that were floated to pay for the deficits of the 2000s under Governor Schwarzenegger. It would be better to reform California's tax system, but this possibility is remote; any meaningful reform would engender substantial opposition. Another positive factor is the realistic possibility of closing a major loophole in the Proposition 13 system of property tax assessment, as described in the box on p. 189–90.

The biggest fiscal problem facing the state is the voters' willingness to approve propositions (initiatives) that allocate money from the general fund or establish a special fund without having a funding source. Some of these are self-serving; others have more merit. While some initiatives divert funds from the general fund by setting up special funds, others simply state that the money for this purpose shall be "X" amount and shall be paid from the general fund, which reduces the funds available for existing programs. Higher education in particular has been hurt by these actions.

Study Guide

FOR FURTHER READING

Barrett, Katherine, Richard Greene, Michele Mariani, and Anya Sostek. "The Way We Tax." *Governing* (February 2003): 20.

Baldassare, Mark, and Christopher Hoene. *Local Budgets and Tax Policies in California and U.S. Cities: Surveys of City Officials.* San Francisco: Public Policy Institute of California, December 2004.

Baldassare, Mark, and Matthew Newman. *The State Budget and Local Health Services in California: Surveys of Local Health Officials.* San Francisco: Public Policy Institute of California, September 2005.

California Budget Project. "Budget Backgrounder, A Mini-Primer on Bonds." Sacramento: California Budget Project, February 2006.

California Budget Project. *An Incomplete Vision: Putting the Governor's Proposed 2014–15 Budget in Context.* Sacramento: California Budget Project, February 2014. www.cbp.org/pdfs/2014/140219_budget_chartbook.pdf. Accessed July 31, 2014.

California Budget Project. "Principles and Policy: A Guide to California's Tax System." Sacramento: California Budget Project, April 2013. www.cbp.org/pdfs/2013/130411_California's_Tax_System.pdf. Accessed July 31, 2014.

California Budget Project. "Who Pays Taxes in California?" Sacramento: California Budget Project, April 2014. www.cbp.org/pdfs/2014/140410_Who_Pays_Taxes.pdf. Accessed July 31, 2014.

California Taxpayers Association. "Cal-Tax: Taxes Are Heavy Burden in California." www.caltax.org/California.htm. Accessed July 30, 2014.

Johnson, Hans. "Defunding Higher Education. What are the Effects on College Enrollment?" San Francisco: Public Policy Institute of California, 2012. www.ppic.org/main /publication.asp?i=988. Accessed July 28, 2014.

League of Women Voters of California. *Guide to California Government*. 15th ed. Sacramento: League of Women Voters of California, 2013.

Legislative Analyst's Office. "California's Tax System: A Primer," April 2007. www.lao.ca.gov/2007/tax_primer/tax_primer _040907.aspx. Accessed July 30, 2014.

Oliff, Phil, Vincent Palacios, Ingrid Johnson, and Michael Leachman. "Recent Deep State Higher Education Cuts May Harm Students and the Economy for Years to Come." Washington, D.C.: Center on Budget and Policy Priorities, May 2013.

Public Policy Institute of California. "Just the Facts: California's State Budget: The Enacted 2014–15 Budget." San Francisco: Public Policy Institute of California, July 2014. www.ppic.org. Accessed July 30, 2014.

———. "Just the Facts: Proposition 13, 30 Years Later." San Francisco: Public Policy Institute of California, June 2008. www.ppic.org. Accessed July 30, 2014.

ON THE WEB

California Budget Project: www.cbp.org. Accessed July 30, 2014.

California Forward: www.cafwd.org. Accessed July 30, 2014.

Howard Jarvis Taxpayers Association: www.hjta.org. Accessed July 30, 2014.

Legislative Analyst's Office: www.lao.ca.gov. Accessed July 30, 2014.

Public Policy Institute of California: www.ppic.org. Accessed July 31, 2014.

State of California, Department of Finance, Budget Update site: www.ebudget.ca.gov. Accessed July 30, 2014.

State of California, Department of Finance: www.dof.ca.gov /research/. Accessed July 30, 2014. California statistics and demographic information.

SUMMARY

I. How is the budget formulated?
   A. Agencies send their requests to the governor each fall.
   B. The governor sends a balanced budget request to the legislature each January for the fiscal year starting the next July 1.
   C. The legislature adopts a balanced budget by June 15 each year, for the fiscal year to start July 1.
      1. In recent years, the volatility of the state's revenues has caused the budget to be substantially readjusted during the fiscal year.
   D. The governor has a line-item veto, allowing him or her to reduce any line-item dollar amount downward, even to zero. However, the governor may not raise any line item.
   E. The legislature is assisted by its own neutral budget office—the Legislative Analyst's Office.
   F. If the Assembly and state Senate versions of the budget differ, a "budget conference committee" will attempt to iron out the differences.
   G. Agencies then implement the approved budget, including studies to be carried out and presented to the legislature.

II. What is the California budget?
   A. The governor's and legislature's views of the future.
      1. The future of the state's economy (economic assumptions).
      2. The future income of the state (revenues).
      3. The future spending of the state (expenditures).
   B. The budget is at the center of the state's activities each year.

III. Revenues.
   A. Personal income tax—the largest source of income for the general fund, highly progressive, and subject to volatility because of its dependence on taxes derived from capital gains.
   B. Sales tax—the next largest source of income. Local governments can add a small amount to the state sales tax. A portion of the tax is refunded to them. Many localities have added businesses to their communities that produce sales tax, such as big-box shopping centers and automobile dealerships, specifically because of the revenues they then receive from the state.
   C. Corporate tax—the third largest source of revenues. Most corporate taxes are paid by the larger corporations.
   D. Property tax—severely limited by Proposition 13, composes only 22 percent of California's tax revenues.
   E. The California tax system is volatile compared to other states. It depends on the ups and downs of the economy and produces surges in revenue and precipitous falls when the economy booms or a recession takes place.

IV. Expenditures.
   A. Health and Human Services is the largest category, driven by the state expenditures for Medi-Cal and other health programs.
   B. Education (K–12) is the second largest single expenditure. Proposition 98 requires that 40 percent of the state general fund be designated for K–12 expenditures.
   C. Higher education is the third largest category, including expenditures for the community colleges, the California State University, and the University of California.
   D. The fourth largest category is business, transportation, and housing.

V. Limitations on the budget.
   A. The most substantial limitations have come from initiatives passed by the voters.
   B. Proposition 13, which limits the property tax to 1 percent of the value of one's house, and Proposition 98, which guarantees a certain amount to K–12 education, are the most important of these limitations.
   C. Cumulatively, the limitations have guaranteed well over half the general fund and at least half of all expenditures, giving the governor and legislature less flexibility than they would have in other states. This is precisely the intended goal of initiatives—to limit what the powers of the governor and legislature. The level of distrust the voters have for the governor and legislature is very high in California.

VI. Recent state budgets have been characterized by huge and fluctuating gaps between revenues and expenditures.

A. These have made it difficult to find the middle ground necessary to obtain a two-thirds vote in the legislature for a budget. But starting in 2011, with only a majority required, the budget was passed four years in a row more or less on time. The last two years, 2013–14 and 2014–15, had surpluses because of a surge in income tax (capital gains) revenues. Governor Brown insisted that some of this money be used for a "rainy-day" fund when revenues inevitably turn downward, and some to repay the bonds used to balance the budget during the 2000s.

VII. The box on p. 189 describes Proposition 13 and its restrictions on how property is taxed in California. Among the effects of Prop. 13 was an increased power for the state over local government and the "fiscalization of land use." Prop. 13 has resisted change, but 2014 may mark the closing of a loophole enabling large landowners and corporations to avoid the increased tax that is supposed to result when property is resold. Another proposal, to split the roll and place a higher rate on commercial property, has faced great opposition from the business community.

VIII. The future of budgeting in California?
   A. California seems to have turned a corner, with four budgets in a row passed on time and more or less balanced. The surge in revenues from the capital gains tax is being used to pay back old debt and to create a "rainy day" fund for the future.
   B. The biggest fiscal problem facing the state continues to be the willingness of the voters to approve propositions (initiatives) that allocate money from the general fund or establish a special fund without having a funding source.

PRACTICE QUIZ

1. Both the governor and the legislature are obliged by the California Constitution to pass a balanced budget.
   a) true
   b) false

2. The state of California cannot pass its budget in 2014–15 unless the Assembly and state Senate pass the budget by
   a) 50 percent plus 1 vote.
   b) 55 percent.
   c) 66.7 percent.
   d) 75 percent.

3. The state of California cannot raise state taxes unless the Assembly and state senate pass the relevant law by
   a) 50 percent plus 1 vote.
   b) 55 percent.
   c) 66.7 percent.
   d) 75 percent.

4. Proposition 13 requires
   a) property taxes to be lowered to the level when the property was last sold. Property tax values can rise 2 percent per year.

b) property taxes to be set at 1975 levels; property is reassessed when it is sold. Property tax values can rise as mush as 2 percent per year.

c) property taxes to be lowered to 1945 levels; property is reassessed when it is sold. The level of the tax can rise 3 percent per year.

d) Property taxes to be raised to the appropriate level when the property on both sides of a house or business has been sold—all the property is then reassessed at current values. The level of the tax can rise 2 percent per year if the property is not sold.

5. Proposition 98 requires education spending to be at least
   a) 50 percent of the entire state budget.
   b) 50 percent of the general fund.
   c) 33.3 percent of the general fund.
   d) 40 percent of the general fund.

6. What is the general fund?
   a) The general fund includes all revenues that are not otherwise allocated into special or bond funds, including federal revenues.
   b) The general fund includes all revenues that are not otherwise allocated into special or bond funds, not including federal revenues.
   c) The general fund includes all state revenue, including special and bond funds.
   d) The general fund includes all state revenue except bond funds, because these are used to construct state facilities and are paid back over a several decade period.

7. The governor's line-item veto allows
   a) the governor, if he or she wishes, to lower any appropriation item.

b) the governor, in conjunction with an agency, to veto any bill in its entirety.

c) the governor to "pencil out" any line or sentence in any bill.

d) the governor to raise or lower any appropriation item, including lowering the item to zero.

8. The governor's line-item veto may be overridden by a 50 percent plus one vote in both houses of the legislature.
   a) true
   b) false

9. The credit rating assigned to the state of California by Moody's, Fitch Ratings, or Standard & Poor's is important because
   a) the credit rating influences the size of California's deficit or surplus in any given fiscal year.
   b) when the credit rating goes down, the interest rate that the state pays to float its bonds goes up.
   c) when the credit rating goes up, the amount of interest the state pays goes down.
   d) all of the above

10. Indian gambling revenues have become a significant source of income for the state of California.
    a) true
    b) false

11. Until 2014, you could avoid being reassessed under Proposition 13 if the property you purchased had several owners, each owning less than 49 percent of the property.
    a) true
    b) false

CRITICAL-THINKING QUESTIONS

1. How might California's tax system be made more predictable and less dependent on the economy than it is now? How might *Governing* magazine rate your proposed changes?

2. How should the budget process in California be reformed, assuming it should be reformed? What goals are important in reforming the process, and what changes in the process might achieve those goals?

3. Should the governor have more authority in the budget process? Leaving aside the opinion you might have of the current incumbent, what reforms might help with the long-term budget process in California?

4. The other major player in the budget process is the legislature. How might the legislature's consideration of the budget be changed to make California's budget more predictable and timely?

KEY TERMS

big-box shopping centers/automobile
  dealerships (p. 187)
bond funds (p. 185)
Budget Conference Committee
  (p. 181)
capital gains (p. 187)
Department of Finance (p. 181)
federal funds (p. 197)

fiscalization of land use (p. 187)
general fund (p. 184)
governor's budget (p. 181)
Legislative Analyst's Office (p. 181)
line-item veto (p. 183)
May revise (p. 181)
Moody's, Fitch Ratings, Standard &
  Poor's ratings (p. 183)

personal income tax (p. 185)
progressive (p. 185)
regressive (p. 187)
sales tax (p. 187)
special funds (p. 185)
split roll property tax reform (p. 190)
student success fees (p. 179)
unified budget (p. 181)

9 Local Government

WHAT CALIFORNIA'S LOCAL GOVERNMENTS DO AND WHY THEY MATTER

Governing California would be hard to imagine without the more than 5,000 local governments that help run the state. Local officials and workers in cities, counties, school districts, special districts, and regional bodies all play an essential role. The complexity of the state's local government system makes it hard to generalize about what local governments do. But a short list would include the following:

- General-purpose local governments, like cities and counties, do everything from putting out fires to cleaning the streets and ensuring that the buses run on time. They protect the health, safety, welfare, and overall quality of life of all who live within their jurisdictions.

- Limited-purpose governments, such as school districts and other special districts, deliver specific public services such as public education, pest abatement, and irrigation to meet particular needs within defined territorial boundaries.

- Regional governments address problems such as air pollution and population growth that affect broad areas across many jurisdictions and that require comprehensive study and planning to solve.

- Many local governments do the actual work involved in implementing state and federal laws, from control of water quality and production of affordable housing to homeland security.

- Most local governments provide citizens with opportunities to learn about public problems, express their opinions, practice hands-on democracy, and collectively exercise some degree of popular control on issues they really care about close to home.

- Some local governments experiment and innovate to pioneer new ways of serving citizens better or improving the democratic process. Often these local initiatives spread and can have major impacts on how government works at the state and national levels.

California's local governments have been subjected to a severe stress test over the last few years, thanks to both the Great Recession and the political responses to it both inside and outside the system—a system that has evolved over decades to help different levels and facets of local government fit and work together. This chapter offers a description and analysis of the essential parts of that system and its capacity to solve problems and function effectively in serving the public.

The recession affected nearly every aspect of local government. For example, the cities of Vallejo, Stockton, and San Bernardino were driven into bankruptcy and as of November 2014 were still trying to recover. California's 435 redevelopment agencies were terminated, and city and county governments across the state are still picking up the pieces. Many local government pension programs, already in bad shape, were damaged and depleted.

On the other hand, the Occupy Movement, born out of the recession and now largely melted away, became one of the wellsprings of an emerging urban-based progressive movement now taking root in some of the state's largest cities. And a new push for effective regional government, long considered quixotic and futile, has grown out of the need to solve problems of affordable housing production, transportation, economic development, decaying public infrastructure, climate change, and social equity.

California's local governments have been on the front lines in coping with all these challenges while seizing the opportunity to test alternative solutions to old and new problems. In general, the recession, despite its negative impact on California's state and local governments, has also been the mother of invention, innovation, and democratic renewal. The goal of this chapter is to give the reader basic knowledge and appreciation of local governments in all their variety, what they do, and why they matter.

The Legal Framework: Dillon's Rule, Home Rule, and Local Powers of Governance

The U.S. Constitution assigns power and authority to the national and state governments, but it says nothing about local governments. **Counties**, **cities**, **special districts**, and other forms of local government have no inherent rights or powers. What rights and powers they do have are conferred on them by the state constitution or state legislature.

The constitutional doctrine that gives state governments ultimate authority over local governments is known as **Dillon's Rule**. In 1868, Iowa judge John F. Dillon ruled that "municipal corporations" such as counties and cities were mere "creatures of the state" and could exercise only those powers delegated to them by the state.[1] Upheld by the U.S. Supreme Court in 1903 and again in 1923, Dillon's Rule is firmly established, at least in theory, as the basic legal framework for relations between state and local governments. In practice, however, only a few states, including Alabama, Idaho, and Nebraska, demand strict obedience to Dillon's Rule and require local governments to seek their permission in order to act. California, like most states, has passed government codes and **home-rule** laws that allow significant local discretion and autonomy. Within broad limits, county and city residents can select their own form of government, manage their own elections, raise their own revenues, and choose what kinds of functions to perform and at what levels of service.[2]

In California, under the provisions of Article 11, Section 5, of the state constitution and various court rulings,[3] most of the more populous cities and counties have adopted home-rule charters. The others are designated as general law cities and counties that fall more directly under state authority and control. To get an idea of just how far home-rule powers can be taken in asserting local autonomy, see Box 9.1 on home rule and local autonomy in San Francisco.

A more practical restraint on state meddling in local government is based on the maxim that all politics is local. State legislators, after all, are elected by local constituencies to protect their local interests, and they won't last long if they forget who brought them to the dance. These political realities have kept state power over local governments in check.[4] Finally, as part of the so-called devolution revolution that began in the 1970s, federal and state authorities have increasingly delegated responsibility to local governments to solve their own problems, using their own money.

In sum, Dillon's Rule is very liberally construed in California. The state's constitutional and legal framework confers broad formal powers of local governance, especially in charter cities and counties. Home rule on paper, however, does not necessarily translate into home rule in reality. In recent years, for example, the state's budget crises, public employee pensions, and other financial stresses have seriously limited the capacity of some local governments to govern effectively and serve the public well. Formal authority minus needed resources weakens home rule and diminishes local autonomy.

BOX 9.1 ● San Francisco: Pushing the Envelope of Home-Rule Powers

As a consolidated city and county, San Francisco has pushed the limits of home-rule powers about as far as they can go. Some examples:

LIMITS ON GROWTH AND NEW LABOR STANDARDS

Since the 1980s, San Francisco has imposed increasingly severe restrictions on high-rise construction, waterfront development, and land use generally. The city also began charging developer fees to raise new local revenues for affordable housing and public-transit improvements. In 2003, the city required all city employers to pay a high minimum wage and has increased that wage annually since 2004. In 2006, the city required employers to provide paid sick leave to all employees, and in 2007, the city began offering affordable health care to all uninsured city residents.

GOVERNMENT REORGANIZATION AND ELECTORAL REFORMS

In 1995, San Francisco voters approved charter reform that consolidated the city's divided bureaucracy under mayoral authority. The following year, voters approved a change from the at-large system to a district system for electing their board of supervisors. In 2002, the city adopted ranked choice voting for district elections and citywide offices, the first major city in the nation to do so.

SOCIAL AND CULTURAL POLICY

In 1996, San Francisco passed its landmark Equal Benefits Ordinance, which requires all businesses and nonprofits that have contracts with the city to provide equal benefits to married employees and those with same-sex domestic partners. In February 2004, Mayor Gavin Newsom directed that official marriage licenses be granted to same-sex couples. A month later, more than 4,000 gay and lesbian couples had been married under the new local policy. The California Supreme Court ordered the city to halt the practice, and ruled in May 2008 that the state's ban on same-sex marriage was unconstitutional. In November 2008, state residents voted to approve Proposition 8, an initiative that eliminated by constitutional amendment the right of same-sex couples to marry. Following the California Supreme Court's ruling in 2009 that Proposition 8 was constitutional, opponents of the proposition appealed through the federal court system and eventually succeeded in defeating it in 2013, when the United States Supreme Court struck down the law on the grounds that it violated the U.S. Constitution.

As these examples illustrate, San Francisco often pushes the limits of its home-rule powers and sometimes creates a storm of national political controversy as a consequence.

SOURCES: Richard Edward DeLeon, *Left Coast City: Progressive Politics in San Francisco, 1975–1991* (Lawrence: University Press of Kansas, 1992); "San Francisco and Domestic Partners: New Fields of Battle in the Culture War," in *Culture Wars and Local Politics*, ed. Elaine B. Sharp (Lawrence: University Press of Kansas, 1999), 117–36; Richard Edward DeLeon, "Only in San Francisco? The City's Political Culture in Comparative Perspective," *SPUR Newsletter*, Report 411, November 12, 2002, www.spur.org/documents/pdf/021101_article_01.pdf (accessed 8/2/12); "San Francisco: The Politics of Race, Land Use, and Ideology," in *Racial Politics in American Cities*, 3rd ed., ed. Rufus P. Browning, Dale Rogers Marshall, and David H. Tabb (New York: Longman, 2003), 167–98; Dean E. Murphy, "San Francisco Mayor Exults in Move on Gay Marriage," *New York Times*, February 19, 2004.

County Governments

At the first meeting of the California legislature in 1850, lawmakers divided the state into 27 counties for the purpose of administering state laws. Since then many new counties have been created, mostly by subdivision. The state's current 58 counties have been with us since 1907, when the last addition, Imperial County, was carved out of the old San Diego County (see Figure 9.1). Political movements have arisen from time to time that attempted to split an existing county to make a new one. An 1894 amendment to the state constitution, however, made it virtually

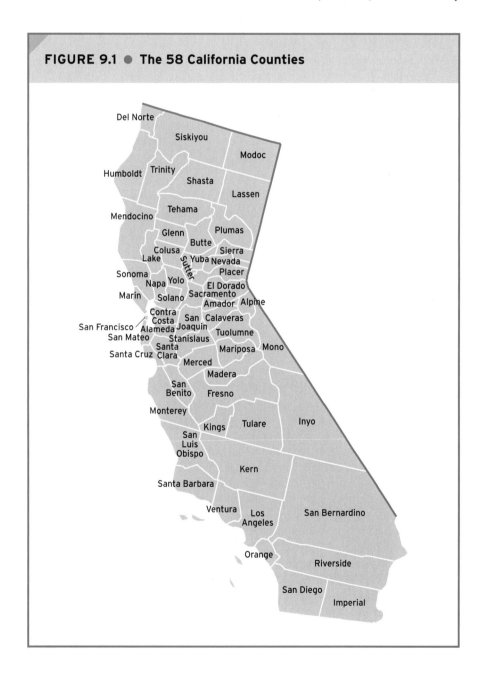

FIGURE 9.1 ● The 58 California Counties

impossible to do so by requiring a favorable majority vote in both the entire county affected and the territory of the proposed new county.[5]

California's 58 counties vary greatly in their territory, population, and demographic characteristics.

- **Territory**   Just in terms of size, the differences are vast. You could fit 427 areas the size of San Francisco County (at just 47 square miles, the smallest county in California) within the borders of San Bernardino County (the largest county in California, at 20,053 square miles). The differences in physical geography are also striking, ranging from deserts to rain forests, flat farmlands to tall mountains. Some counties are densely urban and covered with cities, whereas others are so rural that coyotes outnumber people.

- **Population**   Alpine County's grand total of 1,079 residents could all live comfortably in one San Francisco precinct. Los Angeles County, at the other extreme, is bursting with more than 10 million people, representing over 26 percent of the state's entire population. The lowest-ranking 29 counties combined contain only about 5 percent of the state's total population, while the 5 most populous counties (Los Angeles, Orange, San Diego, San Bernardino, and Riverside) hold about 54 percent of the state's total.

- **Demography**   If you tour the state's 58 counties, you'll discover vastly different social and economic worlds. The populations of some counties are relatively poor, others relatively rich. Some are mostly white, others mainly nonwhite. Some are dominated by homeowners, others—for example, San Francisco—by renters.

The Who Are Californians feature in this chapter reports the lowest- and highest-ranking counties on these and other selected indicators to illustrate the extremes observed among California's counties.

Legal Framework

The state constitution provides a general legal framework for the governing of most counties, which are known as **general-law counties**. It prescribes the number and functions of elected county officials, how they are selected, and what they may or may not do as they raise revenue, spend money, deliver services, and so on. Fourteen counties, however, have adopted a home-rule charter, which gives voters greater control over the selection of governing bodies and officers, more flexibility in raising taxes and revenues, and broader discretion in organizing to deliver services. All of the state's most populous counties and one small county, Tehama, with its 57,000 residents, are now **charter counties**. Voters can adopt a charter for their county government by a majority vote.

Long content to live without a charter, the voters of Orange County finally adopted one in March 2002. They did so mainly to prevent the governor from filling a vacancy on the county board of supervisors with his own choice of representative, an act within his authority under the general-law provisions.

San Francisco is an unusual case. It is governed under a single charter as a consolidated county and city, an arrangement that is unique in the state and rare in the country.

Who Lives in California's Counties?

Total Population

- Under 50,000
- 50,000–249,999
- 250,000–499,999
- 500,000–999,999
- 1,000,000 or more

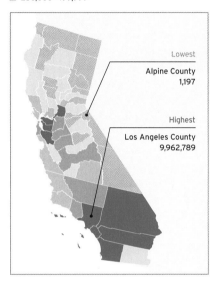

Lowest
Alpine County
1,197

Highest
Los Angeles County
9,962,789

Non-Latino White Population

- Under 30%
- 30–44.9%
- 45–59.9%
- 60–74.9%
- 75% or more

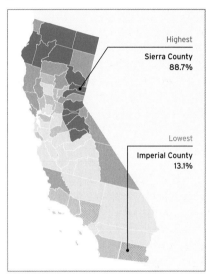

Highest
Sierra County
88.7%

Lowest
Imperial County
13.1%

California's 58 counties are extremely diverse in terms of their population size, ethnoracial composition, and economic conditions. Los Angeles, for instance, has the largest population at almost 10 million residents and the second smallest white population, at 27 percent. In other ways, Los Angeles falls roughly in the middle: 30 percent of its residents have a bachelor's degree and the median household income is $53,000.

SOURCE: U.S. Census Bureau

Bachelor's Degree or Higher

- Under 15%
- 15–24.9%
- 25–34.9%
- 35–44.9%
- 45% or more

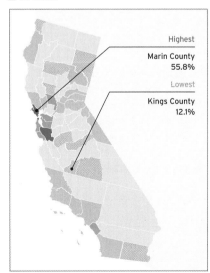

Highest
Marin County
55.8%

Lowest
Kings County
12.1%

Median Household Income

- Under $40,000
- $40,000–$49,999
- $50,000–$59,999
- $60,000–$69,999
- $70,000 or more

Lowest
Lake County
$33,219

Highest
Santa Clara County
$91,425

forcriticalanalysis

1. Why are the counties of California so different from one another? Are the variables related to each other, or to other factors not included here?

2. How do you think this range of ethnoracial diversity, educational attainment, and economic conditions affects California politics? How might this diversity affect local politics vs. state politics?

County charters vary widely in content and in the range of powers claimed for local control. Anything that goes unmentioned within a charter is governed by the general law.

County Government Organization

In all counties except San Francisco, an elected five-member board of supervisors exercises both legislative and executive authority. Given the extremes in the size of county populations, it shouldn't surprise you that small five-member boards yield huge disparities in political representation. For example, each board member in tiny Alpine County represents, on average, only 216 residents. In mammoth Los Angeles County, on the other hand, each board member represents more than 2 million people, nearly equivalent to the entire population of New Mexico.

County boards of supervisors, whose members are elected by districts for staggered four-year terms, not only pass laws, called **ordinances** at the local level, but also control and supervise the departments charged with administering them. This combination of legislative and executive authority gives county supervisors great power.

Several departments report directly to the board of supervisors or are headed by elected officials, but work with the chief executive office through the clusters. These are assessor, auditor-controller, executive office of the board of supervisors, county counsel (operations), community development commission (community and municipal services); sheriff, district attorney, and fire (public safety).

There is an exception: In the consolidated city and county government of San Francisco, an elected 11-member board of supervisors has legislative authority. An independently elected mayor has executive authority and some control, shared with many boards and commissions, over the bureaucracy.

In addition to the board of supervisors, other elected or appointed county officers required by general law include a sheriff, who enforces the law in areas outside the cities; a district attorney; and an assessor. A 1998 constitutional amendment consolidated municipal and superior trial courts into a single layer of superior court judges elected by county voters. Elections for all offices are nonpartisan. In terms of appointed positions, charter counties have considerable latitude in creating departments and agencies to serve their needs, either by charter provision or by ordinance. Other offices are required or authorized by state law. Some charter counties, like Los Angeles County, have appointed a chief executive officer to manage their sprawling bureaucracies under board supervision.

Figure 9.2 shows Placer County's organizational chart, which is very simple and typical of counties with small populations. By way of contrast, Figure 9.3 shows Los Angeles County's organization chart. It illustrates the complexity of local government authority and responsibility that can be found in counties with large and diverse populations.

County Government Functions and Responsibilities

County governments have major functions and responsibilities, most of them mandated by state or federal law, especially outside the jurisdictions of cities. County responsibilities include bridges and highways, public safety, public health, employment, parks and recreation, welfare and public assistance, public records, tax collection, general government, court administration, and land use. In the largest counties, the public workforce required to manage this and the budget needed

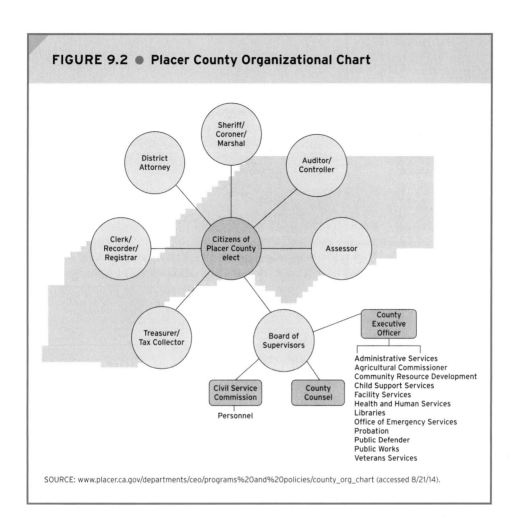

FIGURE 9.2 ● Placer County Organizational Chart

Sheriff/ Coroner/ Marshal

District Attorney

Auditor/ Controller

Clerk/ Recorder/ Registrar

Citizens of Placer County elect

Assessor

Treasurer/ Tax Collector

Board of Supervisors

County Executive Officer

Civil Service Commission

County Counsel

Personnel

Administrative Services
Agricultural Commissioner
Community Resource Development
Child Support Services
Facility Services
Health and Human Services
Libraries
Office of Emergency Services
Probation
Public Defender
Public Works
Veterans Services

SOURCE: www.placer.ca.gov/departments/ceo/programs%20and%20policies/county_org_chart (accessed 8/21/14).

to pay for it can be truly massive. In 2014, for example, Los Angeles County had 105,348 employees and an adopted budget of $26.35 billion.[6]

Decisions on land-use policy are perhaps the most important and controversial ones a county board of supervisors can make. If you're ever in the mood to watch a good political fight, attend a typical county board of supervisors meeting in a place like Napa County or San Diego County. Areas like these still have plenty of open land outside the cities and fast-growing populations that fuel a demand for new housing construction, schools, and public infrastructure (sewers, highways, etc.). Landowners and developers typically badger the county board of supervisors to allow them to build, often with the result that conservationists, environmentalists, and other groups mobilize in opposition to push them back.

For example, in January 2010, Napa County supervisors were the target of several developer and environmentalist lawsuits related to land use. The economic downturn in the Napa Valley wine industry had created pressure to convert agricultural lands into homes. The developers sued the county to block overregulation of such lands and to protect private property rights. The environmentalists sued the county, charging that officials were failing to protect such lands from development.[7]

FIGURE 9.3 ● Los Angeles County Organizational Chart

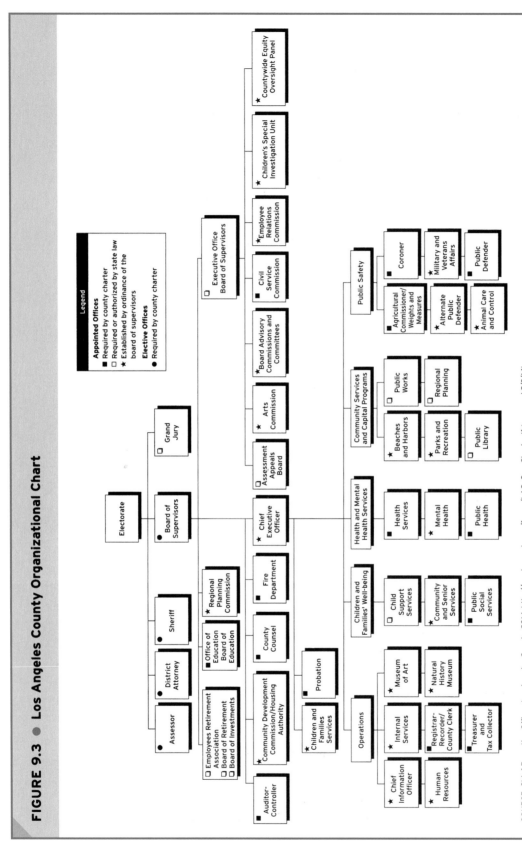

SOURCE: *Chief Executive Officer, Los Angeles County*, 2014, http://ceo.lacounty.gov/forms/LAC_Org_Chart.pdf (accessed 9/3/14).

NOTE: Several departments report directly to the Board of Supervisors or are headed by elected officials, but work with the Chief Executive Office through the clusters. These are: assessor, auditor-controller, executive office of the board of supervisors, county counsel (Operations); community development commission (community services and capital programs); Children and Family Services (Children and Families' Well-Being); sheriff, district attorney, fire, Probation (Public Safety).

More recently, on July 31, 2012, the Riverside County Board of Supervisors met to decide whether to "fast-track" approval of Granite Construction's application to build a surface mine known as Liberty Quarry near the small town of Temecula. Fast-tracking would allow the project to skip the standard review of the county planning commission and thus expedite the board's final decision. The debate at the crowded public meeting was impassioned on both sides. Orange-shirted opponents faced off against green-shirted supporters. Representatives of the chamber of commerce, labor unions, and other groups backed the proposal, arguing that the quarry would stimulate the local economy and create badly needed jobs. Temecula city officials, environmentalists, and leaders of the Pechanga Band of Luiseño Indians contended that the quarry would pollute the air, wreck the economy, and destroy a nearby sacred tribal site. One supervisor called Liberty Quarry "the most divisive project in county history." The board voted 3-to-2 to fast-track approval, prompting cheers from the green shirts and cries of outrage from the orange shirts. This story then ended abruptly and happily for all concerned. On November 15, 2012, just days before the board was scheduled to give its final approval, leaders of the Pechanga Band announced that they had reached an agreement with Granite Construction to purchase the Liberty Quarry site for $3 million and pay the firm an additional $17.35 million to cover its project costs. Granite was permitted to build its mine elsewhere, miles from Temecula and the sacred tribal lands. The Pechanga Band promised to preserve the original site as it was. Temecula officials pledged to drop their lawsuit to stop the board from voting on a controversial decision it no longer had to make.[8]

As California's population continues to grow and spread from the cities into the state's remaining farmlands and rural areas, you can expect to see more land-use battles erupting in the political arenas of county governments.

Local Agency Formation Commissions

All 58 California counties have a **local agency formation commission (LAFCo)**, whose members are appointed by the county board of supervisors. These commissions play a critical role in resolving conflicts among the many local governments that often compete with one another for power and resources within their county jurisdictions. A county's LAFCo is responsible for:

- reviewing and approving the incorporations of new cities, the formation of new special districts, and any proposed changes of jurisdictional boundaries, including annexations and detachments of territory, secessions, consolidations, mergers, and dissolutions.

- reviewing and approving contractual service agreements between local governments and between local governments and the private sector.

- defining the official spheres of influence for each city and special district.

- initiating proposals for consolidation, dissolution, mergers, and reorganizations if such changes seem necessary or desirable.

These powerful commissions are especially busy in counties that are rocked by large-scale land-use battles, such as Napa County and Riverside County, or that teem with masses of people and a multitude of governments, such as Los Angeles County. In the not-so-distant past, LAFCos were also heavily engaged in facilitating the birth of new cities, but more recently have been called upon to preside at their funerals (see the case of Jurupa Valley below).[9]

City Governments

Legal Framework

Like counties, California's cities derive their powers as municipal corporations from the state constitution and state legislature. Within that legal framework, as of August 2014, the state's 482 incorporated cities fell into three categories: **general-law cities** (372), **charter cities** (109), and the unique case of San Francisco's consolidated city and county. The California Government Code, enacted by the legislature, specifies the general powers and structure of general-law cities. Broader home-rule powers are granted to charter cities, giving citizens more direct control over local affairs. Under these different arrangements, all cities have the power to legislate, as long as their local policies don't conflict with state or federal law. They have the power to raise revenues, levy taxes, charge license and service fees, and borrow. They may also hire personnel as needed; exercise police powers to enforce local, state, and federal laws; and condemn property for public use.

Incorporation and Dissolution

The state grants powers to cities, and in that sense cities are indeed creatures of the state. But cities themselves are created only by the request, and with the consent, of the residents in a given area. In California, this process of **municipal incorporation** is typically initiated by a citizen petition or by a resolution of the county board of supervisors. Landowner petitions are also possible but rare. Some of the more important reasons that motivate residents to seek incorporation are:

- to limit or accelerate population growth.
- to provide more or better-quality services than those provided by the county.
- to prevent annexation by a nearby city.
- to create a unit of government more responsive to local needs and concerns.
- to escape the tax and spending burdens imposed by county government rule.

A petition for municipal incorporation must be submitted to the county's LAFCo. The LAFCo panel reviews the proposed plans for the new city, its boundaries, service provisions, governing capacity, and financial viability. The LAFCo also studies the likely financial and other impacts of the proposed incorporation on neighboring local governments, including the county itself. If the petition for incorporation survives this initial review and a later public hearing and possible protests, it moves to an election. If a majority of voters living within the boundaries of the proposed new city approve, a new city is legally born.[10] The rate of incorporation of new cities has fallen dramatically in recent years. Only 9 have incorporated since 1999, raising the total number of cities in 2014 to 482.[11]

As the case of California's youngest city, Jurupa Valley, will demonstrate, the substantial shift in legal obligations and fiduciary responsibilities inherent to incorporation can be difficult for municipalities to handle, particularly in times of widespread financial stress. Jurupa Valley, a community of 91,000 people located in Riverside County, formally became an incorporated, general-law city in July 2011. The community gained home-rule powers and greater local control over land use and service provision within its borders. The summer of 2011 proved an inopportune time for the city of Jurupa Valley to be born, however, as the governor and state legislators faced yet another budget crisis. Only days after the community's incorporation, the state government diverted all of its vehicle license fee revenues away from local governments to bolster budgets for prisons and other law enforcement programs at the state level. This sudden diversion of funds hurt all California cities, but it hit Jurupa Valley especially hard; city officials had counted on their share of that money, totaling several millions of dollars, to make ends meet. On January 16, 2014, after months of cutting staffing and services to the bone while searching in vain for state financial support, Jurupa Valley's city council members voted unanimously to petition Riverside County's LAFCo for municipal dissolution and a return to county rule.

It was the first such petition received by the state in more than forty years, and it triggered a legal process of disincorporation that could take up to two years to complete.[12] A local reporter warned her readers of some of the implications: "If home rule goes away, decision-making on land-use and other issues like code enforcement, public works and road repairs will revert to Riverside County. Traffic enforcement will be handled by the California Highway Patrol."[13]

By late summer 2014, officials of the financially beleaguered cities of Adelanto (San Bernardino County) and Guadalupe (Santa Barbara County) were reluctantly considering following in Jurupa Valley's footsteps.[14] If this trend continues, it seems likely that more California cities will die in the future than be born.

City Government Functions and Responsibilities

City governments provide a wide range of services and facilities that directly affect the lives of their residents: fire and police protection; street construction and maintenance; sewage and waste disposal; health, social, and recreational programs; and planning and zoning to determine land use consistent with the community's needs and values. Most city governments provide water, and some run public transit systems. A few, such as Los Angeles and Sacramento, own and manage municipal electricity or natural gas utilities.

Residents in most cities are content if basic services such as police, fire, and waste management are provided reliably and efficiently, either directly by the municipality itself or, as in many smaller cities, by contracting services from other local governments and the private sector.[15] In some places, however, residents demand more from their city government than just the basics. In some cities, business leaders and entrepreneurs often pressure city hall to promote rapid economic growth and development. In other cities, such as Berkeley and San Francisco, community activists often pressure city hall to limit growth and development and to pursue ambitious social agendas on the world stage.

City Government Revenues and Expenditures

As shown in Table 9.1, the typical city budget in California relies most heavily on current service charges and taxes for most of its revenues. Most of what it spends goes toward public safety, community development and health, public utilities, and transportation. We will have more to say about city finances later in this chapter in the context of the state's continuing budget crisis.

Forms of City Government and the Legacy of Progressive Structural Reforms

The overall vision and structural reforms advanced by the Progressives nearly a century ago have had an enduring impact on the form of municipal government in California. Progressive reformers sought to replace the corrupt bosses running partisan, ward-based, big-city political machines with government by reputable civic leaders and nonpartisan experts managing local affairs in the public interest. The structural reforms implementing that vision called for:

- strong managers and weak mayors.
- nonpartisan elections.
- at-large council elections.
- the tools of direct democracy (the initiative, referendum, and recall).

Other Progressive reforms included civil service (merit-based) systems of municipal employment and, especially in the larger cities, professionally run city planning commissions and departments.[16] Reformers were particularly successful in the southwestern states, where populations were growing fast and new cities

---

TABLE 9.1 ● Typical Sources and Uses of Municipal Funding (Excluding City and County of San Francisco)

Revenues (%)		Expenses (%)	
Current service charges	35.6%	Public safety	26.4%
Taxes	41.5	Community development	16.9
Intergovernmental agencies	9.3	and health	
Special benefit assessments,	2.3	Public utilities	20.5
licenses and permits, fines		Transportation	18.0
and forfeitures		Culture and leisure	9.5
Revenues from use of money	3.7	General government	7.8
and property		Other	0.9
Other revenues and other	7.5		
financing sources			

SOURCE: California State Controller's Office, www.sco.ca.gov/Files-ARD-Local/LocRep/1112cities.pdf (accessed 9/3/14).

were popping up everywhere, isolated from the influence of eastern-style partisanship and urban machine politics.[17] Municipalities that have all or most of these institutional features are known as **reform governments**. Most medium-size American cities and nearly all of California's cities qualify for that label.

COUNCIL-MANAGER PLAN VERSUS MAYOR-COUNCIL SYSTEM Under the **council-manager** form of government, the voters elect a city council, which in turn appoints a professionally trained city manager to run the administration. The city manager directly controls the bureaucracy and supervises the performance of department heads. The council restricts itself to legislative policy making, while retaining the ultimate authority to fire or replace the appointed manager. Nearly all small- and medium-sized California cities, as well as San Jose and Sacramento, are governed by the council-manager plan.[18] Mayors are directly elected in about a third of these cities, but they perform mainly ceremonial duties and have no independent executive powers, such as the veto or budget control. (A partial exception is San Jose, whose mayor has very limited control of the budget and bureaucracy.)

The rest of California's cities are governed by **mayor-council systems**. Most are very small cities that can't afford a professional city manager and have weak mayors of the purely ceremonial type. Most of the state's largest cities, however, have strong mayor-council systems in which the mayor is elected independently of the council and serves as the city's overall chief executive. These are often called strong-mayor systems because the mayor proposes the city's budget, appoints department heads, and has veto power over council legislation. The council (or, in the case of San Francisco, the board of supervisors) is responsible for legislative policy making. Typically, as in Los Angeles and San Francisco, various appointive boards and commissions set overall policy and supervise administration of important city departments, such as police and fire, thus limiting the mayor's direct control of the bureaucracy.

In recent years, the voters in some council-manager cities have approved the switch to a strong-mayor system to make local government decision making more accountable, nimble, and responsive to changing political environments. When former governor Jerry Brown ran for mayor of Oakland in 1998, for example, he insisted that the voters support Measure X, which he had helped to draft, that would give the mayor the veto, control over budget preparation, and extensive appointment powers while reducing the then-powerful city manager to an administrator under mayoral authority. Oakland's voters approved the measure by a 3-to-1 margin and elected Brown as the city's new mayor. In 2004, San Diego's voters followed suit, changing one of the nation's largest council-manager systems into a strong-mayor system on a trial run basis, and voted again in 2010 to make that new system permanent. On November 4, 2014, however, Sacramento's voters soundly rejected (57 to 43 percent) Measure L, a proposed charter amendment that would have changed the city's current council-manager plan to a strong-mayor system. It seems likely that Sacramento and San Jose will remain dug in as the state's two largest cities still sticking with the council-manager system in the years ahead.

In practice, formal and informal power arrangements vary widely across both the council-manager and mayor-council systems. Personal ambition, political skill, and leadership style are key factors that influence the degree of power accorded to a given mayor or manager to run local government and shape public policy.[19]

NONPARTISAN ELECTIONS California law requires that all local elections be officially **nonpartisan**. In nonpartisan elections, no information about a candidate's political party membership is shown on the ballot. In practice, of course, many local contests are fiercely partisan. And they have become even more so in the nation's big cities, where economic hard times and long-term demographic and social changes have shifted their partisan complexion from "red" (Republican) toward "blue" (Democratic). In officially nonpartisan systems, such as San Francisco and San Diego, the voters will not see a "D" or an "R" next to the candidates' names on the ballot, but the partisan combat is sharp and often plays out on a national stage.

For example, in November 2010, Democrat Bob Filner faced Republican Carl DeMaio in San Diego's nonpartisan runoff election for mayor. When Filner won, becoming San Diego's first Democratic mayor since 1992 and second since 1971, Democratic Party leaders around the country were proud, loud, and triumphant about this breakthrough in what had long been a Republican urban stronghold. The national media spotlight tracked Mayor Filner's populist initiatives and bold political moves in taking on the city's Republican establishment. All of that turned sour only months after Filner's inauguration when three former supporters alleged that Filner had sexually harassed them and other women. The national Democratic Party's support turned to strong condemnation, as high-profile Democrats Barbara Boxer, Dianne Feinstein, Nancy Pelosi, and Debbie Wasserman Schultz, along with all nine members of San Diego's city council, demanded Filner's resignation. In August 2013, shortly after the launch of a signature-gathering campaign to force a recall election, Filner resigned. In November, Republican Kevin Faulconer won a special (nonpartisan) election and became the city's new mayor.[20]

The Progressive Era reformers had pushed for nonpartisan elections as a means to insulate the important business of local government from the distracting and corrupting influence of partisan politics. As California's big cities increasingly become arenas for national party politics and platforms for mobilizing insurgencies, and as the trend away from professional city management toward greater mayoral power continues in local government, the practical effect of nonpartisan elections is nearly insignificant.

AT-LARGE VERSUS DISTRICT COUNCIL ELECTIONS More than 90 percent of California cities conduct at-large council elections, in which voters elect council members citywide rather than by districts or wards.[21] Under the **at-large elections** system, for example, if a number of candidates compete for one of the three vacant seats on the council, all of the city's voters have the opportunity to vote for any three of them, and the top three vote-getters are declared the winners. About 5 percent of cities use the **district election** method, which divides the city into districts and requires the voters in each district to elect one of the candidates running in that district to represent them on the council. The remaining cities—Oakland is an example—use some hybrid combination of at-large and district elections to elect their councils.

Local governments change their electoral systems infrequently if at all, and usually they do so after being pressured by political reform movements or litigation. In 2000, for example, San Francisco switched from at-large to district elections for electing its board of supervisors. The city's move to the district system was a response to voter demand for greater representation of neighborhoods and minority groups, reduced influence of big money on elections, and a wider field of candidates who otherwise could not afford to run citywide campaigns.[22] Of course, the district system by itself doesn't guarantee a more neighborhood-oriented council, less costly campaigns, or political life on a smaller scale. The 15 members of the Los Angeles City Council, for example, are elected by districts. But each council member represents nearly a quarter of a million residents on average and must run expensive campaigns over vast territories to get elected.

The California Voting Rights Act of 2001 (CVRA) has catalyzed a recent wave of lawsuits throughout the state, with plaintiffs claiming racial disparities in representation under at-large systems. The CVRA expands on the federal Voting Rights Act of 1965 by eliminating the need for minority plaintiffs to identify a particular geographic district in their city in which a minority is sufficiently concentrated to result in a majority of voters. This crucial distinction makes it easier for plaintiffs to claim that at-large elections dilute their votes. CVRA-based lawsuits by minority groups in Modesto, Compton, Anaheim, Escondido, Whittier, Palmdale, and other cities have been successful, and more are coming. Many lawsuits are now calling for court mandates to require local governments, including community colleges and school districts, to change from at-large to district-based election systems. Local governments using at-large elections in racially diverse communities have been put on the defensive, and it's not hard to see why: consider the egregious case of Palmdale, whose mayor, according to the *Los Angeles Times*, could not "explain why Palmdale, whose population is almost 55% Latino and nearly 15% black, has elected only one Latino and no African Americans to its council."[23]

The switch from at-large to district elections, of course, offers no guarantee of a remedy for underrepresentation of minorities. Such a change can actually make things worse, at least in the short run, as illustrated by San Francisco's move from at-large to district elections in 2000. The election that year produced a progressive supermajority on the 11-member board of supervisors. Soon to be known as the "Class of 2000," it passed a slew of trailblazing policy reforms, including citywide mandates requiring employers to pay what is still the nation's highest minimum wage, provide employees with paid sick leave, contribute to the funding of the city's own health care system, and so on. However, the resulting shuffle in board membership did nothing to improve minority representation: Representation of Asian Americans, who make up about a third of the city's population, dropped from 3 to 1; Latino representation increased from 1 to 2 members; African American representation stayed the same at 1; LGBT members fell from 3 to 2, and, most glaringly, 5 women dwindled to only 1. These results were in part the fallout of a neighborhood revolt against Mayor Willie Brown and the displacement resulting from the dotcom boom of that era, conflicts in which identity politics were virtually suspended. These imbalances in representation have since been corrected over a series of elections, and board membership now looks more like the population of San Francisco.[24]

DIRECT DEMOCRACY At the local level of government, just as at the state level, ordinary citizens have access to the tools of **direct democracy** (the initiative, referendum, and recall) bequeathed to them by Progressive Era reformers. Specifically, if citizens gather the required number of valid signatures on formal petitions, they can:

- initiate direct legislation, including proposed ordinances and charter amendments, by placing such measures on the ballot for voter approval.

- suspend implementation of council legislation until the voters approve it at a referendum election.

- subject incumbent elected officials to a recall vote and possible dismissal before the next scheduled regular election.

Local referenda are quite rare. Local recall elections are also rare, but occur more often than statewide recalls. For example, in the contentious town of Pacifica, voters have successfully petitioned for five recall elections over the last 35 years. The use of local ballot initiatives, however, is much more frequent and widespread, although not nearly to the extent observed at the state level. Direct legislation by citizen ballot initiative has become almost routine in a few cities, such as San Francisco, especially around land-use issues. Citizen initiatives appear on ballots less frequently in most other cities, but they are not uncommon. A 2002 study, for example, found that only 43 of 387 cities surveyed (11 percent) had even one citizen initiative on their most recent ballot.[25] A replication of that survey in 2014 would probably show a higher rate of citizen initiatives, given the rise of contentious politics and anti-establishment movements at all levels of American government.

Legal scholars Matthew Melone and George Nation III offer an important insight into the relationship between direct democracy and representative government:

> The importance of direct democracy is not diminished by the fact that representative democracy is the primary form of government because the importance of direct democracy is not determined by the frequency of its use. . . . [T]he mere fact that the tools of direct democracy are readily available in a state prevents many of the abuses associated with representative government despite the fact that such tools are actually used infrequently. . . . The institutions of representative democracy and the representatives themselves function better due to the possibility of the voters' resort to direct democracy.[26]

This point seems particularly salient in San Francisco politics. While the city's labor and community activists have made extensive use of the tools of direct democracy over the years, they have probably achieved more success by credibly threatening to use these tools than by actually using them. To cite one example, in April 2014 leaders of the Service Employees International Union (SEIU) 1021 announced they would mount a signature-gathering campaign to place a proposal on the November 2014 ballot to raise the minimum wage. Mayor Ed Lee, who up until this point appeared to be dragging his feet on his earlier promise to raise the city's minimum wage, moved quickly to forge a consensus measure for the ballot that would give SEIU 1021 much but not all that it demanded. The union

BOX 9.2 ● The Brown Act

The Ralph M. Brown Act of 1953 required that "all meetings of the legislative body of a local agency shall be open and public, and all persons shall be permitted to attend any meeting of the legislative body of a local agency, except as otherwise provided in this chapter." The intent of the Brown Act, also known as the "open meetings law," was to support transparency and prevent secret meetings and backroom dealings of local government officials conducting public business. (The Bagley-Keene Act of 1967 later extended the same open-meetings requirement to state government agencies.) The Brown Act did allow closed meetings for personnel decisions and the like to protect community and individual rights. Critics such as Peter Scheer, however, argue that the original narrow exemptions were stretched too far in the 1990s to include meetings negotiating local collective-bargaining agreements, which the public may see only after they are signed—often too late to raise hard questions and objections about the financial implications. Despite its limitations, the Brown Act is consistent with the state's Progressive reform tradition. It gives citizens timely access to vital information about what local government officials say and do in their name.

SOURCE: League of California Cities, *Open & Public IV: A Guide to the Ralph M. Brown Act* (2007); Peter Scheer, "Public Employee Unions: Losing the Image Battle," *San Francisco Chronicle*, June 13, 2010, p. N5.

then stopped the campaign and backed Mayor Lee's alternative, which passed in November with overwhelming voter support.[27]

Also see Box 9.2 on the Brown Act, the "open meetings law" that gives citizens yet another tool of direct democracy for becoming more informed about the decision-making process and for holding their local government officials accountable.

LOCAL VOTER TURNOUT AND POLITICAL REPRESENTATION Despite the surge in voter turnout in the 2008 presidential election, the overall trend in voter participation since 1960 has been gradually downwards in national elections (see Chapter 4). Voter turnout rates in California's local elections tend to be much lower. A survey conducted in 2002, the most recent available, found that only 48 percent of a city's registered voters, on average, had cast ballots in the most recent council elections. It also revealed that "California residents who are highly educated, wealthy, old, and white are much more likely to participate than residents who are poor, young, less educated, and nonwhite."[28] As noted in Chapter 4, that same pattern holds for voter turnout in high-profile presidential election years, but the available evidence suggests that the active electorates (eligible voters who actually register and vote) in strictly local elections are smaller in size and even more demographically unrepresentative.

Certain institutional reforms could boost voter turnout and eventually produce more representative and responsive local government. Rescheduling local nonconcurrent elections to coincide with high-turnout presidential elections, for example, would likely have a major impact. Doing so in any given city, according to one study, "could well mean a doubling of voter turnout."[29]

Similar reasoning lies behind one of the arguments for ranked-choice voting, also known as the alternative vote or "instant runoff voting," which San Francisco adopted in 2002 (soon followed by Berkeley, Oakland, and San Leandro). Under ranked-choice voting, voters in the November general election rank the candidates for an office by order of preference (first choice, second choice, and so on). When all the ballots are counted, if no candidate receives a majority of first-choice preferences, the candidate receiving the fewest is dropped from the list and his or her ballots are transferred to the remaining candidates according to voters' rankings. (If a voter's lower-ranked candidates aren't among the survivors, his or her ballot is classified as "exhausted" and removed from the transfer flow of "continuing" ballots to be counted again in the next round.) Another tally is taken of continuing ballots, and if there is still no majority winner, the process is repeated until a majority winner is declared.

This system presents an alternative to the typical local election in California, in which the top two vote-getters face off in a typically low-turnout, low-interest runoff election in December if no candidate receives a majority of the votes cast in November. Under the ranked-choice system, these elections can be avoided.

Some critics of ranked-choice voting argue that many voters actually prefer December runoffs because they winnow the field of candidates and sharpen the voter's focus on only two choices. Further, voter turnout for mayoral elections and other high-profile local contests is sometimes even higher in the December runoff than in the November general election. These kinds of debates about the merits of ranked-choice voting and other proposed electoral reforms will continue.[30] This is considered a benefit by scholars who view local governments as ideal "laboratories of democracy" where innovations like ranked-choice voting can be tried and tested before being recommended to a wider public.[31]

Finally, and more controversially, a case can be made for greater political representation of noncitizens in local government. Noncitizens are not only tolerated but respected in many California cities, and their voices are heard and heeded by local officials. Leaders of immigrant-serving nonprofit agencies, community-based organizations, and worker centers are highly politically active in self-declared "sanctuary cities" such as San Francisco, where their efforts have led to assured equal access to city services regardless of immigrant status, the provision of municipal identification cards, and passage of wage-theft legislation to deter the economic exploitation of this vulnerable population. In 2004, with the knowledge that the California Constitution banned noncitizens from voting, advocacy groups and a broad coalition of supporters advanced a ballot measure giving noncitizen parents of children enrolled in the public schools the right to vote in the city's school board elections. That measure failed, just barely, in 2004, and it failed again in 2010 by a slightly larger margin. In the absence of comprehensive immigration reform at the federal government level, however, these kinds of initiatives in California's local laboratories of democracy will likely continue.[32]

Special Districts

Special districts are limited-purpose local governments. They fill the need or desire for services that general-purpose governments such as counties and cities cannot or will not provide. If residents or landowners desire new or better services, they can take steps to establish a special district to pay for them. As a popular guide to special districts notes: "Special districts *localize* the costs and benefits of public services. Special districts allow local citizens to obtain the services they want at a price they are willing to pay."[33] Examples of special districts include fire protection districts, cemetery districts, water districts, recreation and park districts, storm water drainage and conservation districts, irrigation districts, and mosquito abatement districts.

School and Community College Districts

California's **school and community college districts** are a unique type of special district. As of 2012–13 there were 1,028 K–12 school districts in the state, a number whittled down, mostly by consolidation, from the 1,630 districts that operated in 1962.[34] School districts derive their authority from the state's Education Code and are governed by locally elected school boards. Each board sets general policies and appoints a superintendent as chief executive officer, who serves at the pleasure of the board. The superintendent has overall responsibility for managing the system and its various schools and programs. In 2014, the state's community college system of two-year public institutions comprised 112 colleges organized into 72 districts. Serving more than 2.1 million students, it is the largest system of higher education in the nation. In 1988, the California legislature enacted Assembly Bill 1725, giving community colleges status as institutions of higher education. AB 1725 also strengthened the advisory role of local academic senates and of the Student Senate for California Community Colleges in working with state government officials to make higher-education policy. Each community college district is governed by a locally elected board of trustees that sets general policies and appoints a chancellor as chief executive officer. As discussed elsewhere in this book, the state of California's K–14 public education system and especially the financial crises that surround it continue to be a major focus of policy debate and political battle.

Nonschool Special Districts

Excluding the school districts, the state had 4,711 special districts in 2011–12 according to the most recent California State Controller's report on special districts.[35] These special districts can be classified in three different ways: single-purpose versus multiple-purpose special districts, enterprise versus nonenterprise special districts, and independent versus dependent special districts.

- About 85 percent of the state's special districts perform a single function, such as sewage management, water management, fire protection, or mosquito abatement. The others are multifunctional, such as the state's more than 800 County Service Areas (CSAs), which provide two or more services, such as enhanced recreation services and extended police protection.

- About one in four special districts are **enterprise districts**, which are run like businesses and charge **user fees** for services. Nearly all airport, harbor and port, transit, water, waste, and hospital districts are enterprise districts of this sort. In FY 2011–12, the state's enterprise districts generated a total of $26.7 billion in user fees.[36] The state's many nonenterprise districts provide public services such as fire protection and pest control that benefit the entire community, not just individual residents. Typically, property taxes rather than user fees pay the costs.

- About two-thirds of the state's special districts are **independent districts**. An independent district is governed by its own separate board of directors appointed by an authorizing agency or elected directly by the district's voters. Dependent districts are governed by existing legislative bodies. Nearly all CSAs, for example, are governed by a county board of supervisors.

These three ways of classifying special districts are not mutually exclusive, and examples of all possible combinations exist.

Legal Framework

Like all local governments in the state, special districts must conform to the state constitution and the legislature's Government Code. Statutory authority for special districts derives from either a principal act or a special act of the state legislature. A *principal act* is a general law that applies to all special districts of a given type. For example, the Fire Protection District Law of 1987 in the state's Health and Safety Code governs all 386 fire districts. About 60 of these principal law statutes are on the books and can be used to create a special district anywhere in the state. Another 120 or so *special acts* have been passed by the legislature to adapt a special district's structure, financing, and authority to unique local circumstances. The Alameda County Flood Control and Water District, for example, was formed under such a special act.

How Special Districts Are Created

To form a special district, the voters in the proposed district must apply to their county's LAFCo. After the LAFCo reviews and approves the proposal, it moves to an election in which only the voters residing inside the proposed district boundaries may vote. A simple majority is required for approval in most cases. A two-thirds majority is required if new special taxes are involved. The total number of special districts has decreased slightly in recent years, from 4,776 in 2007–08 to 4,711 in 2011–12, according to the latest available reports. However, the modest net change in total numbers can conceal a considerable churning of old districts dying and new ones being born. During the 2011–12 fiscal year, for example, 13 new districts were created and 74 were dissolved.[37]

The Advantages and Disadvantages of Special Districts

The advantages claimed for special districts by advocates include:[38]

- the flexibility that such districts allow in tailoring the level and quality of service to citizen demands.

- the linking of costs to benefits, so that those who don't benefit from a district's services don't have to pay for them.

- the greater responsiveness of special districts to their constituents, who often reside in smaller geographic areas of larger city and county jurisdictions.

The disadvantages of special districts include:

- the overlapping of jurisdictions and the resulting duplication of services already provided by cities and counties or by other special districts.

- the reduced incentives for needed regional planning, especially in providing water, sewer, and fire protection services, which are typically offered by a host of special districts governed by independent boards without any central coordination.

- the decreased accountability that results from the sheer multiplicity of limited special districts, which overwhelms the average citizen's ability to find out who is in charge of delivering specific services.

Some of the critics who make these kinds of arguments would abolish most special districts and centralize their functions in established general-purpose city and county governments. One contends that special districts "make a mockery of the natural connections that people have with a specific place. Special districts lie beyond the commonsense experience of most citizens; their very purpose is to divorce a narrow element of policy from the consideration of those charged with the maintenance of the common interest."[39]

Regional Governments

A number of **regional governments** have formed in California to cope with problems such as air pollution, waste management, growth control, affordable housing production, and transportation gridlock—problems that affect large geographical areas and millions of people living in many different city and county jurisdictions. Some of these regional bodies have strong regulatory powers. Others are mainly advisory in function.

Regulatory Regional Governments

Examples of state **regulatory regional governments** include the California Coastal Commission, the South Coast Air Quality Management District, and the San Francisco Bay Conservation and Development Commission.

CALIFORNIA COASTAL COMMISSION (CCC) Appointed by the governor and the state legislature, the 12-member CCC has state-empowered regulatory authority to control all development within the 1,000-yard-wide shoreline zone along the entire California coast. Exercising its powers to grant or withhold permits for development, the CCC has succeeded over the years in opening public access to beaches, protecting scenic views, and restoring wetlands.

SOUTH COAST AIR QUALITY MANAGEMENT DISTRICT (SCAQMD) The 12-member SCAQMD board has state-granted regulatory authority to control emissions from stationary sources of air pollution (e.g., power plants, refineries, gas stations) in the state's south coast air basin. This region encompasses all of Los Angeles and Orange Counties and parts of Riverside and San Bernardino Counties, an area of 12,000 square miles and home to more than 12 million people, nearly half the state's total population. This area also has the worst smog problem in the nation. Over the years, the board, which is appointed by city governments in the basin area, has conducted many studies, monitored air pollution levels, developed

The California Coastal Commission, one of California's regulatory regional governments, can bring citizens from throughout the state together through events like the annual California Coastal Cleanup Day, which encompasses the entire area under the CCC's jurisdiction—the length of California's coast.

regional pollution abatement plans, and vigorously enforced federal and state air pollution laws. Thanks in large part to its efforts, the maximum level of ozone in the basin has been cut to less than half of what it was in the 1950s, despite the tripling of the population and quadrupling of vehicles in the region over that same period.

SAN FRANCISCO BAY CONSERVATION AND DEVELOPMENT COMMISSION (BCDC) The 27-member BCDC was created by the state legislature in 1965 in response to growing public concern about the future of San Francisco Bay, which was rapidly being dredged and polluted at an alarming rate by landfill projects. The commission includes members appointed by the governor, legislature, and various state and federal agencies, as well as four city representatives appointed by the Association of Bay Area Governments and nine county supervisors—one from each of the nine Bay Area counties. The commission is charged with regulating all filling and dredging in the bay; protecting the Suisun Marsh, the largest wetlands in California; regulating proposed new development within the first 100 feet inland from the bay to ensure maximum public access; enforcing the federal Coastal Zone Management Act; and other regulatory functions. By exercising its permit powers, BCDC not only stopped development that could have reduced the bay to a pond but also added hundreds of acres of new open water.

Advisory Regional Governments

In addition to regional regulatory bodies, the state also has a number of regional planning, research, and advisory institutions called **advisory regional governments**. The most important are various regional **councils of government (COGs)**. COGs are assemblies of delegates representing a region's counties and cities who join voluntarily and meet regularly to discuss common problems and regional issues. The state's two most prominent COGs are the Southern California Association of Governments (SCAG), the nation's largest COG, and the Association of Bay Area Governments (ABAG).

SCAG's regional jurisdiction encompasses 15 million people living in an area of more than 38,000 square miles, while ABAG's boundaries include 6 million people living in an area of 7,000 square miles. Both SCAG and ABAG have general assemblies that represent the broad membership of counties and cities located in each region. In both COGs, the serious work is done by smaller executive committees, a 75-member regional council in the case of SCAG and a 38-member executive board in the case of ABAG. Like most COGs, both SCAG and ABAG have professional staffs that conduct extensive research and planning studies of regional problems. Both regularly host regional conferences and forums on a range of substantive issues. And both have been designated by the federal government as metropolitan planning organizations for their regions, with the mandate to draw up plans for regional transportation, air quality, growth management, hazardous waste management, and production of affordable housing.

Both SCAG and ABAG have raised public awareness of regional problems and issues. They have also encouraged more regional planning and collaborative decision making. Neither COG, however, has the effective power or authority to enforce its policy recommendations on other local governments in their regions. Many Bay Area local officials, for example, pay lip service to ABAG's recommended fair-share quotas for production of affordable housing but then routinely ignore them when making decisions.

Occasionally, a serious organized effort is made to create a truly comprehensive regional government with broad regulatory authority and strong enforcement powers. In the early 1990s, for example, an attempt was made to establish a powerful Bay Area regional government under the banner of BayVision 2020.[40] That proposal failed, like all the others, because most of the region's local governments were unwilling to surrender local autonomy and delegate some of their powers to a new, higher authority.

On a more hopeful note, Governor Schwarzenegger signed Senate Bill 375, the Sustainable Communities Act, into law in September 2008, moving the state at least a few steps in the direction of creating stronger regional governments, particularly in the areas of transportation, housing, and environmental protection. This landmark legislation requires the state's Air Resources Board to collaborate with metropolitan planning organizations (MPOs) and local government officials in developing "sustainable community strategies" and setting regional targets for the reduction of greenhouse gas emissions. Progress in implementing SB 375 over the last few years has depended on economic conditions and mostly voluntary cooperation from city and county officials. Winning this voluntary cooperation, however, might prove to be an uphill climb. For example, the small Marin County town of Corte Madera in 2012 became the first city ever to secede from ABAG on grounds that the Bay Area plan engendered by SB 375 would turn their small town into a big city. Corte Madera's city council voted to make their **secession** permanent in 2013. But SB 375 also comes armed with an array of penalties and incentives that could nudge local officials into significant exertion of regional governance.[41]

California's Community Redevelopment Agencies

In late December 2011, 435 **redevelopment agencies** operated throughout the state in sponsoring cities and counties. By May 2012, only a few months later, they were all gone. These agencies, a distinct species of local government now extinct in California, played an important role, for both better and worse, in the history of the state's physical and economic development. Here we'll offer a short obituary explaining how they were born, what they did, how they died, and why their abrupt death created both crises and opportunities in the state's urban areas.

California's redevelopment agencies were born on paper in 1945 when the state legislature passed the Community Redevelopment Act, which authorized the formation of such agencies "to prepare and carry out plans for the improvement, rehabilitation, and redevelopment of blighted areas."[42] These new agencies were to be placed under the control of sponsoring local governments, mainly cities and counties, and were authorized to acquire property by the power of eminent domain, dispose of it by lease or sale without public bidding, clear the land, construct infrastructure needed for building on project sites, and make other improvements. Typically, the agencies would then transfer the developed land to private parties on what were supposed to be "favorable terms for residential and/or commercial development."[43] To ensure that these powerful agencies served a public interest priority, they were required to spend at least 20 percent of their funds on affordable housing.

As to their funding, redevelopment agencies did not have the power to tax, but they could issue revenue bonds. The first redevelopment agencies received most of their funding from federal grants. Later they would be allowed to earn revenues through property **tax-increment financing (TIF)**. If a project site generated higher property tax revenues than it otherwise might have produced without redevelopment, the increment in revenues over the baseline would be returned to the agency to pay for the project site investments. As one recent study shows, the officials who ran some of these agencies would pay off the debt of one project and then invest not only their own TIF proceeds but those of other agencies, such as school districts, into new projects they would invent without consultation or voter approval.[44] In time, many of these agencies became flush with cash and masters of perpetuating their own power.

Following passage of Proposition 13 in 1978 (see Chapter 8), fiscally starved cities and counties began using their redevelopment agencies as an easier way to raise additional property tax revenues rather than trying to muster a two-thirds vote of approval from their local taxpayers under the harsh restrictions imposed by Prop. 13.

Over the years, the state's redevelopment agencies did produce a lot of affordable housing, rescued a lot of land from blight and decay, and often became engines of local economic development. Their collective track record was blemished, however, by the abuse of agency power and misuse of funds. Redevelopment projects often had little to do with reducing blight and decay, and many served only the private interests and profits of landlords, investors, and developers. Some of these projects actually destroyed more affordable housing than they created. Early in its history, for example, San Francisco's redevelopment agency bulldozed entire low-income and minority communities out of their neighbourhoods. That city's community activists fought back and eventually forced the city's redevelopment agency to raise its commitment to affordable housing production from the minimum required 20 percent to 50 percent, and to devote more resources to building communities than to tearing them down.[45] Moreover, some studies showed that redevelopment projects really didn't stimulate new economic development but merely relocated it from one poor area to another within a region with no net gain in jobs or tax revenues. Madeline Janis, a former commissioner on the Los Angeles Community Redevelopment Agency, offers the example of "a garment factory that was given CRA/LA-owned land and a $2-million subsidy in 2009 to move from South Gate to South Los Angeles, creating very few new jobs—and taking jobs away from another needy community."[46]

By 2010, redevelopment agencies had become chronically controversial, loved by some and hated by others. The precise mix of love and hate was determined by an agency's location and its history there. When the state government once again took from redevelopment funds to balance its own budget that year, redevelopment officials and their allies chose to fight rather than compromise. It was a political battle they couldn't win.

In early 2010, motivated by anger toward the state government for its continuing practice of raiding local property tax revenues to balance state budgets, a statewide coalition of cities, counties, professional associations, and redevelopment agencies gathered 1.1 million qualifying signatures to place an initiative constitutional amendment, Proposition 22, on the November 2010 election ballot. The official voter guide summarized the proposition's intent: "Prohibits the State, even during a period of severe fiscal hardship, from delaying the distribution of tax revenues for transportation, redevelopment, or local government projects and services."[47] If approved by the voters, the proposed constitutional amendment would prevent the state from "borrowing" local property tax revenues even under conditions of "severe fiscal hardship." Furthermore, Proposition 22 explicitly protected the state's redevelopment agencies. Property tax revenues would be reserved for local government use only, safe from the sticky fingers of desperate state legislators.

Representatives of the state's teachers, nurses, and firefighters wrote the argument against Proposition 22 in the official voter guide. They warned that the proposed amendment would significantly reduce funding for public schools, affordable health care, and public safety. The prohibition on state borrowing of local funds particularly worried them because in a "real fiscal crisis" such inflexibility would leave "schools, children's health care, seniors, the blind and disabled with even less hope." Their most vehement objection to Proposition 22, however, was that it "locks protections for redevelopment agencies into the State Constitution forever. These agencies have the power to take your property away with eminent domain. They skim off billions in local property taxes, with much of that money ending up in the hands of local developers." "Your tax dollars," they concluded, "should go first to schools, public safety, and health care. They should go LAST to the developers and the redevelopment agencies that support this proposal."[48]

On November 2, 2010, Proposition 22 passed easily with 61 percent of the vote. State legislators could never again balance their state budgets on the backs of the cities, counties, and redevelopment agencies. Or so it might have seemed to the victors. Perhaps forgotten, however, was a very important point made at the beginning of this chapter. Dillon's Rule established that local governments are creatures of the state. And the state's power to create local political entities also allows it to destroy them.

When Jerry Brown became governor in January 2011, he faced a huge budget deficit of $25 billion. As part of his response, he announced a plan to terminate all of the state's redevelopment agencies and redirect their property tax revenues to pay for schools, health services, and other programs placed in jeopardy by the budget crisis. Those property tax revenues totaled $5.7 billion (about 12 percent of all property tax revenues collected by the state). Governor Brown's goal the first year, however, was to transfer only $1.7 billion to the state, leaving the remaining funds to affected local governments to complete redevelopment projects already underway and to close up shop.

To execute Governor Brown's plan, two bills were introduced in the state Assembly. The first, AB 26, would dissolve all the redevelopment agencies. The second, AB 27, was a compromise measure pushed mainly by legislators who worried that killing the redevelopment agencies would eliminate a major source of funding for new affordable housing. This bill would allow cities and counties to reconstitute their redevelopment agencies on a smaller scale but only on the condition that they made substantial payments twice a year to a state fund set up to benefit schools and other programs. Redevelopment officials might have worked with legislators at this stage to make a better deal, but they were in no mood to compromise. As AB 26 and AB 27 made their way through the legislative process, local redevelopment officials across the state, seeing the writing on the wall, rushed to lock in funds before the curtain came down and their money was taken. In San Diego, for example, these preemptive lock-in moves were made to guarantee funding not only for current projects but also for those set to start in the distant future, as far away as 2048.[49]

After AB 26 and AB 27 became law in June 2011, the California Redevelopment Association, League of California Cities, and other petitioners promptly sued the state and took their case to the California Supreme Court. Based in large part on their claim that these two laws violated the provisions of Proposition 22, they challenged the constitutionality of both laws and requested a stay of action. The justices of the Supreme Court granted the stay, heard oral arguments in November, and announced their ruling on December 29, 2011.[50]

First, the court ruled that AB 26 was constitutional. As creatures of the state, redevelopment agencies could be dissolved by the state. Nothing in Proposition 22 or the rest of the state constitution explicitly protected these agencies from dissolution.

Second, the court ruled that AB 27 was unconstitutional because it required newly reconstituted redevelopment agencies to make payments to the state as a condition for survival. Such mandatory "pay to play" payments violated Proposition 22, which prohibited the state from making such "raids" on redevelopment funds.

The court's decision was the worst possible outcome for redevelopment agency supporters. The state could kill redevelopment agencies with AB 26, but it could not resurrect them with AB 27 because of Proposition 22. Redevelopment agency officials, the most aggressive advocates of Proposition 22, were thus hoisted by their own petard.[51]

City and county officials pleaded with state legislators to pass a new and improved version of the old redevelopment program that might survive legal scrutiny. Their pleas were in vain.

By May 2012, redevelopment agencies no longer existed in California. The 1,500 or so employees who had worked for them were laid off or reassigned to other positions. A big chunk of redevelopment agency funds, about $1.5 billion, was redirected to support the state's public schools, health care services, and public safety programs. The remaining funds were assigned to counties for distribution to cities and their designated "successor agencies" to wind down existing redevelopment projects under the watchful eyes of the state controller. The actual process of phasing out 435 redevelopment agencies, however, would prove extremely messy, highly contentious, and take many years to complete.

Local Government: Where Are We Now?

By early November 2014, California's local governments had survived a gauntlet of economic and political crises. The Great Recession had severely weakened local economies and hit most of the state's city and county governments hard as tax revenues plummeted, which resulted in austerity in the form of slashed budgets, staff layoffs, and cutbacks in services. No financial rescue had come from the federal government, which had bailed out the nation's leading financial institutions and the automobile industry but not its crippled public sector or struggling cities. Nor had the state government been of much help during the worst of it. Faced with its own budget crisis, the state abolished California's 435 redevelopment agencies to extract new revenues to help make ends meet. For some struggling cities, the loss of those revenues had been a crushing financial blow. Protesters in the Occupy Movement had put down stakes and organized rallies in many of the state's larger cities. For the most part they had no clear agenda or even leaders, but they gave voice to widespread rage against America's growing inequality, political domination by economic elites, and the failure of government to do anything about it. Against this backdrop of conflict and inter-city competition, visionary plans for regional alliances and inter-city cooperation had been placed on hold.

However, the state's local governments are now in a much better place than they were even a year or two ago. The state's economy is slowly recovering from the recession. California's state government and the voters have become more responsive to the plight of cities and the need for change. Voter approval of Proposition 30 in November 2012 provided new tax revenues to financially starved local governments. The election of Democratic supermajorities in both houses of the state's legislature loosened the legislative gridlock and cleared a path to passage of a paid sick leave bill and a modest increase in the minimum wage in 2014. The state's budget became flush; this meant funding was restored for public schools, health care, and social services. Ambitious plans for creating sustainable communities, improving transportation infrastructure, producing affordable housing, and controlling greenhouse gas emissions were reactivated.

Against this increasingly optimistic backdrop, many of the state's local government leaders and citizens have moved forward to solve the problems left unsolved by governments at higher levels. Four major transitions are underway that will change local government as we know it now and shape California's economic and political future:

- The transition from the Great Recession to geographically uneven economic recovery and prosperity.

- The transition from the death of urban redevelopment agencies to new institutions of physical and economic development in our cities.

- The transition from the massive but ephemeral Occupy Movement to a growing and durable network of progressive cities pushing for reforms at the local level.

- The transition from mutually destructive inter-city competition to a world of regional cooperation and sustainable communities.

From the Great Recession to Uneven Economic Recovery and Prosperity

The Great Recession, which officially began in December 2007, hit California especially hard. Across the state, 95 percent of voters surveyed in January 2010 reported that California's economy was in "bad times" (up from 52 percent in 2007), 79 percent that unemployment was a "very serious" problem (up from 39 percent in 2007), and 59 percent that their personal financial well-being was "worse off" than the year before (up from 33 percent in 2007).[52] The Associated Press reported that between October 2007 and April 2010 the state's unemployment rate increased from 5.4 to 12.3 percent, residential and commercial property foreclosure rates from 1.5 to 3.2 percent, and bankruptcy filings from 0.5 to 1.7 percent.[53] All the state's 58 counties suffered economic hardship during this period, but some much more than others. The recession's impacts were so severe that some local governments were forced into bankruptcy. The city of Vallejo, for example, buckled under the burden of overspending, reduced tax revenues, and out-of-control pension and benefit costs. In 2008, this city of 117,000 declared bankruptcy. In spring 2012, Stockton, a city of 290,000, was in dire financial straits because of its depressed local economy, 20 percent unemployment rate, large projected budget deficits with no reserves, and unsustainable pension and benefit liabilities. Most daunting were the mounting debt-service costs to be paid on gross overinvestment in redevelopment projects like a new baseball park, marina, sports arena, and city hall.[54] After negotiations with creditors failed to produce a better solution, the city council voted on June 26, 2012, to declare bankruptcy. That decision, according to *The Economist*, made Stockton, at the time, "the biggest municipal insolvency in American history."[55] Only a month later, San Bernardino, a city of 210,000 coping with its own financial emergency, also filed for bankruptcy protection.[56]

In June 2014, a statewide survey found that California's voters, for the first time since 2007, saw themselves as financially better off than they were during the previous year. Yet 53 percent still described the state as being in economic bad times and only 25 percent described the state as being in good times. A breakdown of voter responses by region also revealed how geographically uneven the state's economic recovery was perceived to be. For example, only 35 percent of voters in the San Francisco Bay Area and 44 percent of those in Los Angeles County said the state was in bad times. But between 60 and 65 percent of voters in the other major regions said the state's economy remained mired in bad times. In general, things were looking up for those who lived in the Bay Area or Los Angeles region. For those living outside those two large metropolitan areas, however, the economic future continued to look bleak.[57]

A comparison of San Francisco's economic recovery to that of cities like Vallejo, Stockton, and San Bernardino reveals just how stark the geographical disparities had become. San Francisco's unemployment rate had dropped from 9.6 percent to 4.9 percent between July 2010 and July 2014.[58] The flood of high-tech startup firms and venture capital into the city had put people to work and filled city hall's coffers with new tax revenues. The mayor and other elected officials used those new resources to balance the budget, restore service cuts, make a healthy dent in pension obligations, boost affordable housing production, and earn the city its highest ratings ever from Moody's and Fitch. Richard Florida, the urban economic development guru, even declared that San Francisco now deserved the title of "Silicon Valley North" as the new driver of technological innovation and economic prosperity for the entire region.[59] Only four years earlier, the city had been coping with its highest unemployment rate in living memory, huge budget deficits, a pension tsunami that threatened to devour the city's entire budget within a decade, conflict and rancor among public employees, and the realistic prospect of bankruptcy. But now, four years later, it was on top of the world.

Those same four years did not treat Vallejo, Stockton, and San Bernardino so kindly. All three cities made at least some progress toward economic recovery. Vallejo's unemployment rate, for example, had dropped from 14.9 percent to 9.0 percent, Stockton's from 20.9 percent to 13.5 percent, and San Bernardino's from 19.7 percent to 12.2 percent. But all three still lagged far behind San Francisco and the state as a whole, and the prospects of catching up any time soon seemed dim. That outlook was reinforced by Wallet Hub's 2014 survey of the nation's 150 largest cities and their relative pace in recovering from the recession. Using 18 metrics to rank cities from highest to lowest in recovery, Wallet Hub's team of university economists found that Stockton ranked 149 and San Bernardino 150. The struggling cities of Riverside and Modesto ranked 140 and 146, respectively, while San Francisco ranked 20, and San Jose, in the heart of Silicon Valley, ranked 35.[60]

The burdens of municipal bankruptcy have made the climb toward economic recovery even steeper for Vallejo, Stockton, and San Bernardino. City officials in all three cities continue to wrestle in courts and council chambers with angry creditors, combative labor unions, anxious business leaders, and aggrieved citizens. And in all three they have had to cope with the long-term consequences of their public employee pension and health benefit obligations. A major player in this process has been the California Public Employees' Retirement System (CalPERS). Backed by state labor law, the labor unions and the courts, CalPERS has fought off all attempts by city leaders to reduce their contributions to the CalPERS pension fund. Such reductions, if agreed to, would allow them to avoid the pain of making further staffing and service cuts. In all cases, however, CalPERS insisted on receiving 100 percent of what it was due. All other creditors holding city debt, therefore, would be asked to accept much less than they were owed (known as "taking a haircut") to give the city any chance of exiting bankruptcy.

In Stockton, a major creditor, Franklin Templeton Investments, demanded more than the city had offered as part of its bankruptcy exit plan to retire Franklin's $350 million loan. The city had used that loan to buy fire stations, a police station, bridges, street improvements and parks. Franklin's actuaries were extremely upset that CalPERS got 100 percent of what it was due while Franklin had to accept a 99 percent haircut, and Franklin sued the city. In late summer 2014, these various parties began battling it out in a federal bankruptcy court. Leaders of other financially distressed cities closely observed the court proceedings. As a *Wall Street Journal* reporter noted: "A ruling that Stockton's pensions can be curtailed could embolden more cities to use bankruptcy as a way to seek retirement concessions."[70] On October 30, 2014, the federal bankruptcy judge approved Stockton's bankruptcy exit plan, did not ask CalPERS for a dime (arguing that the city's workers already had made sufficient concessions), and ordered the city to pay more than one percent on its debt to Franklin.[71]

The court's approval of Stockton's exit plan released the city from bankruptcy. For the short run, that decision satisfied CalPERS, the labor unions, city officials, and (to a degree) Franklin. It also no doubt disappointed other interested parties, including leaders of other cities facing the same kinds of problems and hoping for a court-sanctioned short-cut allowing them to tap CalPERS in repaying their own debts. The court's ruling did little, however, to help solve Stockton's long-run challenge of meeting its rapidly growing pension obligations. One analysis of the city's own projections, for example, showed that by 2019 more than 18 percent of the city's general revenues would go to CalPERS, up from 11 percent in 2014, thus placing the city in peril of being forced to file for a second bankruptcy.[72]

In Vallejo, three years after a federal bankruptcy judge released that city from bankruptcy, the same spectre haunts its future. The city's fiscal condition has improved since declaring bankruptcy in 2008 but city leaders continue to grapple with austerity budgets, reduced staff, unhappy citizens, and lingering anger from the public employee labor union leaders who had sued to stop the bankruptcy in the first place. They also continue to search for new revenue sources while coping with the stigma of management failure. Their biggest problem, however, remains that of controlling pension costs, which had grown by nearly 40 percent in just the last two years and are projected to grow by another 42 percent over the next five years. Financial experts predict a relapse into bankruptcy if those growth trends continue.[73] City officials in bankrupt San Bernardino, which has yet to submit its own exit plan, have reason to worry, as do leaders in other California cities facing similar dire straits.

These snapshots of struggle for financial survival in three California cities suggest the possibility of a death spiral in their futures. The author of the Wallet Hub report spelled out what the "collateral effects" of economic recovery might look like: "Crime rises, education suffers, local administrations collapse. In the private sector, property values decline and businesses shut down. If and when that happens, skilled workers are forced to seek better opportunities in more thriving communities. And a town that had little hope remaining is completely crippled."[74] That discouraging scenario prompts an even deeper concern about long-term trends pointing to the bifurcation of California's cities into affluent, high-tech "brain hub" cities like San Francisco and San Jose, and cities like Vallejo, Stockton and San Bernardino, which are likely to be abandoned by ambitious and talented youth and left behind.[75]

From the Death to the Rebirth of Urban Redevelopment

The legal death of the state's 435 redevelopment agencies (RDAs) in late 2011 confronted local and state government officials with two major challenges. At the local level, the first challenge was to create a "successor agency" to take over a city's existing redevelopment projects and then submit a transition plan for managing RDA assets and funds to the State Controller's Office for approval. The second challenge, for many local leaders, was to invent new ways to achieve redevelopment goals without resurrecting the powerful but controversial RDAs in the face of strong opposition.

By late summer 2014, the State Controller's Office had reviewed and approved only about half of the county and city plans for winding down and phasing out their RDAs.[76] A key motivation behind most plans was the desire of local officials to keep as many of the RDA's assets and funds as possible under local government control. The state government's interest was to make sure those plans complied with the law and met its objectives. Conflicts were inevitable and will continue for some time.

The small city of Cerritos, for example, balked when the state controller ordered it to liquidate $171 million in assets, including the land beneath an auto mall and performing arts center that had been leased from the city's redevelopment agency. The order also required the city to use the proceeds from selling those assets to pay off its redevelopment agency's debts and then give any remaining funds to the state or show how they would be spent locally to support public schools, health care, and public safety. This order shocked and outraged the city's government and business leaders. The auto mall, in particular, generated badly needed sales tax revenues for the city. Cerritos had laid claim to the land after its redevelopment agency was abolished, but the controller rejected that claim, as he did in dozens of similar cases in cities throughout the state. A spokesman for the controller explained: "While we appreciate [the cities'] frustration, the legislature and the courts have made it clear that redevelopment assets must be used to pay off the RDA debts and support other community services." Many cities defaulted on their RDA debts, however, causing Moody's and other rating agencies to downgrade their bonds to junk. And for some cities, like Stockton and San Bernardino, the loss of RDA revenues had been the last straw that toppled them into bankruptcy.[77]

A few of the state's larger cities, like San Diego and San Francisco, have robust local economies and have been able to launch new redevelopment initiatives using their own limited authority and investment funds. But life in the post-RDA era has been a struggle for many other local governments. By late summer 2014, the resulting political pressure on state legislators to do something about it had grown fierce.

Responding to that pressure, on September 29, 2014, Governor Brown signed two bills but vetoed a third intended to restore local redevelopment authority at least in part. The two he signed into law were AB 229, which allowed local governments to create "Infrastructure and Revitalization Financing Districts" to revive old military bases, and SB 628, which established "Enhanced Infrastructure Financing Districts" allowing local governments to "finance public capital facilities or other specified projects of community-wide significance" with the approval of 55 percent of voters in the district. The bill he vetoed, AB 2280, would have allowed local governments to create a "Community Revitalization and Investment Authority" with the power to use RDA-style tax-increment financing in narrowly defined disadvantaged communities with 25 percent of funding earmarked for affordable housing. According to one reporter, the governor opposed resurrecting the "former redevelopment mechanisms" and was skeptical about housing affordability restrictions.[78] By early November 2014, the political forces supporting and opposing the rebirth of redevelopment agencies seemed equally matched. Thus, many more collisions and battles are likely in the years ahead, with the fiscal fate of some local governments hanging in the balance.

From the Occupy Movement to a Growing Network of Progressive Cities

Erupting from the depths of the Great Recession, the Occupy Wall Street movement spread rapidly from New York City to many California cities and college campuses in September 2011. As an urban-based protest movement, its impact varied greatly with the local political culture, economic circumstances, and leadership skills

found in each city. In San Francisco, for example, most of the city's elected officials supported the first Occupy San Francisco demonstrations and encampments. Interim Mayor Edwin Lee and his police chief waited a long time and negotiated patiently with the occupiers before dismantling the encampments in December 2011 with relatively few arrests. In Oakland, on the other hand, the Occupy Oakland movement took root in a more economically distressed city and with many more working-class and unemployed participants than in San Francisco. Occupy Oakland was also characterized by more outbreaks of violence and greater economic disruption, including a general strike that closed down the city's port for a day, and with a more repressive response from city officials, especially the police. The dismantling of the protesters' main encampment was accompanied by violent resistance and many arrests. As this brief comparison illustrates, the Occupy Movement itself was too volatile, uncoordinated, and leaderless to have much of a direct impact in transforming America's political system and governing institutions. By late 2012, the Occupy encampments in California cities had disappeared. Many of the original protesters had moved on to agitate for social change in more conventional ways.

In future hindsight, the **Occupy Movement** may come to be seen as a short-lived but vital catalyst of urban-based democratic renewal and progressive reform. It forced the issues of income inequality and economic justice into the spotlight of the 2012 presidential election. It moved many government leaders at all levels, including the local, to pay more attention to the forgotten 99 percent. And it helped to inspire the formation of broad-based and well-led political coalitions demanding immediate and achievable economic justice reforms, such as an increase in the minimum wage, in the only public arenas where success was even possible at this time: local governments. Nowhere was that success greater than in California's cities.

SAN JOSE In Spring 2011, Marisela Castro and other students in a sociology class at San Jose State University persuaded their professor, Scott Myers-Lipton, to organize a class project aimed at raising the mandated minimum wage for all employers in the city of San Jose from $8 to $10 an hour. Their model legislation was a minimum wage ordinance passed by San Francisco voters in 2003. Studies by labor economists at the University of California at Berkeley had shown that the law significantly improved the economic well-being of low-income workers with no major negative effects on business profits, prices or employment.[79] The student research team raised $6,000 to pay for a survey of voters, and found overwhelming support for a minimum wage increase in San Jose. Their survey results convinced the city's Labor Council to sponsor a successful signature-gathering campaign to place a citizen initiative for a higher minimum wage (Measure D) on the November 2012 ballot. A broad-based coalition was organized to educate and mobilize voters. On Election Day, despite opposition from many members of the city's government, Measure D won with 59 percent of the vote. As a result, San Jose became the state's largest city with an advanced minimum wage law.[80]

SAN DIEGO In July 2014, San Diego's city council voted 6 to 3 to pass an ordinance mandating that all city employers pay a higher minimum wage rising to $11.50 an hour over three years. The ordinance also required employers to provide their employees with paid sick leave. This ordinance, too, was inspired by San Francisco laws passed years earlier. San Diego's Republican mayor vetoed the proposed ordinance, but the council overrode his veto by the same 6 to 3 vote. Before the ordinance could be implemented, however, a coalition of business groups led by the city's chamber of commerce ran a successful signature-gathering campaign calling for a referendum on the measure at the June 2016 primary election. Under state law, the council was required to reconsider the original ordinance before the referendum could move forward. If the council voted against it in this second round, the referendum would be withdrawn. The council members did not change their minds, the referendum was scheduled for June 2016, and actual implementation of the ordinance was therefore delayed until the voters have their say.[81]

BAY AREA CITIES, EUREKA, AND THE NOVEMBER 2014 ELECTIONS In summer 2014, city councils in the Bay Area cities of Richmond and Berkeley passed citywide employer mandates for a higher minimum wage. San Francisco's mayor and board of supervisors placed a compromise measure on the November 2014 ballot, Proposition J, which would raise the city's already very high minimum wage to become the highest in the land. Polls showed overwhelming voter support for the measure. The city's chamber of commerce, restaurant owner lobbying organization, and other traditional business groups chose not to oppose the measure, while the city's top high-tech CEOs and investors endorsed it enthusiastically. In Oakland, a minimum wage measure almost identical to Berkeley's, Proposition FF, was placed on the November 2014 ballot. One reason the Berkeley and Oakland initiatives were so similar is that Berkeley's mayor, Tom Bates, modeled his city's ordinance on what Oakland intended to do with Proposition FF. He argued that Berkeley, Oakland, and other East Bay cities should coordinate their proposed minimum wage laws to help create a uniform regional minimum wage standard. "It makes so much more sense if we were all on the same page, for the same amount," Bates said. "This way we can share enforcement duties, and no city would be at an economic disadvantage."[82] Far to the north of the Bay Area, the small city of Eureka also placed a minimum wage measure, Proposition R, on the November 2014 ballot. The inspiring model, once again, was San Francisco's 2003 law and also the one passed by San Jose voters in 2012.[83] On November 4, 2014, after the votes were tallied, San Francisco's Proposition J had passed with 76 percent of the votes, and Oakland's Measure FF had won even more resoundingly with 81 percent. Eureka's Measure R, however, had failed, receiving only 38 percent of the votes.

In the wake of the Occupy Movement, a growing number of California cities have passed progressive policy reforms on their own turf and are increasingly coordinating their strategies and actions at the regional level. Cities as "laboratories of democracy" are conducting important policy experiments, sharing their results, and having an impact both inside and beyond California's borders. It seems likely that the urban-based progressive movement born in California cities will continue to grow and spread throughout the nation.

From Inter-City Competition to Regional Cooperation and Sustainable Communities

Passage of California's Sustainable Communities Act of 2008 (SB 375) gave hope to advocates of stronger regional governance. A major goal of the legislation was to encourage collaboration between the state's Air Resources Board and metropolitan planning organizations (MPOs) in developing regional plans and setting regional targets for reducing the state's greenhouse gas emissions. The state's COGs, such as SCAG and ABAG, although still mainly advisory in their powers, have played a leading role in organizing MPOs to achieve that goal. By early 2014, the Air Resources Board had certified that nearly all of the 18 MPO plans submitted could meet their specified targets for 2020 and 2035. California Senate Leader Darrell Steinberg (D-Sacramento), legislative author of SB 375, then announced in April that a large share of the projected billions of dollars to be generated annually by the state's cap and trade program would be available to support MPOs and participating local governments in implementing their regional plans. When local government officials heard that, their level of interest in voluntary cooperation rose noticeably.[84] Local interest grew even more in June when the legislature and governor approved a budget for FY 2014–15 that included sizable funds earmarked for affordable housing, transit improvements, and equity programs supportive of MPO plans.[85] The challenge of getting the state's local leaders to collaborate in thinking and acting regionally has often been likened to that of "herding cats." But with potentially large sums of new money on the table to help financially strapped cities, that challenge may now prove easier to meet. As the populist Jim Hightower once quipped, "those who say you can't herd cats never tried a can opener."[86] Years from now, if these trends continue, SB 375 may be viewed in hindsight as the legislative "can opener" that helped to reduce inter-city competition, encourage cooperation, strengthen regional government, and turn California into even more of an economic powerhouse than it already is.

Over the years ahead, different pieces of the future of California's local governments will be legislated in the state capitol, adjudicated in bankruptcy courts, calculated in the state's controller's office, envisioned in metropolitan planning organizations, and contested in city halls or on the streets alive with direct democracy. It is possible that these pieces might actually fit together in some coherent way, especially if the state's economy continues to recover and renewed prosperity spreads beyond the Bay Area and Los Angeles regions. But even if not, experiments are taking place and change is afoot in California, much of it in the laboratories of local democracy.

Study Guide

FOR FURTHER READING

Baldassare, Mark. *A California State of Mind: The Conflicted Voter in a Changing World*. Berkeley, CA: University of California Press, 2002.

Bridges, Amy. *Morning Glories: Municipal Reform in the Southwest*. Princeton, NJ: Princeton University Press, 1997.

DeLeon, Richard Edward. *Left Coast City: Progressive Politics in San Francisco, 1975–1991*. Lawrence: University Press of Kansas, 1992.

Hajnal, Zoltan L., Paul G. Lewis, and Hugh Louch. *Municipal Elections in California: Turnout, Timing, and Competition*. San Francisco: Public Policy Institute of California, 2002.

Rodriguez, Daniel B. "State Supremacy, Local Sovereignty: Reconstructing State/Local Relations under the California Constitution." In *Constitutional Reform in California: Making State Government More Effective and Responsive*, ed. Bruce E. Cain and Roger G. Noll. Berkeley, CA: Institute of Governmental Studies Press, University of California, 1995, 401–29.

Sonenshein, Raphael J. *Politics in Black and White: Race and Power in Los Angeles*. Princeton, NJ: Princeton University Press, 1993.

ON THE WEB

California Department of Finance: www.dof.ca.gov/Research /Research.php. Accessed July 6, 2012. The Department of Finance produces detailed and up-to-date statistical reports and studies on local government finances, the state budget process and its impacts on localities, and a wide range of demographic and economic information on cities and counties.

California Employment Development Department: www.edd .ca.gov. Accessed July 7, 2012. Valuable source of up-to-date statewide and county-level information on employment and labor market conditions.

California Secretary of State: www.sos.ca.gov/elections. Accessed July 7, 2012. Excellent source of information on county-level election results for statewide candidate races and ballot propositions.

California Special Districts Association: www.csda.net. Accessed July 7, 2012.

California State Association of Counties: www.csac.counties .org. Accessed July 7, 2012. Useful source of wide-ranging news and information on California's counties, with a main focus on policy and administration.

Institute for Local Government: www.ca-ilg.org. Accessed August 4, 2012. The research arm and affiliate of the League of California Cities and the California State Association of Counties. Very good source for in-depth studies of key policy issues facing the state's local governments.

League of California Cities: www.cacities.org/index.jsp. Accessed July 7, 2012. An excellent source of news, information, and data on all aspects of governing California's cities.

U.S. Conference of Mayors: www.usmayors.org. Accessed July 7, 2012.

SUMMARY

I. Overview of California local governments.
   A. California has more than 5,000 local governments of various types, including general-purpose governments such as those in counties and cities, specific-purpose governments such as those for school districts and special districts, and regional governments.
   B. Local governments provide essential services, ranging from law enforcement and fire protection to waste management and street maintenance to air- and water-quality control.

II. Legal framework for local government: the state has ultimate authority over local governments.
   A. Under Dillon's Rule, local governments are "creatures of the state" and have no inherent rights or powers except those given to them by the state constitution or legislature.
   B. California, like most states, gives counties and cities significant powers to govern themselves, make policies, enforce laws, raise revenues, borrow, and generally control local affairs as long as their decisions don't conflict with state or federal laws.
   C. The more populous cities and counties have adopted home-rule charters, which allow maximum local autonomy in self-governance.
   D. The other cities and counties operate as general-law counties and cities, which have to abide more strictly by the state legislature's local government code.

III. County governments.
   A. California's 58 counties are extremely diverse in terms of territorial extent, population size, demographic characteristics, and political culture.
   B. Except for the unique case of San Francisco's consolidated county/city government, all counties are governed by five-member boards of supervisors that exercise both legislative and executive powers.
   C. Counties perform important functions, many of them required by state government laws and mandates.
   D. Counties also provide essential services, especially in unincorporated areas outside the cities and other jurisdictions, and they are major arenas for making large-scale land-use and development policies.
   E. Each county also has a local agency formation commission (LAFCo), which plays a critical role in creating, merging, or dissolving new local governments, such as those in cities and special districts, and resolving disputes among competing jurisdictions.

IV. City governments.
   A. The state has 482 cities, most of them general-law cities, the rest charter cities with significant home-rule powers and local autonomy.
   B. Cities are legally created through a process of municipal incorporation that requires LAFCo review and approval, and a final majority vote of the community seeking formal city status.
   C. Nearly all cities have a form of government modeled on the vision of Progressive Era reformers. Called reform cities, most have strong city managers, weak mayors, nonpartisan elections, at-large council elections, nonconcurrent elections, and direct democracy procedures (the initiative, referendum, and recall). Important exceptions to such reform cities are cities such as Los Angeles and San Francisco, which have strong mayors and, in the case of San Francisco, district elections.

V. Citizen participation in local government.
   A. The Brown Act of 1953, known as the "open meetings law," requires that all meetings of local legislative bodies be open and public unless specifically exempted, and that all citizens be permitted to attend such meetings.
   B. Voter turnout in city elections has been steadily declining in recent years.
      1. Those who do vote in city elections tend to be whiter, older, richer, and more educated than those who don't.
      2. In particular, the state's growing population of noncitizens have little political voice or formal representation in local government.

      3. Certain electoral reforms, such as a shift from nonconcurrent to concurrent elections, could markedly increase voter turnout levels.

VI. Special districts.
   A. Special districts are limited-purpose local governments.
   B. Excluding the state's 1,028 K–12 school districts and 72 community-college districts, California has nearly 5,000 special districts.
   C. Special districts provide a range of services—for example, irrigation, pest abatement, parks and recreation, water, and fire protection—which are not provided at all (or in sufficient amounts) by general-purpose governments such as those for counties and cities.
   D. Special districts are created by a LAFCo-approved citizen petition and a majority vote.
   E. Most special districts are independent agencies that provide one type of service received and paid for by residents in smaller territories of larger jurisdictions, like counties.
   F. Some special districts are enterprise districts that charge individual user fees for service.
   G. Most special districts are funded by taxes or special assessments from service recipients.
   H. The advantages of special districts include greater flexibility and responsiveness in tailoring service and the levels of cost and benefit to citizen demands.
   I. The disadvantages of special districts include duplication of services, lack of coordination, and unclear structures of authority and accountability.

VII. Regional governments.
   A. The state's regional governments address problems like air pollution and population growth that affect large areas and multiple local government jurisdictions.
   B. Some regional governments, such as the San Francisco Bay Conservation and Development Commission and the California Coastal Commission, have strong regulatory authority and enforcement powers.
   C. Other regional governments, such as the Southern California Association of Governments, the Association of Bay Area Governments, and other councils of government (COGs), mainly perform research, planning, and advisory functions and have little or no power or authority to impose their decisions on local jurisdictions.

VIII. Community redevelopment agencies.
   A. Over 400 redevelopment agencies were active throughout the state in 2011.
   B. They no longer exist. How and why they disappeared are discussed in the text.

IX. Four major transitions facing local governments.
   A. The transition from the Great Recession to geographically uneven economic recovery and prosperity.
   B. The transition from the death of urban redevelopment agencies to new institutions of physical and economic development in our cities.
   C. The transition from the massive but ephemeral Occupy Movement to a growing and durable network of progressive cities pushing for reforms at the local level.
   D. The transition from mutually destructive inter-city competition to a world of regional cooperation and sustainable economies.

PRACTICE QUIZ

1. Cities and counties that have home-rule charters have the authority to make their own laws even if they violate state and federal laws.
   a) true
   b) false

2. The U.S. Constitution gives local governments inherent rights and powers that cannot be taken away by state governments.
   a) true
   b) false

3. County boards of supervisors have both legislative and executive authority.
   a) true
   b) false

4. Most cities are governed by council-manager systems.
   a) true
   b) false

5. At the local government level, citizens cannot petition for a referendum or recall election.
   a) true
   b) false

6. Which of the following is *not* a characteristic of reform government at the local level?
   a) at-large council elections
   b) nonpartisanship
   c) city manager plan
   d) concurrent elections

7. Which of the following counties operates under a single charter as a consolidated city and county?
   a) Los Angeles
   b) Sacramento
   c) San Francisco
   d) Orange

8. Which of the following elected officials can be found only in county governments?
   a) sheriff
   b) mayor
   c) council member
   d) manager

9. ABAG is an example of a COG.
   a) true
   b) false

10. The Sustainable Communities Act (SB 375) prohibits California cities from making regional alliances with other cities.
   a) true
   b) false

CRITICAL-THINKING QUESTIONS

1. Do you think the Progressive Era reform vision for local governments is still a good one today? Should the state's local governments continue to be run by professional managers and insulated as much as possible from state and national party politics? Why or why not?

2. Should local governments, such as cities, be given more home-rule powers and greater local autonomy free of state interference? Test case: Would you support all California cities asserting their home-rule powers and local autonomy to the extent that San Francisco has? Why or why not?

3. Do you agree with some critics that most special districts should be abolished and their functions centralized under the control of county and city governments? Why or why not?

4. Do you agree with some observers that California needs more and stronger regional governments? Why or why not? If you agree, what are some of the problems facing those who seek to form such governments, and what steps would you take to create them? How would you balance your recommendations with the principles of home rule and local autonomy?

5. Do you support or oppose the rebellion of local governments against the state as a response to the state's attempt to use local government property tax revenues to solve its budget deficit problems? Why or why not?

KEY TERMS

At this point you should have a general understanding of the following concepts and terms:

advisory regional governments (p. 226)
at-large elections (p. 218)
charter cities (p. 214)
charter counties (p. 208)
cities (p. 205)
council-manager plan (p. 217)
councils of government (COGs) (p. 226)
counties (p. 205)
Dillon's Rule (p. 205)
direct democracy (p. 220)
district elections (p. 218)

enterprise districts (p. 223)
general-law cities (p. 214)
general-law counties (p. 208)
home rule (p. 205)
independent districts (p. 223)
local agency formation commission (LAFCo) (p. 213)
mayor-council plan (p. 217)
municipal incorporation (p. 214)
nonpartisanship (p. 218)
Occupy Movement (p. 236)
ordinances (p. 210)

redevelopment agencies (p. 228)
reform governments (p. 217)
regional governments (p. 225)
regulatory regional governments (p. 225)
school and community college districts (p. 223)
secession (p. 227)
special districts (p. 205)
tax-increment financing (p. 228)
user fees (p. 223)

Public Policy in California

WHAT CALIFORNIA GOVERNMENT DOES AND WHY IT MATTERS

Riverside County, east of Los Angeles, has over 300 trailer parks, many inhabited by migrant agricultural workers who pick the vegetables and fruit that grow abundantly in the county's irrigated valleys. In 1999, the county accused several trailer parks that catered to migrant workers of substandard and dangerous conditions. Harvey Duro, Sr., a member of the Torres Martinez Desert Cahuilla Indian Reservation, spread the word of a new trailer park on reservation land where the displaced workers could reside. Many farmworkers moved in, paying about $500 a month per trailer to live there.[1]

The conditions weren't good. The trailer park, officially called Desert Mobile Home Park but unofficially known as Duroville or Duros, was next to a dump that burned from time to time. Heaps of tires and construction debris littered the area, the streets were dusty (and muddy when it rained), and the area's sewage flowed into a pond next door. In 2002, the teachers in the local schools noticed that many of their students from the park were suffering from asthma and rashes, and determined that the dump was the likely cause. The Bureau of Indian Affairs, which had jurisdiction because the trailer park was on the reservation, moved to close the park because of the unsanitary conditions. In 2009 the local U.S. attorney cited in court the park's "leaking sewage, 800 feral dogs, piles of debris and fire hazards," as well as 5,000 tenants. The cost of bringing it into compliance would be more than $4 million, which the owner could not afford.

After several years of litigation, a federal judge in 2009 decreed that since there was no other place for the residents to go, the park could stay open. The population of the park numbered between 2,000 to 6,000 people, depending on the time of year and economic conditions. Many residents were undocumented. Many earned less than $10,000 per year. And many of them were Purépechas, an indigenous people from Michoacán, Mexico. Many, in fact, were from a single town in Michoacán.

By 2010, most of those selling drugs in the park were gone, the feral dog problem was substantially reduced, and the rotting garbage had been cleared. But there was still no place for the residents to move, and the quality of the trailers was no better.

Riverside County then completed a public housing project for the residents, Mountain View Estates, six miles away from Duroville and composed of 181 units.[2] Duroville finally closed in June 2014, 15 years after it opened. Public housing projects require residents to be in the United States legally, so many undocumented former residents of Duroville moved to other trailer parks in the area. While it was open, Duroville had its own Wikipedia entry and new resident councils and representatives to help ensure residents' adherance to the rules. Articles about the community occasionally appeared in the *New York Times* and *Los Angeles Times* as well as in the local newspapers.

The issue of housing and many other policy areas in California politics exemplify the challenges posed throughout this book—challenges related to California's enormous diversity and unique institutions. Sites like Duroville can exist on Indian reservations, which have jurisdiction over most governmental areas except law enforcement. If not for this jurisdiction, zoning and other laws in most areas of California would have shut Duroville down much sooner.

You may have concluded by now that California is a land of contrasts. The same state that includes Beverly Hills and Silicon Valley also has its Durovilles. Public policy in California governs areas that are like Duroville—that is, areas that are not doing so well—and other areas that are in better shape. It is difficult to generalize as to the average state of affairs. California's high degree of heterogeneity is evident in the proposal to divide California into six states, an initiative that failed to collect enough signatures in 2014 to make the ballot. This plan would have created the richest state in the United States (in the state that encompassed Silicon Valley) as well as the poorest (the state that included the Central Valley).

We know from earlier chapters in this book that California has come close to being ungovernable during the last two decades. We have a public that demands a high level of services but consistently refuses to pay for them. Many members of the public still feel that the free tuition and low fees in higher education during the Pat Brown era are still possible at a time when the state's people and politics have changed profoundly. Proposition 30, passed in November 2012, is one of the few exceptions, with a small permanent sales tax increase and larger temporary income tax increases on the wealthy, expiring in 2018. The public is sometimes willing to approve initiatives to undertake new projects that lack funding. It is also willing to pass special taxes earmarked for special purposes, many of which benefit the interests sponsoring the relevant initiative.

The lack of consensus among the public is reflected in our institutions, which in some cases barely function. However, major steps have been taken to improve the quality of the political process in California. While the legislature has been unable to change the state's tax structure, now over 50 years old, some new institutional changes—most notably, the top-two primary system and the new nonpartisan legislative redistricting system—are designed to improve the functioning of our political system. The 50 percent majority now necessary to pass a budget has ended the budget haggling that used to paralyze Sacramento all summer and for part of the fall, but the cost of limited revenues in 2011 and 2012 was a substantial reduction in funds for the state's public schools. The top-two primary, the 50 percent rule for passing the state's budget in the legislature, and the commission to handle redistricting every 10 years in a neutral and nonpartisan fashion may be just the beginning of a wave of reform, though these reforms will take years to assess.

Meanwhile, our focus in this chapter is the current state of public policy in California. **Public policy** means what government actually does or "produces" in various policy areas, such as health, welfare, education, higher education, water, and the like. The policies in each of these areas are different in each state. For the California of the 1950s and 1960s, education and water policy were proud, if politically difficult, achievements, and the state was one of the nation's leaders in solving its problems and supporting its schools and colleges. For the California of the 2000s, these are areas of profound disappointment.

For example, even with Proposition 98 (1988) "guaranteeing" the public schools some 40 percent of the general fund, California's finances have been so tight that K-12 spending is below average, sometimes ranking in the bottom 40 percent of states.[3] Likewise, the University of California, the California State University, and the state's extensive community college system have all seen cutbacks in pay and course offerings as well as substantially higher tuition and fee payments. How much higher these can go is a major, unanswered question, but there were few alternatives in the severe recession of 2009–2010.

One could write several books about California public policy, so in this chapter we have confined ourselves to four areas of interest. They are typical in the sense that they show some of the best and worst areas in which the state is involved. The first of these is water policy. The second is health insurance. The third is the state's infrastructure, which has experienced spending issues similar to those endured by K-12 education. And the fourth is gambling, specifically the complex negotiations between the state and Indian tribes regarding Indian casinos.

Water Policy

Of the water that humans use in California, 20 percent is for households, business, and industry, while 80 percent is for agricultural purposes, including irrigation. Farm production and food processing compose about 2 percent of the California economy, down from 5 percent in 1960. Over the past decade or more, higher revenue perennial crops that require annual watering, such as grapes, nuts, and other fruits, have increased as a proportion of California's total agricultural output (as compared to annual crops, where land can be left fallow in times of drought). As a consequence, **agricultural water use** has been creeping up.[4]

Household water use is dominated by the two megalopolises of California: the San Francisco Bay region and Southern California. Residential and commercial water use is split 50–50 between use inside the house and landscaping outside. Total urban water use has been constant for the last two decades, in spite of increases in population, because water districts have instituted water conservation programs. Some of these are tiered pricing programs, so that large users pay more per unit, and some incorporate legal requirements to install low-flow toilets and showerheads. Even so, substantial differences among similar cities exist, depending on their closeness to the Pacific coast, density of the population, typical climate, and amount of industry. Coastal cities use less water; a dense population means smaller yards. Hot weather means more watering, and more industry can skew statistics because some industries may use a lot more water than others. A 2004 law requires that water meters be installed statewide by 2025. As of 2014, there are still cities with some customers unmetered; generally the latter are billed a flat rate each month.[5] (See the Who Are Californians feature for more on variation in water use across California.)

The major **2013–14 drought** exposed the problems in the existing system of water rights and uses. Governor Jerry Brown proclaimed a statewide water emergency in January 2014, and local water agencies, depending on their particular situations, gradually imposed measures to restrict the use of water.

The drought has also highlighted problems in the water supply. A study by several University of California researchers released in 2014 pinpointed the central problem: California's freshwater runoff in an average year is about 70 million acre-feet, but since 1914, the state has handed out water rights totaling 370 million acre-feet. That's five times more water than nature, on average, produces.[6] An acre-foot of water (one foot of water in depth on an acre of land) is sufficient for two average households for a year.

Many solutions have been proposed, among them the following: building two 35-mile tunnels around the Sacramento–San Joaquin Delta to bring water to the California aqueduct, importing water from new sources, increasing water conservation efforts, and using rainwater or gray water at home. Four practical solutions were suggested in major studies released in June 2014 by Oakland's Pacific Institute, the Natural Resource Defense Council, and researchers from UC Santa Barbara. Taken together, they point to the future of water supply.[7]

1. Increasing efficiency in homes and industries by replacing or improving inefficient appliances, reducing waste and leaks, and replacing traditional landscapes with low–water-use plants and gardens. The potential savings are 2.9 to 5.2 million acre-feet per year.
2. Increasing efficiency in agriculture through better irrigation techniques and practices, with potential savings of 5.6 to 6.6 million acre-feet per year.
3. Reusing treated wastewater for irrigation, landscapes, industry, and recharging groundwater basins. Savings here could total 1.2 to 1.8 million acre-feet.
4. Capturing storm water at homes and businesses, using it locally or to recharge groundwater basins. Savings could total 0.4 to 0.6 million acre-feet.[8]

Who Gets Water in California?

California gets its water from two major sources: surface water and groundwater. Most water in California goes to agriculture: in an average year, California agriculture irrigates 9.6 million acres of land using approximately 34 million acre-feet of water, while only 9 million acre-feet goes to urban uses including residential use. Water use became especially controversial in 2014 when the state experienced a historic drought, with groundwater at an all-time low (in the 119 years that the state has kept records). The lack of water led to increased calls for conservation and political action, but as the map shows, the response has varied across communities and water districts. As the table shows, per capita water use varies significantly by region.

Restrictions on Water Use, July 2014

● Mandatory restrictions   ● Agricultural restrictions

Note: Many areas also imposed voluntary restrictions.

SOURCES:
Association of California Water Agencies,
Status of Response to 2014 Drought,
http://www.acwa.com/content/drought-map (accessed 7/17/14);
Department of Water Resources, 2014 WY Precipitation Summary,
http://cdec.water.ca.gov/cgi-progs/reports/PRECIPSUM.2014
(accessed 5/1/14);
Department of Water Resources, Draft California Water Plan Update
2013, http://cdec.water.ca.gov/cgi-progs/snowsurvey_sno/COURSES
(accessed 5/1/14).

Water Supply and Use by Region

💧 100 gallons of water

Hydrologic Region	Precipitation %, (2014)*	Snowpack % (2014)*	Gallons per day (2010)**
North Coast	51%	0%	160
San Francisco Bay	73%	N/A	156
Central Coast	46%	N/A	145
South Coast	45%	N/A	189
Sacramento River	54%	9%	280
San Joaquin	47%	21%	239
Tulare Lake	45%	13%	272
North Lahontan	51%	10%	253
South Lahontan	44%	20%	272
Colorado River	24%	N/A	372
State average†	50%	13%	300

* % of historic average   ** Per capita   † Weighted average

forcriticalanalysis

1. Why do some regions of California use more water than others? What drives the different rates of use in the ten hydrologic regions of the state?

2. Given the historic shortage of water, should restrictions be placed on urban/residential use, agricultural use, or both? What other strategies might California use to meet its water needs?

Governor Brown's proposed plan to build two massive tunnels to carry water from the Sacramento–San Joaquin Delta to farmland and cities has been met with opposition from those who fear the plan will destroy the Delta's ecosystem.

At a minimum, the new sources over time could add 10 million acre-feet of water.

The other side of the water quantity problem is the water *quality* problem, involving problems of **groundwater management**, naturally occurring minerals such as arsenic in California's water and, in the eyes of many Californians, hardness. (The latter isn't a water quality issue, but many feel that it is.)

Groundwater composes 35 percent of the total water used in California in an average year. In a drought year, pumping groundwater increases as users attempt to compensate for the lack of rain. While surface water is regulated in California, until September 2014, groundwater was largely unregulated. Some groundwater basins have been so heavily used that the amount taken out each year exceeds what can be reasonably replenished even in El Niño years with relatively heavy rainfall totals. When groundwater declines, the energy costs of pumping water from deeper wells increase and land can actually sink, damaging surface infrastructure such as roads and canals.[9]

Contamination of groundwater is a growing problem in California, with some basins contaminated from fertilizers and manure, and others suffering because of salinity. Changes in water-use practices will help in the future, but some existing basins will need to be cleaned up.

Until 2014, California was the only western state in the U.S. without some level of state regulation of groundwater. The state took a major step in this direction as a result of the 2013–14 drought: the Assembly and state Senate passed three bills to compel water-basin managers in certain areas of the state to design groundwater management plans that would prevent overdrafting. The state will review the plans and can step in if they are inadequate.

In addition, a water bond issue of more than $7 billion was placed on the November 2014 ballot, as the drought provided the catalyst for the legislature to agree on a series of projects in the water policy area. The bond issue had previously been stalled in the legislature for several years. The water bond was approved by almost 67 percent of the voters.

Health Insurance

While many Californians are still without health insurance coverage, President Obama's Affordable Care Act (ACA) has already had a significant impact in California. During the first six months of enrollment, 1.4 million people purchased a health insurance policy on Covered California, the state's health insurance exchange.[10] Another 1.9 million people enrolled in Medi-Cal, now open to single adults and couples without children who qualify on the basis of poverty. These enrollments should reduce the number of people without health insurance in California by about 3 million; the exact number is unclear because some new enrollees replaced their private insurance plans with insurance through the exchange or Medi-Cal. Gallup polls taken in 2013 and in mid-2014 showed a reduction in those without health insurance in California from 21.6 percent to 16.3 percent, which is "in the ballpark" of what can be reasonably expected—a good start toward reducing the very high proportion of people in California without health insurance.

There are three major reasons why the number of uninsured is so high in California. One is that many people in California, more than the national average, work in small firms, and small firms tend not to offer health insurance nearly as often as large firms. The second is that California's population has a large proportion of immigrants, and immigrants are much less likely to have health insurance than native-born Americans. The third reason is that undocumented immigrants are not eligible to enroll in Medicaid (Medi-Cal is California's Medicaid program, see below), nor are they eligible to purchase health insurance through the ACA exchanges. About 2.5 million people are undocumented in California, a figure that has remained constant for over a decade.

Employer-Sponsored Insurance

In 2012, about 53 percent of Californians under age 65 had **employer-sponsored insurance (ESI)**—that is, they obtained their insurance through their employer, who typically subsidized some of the cost. ESI has been declining nationally, and the recession of 2008–09 accelerated the process. In California, ESI has historically been lower than in other states because of the size and structure of California's employers and the number of non-citizens in the state. As of 2014, the ESI numbers had stayed more or less the same after the first round of enrollment in the ACA.

Individual Health Insurance Marketplace

In California's state **individual insurance marketplace**, people purchase a health insurance policy directly from the insurance company. This is the market expected to be most directly affected by the ACA. Several provisions in the Act reformed this market, which has been characterized in the past by extremely large price increases from year to year (one large insurer asked for a 39 percent price increase from 2010 to 2011) and by **rescissions**, cases in which insurers have dropped policyholders who have become sick and filed large claims, on the grounds that their applications were not truthful. The extent of these price increases and recissions enabled by California's pre-ACA marketplace meant that it was a model other states would not want to emulate. The ACA now prohibits companies providing insurance on the marketplace from charging higher rates for preexisting conditions, rescinding policies after policyholders file insurance claims, rating users by health status so that those with fair or poor health pay a higher rate, and enforcing lifetime limits on policies. In 2012, about 8 percent of California's population participated in this market. Most of the people in the market should eventually be receiving their health insurance through Covered California, the state's health insurance exchange.

Medi-Cal

Medi-Cal is California's version of the federal Medicaid plan for the poor. The federal government sponsors two large federal health insurance programs, **Medicare** and **Medicaid**. Medicare, aimed primarily at senior citizens, is paid for with federal funds, a tax on workers and their employers, and beneficiary premiums, deductibles, and co-pays. Medicaid, in contrast, is aimed at low-income people, and the financing is split between the federal government and the states, with the federal government providing an average of 57 percent of the funding and some national standards, and the states providing the other 43 percent of the funding plus basic program administration and decision making. The proportion of the funding that each state provides is determined by a formula based on state per capita income, and because California is a relatively rich state, it receives 50 percent federal funding, the minimum rate. Mississippi will receive the maximum federal funding rate at 73.6 percent in fiscal year 2015.

Under the ACA, Medicaid/Medi-Cal will expand by dropping requirements that excluded single individuals and couples without children and by accepting Medi-Cal enrollees solely on the basis of their income. These changes resulted in 1.9 million people signing up for Medi-Cal during the first enrollment period for the ACA, from November 2013 to March 2014. Medi-Cal now covers about 11.5 million Californians, almost 30 percent of the population.[11]

However, the downside to this expansion is that California's average cost per Medi-Cal recipient is the lowest of any state, mostly because provider payments—the payment to each hospital and doctor for providing a Medi-Cal–covered service—are the lowest in the country. Consequently, access to doctors, particularly specialists, is limited for Medi-Cal beneficiaries in many parts of the state because, for financial reasons, many medical practices either will not take Medi-Cal beneficiaries at all or limit the number of Medi-Cal patients they will see.[12]

Medicare

Some 12.5 percent of Californians are over 65, and almost all of the 4.5 million people in that category are on Medicare. In addition, 2.4 percent of Californians under 65 also qualify for Medicare. All those under 65 who are on Medicare have a disability of some kind (although not all those with disabilities are eligible for Medicare): anyone with ALS (Lou Gehrig's disease) or end-stage renal disease is immediately eligible for Medicare, and those who are on Social Security disability are eligible for Medicare after a two-year wait. The Medicare numbers are not expected to be affected by the ACA.

TRICARE

TRICARE and other military-related programs are the health care programs for military retirees and their dependents, including some members of the military reserves, with some civilian health benefits for military personnel as well. The category also includes those who receive their health care from the U.S. Department of Veterans Affairs (VA). About 2.4 percent of those under 65, some 800,000 Californians, are on TRICARE. The ACA does not affect TRICARE.

The Uninsured

The California HealthCare Foundation, using census data from the federal government, calculated the proportion of uninsured Californians under age 65 from 2010 to 2012 at 21.2 percent.[13] Gallup, using its own surveys and a much simpler question, calculates the proportion as 21.6 percent in 2013 and 16.3 percent in mid-2014. Clearly, the implementation of the ACA in early 2014 has resulted in a major drop in the number and proportion of the uninsured. Just as surely, there is still a long way to go. Basic information about those without insurance follows, although any specific numbers cited are from *before* the ACA.

- Some 23 percent of workers lacked insurance in California, compared with 19 percent in the nation.

- Most heads of household without insurance have a job, and most of those jobs are full-time.

- It is estimated that most *children* without insurance are eligible for Medi-Cal or Healthy Families, California's State Children's Health Insurance Program (SCHIP, which is a federal program aimed at those whose incomes are just above the Medicaid/Medi-Cal eligibility levels).

- 25- to 34-year-olds are the largest age group represented among the uninsured (26 percent), but every age group under 65 is represented. So-called pre-retirees, 55- to 64-year-olds, comprise 9 percent of the total.

- In terms of ethnicity, most people without health insurance in California are Latino (about 58 percent). Whites represent the next most frequent group, at 24 percent. Asians compose 11 percent of the total, and African Americans 5 percent.

- Of those without health insurance, 63 percent are American citizens and 37 percent are not.

California's Infrastructure

Infrastructure is the part of government with which citizens come into contact the most—highways, schools, universities, commuter buses, and railways. California's infrastructure deteriorated significantly from the 1970s into the 2000s, although recently some progress toward improving the system has been made. One factor complicating the successful maintenance of the state's infrastructure is what

The new stretch of the Bay Bridge connecting Oakland and San Francisco (shown here alongside the old, structurally deficient stretch of the bridge that it is designed to replace) has been beset by construction and management problems that catalyzed a government investigation into Caltrans.

Bruce Cain of U.C. Berkeley's Institute of Governmental Studies calls California's "infrastructure ambivalence." On the one hand, Californians want modern facilities and infrastructure, but "we don't want what often comes with those things. There are, for instance, unavoidable environmental costs. Water projects can endanger fisheries in the Delta. New roads and housing can separate and destroy ecosystems."[14] And, of course, we don't want to pay for them. Consider the following examples.

Highways

California's highway system was close to the best in the nation after World War II and into the 1950s and 1960s. Beginning with the 1970s, however, it declined severely. The "California Infrastructure Report Card 2012," issued by the American Society of Civil Engineers, gave California's infrastructure a grade of "C," which is a bit better than the D grade for the nation as a whole.[15] A 2011 report on pavement conditions in the United States found 37 percent of California's roads to be "poor," with only 21 percent "good," making California the state ranked sixth from the bottom of the list.[16] A study of the structural quality of California's bridges found an improvement overall from 2007 to 2013. In 2007, 3,249, or 13.4 percent, of California's 24,189 bridges were structurally deficient; this number declined to 2,769, or 11.1 percent, in 2013.[17] There has been progress, the result in part of bond issues approved by the voters during the Schwarzenegger administration, but there is still much to be done.

The rebuilding of the Bay Bridge connecting San Francisco and Oakland is an extreme example of the substantial problems that have plagued the California state government's management of infrastructure projects. A 2014 report published in the *Sacramento Bee* indicated that the state agency responsible for the bridge construction chose a Chinese contractor who had never built parts for a bridge before to fabricate the steel structure of the bridge. The contractor ignored quality requirements built into the contract and fell behind schedule, necessitating the expenditure of hundreds of millions of dollars above the contract level. The result was a bridge built years behind schedule, costing more than twice the original price, and inspiring significant doubts about its quality.[18]

The management of California's transportation funds is clearly an issue. Dan Walters, who has been writing about California politics and management issues for the *Sacramento Bee* for several decades, points to "the labyrinth of interlocking transportation accounts" directing money to infrastructure projects as the root of the mismanagement. Others locate the problem in the increase in hybrid automobiles that use less gasoline, resulting in less income for the state from the gasoline tax. Another factor is the politicians who find few political benefits from maintaining infrastructure compared with building new projects. Additionally, there are governance problems. For example, when a water main broke in Los Angeles in 2014, it turned out that the main was 100 years old and that water rates were too low to keep up on maintenance, because the city council, not a water agency, sets the rates. Although California's infrastructure is clearly beset by numerous problems, few people consider the maintenance of California's infrastructure, so critical to the movement of citizens, to be a top priority.

Levees

In 1986, a levee broke along the Yuba River and inundated the small town of Linda in the Central Valley, causing several hundred million dollars' worth of damage. In 2004, 18 years later, the state Supreme Court ratified a Court of Appeal decision that found the state of California liable because it had not repaired the broken stretch of levee. While the state resisted liability for the break and its consequences, the courts have determined that the state must pay for the consequences of its neglect.[19]

The *Sacramento Bee* published a series of articles detailing several governmental agencies that were responsible for flood control and maintenance of the levees along the Sacramento River. Although the agencies have not been able to find the funds to repair over 150 sites where the levees could fail during a major flood, builders and developers have continued to construct large developments in the Central Valley near Sacramento in areas where levees hold back rivers that are capable of flood damage to thousands of homes and businesses.[20]

In mid-2004, just after the publication of the *Sacramento Bee* series, a dirt levee broke suddenly in the Delta region, instantly changing 12,000 acres of farmland into a 12,000-acre lake. Officials found that a second levee was in danger of breaking, and a third needed to be shored up to prevent a road from being flooded, cutting the only connection to two islands housing 178 residents.[21] The total damage amounted to $35 million in damages to buildings and crops, plus another $36.5 million to fix the levees. Some of this changed when California lawmakers prioritized levee reconstruction after the destruction wreaked by Hurricane Katrina on the Gulf Coast and the subsequent failure of government in many places to fulfill its emergency responsibilities. The public-works package of bond issues approved by the voters in November 2006 included Proposition 1E, the Disaster Preparedness and Flood Prevention Act, which authorized $4.1 billion in bonds to rebuild flood-control structures, including the Delta levees. The money authorized has provided a starting point for rebuilding the eroding facilities.

In late 2013, Governor Jerry Brown proposed a $25 billion plan to build two 35-mile-long tunnels to carry water under and around the Delta and to rebuild the Delta levees, with construction starting in 2017. The plan would restore wetlands and, in the eyes of supporters, provide a more reliable source for those 25 million Californians who use the Delta's water. Opponents, however, are concerned about the cost of the tunnels, possible ecological damage from the additional water pumped out of the Delta, and questionable financing. Whether the plan will be implemented is a question only time will answer.

The Future of California's Infrastructure

In addition to the Delta tunnels, Governor Brown's second long-term infrastructure priority is the high-speed rail system that would connect San Francisco,

Sacramento, and Los Angeles. As of 2014, construction had not begun, delayed by numerous lawsuits over the system's funding and other design and implementation problems. Currently the plan is projected to cost $68 billion, and the voters have authorized about $10 billion in bonds for the first phase of construction, along with federal stimulus funds from the 2009 recession. Many argue that the state cannot afford a project this large on top of its other needs.

The neglect of the state's infrastructure over time is obvious. There are many reasons why infrastructure repair and upkeep are not more pressing concerns, but the priorities of both politicians and the public are clearly part of the problem. Infrastructure is a long-term problem, and our political system, based on two- and four-year terms of office, thinks short term. This factor is magnified by the term limits imposed on the legislature, traditionally a body in which legislators spent several decades of their careers and could think in longer terms than the governor and the executive-branch officials, who are elected for only one or two four-year terms. Now with term limits, the members of the legislature are subject to the same short-term time constraints.

Indian Gaming in California

In 1931 the first casino opened in Nevada, which remained the only state with gambling casinos until 1976, when New Jersey voters legalized gambling in Atlantic City. Nine more states legalized gambling between 1989 and 1998, and some type of gambling, whether charitable, pari-mutuel, lotteries, commercial casinos, Indian casinos, or racetracks, is now legal in every state except Utah. In the early 1980s, Indian tribes in Florida and California began to operate bingo games with larger prizes than state regulators allowed. The cases in both states went to court resulting in a Supreme Court decision in 1987 and congressional passage of the **Indian Gambling Regulatory Act (IGRA)** in 1998. The act requires tribes to have a compact with the state specifying the type of gambling permitted on their lands. As of September 2014, according to an Indian casino web site, at least 242 of the 562 federally recognized tribes run about 470 gaming operations in 28 of the 50 states.[22] Total national Indian gaming revenues in 2012 were $28.1 billion.

In California, former governor Pete Wilson was reluctant to negotiate any compacts with the Indian tribes, asserting that any compact including slot machines violated the state constitution's prohibition on Nevada- and New Jersey–style casinos. The California Supreme Court subsequently suggested that some electronic gaming devices might qualify, possibly including slot machines. If so, then Wilson would have violated the IGRA's good faith requirement in his reluctance to approve any compacts. After Wilson "begrudgingly" negotiated an agreement with one tribe, citizens who found the agreement unacceptable launched **Proposition 5** in the November 1998 election to force his hand.[23] Prop. 5, approved by a two-thirds vote in a hotly contested proposition battle, guaranteed that any tribe eligible for a gambling compact could have one with Class III games, including slot machines. However, the California Supreme Court overturned Prop. 5 on the grounds that its authorization of slot machines violated the constitutional prohibition against Nevada- or New Jersey–style casinos.

In the 1998 election, Wilson left office, and Gray Davis was elected governor. Davis was much more supportive of **tribal casinos** and drafted a model compact, accepted by the tribes pending the approval of Prop. 1A in 2000. Prop. 1A amended the California Constitution to exempt Indian tribes from the prohibition against Nevada- or New Jersey–style casinos and to authorize the governor to negotiate gambling compacts, placing casinos with slot machines and other gambling games in the same category. The proposition passed overwhelmingly. In 2014, the state's 109 tribes operated 68 casinos. The tribes are estimated to generate revenues of approximately $7 billion per year, and they have become major contributors to California election campaigns.[24]

The major policy issue in the past was the percentage of gaming revenues due to the state of California. At present, the tribes pay approximately $130 million per year to the state, about 2 percent of their revenues, to help other tribes that do not have gaming operations. They also make voluntary (often small) contributions to the local governments in the area of their casinos to offset increased expenses that may result from the casino. A California court decision involving the Rincon tribe of San Diego County held that California could not extract taxes from Indian casinos in return for permission to expand.

Tribal casinos are not required to address environmental problems, such as "damage to local roads, animal and plant life, and water supplies and for public services." On his last day in office, after being recalled, Governor Davis wrote a letter releasing the tribes from any obligation to negotiate over these issues.[25] Another contentious issue is the exclusion of hundreds of persons who thought they were members of Indian tribes and thus entitled to receive the substantial annual payments generated from casino profits that go to lawful members. Several tribes in recent years voted former members out of membership on the grounds that they were not lineal descendants of the original members of the tribe. The governor has been urged to investigate the disenrollments, which in some cases are contravened by DNA evidence, and the disenrolled members have threatened to sue in state, federal, or Bureau of Indian Affairs courts; the courts have left membership issues to the tribes, however, and so the suits have not been successful.

One interesting feature of Indian casinos in California is that the tribes have **sovereign immunity** from lawsuits filed by those who work in the casino or by patrons of the casino. Injured employees and customers have sued the casinos, but the suits have been routinely dismissed because of sovereign immunity. Congress has been unable or unwilling to attempt any changes, and the Supreme Court might well refuse to uphold them, meaning that the tribes are not required to obey laws relating to environmental quality, workers' compensation, and so forth. (They are required to obey alcohol control laws, however.)

Another major issue currently facing the state and federal government is that some of the tribes want to expand their casinos closer to urban areas. The Obama Administration has loosened the rules on adding land to existing reservations. The U.S. Supreme Court in 2009 issued a ruling that the Interior Department, which houses the Bureau of Indian Affairs, could not create reservations for tribes that were not recognized in 1914, but legislation could overturn that ruling. Indian gaming, then, raises a host of issues about the relations between historically deprived targets of discrimination and the current state and federal governments. These are difficult issues, particularly given the history of the treatment of Native Americans in California, and they promise to be in the news for years to come.

Conclusion

The Duroville case study illustrates the problems that arise in California because of fractured interests, complications of land (Indian reservations) that the state cannot control or regulate, and problems resulting from undocumented immigration. The fact that a disgraceful trailer park finally closed after many years of dysfunction is good. The fact that it took so many years to find a substitute location for the people who lived in the park is not good. One characteristic of contemporary California is that it can be years or decades before even modest starts are made on solving problems.

Water policy and health insurance illustrate how external changes, such as climate fluctuations or new federal policy, can dramatically affect state policy. When these kinds of catalysts do not exist, California is often slow or unable to make headway. For example, the health insurance situation only worsened in the two decades before the passage of the ACA, and the last great pieces of infrastructure affecting water policy were decided upon during the administration of Governor Edmund G. "Pat" Brown, from 1959 to 1967. Recent external events have finally prompted movement in both policy areas. The 2013–14 drought stimulated California's state government to pass pathbreaking legislation in August 2014, making it the last western state to enact groundwater regulations. Regarding health insurance, the passage of the federal Affordable Care Act gave California the opportunity to insure a substantial proportion of its uninsured population at the minimum cost. California was wise to take advantage of this opportunity.

Water policy has become immensely more complicated with the growth of the environmental movement since the first Earth Day in 1969. But even under the senior Governor Brown in the early 1960s, the decisions made on water were not easy and involved prolonged political conflict. We often hear commentators discussing the "cultural breakup" of the old political consensus in the state, but the truth is, we are better for the multiplicity of voices that continually debate the best course of action for California to pursue. It is more difficult to achieve public policy consensus and make decisions, some long overdue, but these are interests that need to be considered in the present day. We have begun the long road to reform on many issues discussed in this chapter and the book as a whole, and there is hope for a state more governable in the future. But more steps have to be taken, and we need both visionary leadership and voters who pay attention and are interested in change. We hope the readers of this book will be those voters.

Study Guide

FOR FURTHER READING

"Arnold's Big Chance: A Survey of California." *The Economist*, May 1, 2004, pp. 1–16.

Gleick, Peter H. "Solving California's Water Problems." *Huffington Post*, June 10, 2014. www.huffingtonpost.com/peter-h-gleick/solving-californias-water_b_5479569.html. Accessed September 3, 2014.

Hanak, Ellen, Jeffrey Mount, and Caitrin Chappelle. "Just the Facts: California's Latest Drought." Public Policy Institute of California, February 2014. www.ppic.org. Accessed September 3, 2014.

Maiman, Bruce. "Priorities Are Not on Infrastructure Repair." *Sacramento Bee*, March 18, 2014.

Walters, Dan. "Politicians Often Ignore California's Aging Infrastructure." *Sacramento Bee*, August 9, 2014.

Rogers, Paul. "Is Jerry Brown's Delta Tunnels Plan Repeating the Errors of High-Speed Rail?" *San Jose Mercury-News*, December 9, 2013.

Barrera, E. A. "A Firestorm of Controversy—Still No County Fire Department Five Years after Cedar Blaze." *East County Magazine*, August 2008, www.eastcountymagazine.org. Accessed August 17, 2012.

Hill, Laura E., Magnus Lofstrom, and Joseph M. Hayes. "Immigrant Legalization: Assessing the Labor Market Effects." San Francisco: Public Policy Institute of California, 2010, www.ppic.org/content/pubs/report/R_410LHR.pdf. Accessed August 17, 2012.

Johnson, Hans, and Laura Hill. "At Issue, Illegal Immigration." San Francisco: Public Policy Institute of California, July 2011. www.ppic.org/content/pubs/atissue/AI_711HJAI.pdf. Accessed August 17, 2012.

Light, Steven Andrew, and Kathryn R. L. Rand. *Indian Gaming and Tribal Sovereignty: The Casino Compromise*. Lawrence: University Press of Kansas, 2005.

Lustig, R. Jeffrey. *Remaking California, Reclaiming the Public Good*. Berkeley: Heyday Books, 2010.

Matthews, Joe, and Mark Paul. *California Crack-Up, How Reform Broke the Golden State and How We Can Fix It*. Berkeley, CA: University of California, 2010.

Pear, Robert. "Lacking Papers, Citizens Are Cut from Medicaid." *New York Times*, March 12, 2007.

Piller, C. "Bay Bridge's Troubled China Connection," *Sacramento Bee*, June 8, 2014.

Schrag, Peter. *California: America's High-Stakes Experiment*. Berkeley: University of California Press, 2006.

Simmons, Charlene Wear. *Gambling in the Golden State, 1998 Forward*. Sacramento: California Research Bureau, California State Library, May 2006.

"Special Report: Democracy in California, The People's Will." *The Economist*, April 23, 2011.

State of California, Legislative Analyst's Office. *A Primer: The State's Infrastructure and the Use of Bonds*. Sacramento: Legislative Analyst's Office, January 2006.

"The Drying of the West," *The Economist*, February 22, 2014, pp. 22–23.

ON THE WEB

American Association of State Highway and Transportation Officials: www.transportation.org/Pages/Default.aspx. Accessed September 3, 2014.

California HealthCare Foundation: www.chcf.org. Accessed September 3, 2014.

California Progress Report: www.californiaprogressreport.com/site/. Accessed September 3, 2014. A daily briefing on politics and policy.

Field Poll of Californians: www.field.com/fieldpollonline/subscribers/. Accessed September 3, 2014.

Huffington Post: www.huffingtonpost.com. Accessed September 3, 2014.

Kaiser Family Foundation: http://kff.org/. Accessed September 3, 2014. Health insurance information.

Pacific Institute: http://pacinst.org/ or www.californiadrought.org/. Accessed September 3, 2014.

Public Policy Institute of California: www.ppic.org. Accessed September 3, 2014.

State of California, Legislative Analyst's Office: www.lao.ca.gov. Accessed September 3, 2014.

SUMMARY

I. Duroville was a trailer park located on an Indian reservation in Riverside County. Many of its residents were agricultural workers, and the park were experienced particularly squalid conditions in its 12 years of existence.

A. The federal government filed suit to close it, but the lack of an alternative location that the several thousand residents could afford stymied federal and state efforts to do so.

B. The state and county have constructed a new trailer park using redevelopment funds, and the Duroville trailer park was finally closed in 2014.

II. The 2013–14 drought worsened California's water supply problem.
A. 20 percent of the water humans use in California is for household use, of which half is used for landscaping. The other 80 percent is for agriculture.
B. Urban water use has been constant, reflecting the water conservation programs implemented in water districts in California.
C. California water agencies have vastly overpromised the average amount of water that runs off each year in California.
D. Practical solutions to increase the amount of water that humans can use in California include: increased efficiency at home or in industry, increased efficiency in agriculture, reusing treated wastewater on landscapes and recharging groundwater basins, and capturing storm water.
E. Water quality is also an issue in California, because of pollution and naturally occurring minerals such as arsenic.
F. Groundwater makes up 35 percent of the water used in an average year, and more in drought years. California was the last state not to regulate groundwater in the western United States, until in August 2014 the legislature passed a bill to allow the state to review groundwater management plans to be produced by many water districts in the state.

III. The lack of health insurance among Californians is a major problem, but President Obama's Affordable Care Act has had a major impact in California, with 1.4 million people purchasing health insurance policies and another 1.9 million enrolling in Medi-Cal, California's Medicaid program.
A. Employers insure a lower proportion of people in California compared with other states because California has more small firms and the state has so many noncitizens.
B. Proportionally, more people buy their own health insurance in California than in other states. The health insurance market has been characterized by a large percentage of price increases from year to year and by "rescissions," the cancellation of policies because of inaccurate applications (from the perspective of the insurance companies) or because high claims have been filed (from the perspective of the state). This is the market that the Affordable Care Act will affect the most, by eliminating rescissions and more closely standardizing policies.
C. Medi-Cal covers 30 percent of Californians, a larger proportion than in other states, but the average cost per beneficiary is among the lowest among the states because provider payments are so low. Access to providers is a major problem in some areas of the state.
D. In California, Medicare covers some 600,000 persons under 65 with disabilities. A similar number is covered by TRICARE or the Department of Veterans Affairs (VA).
E. Because of the Affordable Care Act, the 21 percent of adult Californians under 65 who lack health insurance has fallen to 16 percent or less, although we do not have good quality data on the statistics at this point.

IV. California's infrastructure has noticeably deteriorated in the last 50 years.
A. The state's highways were in poor condition but are being gradually upgraded through bond issues passed in 2006 at Governor Schwarzenegger's urging and through federal Recovery Act funds.
B. The management of transportation funds is an issue, with the major contemporary example being the problems with the new San Francisco–Oakland Bay Bridge.
C. The levees in the Delta and the Central Valley of California are the subject of a major and controversial plan being urged by Governor Jerry Brown in 2014. Some levee work is being attended to by state funds provided in bond issues passed in 2006.

V. Indian casinos are widespread in California.
A. There are presently 68 Indian casinos, with over 60,000 slot machines. Some 2 to 3 percent of the proceeds from the casinos are paid to the state, mostly to a fund that compensates tribes that do not have casinos.
B. *Sovereign immunity* for Indian tribes means that they control most areas of government that would otherwise be subject to the control of the state. One implication of this is that those who work at or patronize Indian casinos do not have the right to sue casino management for injuries or other problems.
C. The tribes determine who is and is not a member, and some tribes have excluded previous members after the casino has opened, thus increasing the money received by the other members.

PRACTICE QUIZ

1. Medicaid is
   a) a national program, administered by the federal government, with little state input.
   b) a state program, administered with little federal government guidance or funds.
   c) a federal/state program, with over half the money coming from the federal government.
   d) a federal/state program, with over half the money coming from the states.

2. Duroville was a particularly difficult public policy problem because
   a) the trailer park was located on an Indian reservation, where the state has little jurisdiction.
   b) many of the residents were undocumented, meaning they will have a difficult time qualifying for public housing.
   c) the many other trailer parks in Riverside County indicate that the problems symbolized by Duroville may be widespread.
   d) all of the above

3. In California, employer-sponsored health insurance or ESI
   a) has historically been higher proportionately than in other states because of the size and structure of California's employers and the number of noncitizens in the state.
   b) has historically been about the same as in other states.
   c) has historically been lower than in other states because of the size and structure of California's employers and the number of noncitizens in the state.
   d) has historically been higher than in other states because of the generosity of the state's medical programs.

4. The individual health insurance market in California, prior to the implementation of the Affordable Care Act, was a model that other states might emulate.
   a) true
   b) false

5. California's basic water allocation is as follows:
   a) Of the water for human use, most is used for households, and only a small amount for agriculture. The water for household use is divided roughly 50–50 between inside and outside use.
   b) Of the water for human use, about half is used for households, with the other half for agriculture. The household portion is dominated by inside use, which is the greater proportion.

   c) Of the water for human use, most is used in agriculture. The portion used for households is divided about 50–50 between inside and outside use.
   d) Of the water for human use, most is used in agriculture. The portion used for households is mostly used outside for landscape watering.

6. The most likely solutions for increasing the water supply in California rely on:
   a) reusing treated wastewater.
   b) capturing storm water.
   c) increased efficiency at homes, businesses, and in agriculture.
   d) all of the above

7. California's infrastructure has been neglected for all of the following reasons *except*
   a) most recent budgets have had to cut expenses, and infrastructure is among the easier items to cut.
   b) the state legislature does not put a high priority on infrastructure issues.
   c) most politicians in California have long-term horizons.
   d) California's transportation funds are often mismanaged.

8. The amount of groundwater pumped during a drought is higher than the average amount pumped in most years.
   a) true
   b) false

9. Indian gaming issues in California have involved the following *except*
   a) tribal-sponsored initiatives.
   b) federal court decisions over the legality of Indian casinos in California.
   c) compacts negotiated by the governor and ratified by the state Senate.
   d) substantial gaming revenues received by local governments in California.

10. The example of the new San Francisco–Oakland Bay Bridge illustrates the following problem:
    a) Not nearly enough money was spent on the bridge.
    b) The management of bridge construction is a major problem for California state government.
    c) The bridge was built far too quickly, although by competent construction workers.
    d) The governor of the state should not be involved in constructing major projects like the new Bay Bridge.

CRITICAL-THINKING QUESTIONS

1. Discuss the condition of California's highways, both in your experience and as presented in the book. What do you think is the nature of the problem at the most fundamental level?
2. The involvement of many different groups makes Indian gaming a significant public-policy problem. Indicate the different groups that are involved; their goals, which may be different or conflicting; and something about their success thus far.
3. What future reforms of California state government might help with the public policy problems illustrated in this chapter?

KEY TERMS

2013–14 drought (p. 246)
agricultural water use (p. 246)
employer-sponsored insurance (ESI) (p. 249)
groundwater management (p. 248)
household water use (p. 246)

Indian Gambling Regulatory Act (p. 254)
individual insurance marketplace (p. 249)
infrastructure (p. 251)
Medicaid (p. 250)
Medi-Cal (p. 250)

Medicare (p. 250)
Proposition 5 (p. 254)
public policy (p. 245)
rescissions (p. 249)
sovereign immunity (p. 255)
tribal casinos (p. 255)

Answer Key

Chapter 1
1. a
2. b
3. d
4. b
5. b
6. d
7. c
8. a
9. c
10. b

Chapter 2
1. b
2. c
3. a
4. c
5. c
6. c
7. a
8. c
9. d
10. b

Chapter 3
1. c
2. b
3. a
4. c
5. b
6. c
7. a
8. d
9. a
10. b

Chapter 4
1. a
2. b
3. d
4. a
5. a
6. d
7. a
8. b
9. a
10. b

Chapter 5
1. a
2. a
3. d
4. c
5. d
6. c
7. a
8. c
9. a
10. d

Chapter 6
1. a
2. b
3. d
4. c
5. d
6. d
7. d
8. b
9. a
10. b

Chapter 7
1. a
2. b
3. a
4. b
5. b
6. a
7. b
8. c
9. a
10. d

Chapter 8
1. a
2. a
3. c
4. b
5. d
6. b
7. a
8. b
9. d
10. b
10. a

Chapter 9
1. b
2. b
3. a
4. a
5. b
6. d
7. c
8. a
9. a
10. b

Chapter 10
1. c
2. d
3. c
4. b
5. c
6. d
7. c
8. a
9. d
10. b

Notes

Chapter 1

1. James Q. Wilson, "A Guide to Schwarzenegger Country," *Commentary* (December 2003): 45–49. Field Institute, *Legislation by Initiative vs. through Elected Representatives*, San Francisco: Field Institute, November 1999, www.field.com/fieldpollonline/subscribers/COI-99-Nov-Legislation.pdf (accessed 7/17/12).
2. Initiative and Referendum Institute, "Initiative Use," Los Angeles: University of Southern California Gould School of Law, September 2010, www.iandrinstitute.org (accessed 7/17/12).
3. Public Policy Institute of California, "Just the Facts: Immigrants in California," May 2013. http://www.ppic.org/main/publication_show.asp?-258 (accessed 10/14/14).
4. Jeffrey S. Passel, Randy Capps, and Michael Fix, *Undocumented Immigrants: Facts and Figures* (Washington, DC: Urban Institute Immigration Studies Program, January 12, 2004), www.urban.org/UploadedPDF/1000587_undoc_immigrants_facts.pdf (accessed 7/17/12).
5. Dan Walters, "Ex-Governors Miss Chance to Discuss Complexities," *Santa Barbara News-Press*, February 21, 2004, p. A11.

Chapter 2

1. Follow the Money, "National Institute on Money in State Politics," www.followthemoney.org (accessed 6/20/12).
2. Joe Matthews and Mark Paul, *California Crackup: How Reform Broke the Golden State and How We Can Fix It* (Berkeley: University of California Press, 2010), 21.
3. Kevin Starr, *California: A History* (New York: Modern Library, 2005), 121.
4. Starr, *California*, 124.
5. Matthews and Paul, *California Crackup*, 23.
6. Carl Brent Swisher, *Motivation and Political Technique in the California Constitutional Convention: 1878–79* (New York: Da Capo Press, 1969).
7. The U.S. Constitution can also be amended by passage in a constitutional convention called by two-thirds of the states, followed by ratification by three-fourths of the states. This method has never been used, however. See Article V of the U.S. Constitution.
8. Spencer C. Olin, Jr., *California's Prodigal Sons: Hiram Johnson and the Progressives, 1911–1917* (Berkeley: University of California Press, 1968), 70.
9. John M. Allswang, *The Initiative and Referendum in California, 1898–1998* (Stanford, CA: Stanford University Press, 2000), 15.
10. George Mowry, *The California Progressives* (Chicago: Quadrangle Paperbacks, 1963), 9, 12–13.
11. Kevin Starr, *Inventing the Dream: California through the Progressive Era* (New York: Oxford University Press, 1985), 242–43.
12. Dean R. Cresap, *Party Politics in the Golden State* (Los Angeles: The Haynes Foundation, 1954), 12.
13. Mowry, *The California Progressives*, 12.
14. Mowry, *The California Progressives*, 15.
15. Quoted in Mowry, *The California Progressives*, 65.
16. Starr, *Inventing the Dream*, 254.
17. Many recalls take place at the local level: volunteer groups organize recalls of city council or school board members because they simply feel strongly about a particular issue. Statewide recalls, however, are rare.
18. California Secretary of State Debra Bowen, "99 Years of California Initiatives, One Day Left to Qualify for June 8 Ballot," www.sos.ca.gov/admin/press-releases/2010/db10-015.pdf (accessed 6/20/12); "Initiative Totals by Summary

Year 1912–September 2014," http://sos.ca.gov/elections/ballot-measures/pdf/initiative-totals-summary-year.pdf (accessed 11/24/14).

19. Allswang, *The Initiative and Referendum in California*, 33.

20. Allswang, *The Initiative and Referendum in California*, 75.

21. California Secretary of State Debra Bowen, "Referendum," www.sos.ca.gov/elections/ballot-measures/referenda.htm (accessed 11/24/14).

22. Jim Puzzanghera, "History of Recall Adds Fuel to Both Sides," *San Jose Mercury News*, June 18, 2003, http://digital.library.ucla.edu/websites/2003_999_022/latest.news/94/index.htm (accessed 8/3/12).

Chapter 3

1. Jay Michael, Dan Walters, and Dan Weintraub, *The Third House: Lobbyists, Power, and Money in Sacramento* (Berkeley, CA: Berkeley Public Policy Press, 2002), 13.

2. Sam Delson, "Some Call Spending Money to Get Money Regrettable but Necessary for Inland Cities and Schools," *Riverside Press Enterprise*, July 6, 1997, p. A2.

3. Debra Bowen, California Secretary of State, "Lobbying Activity: Employers of Lobbyists," http://cal-access.ss.ca.gov/Lobbying/Employers (accessed 6/22/12).

4. Chase Davis, "State Lobby Spending on Pace to Set Records," *California Watch*, November 3, 2011, http://californiawatch.org/dailyreport/state-lobby-spending-pace-set-records-13402 (accessed 6/22/12).

5. "California Lobbyist Control Gets a C," *Silicon Valley/San Jose Business Journal*, May 19, 2003.

6. Cary McWilliams, *California: The Great Exception* (Berkeley: University of California Press, 1999), 198.

7. Mark Sappenfield, "Why Clout of Lobbyists Is Growing," *Christian Science Monitor*, July 23, 2003, www.csmonitor.com/2003/0722/p01s02-uspo.html (accessed 6/22/12).

8. Debra Bowen, California Secretary of State, "Lobbying Activity: Lobbying Firms," 2007–08, http://cal-access.ss.ca.gov/Lobbying/Employers (accessed 6/22/12).

9. Stephen Ansolabehere, James Snyder, Jr., and Mickey Tripathi, "Are PAC Contributions and Lobbying Linked? New Evidence from the 1995 Lobby Disclosure Act," www.tandfonline.com/doi/abs/10.1080/1369525022000015586#preview (accessed 8/4/12).

10. National Institute on Money in State Politics, "State Overview: California 2009–10," www.followthemoney.org.

11. California Fair Political Practices Commission, "Big Money Talks," March 2010, p. 41, www.fppc.ca.gov/reports/Report 31110.pdf (accessed 6/22/12).

12. Maria Lagos, "Result of Furloughs—$1 Billion Liability," *San Francisco Chronicle*, April 23, 2011, www.sfgate.com/cgi-bin/article.cgi?f=/c/a/2011/03/07/MNSQ1I2ASB.DTL&ao=all (accessed 6/22/12).

13. Steven Malanga, "The Beholden State," *City Journal* 20 (Spring 2010), www.city-journal.org/2010/20_2_california-unions.html (accessed 6/22/12).

14. Field Research Corporation, "Statewide Ballot Proposition Elections," October 2011, http://field.com/fieldpollonline/subscribers/COI-11-Oct-California-Ballot-Propositions.pdf (accessed 6/22/12).

15. Elisabeth R. Gerber, "Interest Group Influence in the California Initiative Process," Public Policy Institute of California, 1998, www.ppic.org/main/publication.asp?i=49 (accessed 8/4/12).

16. McWilliams, *California*, 213.

17. Arthur H. Samish and Bob Thomas, *The Secret Boss of California* (New York: Crown Publishers, 1971), 13.

18. Debra Bowen, California Secretary of State, "History of the Political Reform Division," 2004, www.ss.ca.gov/prd/about_the_division/history.htm (accessed 6/22/12).

19. Patrick McGreevy and Nancy Vogel, "Senate Travel Perks for Sale," *Los Angeles Times*, March 16, 2008.

20. Pew Research Center for the People and the Press, "Digital: By the Numbers," *The State of the News Media, 2013*, http://stateofthemedia.org/2013/digital-as-mobile-grows-rapidly-the-pressures-on-news-intensify/digital-by-the-numbers (accessed 7/21/14).

21. Susan F. Rasky, "Covering California: The Press Wrestles with Diversity, Complexity, and Change," in *Governing California: Politics, Government, and Public Policy in the Golden State*, ed. Gerald C. Lubenow and Bruce E. Cain (Berkeley: Institute of Governmental Studies Press, University of California, 1997), 157–88.

22. Rasky, "Covering California," 182.

23. Pew Research Center for the People and the Press, *Future of Mobile News*, October 1, 2012, www.journalism.org/2012/10/01/future-mobile-news/ (accessed 7/21/14).

24. Joe Garofoli, "Labor Beat Prop. 32 via Social Media," *SFGate*, December 25, 2012.

25. Jim Rutenberg, "Working to Spin Distrust of Media into Votes," *New York Times*, October 12, 2003.

Chapter 4

1. Spencer C. Olin, *California's Prodigal Sons: Hiram Johnson and the Progressives, 1911–1917* (Berkeley: University of California Press, 1968).

2. Brian F. Schaffner, Matthew Streb, and Gerald Wright, "Teams without Uniforms: The Nonpartisan Ballot in State and Local Elections," *Political Research Quarterly* 54, no. 1 (2001): 7–30.

3. Michael Finnegan, "The Race for the White House," *Los Angeles Times*, September 8, 2004, p. A1.

4. Roper Center for Public Opinion Research, *Social Capital Community Benchmark Survey: Methodology and Documentation*, February 17, 2001, www.ropercenter.uconn.edu/scc_bench.html (accessed 8/13/12).

5. Mark Baldassare, *A California State of Mind: The Conflicted Voter in a Changing World* (Berkeley: University of California Press, 2002), 47.
6. Stanford Law School, Stanford Three Strikes Project. "Three Strikes Basics." https://www.law.stanford.edu/organizations/programs-and-centers/stanford-three-strikes-project/three-strikes-basics.
7. Richard Edward DeLeon, *Left Coast City: Progressive Politics in San Francisco, 1975–1991* (Lawrence: University Press of Kansas, 1992).
8. "The Mormon Money behind Proposition 8," *The Atlantic*, October 23, 2008, www.theatlantic.com/daily-dish/archive/2008/10/the-mormon-money-behind-proposition-8/209748/ (accessed 8/13/12).
9. Wilson, Reid "The Most Expensive Ballot Initiatives." Gov Beat, http://www.washingtonpost.com/blogs/govbeat/wp/2014/05/17/the-most-expensive-ballot-initiatives.
10. Susan Rasky, "Introduction to 'An Antipolitician, Anti-establishment Groundswell Elected the Candidate of Change,'" in *California Votes: The 2002 Governor's Race and the Recall That Made History*, ed. Gerald Lubenow (Berkeley: Berkeley Public Policy Press, 2003).
11. Rasky, "Introduction."
12. Catherine Decker, "State's Shifting Political Landscape," *Los Angeles Times*, November 6, 2008, p. A1.
13. "Young Voters Help Secure Obama Victory, Passage of Progressive Ballot Measures," *Huffington Post*, November 7, 2012.
14. Phil Willon, "GOP Loses Grip on Inland Empire," *Los Angeles Times*, November 11, 2012, p. A37.
15. George Skelton, "Time for Initiative Reforms," *Los Angeles Times*, November 15, 2012, p. A2.
16. St John, P. "Prop. 47 would cut penalties for 1 in 5 criminals in California." October 11, 2014. http://www.latimes.com/local/politics/la-me-ff-pol-proposition47-20141012-story.html.
17. D. P. Osorio, "The Cost of Winning a Senate Race," DPOsorio.com, May 9, 2012, http://dposorio.com/blog/822/the-cost-of-winning-a-senate-race (accessed 7/20/12).
18. Rasky, "Introduction."
19. William Booth, "In Calif. Governor's Race, It's Ads Infinitum," *Washington Post*, May 29, 1998, p. A1.
20. Carol A. Cassel, "Hispanic Turnout: Estimates from Validated Voting Data," *Political Research Quarterly* 55, no. 2 (June 2002): 391–408. Michael A. Jones-Correa and David L. Leal, "Political Participation: Does Religion Matter?," *Political Research Quarterly* 54, no. 4 (2001): 751–70.

Chapter 5

1. Field Research Corporation, "California Voter Views of the State Legislature Turn Negative after the Arrest of State Senator Leland Yee." Poll release #2464, April 10, 2014, http://field.com/fieldpollonline/subscribers/ (accessed 8/11/14).
2. Andrew Dugan, "Congressional Approval Rating Languishes at low Level," *Gallup Politics*, July 15, 2014 http://www.gallup.com/poll/politics.aspx?ref=b (accessed 8/11/14).
3. State Netz *Session Statistics, 2013–2014 California Session Statistics*, November 7, 2014, and *2011–2012 California Session Statistics*, November 23, 2012 (Accessed 11/7/2014). http://www.statenet.com/resources/session_statistics.php?state=CA.
4. Editorial Board, "Editorial: Stop Disgrace of 'Gut and Amend' in Legislature," *Sacramento Bee*, May 1, 2013, http://www.sacbee.com/2013/05/01/5384661/stop-disgrace-of-gut-and-amend.html (accessed 8/11/14).
5. Lou Cannon, *Governor Reagan: His Rise to Power* (New York: Public Affairs, 2003), 166.
6. Peter Schrag, *Paradise Lost: California's Experience, America's Future* (New York: New Press, 1998), 244.
7. Institute of Governmental Studies, "IGS Goes to Sacramento to Assess Ten Years of Term Limits," *Public Affairs Report* 42, no. 3 (Fall 2001).
8. National Association of Latino Elected and Appointed Officials, http://www.naleo.org/downloads/State_Leg_Table_2012.pdf (accessed 11/7/14) and the National Conference of State Legislatures, http://www.ncsl.org/legislators-staff/legislators/womens-legislative-network/women-in-state-legislatures-for-2014.aspx (accessed 11/7/14).
9. Schrag, *Paradise Lost*, 143.
10. Adam Nagourney, "Political Shift in California Trips Brown," *New York Times*, September 20, 2011, www.nytimes.com/2011/09/21/us/politics/brown-says-california-gop-is-harder-to-work-with-decades-later.html?pagewanted=all (accessed 6/24/12).
11. Anthony York, "Brown and Obama Find Bipartisanship a Difficult Goal to Reach," *Los Angeles Times*, February 24, 2012, http://articles.latimes.com/2012/feb/24/local/la-me-jerry-brown-20120224 (accessed 6/24/12).
12. Nagourney, "Political Shift in California Trips Brown."
13. George Skelton, "California's Capitol—the Long View: A Columnist Looks Back on 50 Years Covering the Ups and Downs of Sacramento," *Los Angeles Times*, December 1, 2011, p. A2.

Chapter 6

1. Timothy Egan, "Jerry Brown's Revenge," *New York Times*, March 6, 2014, www.nytimes.com/2014/03/07/opinion/egan-jerry-browns-revenge.html?module=Search&mabReward=relbias%3As%2C%7B%221%22%3A%22RI%3A6%22%7D&_r=0 (accessed 7/30/2014).
2. Richard E. Neustadt, *Presidential Power and the Modern Presidents: The Politics of Leadership from Roosevelt to Reagan* (New York: Macmillan, 1990).

3. Thomas E. Cronin and Michael A. Genovese, *The Paradoxes of the American Presidency* (New York: Oxford University Press, 1998).

4. Public Policy Institute of California, "PPIC Statewide Survey: Time Trends for Job Approval Ratings for Governor Schwarzenegger," www.ppic.org/main/dataSet.asp?i=927 (accessed 8/1/2014).

5. "Press Release: Governor Brown Delivers Plan to Streamline and Simplify State Government to Little Hoover Commission," March, 30, 2012, http://gov.ca.gov/news.php?id=17476 (accessed 8/1/2014).

6. Joshua Stark, "New Report Calls For Radical Reform of Caltrans," *Transform*, February 4, 2014, www.transformca.org/trblogpost/report-calls-radical-reform-caltrans (accessed 8/4/2014). Charles Piller, "Senate Report: Caltrans 'gagged and banished' Bay Bridge critics," *Sacramento Bee*, July 31, 2014, www.sacbee.com/2014/07/31/6596963/senate-report-caltrans-gagged.html (accessed 8/2/2014). Charles Piller, "Bay Bridge's troubled China connection," *Sacramento Bee*, June 8, 2014, www.sacbee.com/static/sinclair/sinclair.jquery/baybridge/index.html (accessed 8/2/2014). Debra J. Saunders, "Jerry Brown on Bay Bridge: Don't worry, be happy," *SFGate*, May 16, 2014, http://blog.sfgate.com/djsaunders/2014/05/16/jerry-brown-on-bay-bridge-dont-worry-be-happy/ (accessed 8/2/2014).

7. "Gov. Jerry Brown's Veto Rate is now 13%, Gov. Schwarzenegger's was twice that," KPCC, October 2, 2012, Retrieved from http://www.scpr.org/blogs/news/2012/10/02/10286/gov-jerry-browns-veto-rate-13-gov-schwarzeneggers-/ (accessed August 28, 2014). State Net, *Session Statistics, 2013–2014 California Session Statistics*, November 7, 2014, and *2011–2012 California Session Statistics*, November 23, 2012. http://www.statenet.com/resources/session_statistics.php?state=CA (Accessed 11/7/2014).

8. Eric McGhee and Paul Warren, "The Vanishing Line-Item Veto," *Viewpoints: The PPIC Blog* (San Francisco: Public Policy Institute of California, June 26, 2014), www.ppic.org/main/blog_detail.asp?i=1551 (accessed 7/28/2014).

9. Steven Harmon, "Gov. Brown warns Democratic lawmakers not to overreach, overspend," *Vallejo Times-Herald*, January 24, 2013, www.timesheraldonline.com/ci_22439612/gov-brown-warns-democratic-lawmakers-not-overreach-overspend.

10. James Fallows, "Jerry Brown's Political Reboot," *The Atlantic*, May 2013, www.theatlantic.com/magazine/archive/2013/06/the-fixer/309324/ (accessed 7/28/2014).

11. Nicolas Riccardi, "Brown's 2011: Tall Hopes but Taller Hurdles," *Los Angeles Times*, December 27, 2011, p. A1.

12. Fallows, "Jerry Brown's Political Reboot"; Egan, "Jerry Brown's Revenge"; Lou Cannon, "Calif. Comeback: Jerry Brown Leads a Turnaround," *Real Clear Politics*, June 25, 2013, www.realclearpolitics.com/articles/2013/06/25/calif_comeback_jerry_brown_leads_a_turnaround_118943.html (accessed 7/28/2014).

13. Fallows, "Jerry Brown's Political Reboot."

Chapter 7

1. See *In re Sergio C. Garcia* on Admission.

2. Court Statistics Report, *Statewide Caseload Trends, 2000–2001 Through 2009–2010* (2011), www.courts.ca.gov/documents/2011CourtStatisticsReport.pdf (accessed 9/22/14.

3. www.courts.ca.gov

4. *People v. Colvin*, 203 Cal.App.4th 1029 (2012).

5. Unpublished means that it may not be used for purposes of legal citation or precedent. http://gpo.gov/fdsys/pkg/USCOURTS-caed-2_11-cv-02939

6. The memorandum can be found here: *11-2939— Sacramento Nonprofit Collective et al v. Holder et al*, U.S. Government Printing Office, www.gpo.gov/fdsys/granule/USCOURTS-caed-2_11-cv-02939/USCOURTS-caed-2_11-cv-02939-0 (accessed 9/22/14).

7. There are seven seats on the California Supreme Court; however, Justice Joyce L. Kennard retired in April 2014, and her replacement, as of press time, has yet to be appointed.

8. Bob Egelko, "California Supreme Court nomination a 'statement' to U.S.," *SF Gate*, www.sfgate.com/politics/article/Brown-nominates-Stanford-professor-to-state-high-5638237.php (accessed 9/22/14).

9. David Siders, "Gov. Jerry Brown names Obama administration lawyer to California Supreme Court." *Sacramento Bee*, November 24, 2014. http://www.sacbee.com/news/politics-government/capitol-alert/article4123447.html (accessed 12/3/14).

10. Prebloe, Stolz, *Judging Judges: The Investigation of Rose Bird and the California Supreme Court* (New York: Free Press, 1981).

11. "Judicial Council," California Courts, www.courts.ca.gov/policyadmin-jc.htm?genpubtab (accessed 9/22/14).

12. Melanie Mason, "California Supreme Court Blocks Citizens United Measure from Ballot," *Los Angeles Times*, www.latimes.com/local/political/la-me-pc-supreme-court-citizens-united-20140811-story.html (accessed 9/22/14).

13. 2008 Court Statistics Report.

14. Unlimited jurisdiction civil cases are disputes that involve more than $25,000. Limited jurisdiction civil cases are disputes that involve amounts from $10,000 to $25,000. See Court Statistics Report, *Statewide Trends*, 2014.

15. "California Courts Wrestle with Budget Cuts Old and New," *Los Angeles Times*, http://latimesblogs.latimes.com/california-politics/2012/06/california-court.html (accessed 9/22/14).

16. Maria Dinzeo, "IT Project Sinks in Sea of Criticism," *Courthouse News Service*, www.courthousenews.com/2012/03/27/45079.htm (accessed 9/22/14).

17. Cheryl Miller, "Judges Criticize Court Bureaucracy in Blistering Report," *The Recorder*, www.law.com/jsp/ca/PubArticleCA.jsp?id=1202556419264&Judges_Criticize_Court_Bureaucracy_in_Blistering_Report (accessed 5/25/12).

Chapter 8

1. College Board, "Trends in Higher Education," http://trends .collegeboard.org/college-pricing/figures-tables/tuition -and-fees-sector-and-state-over-time (accessed 7/21/2014).
2. California State Budget, 2014–2015, "Enacted Budget Summary," *Higher Education*, June 19, 2014, www.ebudget .ca.gov/2014-15/Enacted/BudgetSummary/BSS/BSS .html (accessed 7/21/14).
3. Marla Dickerson, "State Fiscal Woes Threaten Cities' Budgets and a Leading Job Engine," *Los Angeles Times*, January 17, 2003, pp. C1, C4.
4. California Department of Finance, "History of Budgeting," February 24, 1998, www.dof.ca.gov (accessed 7/27/12).
5. California Department of Finance, "History of Budgeting."
6. George Skelton, "The 'Budget Nun' Earns Her Pay and Bipartisan Respect," *Los Angeles Times*, May 26, 2003, p. B5.
7. California Department of Finance, "California's Budget Process," October 10, 2000, www.dof.ca.gov/fisa/bag /process.htm (accessed 7/27/12).
8. Public Finance Division, California State Treasurer, "California's Current Credit Ratings," www.treasurer.ca.gov/ratings /current.asp (accessed 8/1/14). *Sacramento Bee*, "Moody's Raises California's Credit Rating," June 25, 2014, http:// blogs.sacbee.com/capitolalertlatest/2014/06/moodys -raises-californias-bond-credit-rating.html (accessed 8/1/14).
9. California Budget Project, "Special Report, Principles and Policy: A Guide to California's Tax System. Sacramento: California Budget Project, April 2013. www.cbp.org/pub lications/publications.html (accessed 7/22/2014).
10. Katherine Barrett, Richard Greene, Michele Mariani, and Anya Sostek, "The Way We Tax," *Governing* (February 2003): 20.
11. Franchise Tax Board, State of California, "2012 Annual Report," Table C-8, Corporation Tax, Tax Liability by Net Income Class, Sacramento: Franchise Tax Board, 2011, www.ftb.ca.gov/aboutFTB/Tax_Statistics/2012.shtml (accessed 7/29/2014). See also California Budget Project, "Who Pays Taxes in California?," Sacramento: California Budget Project, April 2013, www.cbp.org (accessed 7/29/14).
12. Barrett et al., "The Way We Tax."
13. Council on State Taxation, "The Best and Worst of State Tax Administration," December 2013, www.cost.org/ (accessed 8/1/14).
14. California Budget Project, "Who Pays Taxes in California?" April 2014, www.cbp.org/pdfs/2014/140410_Who_Pays _Taxes.pdf (accessed 8/1/14).
15. California Taxpayers Association, "Cal-Tax: Taxes Are Heavy Burden in California," www.caltax.org/California .htm (accessed 7/30/12).
16. Elizabeth Malm, and Gerald Prante, "Annual State-Local Tax Burden Rankings, FY 2011," Washington, DC: Tax Foundation, April 2014, http://taxfoundation.org/article /annual-state-local-tax-burden-ranking-fy-2011 (accessed 8/1/14).
17. California Budget Project, "Who Pays Taxes in California?"
18. Carson Bruno, "California: CEOs Rate It Worst U.S. Business Climate for 8 Years Running," March 21, 2014, www.realclearmarkets.com/articles/2014/03/21/california _ceos_rate_it_worst_us_business_climate_for_8_years _running_100963.html (accessed 8/1/14).
19. Institute for Taxation and Economic Policy, "'High Rate' Income Tax States Are Outperforming No-Tax States," February 2012, www.itepnet.org (accessed 7/27/12).
20. Hans Johnson, "Defunding Higher Education" (San Francisco: Public Policy Institute of California, 2012), p. 4.
21. Phil Oliff, Vincent Palacios, Ingrid Johnson, and Michael Leachman. "Recent Deep State Higher Education Cuts May Harm Students and the Economy for Years to Come" (Washington, DC: Center on Budget and Policy Priorities, May 2013).
22. James D. Savage, "California's Structural Deficit Crisis," *Public Budgeting and Finance* 12, no. 2 (Summer 1992): 82–97.
23. California Forward, "Curing Deficits and Creating Value: Principles for Improving State Fiscal Decisions," s3.amazon aws.com/zanran_storage/www.caforward.org/Content Pages/1903423.pdf (accessed 12/3/12).
24. California Forward, "Curing Deficits and Creating Value."
25. Peter Nicholas and Virginia Ellis, "Budget Signals Narrowed Ambitions," *Los Angeles Times*, February 18, 2004, p. A1.

Chapter 9

1. Bernard H. Ross and Myron A. Levine, *Urban Politics: Power in Metropolitan America*, 6th ed. (Itasca, IL: F. E. Peacock, 2001), 90.
2. Dale Krane, Platon N. Rigos, and Melvin B. Hill Jr., *Home Rule in America: A Fifty-State Handbook* (Washington, DC: CQ Press, 2001).
3. Daniel B. Rodriguez, "State Supremacy, Local Sovereignty: Reconstructing State/Local Relations under the California Constitution," in *Constitutional Reform in California: Making State Government More Effective and Responsive*, ed. Bruce E. Cain and Roger G. Noll (Berkeley: Institute of Governmental Studies Press, University of California, 1995), 401–29; Krane, Rigos, and Hill, *Home Rule in America*; Melvin B. Hill, *State Laws Governing Local Government Structure and Administration* (Washington, DC: U.S. Advisory Commission on Intergovernmental Relations [ACIR], 1993).
4. Ross and Levine, *Urban Politics*, 91.
5. John Taylor, "What Happened to Branciforte County?" (Sacramento: California State Association of Counties, 2000), www.counties.org/defaultasp?id=52 (accessed 8/4/12).

6. County of Los Angeles Annual Report 2011–2012, http://lacounty.gov/wps/portal/lac/employees/ (accessed 8/2/12). For budget figures, see http://ceo.lacounty.gov/pdf/11-12/2011-12%20Adopted%20Budget%20Charts.pdf (accessed 8/2/12).

7. Jillian Jones, "County's Legal Troubles Tied to the Value of the Land," *Napa Valley Register*, January 30, 2010, http://napavalleyregister.com/news/local/article_31d6dfe0-0d71-11df-a0e3-001cc4c03286.html (accessed 8/4/12).

8. Aaron Claverie and David Downey, "Pechanga to Buy Quarry Site," *The Californian*, November 15, 2012, www.nctimes.com/news/local/swcounty/region-pechanga-to-buy-quarry-site/article_a17a4dde-0a5a-597d-a8f9-057ba5c3eddf.html (accessed 11/16/12).

9. For an excellent study of the 1963 Knox-Nisbet Act, which created LAFCos to impose order and control on the post–World War II explosion of new cities and annexations in California, see Tom Hogen-Esch, "Fragmentation, Fiscal Federalism, and the Ghost of Dillon's Rule: Municipal Incorporation in Southern California, 1950–2010," *California Journal of Politics & Policy* 3, no. 2 (2011): 1–22.

10. Voters in these elections may, of course, choose not to incorporate as a city and run their own show. The prospect of rapid growth and development, for example, scared many of the 57,000 residents of Castro Valley. In November 2002, they voted three to one against incorporation, opting to remain Northern California's largest unincorporated community and governed locally by the Alameda County Board of Supervisors.

11. U.S. Census Bureau, "2007 Census of Governments" (Washington, DC: Government Printing Office, 2007); California Association of Local Agency Formation Commissions, "California Cities by Incorporation Date," www.calafco.org/resources.htm#incorp (accessed 8/4/12).

12. See John H. Knox and Chris Hutchinson, "Municipal Disincorporation in California," *Public Law Journal* 32, no. 4 (Fall 2009), http://californiacityfinance.com/DisincorporationKnox2010.pdf (accessed 8/23/14).

13. Sandra Stokley, "Understanding the Disincorporation Issue," *The Press Enterprise*, September 18, 2013, http://blog.pe.com/city-government/2013/09/18/jurupa-valley-a-primer-on-disincorporation/ (accessed 8/20/14). For more background on Jurupa Valley's tribulations, see Rick Rojas, "For Jurupa Valley, Cityhood Isn't What It Expected," *Los Angeles Times*, December 1, 2013, http://articles.latimes.com/2013/dec/01/local/la-me-jurupa-valley-20131202 (accessed 8/25/14); Sandra Stokley, "'Bitter' Announcement on Disincorporation," *The Press Enterprise*, December 18, 2013, http://www.pe.com/articles/city-682062-valley-jurupa.html (accessed 8/21/14); Irvin Dawid, "Puff! There Goes California's Newest City," *Planetizen*, January 18, 2014 (accessed 8/21/14).

14. See Brooke Self, "The Vanishing City? Adelanto Officials Say Disincorporation Last Resort," *Daily Press*, August 3, 2014, www.vvdailypress.com/article/20140803/News/140809960 (accessed 8/19/14), and Erin Lennon, "Guadalupe Faces Possibility of Disincorporation," *Santa Maria Times*, August 25, 2014, http://santamariatimes.com/lompoc/news/local/guadalupe-faces-possibility-of-disincorporation/article_e2413824-a0fd-50aa-b0e8-431e7ef75089.html (accessed 8/29/14).

15. Zoltan L. Hajnal, Paul G. Lewis, and Hugh Louch, *Municipal Elections in California: Turnout, Timing, and Competition* (San Francisco: Public Policy Institute of California, 2002), 23–24.

16. Ross and Levine, *Urban Politics*, 165–78.

17. Amy Bridges, *Morning Glories: Municipal Reform in the Southwest* (Princeton, NJ: Princeton University Press, 1997).

18. International City/County Management Association (ICMA), "Officials in U.S. Municipalities 2,500 and Over in Population," in *The Municipal Year Book 2003* (Washington, DC: ICMA, 2003), 195–200.

19. Bruce E. Cain, Megan Mullin, and Gillian Peele, "City Caesars? An Examination of Mayoral Power in California," presented at the 2001 annual meeting of the American Political Science Association, August 29–September 2, San Francisco.

20. See Tony Perry, "A Liberal Mayor Takes on the San Diego Establishment," *Los Angeles Times*, June 1, 2013, http://articles.latimes.com/2013/jun/01/local/la-me-san-diego-mayor-20130602 (accessed 8/3/14); Jonathan Easley, "Wasserman Schultz Calls on San Diego Mayor to Resign," *The Hill*, July 26, 2013, http://thehill.com/blogs/blog-briefing-room/news/313755-wasserman-schultz-calls-on-filner-to-resign-over-sexual-harassment-allegations (accessed 8/3/14).

21. Hajnal et al., *Municipal Elections in California*, 25.

22. Richard DeLeon, *Left Coast City: Progressive Politics in San Francisco*, 1957–1991. (Lawrence, KS: University Press of Kansas, 1992). A recent study of over 7,000 U.S. cities found that district systems were better than at-large systems at achieving diverse city councils only in areas where underrepresented groups were highly concentrated geographically and constituted a sizable share of the population. See Jessica Trounstine and Melody Ellis Valdini, "The Context Matters: The Effects of Single-Member Versus At-Large Districts on City Council Diversity," *American Journal of Political Science* 52, no. 3 (July 2008): 554–69.

23. Jean Merl, "Voting Rights Act Leading California Cities to Dump At-Large Elections," *Los Angeles Times*, September 14, 2013, www.latimes.com/local/la-me-local-elections-20130915-story.html#axzz2tt5grBf9 (accessed 8/27/14).

24. Richard DeLeon, "San Francisco: The Politics of Land Use and Ideology," in *Racial Politics in America*, 3rd ed., ed. Rufus P. Browning, Dale Rogers Marshall, and David H. Tabb (White Plains, N.Y.: Longman, 2003).

25. Hajnal et al., *Municipal Elections in California*, 26.

26. Matthew A. Melone and George A. Nation III, "'Standing' on Formality: *Hollingsworth v. Perry* and the Efficacy of Direct Democracy in the United States," March 2014 [unpublished paper], http://works.bepress.com/matthew_melone/2/ (accessed 5/3/14), 289.

27. See Rebecca Bowe, "New Minimum Wage Proposal Less Ambitious, Has Broader Support," *San Francisco Bay Guardian*, June 10, 2014, www.sfbg.com/politics/2014/06/10/new-minimum-wage-proposal-less-ambitious-has-broader-support (accessed 6/20/14).

28. Hajnal et al., *Municipal Elections in California*, 3.

29. Hajnal et al., *Municipal Elections in California*, 64.

30. Fairvote, a nonprofit advocacy group that promotes ranked-choice voting and other electoral reforms, provides useful background research and discussion of the pros and cons on its web site at www.fairvote.org.

31. For example, see Richard Briffault, "Home Rule and Local Political Innovation," *Journal of Law and Politics* 22 (Winter 2006): 1–32, which uses San Francisco's ranked-choice voting system as a case study exemplifying the idea that local government can act as "laboratories of democracy."

32. For useful studies of these issues and initiatives, see Kathleen M. Coll, *Remaking Citizenship: Latina Immigrants and New American Politics* (Stanford, CA: Stanford University Press, 2010); Els de Graauw, "The Inclusive City: Public-Private Partnerships and Immigrant Rights in San Francisco," in *Remaking Urban Citizenship: Organizations, Institutions, and the Right to the City*, ed. Michael Peter Smith and Michael McQuarrie (New Brunswick: Transaction Publishers, 2012), 135–150; Jennifer Ridgley, "Cities of Refuge: Immigration Enforcement, Police, and the Insurgent Genealogies of Citizens in U.S. Sanctuary Cities," *Urban Geography* 29, no. 2 (2008): 53–77; Joaquin Avila, "Political Apartheid in California: Consequences of Excluding a Growing Noncitizen Population," *Latino Policy & Issues Brief* no. 9, UCLA Chicano Studies Research Center (December 2003); Ron Hayduk, *Democracy for All: Restoring Immigrant Voting Rights in the United States* (New York: Routledge, 2006).

33. Senate Local Government Committee, *What's So Special about Special Districts? A Citizen's Guide to Special Districts in California*, 3rd ed. (Sacramento: California State Senate, 2002), 3.

34. California Department of Education, *Fingertip Facts on Education in California*, www.cde.ca.gov/ds/sd/cb/ceffinger tipfacts.asp (accessed 8/2/12).

35. California State Controller's Office, *Special Districts Annual Report 2009–2010*, www.sco.ca.gov/Files-ARD-Local/LocRep/districts_reports_0910_specialdistricts.pdf (accessed 8/2/12), p. vi.

36. California State Controller's Office, *Special Districts Annual Report 2011–2012*, p. vii.

37. California State Controller's Office, *Special Districts Annual Report 2009–2010*.

38. See, for example, California Special Districts Association, "What is a Special District?" www.csda.net/special-districts/ (accessed 8/22/14).

39. Brian P. Janiskee, "The Problem of Local Government in California," *Nexus* (Spring 2001): 219–33.

40. Gabriel Metcalf, "An Interview with Joe Bodovitz," SPUR report no. 378 (September 1999).

41. The text of the SB 375 law is available at www.leginfo.ca.gov/pub/07-08/bill/sen/sb_0351-0400/sb_375_bill_20080930_chaptered.pdf (accessed 8/2/12). The Institute for Local Government provides a useful resource center with detailed background information on SB 375: see www.ca-ilg.org/sb-375-resource-center (accessed 8/2/12). To track progress in implementing SB 375, see www.arb.ca.gov/cc/sb375/sb375.htm (accessed 8/2/12).

42. California Supreme Court, quoting from the Community Redevelopment Act, in *Cal. Redevelopment Assn. v. Matosantos*, S194861 (December 29, 2011), www.courtinfo.ca.gov/opinions/archive/S194861.PDF (accessed 5/23/12), p. 9.

43. *Cal. Redevelopment Assn. v. Matosantos*, p. 9.

44. George Lefcoe and Charles W. Swenson, "Redevelopment in California: The Demise of TIF-Funded Redevelopment in California and Its Aftermath," *National Tax Journal* 67, no. 3 (September 2014): 719–44. This is a probing, illuminating, and very readable analysis; if you're interested in this topic, it is an excellent place to start.

45. Marcia Rosen and Wendy Sullivan, *From Urban Renewal and Displacement to Economic Inclusion: San Francisco Affordable Housing Policy 1978–2012* (Washington, DC: Poverty & Race Research Action Council and the National Housing Law Project, 2012).

46. Madeline Janis, "Rethinking Redevelopment in California," *Los Angeles Times*, February 8, 2012, http://articles.latimes.com/print/2012/feb/08/opinion/la-oe-janis-redevelopment-20120208 (accessed 5/13/12).

47. California Attorney General, "Proposition 22: Official Title and Summary," http://voterguide.sos.ca.gov/past/2010/general/propositions/22/title-summary.htm (accessed 5/22/12).

48. California Attorney General, "Proposition 22: Arguments and Rebuttals," http://voterguide.sos.ca.gov/past/2010/general/propositions/22/arguments-rebuttals.htm (accessed 5/22/12).

49. Liam Dillon, "San Diego to Brown: How You Like Them $4 Billion?" *Voice of San Diego*, February 17, 2011, www.voiceofsandiego.org/government/thehall/article_95760260-3b01-11e0-bbac-001cc4c03286.html (accessed 5/19/12).

50. *Cal. Redevelopment Assn. v. Matosantos*.

51. See Marisa Lagos, "Calif. Wins OK to Abolish Redevelopment Agencies," *San Francisco Chronicle*, December 30, 2011, p. A-1.

52. Ashok Bardhan and Richard A. Walker, "California, Pivot of the Great Recession," Working Paper Series (Berkeley,

CA: Institute for Research on Labor and Employment, University of California, March 2010).

53. Field Research Corporation, *The Field Poll*, Release #2320, January 19, 2010.

54. Maria LaGanga, "Lessons of Hard Times in Vallejo," *Los Angeles Times*, May 26, 2010; Carolyn Jones, "Vallejo's Bankruptcy Ends after 3 Tough Years," *San Francisco Chronicle*, November 2, 2011, p. C-5.

55. Alison Vekshin, "The Building Boom That's Sinking Stockton," BusinessWeek.com, April 12, 2012, www.business week.com/articles/2012-04-12/the-building-boom-thats -sinking-stockton.html (accessed 5/24/12).

56. "Stockton's Bankruptcy: California's Greece," *The Economist*, June 30, 2012, www.economist.com/node/21557768 (accessed 8/3/12).

57. Field Research Corporation, *California Field Poll Release #2473*, June 26, 2014.

58. All unemployment statistics shown here and below were taken from the California Employment Development Department, http://www.labormarketinfo.edd.ca.gov/cgi/data analysis/labForceReport.asp?menuchoice=LABFORCE (accessed 9/1/14).

59. Richard Florida, "Why San Francisco May Be the New Silicon Valley," *The Atlantic Cities*, August 2013, http://www .theatlanticcities.com/jobs-and-economy/2013/08/why -san-francisco-may-be-new-silicon-valley/6295/ (accessed 8/22/13).

60. Richie Bernardo, "2014's Most & Least Recession-Recovered Cities," *Wallet Hub*, http://wallethub.com/edu/most-least -recession-recovered-cities/5219/ (accessed 9/28/14); Dan Walters, "California Cities Don't Fare Well in Recovery Rankings," *Sacramento Bee*, July 30, 2014, dwalters@sacbee .com (accessed 8/28/14)

70. Dan Fitzpatrick, "Franklin, CalPERS Clash on Stockton Pension Issue, *Wall Street Journal*, July 7, 2014, http://online .wsj.com/articles/franklin-CalPERS-clash-on-stockton -pension-issue-1404772370 (accessed 8/28/14). Also see *The Guardian*, "Stockton Asks Judge to Approve Bankruptcy Plan as City Looks to Shed Fiscal Woes," http://www .theguardian.com/us-news/2014/oct/30/california-city -stockton-bankruptcy-judge-ruling-debt-reorganisation (accessed 10/30/2014).

71. Marc Lifsher and Melody Petersen, "Judge Approves Stockton Bankruptcy Plan; Worker Pensions Safe," *Los Angeles Times*, October 30, 2014, http://www.latimes.com/business /la-fi-stockton-pension-court-ruling-cuts-20141029-story .html (accessed 10/30/2014).).

72. Lifsher and Petersen, "Judge Approves Stockton Bankruptcy Plan."

73. Melanie Hicken, "Once Bankrupt, Vallejo Still Can't Afford its Pricey Pensions," *CNN*, March 10, 2014, http://money .cnn.com/2014/03/10/pf/vallejo-pensions/ (8/28/14).

74. Bernardo, "2014's Most & Least Recession-Recovered Cities."

75. For studies along these lines, see Richard Florida, "High-School Dropouts and College Grads Are Moving to Very Different Places," *CityLab*, June 16, 2014, http://www.citylab .com/work/2014/06/high-school-dropouts-and-college -grads-are-moving-to-very-different-places/372065/ (accessed 7/5/14); Alan Ehrenhalt, *The Great Inversion and the Future of the American City* (New York: Vintage Books, 2013), and Enrico Moretti, *The New Geography of Jobs* (New York: Houghton Mifflin Harcourt, 2012).

76. For details on the process, see California State Controller's Office, "Redevelopment Asset Reviews," http://www .sco.ca.gov/eo_redevelopment_asset_reviews.html (accessed 10/01/14).

77. James Nash, "California Land Grab Threatens Cities From Oakland to LA Suburbs," *Business Week*, November 13, 2013, http://www.businessweek.com/news/2013-11-13 /california-land-grab-threatens-cities-from-oakland-to-la -suburbs (accessed 09/14/14).

78. John Hrabe, "Gov. Brown Rebuilds Redevelopment," *Foxes and Hounds Daily*, October 1, 2014, http://www.foxand houndsdaily.com/2014/10/gov-brown-rebuilds-redevel opment/ (accessed 10/24/14).

79. See Michael Reich, Ken Jacobs, and Miranda Dietz, eds, *When Mandates Work: Raising Labor Standards at the Local Level*. Berkeley, CA: University of California Press, 2014.

80. Peter Jon Shuler, "In San Jose, Once a Class Project, Now a Major Political Battle," *KQED News*, August 28, 2012, http:// blogs.kqed.org/election2012/2012/08/28/in-san-jose -a-class-project-morphs-into-a-major-political-battle/ (accessed 09/21/14); Gabriel Thompson, "How Students in San Jose Raised the Minimum Wage," *The Nation*, November 28, 2012, http://www.thenation.com/article/171510 /how-students-san-jose-raised-minimum-wage# (accessed 09/12/14).

81. Karen Weise, "Business Tries to Stop San Diego's Minimum Wage Hike," *Business Week*, August 21, 2014, http://www .businessweek.com/articles/2014-08-21/business-tries-to -stop-san-diegos-minimum-wage-hike (accessed 08/21/14); Karen Weise, "Businesses Find a Bulwark Against Minimum Wage Hikes," *Business Week*, October 21, 2014, http:// www.businessweek.com/articles/2014-10-21/san-diego -businesses-find-a-bulwark-against-minimum-wage-hikes (accessed 10/24/14); Debbie L. Sklar, "Decisive Vote on Higher Minimum Wage Set for June 2016," *Times of San Diego*, October 20, 2014, http://timesofsandiego.com/poli tics/2014/10/20/crepeal-or-referendum-what-next-for -minimum-wage-hike/ (accessed 10/24/14).

82. Carolyn Jones, "East Bay Mayors Looking to Raise Minimum Wage Together," *San Francisco Chronicle*, June 23, 2014, http://www.sfgate.com/bayarea/article/East-Bay-mayors -looking-to-raise-minimum-wage-5571352.php (accessed 06/23/14).

83. Will Houston, "Measure R: Comparing Wage Hikes in California Cities," *Eureka Times-Standard*, September 9, 2014,

http://www.times-standard.com/localnews/ci_26485119
/measure-r-comparing-wage-hikes-california-cities (accessed
10/30/14).

84. The California Channel, "Senate Pro Tem Steinberg Proposes Permanent Sources of Funding for Housing and
Transit," April 14, 2014, http://www.calchannel.com/senate
-pro-tem-steinberg-proposes-permanent-sources-of-funding
-for-housing-and-transit/ (accessed 10/21/14).

85. California Senate District 6 Newsletter, "Legislature Approves Greenhouse Gas Reduction Plan with Permanent
Funding for Mass Transit," June 15, 2014, http://sd06.senate
.ca.gov/news/2014-06-15-legislature-approves-greenhouse
-gas-reduction-plan-permanent-funding-mass-transit (accessed 10/21/14).

86. Jim Hightower, "Time for a Populist Revival," *The Nation*,
March 24, 2014, 17.

Chapter 10

1. Dan Barry, "Beside a Smoldering Dump, a Refuge of
Sorts," *New York Times*, October 21, 2007, www.nytimes
.com/2007/10/21/us/21land.html?_r=1 (accessed 7/10/12).

2. David Olson, "Duroville: Slum Mobile Home Park Finally
Closes," *Riverside Press-Enterprise*, June 26, 2014, www
.pe.com/articles/duroville-678572-park-mobile.html
(accessed 8/1/14). See also Phil Willon, "Farmworkers' New Home Is Near Duroville, Yet a World Away,"
Los Angeles Times, March 25, 2013, www.latimes.com
/news/local/la-me-duroville-20130325,0,5395710.story
(accessed 8/1/14).

3. California Budget Project, "School Finance Facts, a
Decade of Disinvestment: California Education Spend-
ing Nears the Bottom," Sacramento: California Budget
Project (October 2011), www.cbp.org/pdfs/2011/111012
_Decade_of_Disinvestment_SFF.pdf (accessed 8/10/12).
See also National Education Association, "Rankings and
Estimates, Rankings of the States 2013 and Estimates of
School Statistics 2014," NEA Research (March 2014),
www.nea.org/home/rankings-and-estimates-2013-2014
.html (accessed 8/4/14).

4. Jeffrey Mount, Emma Freeman, and Jay Lund, "Just the
Facts: Water Use in California," San Francisco: Public
Policy Institute of California, July 2014, www.ppic.org
(accessed 9/24/14).

5. Paul Rogers and Nicholas St. Fleur, "California Drought:
Database Shows Big Difference Between Water Guzzlers
and Sippers," February 7, 2014, www.insidebayarea.com
/science/ci_25090363/california-drought-water-use-varies
-widely-around-state (accessed 9/3/14).

6. Matt Weiser, "California Allocates Vastly More Water Than
Supplies Allow, Study Shows," *Sacramento Bee*, August 19,
2014.

7. Peter H. Gleick, "Solving California's Water Problems,"
Huffington Post, June 10, 2014, www.huffingtonpost.com
/peter-h-gleick/solving-californias-water_b_5479569.html
(accessed 9/3/14).

8. Gleick, "Solving California's Water Problems."

9. Caitrin Chappelle, Ellen Hanack, and Jeffrey Mount, "Just
the Facts: Reforming California's Groundwater Management," San Francisco: Public Policy Institute of California, June 2014; Chappelle, Hanack, and Mount, "Just the
Facts: Califorinia's Latest Drought," February 2014; both
at www.ppic.org (accessed 9/3/2014).

10. "Covered California's Historic First Open Enrollment
Finishes with Projections Exceeded," Covered California, April 17, 2014. news.coveredca.com/2014/04/covered
-californias-historic-first-open.html / (accessed 9/24/14).

11. Dan Walters, "Medi-Cal Expands to Cover 30 Percent
of Californians," *Sacramento Bee*, May 20, 2014, www
.sacbee.com/2014/05/20/6416763/dan-walters-medi
-cal-expands-to.html#storylink=cpy (accessed 6/10/14).
For a more cautious view, see Laurel Beck and Shannon
McConville, "Just the Facts: The Affordable Care Act in
California," San Francisco: Public Policy Institute of California, May 2014.

12. For more information about Medi-Cal, see the many pub-
lications of the California HealthCare Foundation at their
web site, www.chcf.org (accessed 8/17/12), or the Kaiser
Family Foundation, www.kff.org (accessed 8/17/12).

13. California Healthcare Foundation, "California's Uninsured: By the Numbers (Charts)," www.chcf.org/chart-cart
/presentations/uninsured (accessed 8/29/14).

14. Bruce E. Cain, "Searching for the Next Pat Brown: California Infrastructure in the Balance," in *California's Future
in the Balance*, California Policy Issues Annual, special ed.
(Los Angeles: Edmund G. "Pat" Brown Institute of Public
Affairs, November 2001).

15. Region 9, American Society for Civil Engineers, "California's Infrastructure Needs $65 Billion in Major Improve-
ments, State's Infrastructure Earns an Overall Grade of 'C'
from Local Civil Engineers," www.ascecareportcard.org
(accessed 9/3/14).

16. Gary Stoller, "U.S. Roads, Bridges Are Decaying Despite
Stimulus Influx," *USA Today*, July 29, 2013.

17. Daniel C. Vock, "Under Scrutiny, States Trim List of Bad
Bridges," *Governing Magazine*, June 4, 2014.

18. C. Piller, "Bay Bridge's Troubled China Connection," *Sacramento Bee*, June 8, 2014.

19. Stuart Leavenworth, "Logjam May Break on Mending
Levees," *Sacramento Bee*, April 2, 2004.

20. Stuart Leavenworth, "Defenses Decayed: Neglected Levees
Pushed Past Limits," *Sacramento Bee*, March 28, 2004.

21. Sara Lin and William Wan, "Crews Shore Up Levees as
Concerns Rise over Upkeep," *Los Angeles Times*, June 10,
2004, pp. B1, B8.

22. 500 Nations, "500 Nations Indian Casinos SuperSite." http://500nations.com/Indian_Casinos.asp (accessed 9/24/14).

23. Steven Andrew Light and Kathryn R. L. Rand, *Indian Gaming and Tribal Sovereignty: The Casino Compromise* (University Press of Kansas, 2005), 67.

24. Howard Stutz, "Indian Casinos Set New Revenue Record, Topping $28.13 Billion," *Las Vegas Review-Journal*, March 26, 2014, www.reviewjournal.com/business/indian-casinos-set-new-revenue-record-topping-2813-billion (accessed 8/31/14).

25. Paul Pringle, "Players at Indian Slots Have No Clue on Payout," *Los Angeles Times*, February 10, 2003, p. B1. See also Fred Dickey, "Going, Going, Gone," Los Angeles Times, February 29, 2004, http://articles.latimes.com/2004/feb/29/magazine/tm=gaming09 (accessed 11/26/14).

Photo Credits

Chapter 1

Pg. 4: Petitions to turn over transgender law in public school restrooms: © Rich Pedroncelli / Associated Press. **Pg. 13:** Governor Jerry Brown unveils his 2014 California state budget in Sacramento: © Max Whittaker / Reuters.

Chapter 2

Pg. 30: *"The Curse of California."* Tinted lithograph. Sourced From Wikimedia Commons: The Wasp, August 19, 1882, vol. 9. No. 316, pp. 520–521. Original Author: G. Frederick Keller. **Pg. 36:** Supporters of same sex marriage protest in San Francisco: © Kimberly White / Reuters.

Chapter 3

Pg. 51: Political cartoon portraying California Lobbyists: © Monte Wolverton / Cagle Cartoons / PoliticalCartoons.com. **Pg. 56:** A prison guard watches inmates at Imperial Valley's Calipatria State Prison in California: © Gregory Bull / Associated Press.

Chapter 4

Pg. 83: Democrats Ro Khanna and Mike Honda shake hands after their general-election debate in San Jose, California: © John Green / Bay Area News Group / The San Jose Mercury News. **Pg. 98:** Woman holds sign against Proposition 30 in California: © Kevork Djansezian / Getty Images.

Chapter 5

Pg. 113: Senator Ted Lieu attending a Pride Parade: © Faye Sadou / UPA / Retna Ltd./Corbis. **Pg. 127:** Toni Atkins smiles as she is sworn in as Assembly Speaker: © Associated Press.

Chapter 6

Pg. 137: Governor Jerry Brown and his wife look over the papers for tax-hike initiative petitions: © Rich Pedroncelli / Associated Press.

Pg. 146: Governor Jerry Brown after authorizing construction of CA's high-speed rail line: © Damian Dovarganes / Associated Press.

Chapter 7

Pg. 161: "Status of Response to 2014 Drought," from the Association of California Water Agencies, www.acwa.com/content /drought-map. Reprinted by permission of the Association of California Water Agencies. **Pg. 163:** U.S. Attorney Laura Duffy displays retail marijuana packaging while announcing enforcement against California's marijuana industry: © Max Whittaker / Reuter. **Pg. 166:** The California State Supreme Court Justices: © Courtesy of the Supreme Court of California. Photo by Wayne Woods.

Chapter 8

Pg. 188: First grade teacher Lynda Jensen at Willow Glenn Elementary School in San Jose, California: © Ben Margot / Associated Press. **Pg. 192:** Los Angeles Mayor Antonio Villaraigosa after signing to exempt all new-car dealerships from the city's gross receipts tax: © Damian Dovarganes / Associated Press.

Chapter 9

Pg. 226: Hundreds of volunteers for the international coastal cleanup day on a San Francisco Beach: © Michael Macor / San Francisco Chronicle / Corbis. **Pg. 236:** Occupy Wall Street Encampment: © Richard DeLeon.

Chapter 10

Pg. 247: "Flow of Cases through the California State Judicial System." Copyright © 2014, Judicial Council of California, used by permission. **Pg. 248:** Protesters rally against a giant twin tunnel system to move water from the Sacramento-San Joaquin River Delta: © Rich Pedroncelli / Associated Press. **Pg. 252:** Construction on the new Bay Bridge, next to the old bridge in Oakland California in 2013: © Jim Wilson / The New York Times / Redux.

Index